THERE IS A DREADFUL HELL,
AND EVERLASTING PAINS;
THERE SINNERS MUST WITH DEVILS DWELL
IN DARKNESS, FIRE, AND CHAINS.

Isaac Watts *(1674-1748) from Divine and Moral Songs for Children. 1720.*

YOU DON'T HAVE TO STAY ANYWHERE FOREVER.

Edwin Paine *(1901-1914), in conversation, December 1990.*

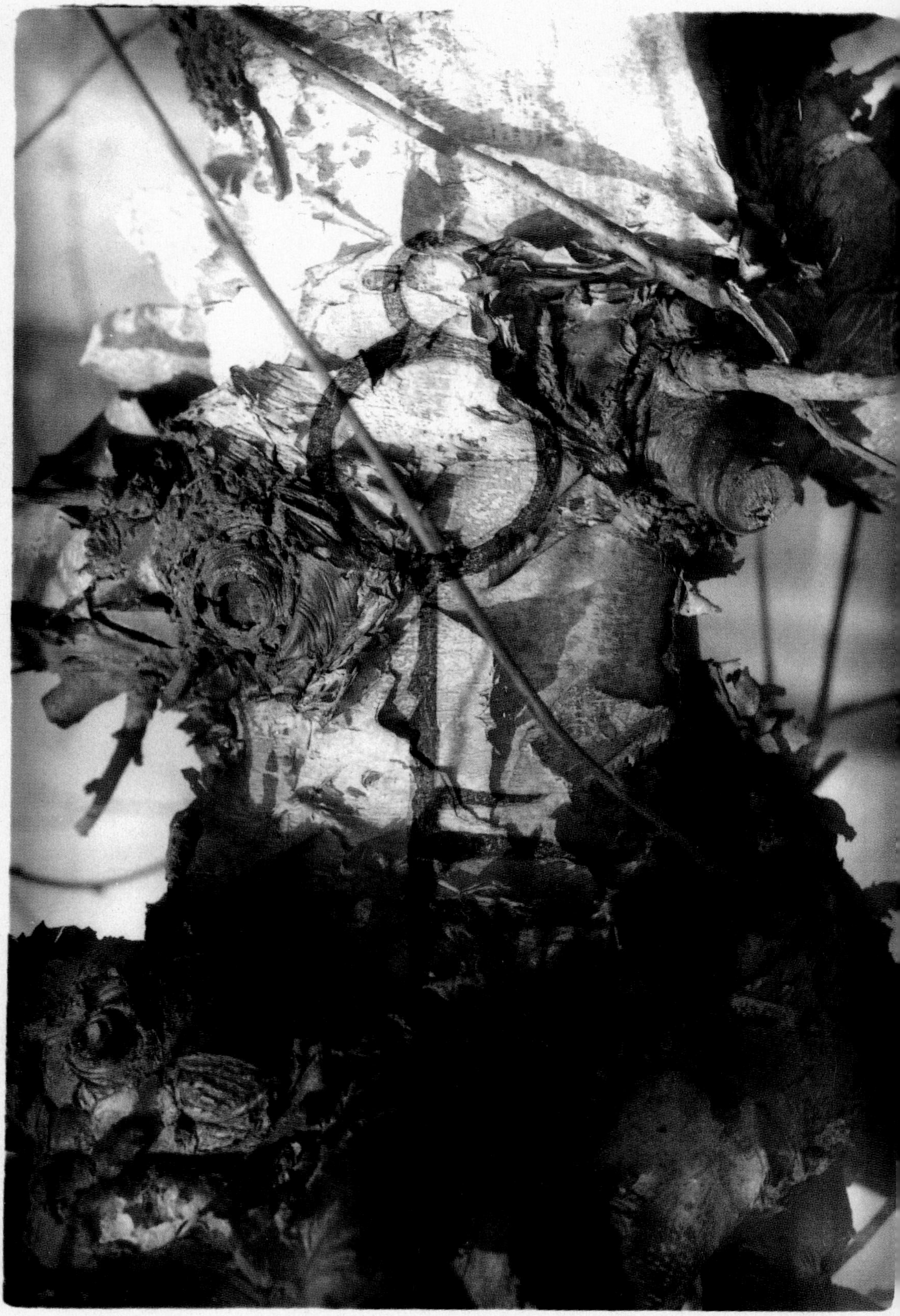

the SANDMAN

SEASON of MISTS

writer	**NEIL GAIMAN**
artists	**KELLEY JONES**
	MIKE DRINGENBERG
	MALCOLM JONES III
	MATT WAGNER
	DICK GIORDANO
	GEORGE PRATT
	P. CRAIG RUSSELL
letterer	**TODD KLEIN**
colorists	**STEVE OLIFF**
	DANIEL VOZZO
covers	**DAVE McKEAN**

Introduction by
HARLAN ELLISON

Featuring characters created by
NEIL GAIMAN, SAM KIETH, MIKE DRINGENBERG

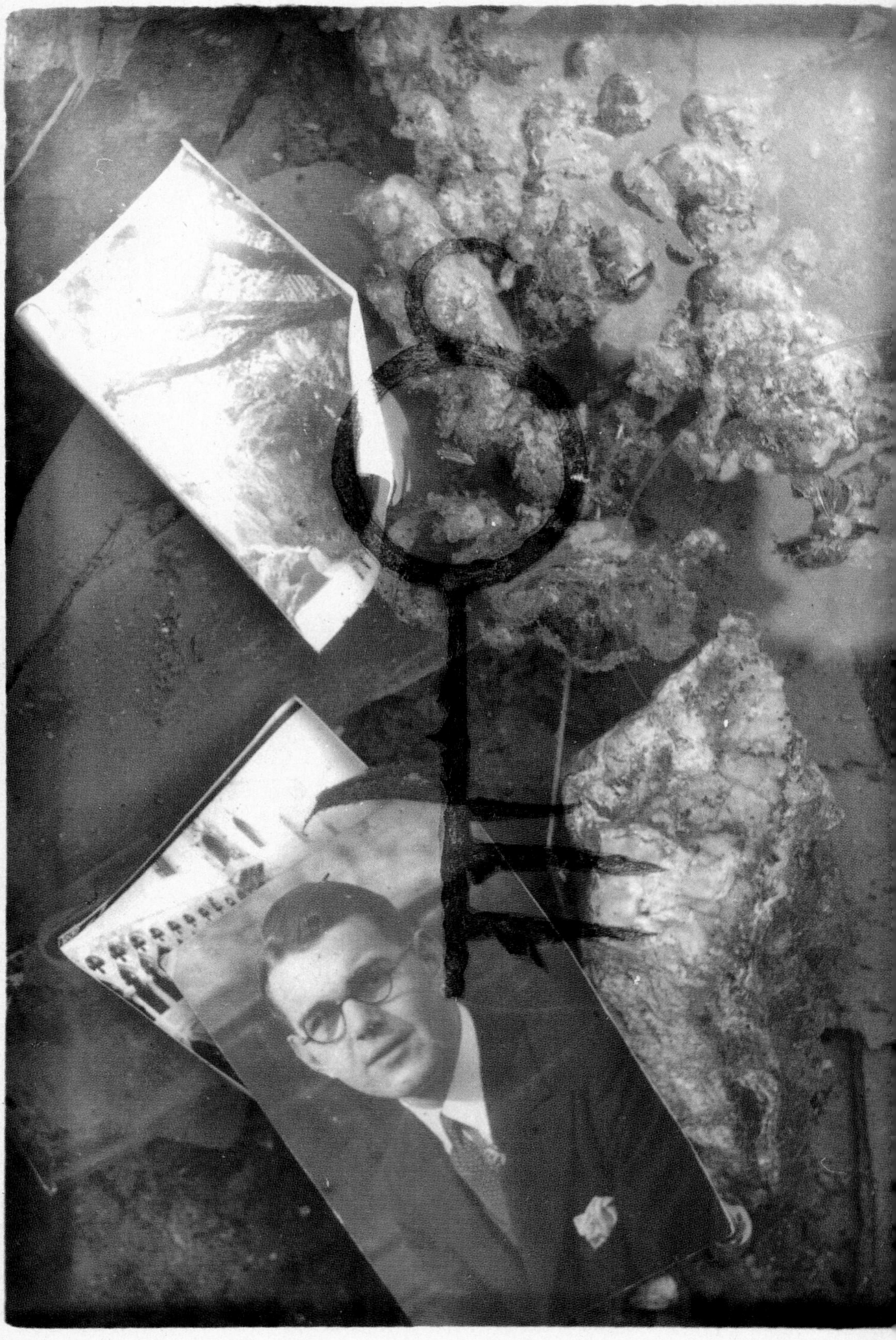

the SANDMAN:
SEASON OF MISTS

Published by DC Comics.
Cover and compilation
copyright © 1992 DC Comics.
All Rights Reserved.

Originally published in single
magazine form as THE SANDMAN
21-28. Copyright © 1990, 1991
DC Comics. All Rights Reserved.

Introduction copyright © 1992
Kilimanjaro Corp.

Cover and publication design
by DAVE McKEAN.

DC Comics
1700 Broadway
New York, NY 10019

A Warner Bros.
Entertainment Company.
Printed in Canada.
Eleventh printing

ISBN: 1-56389-041-0

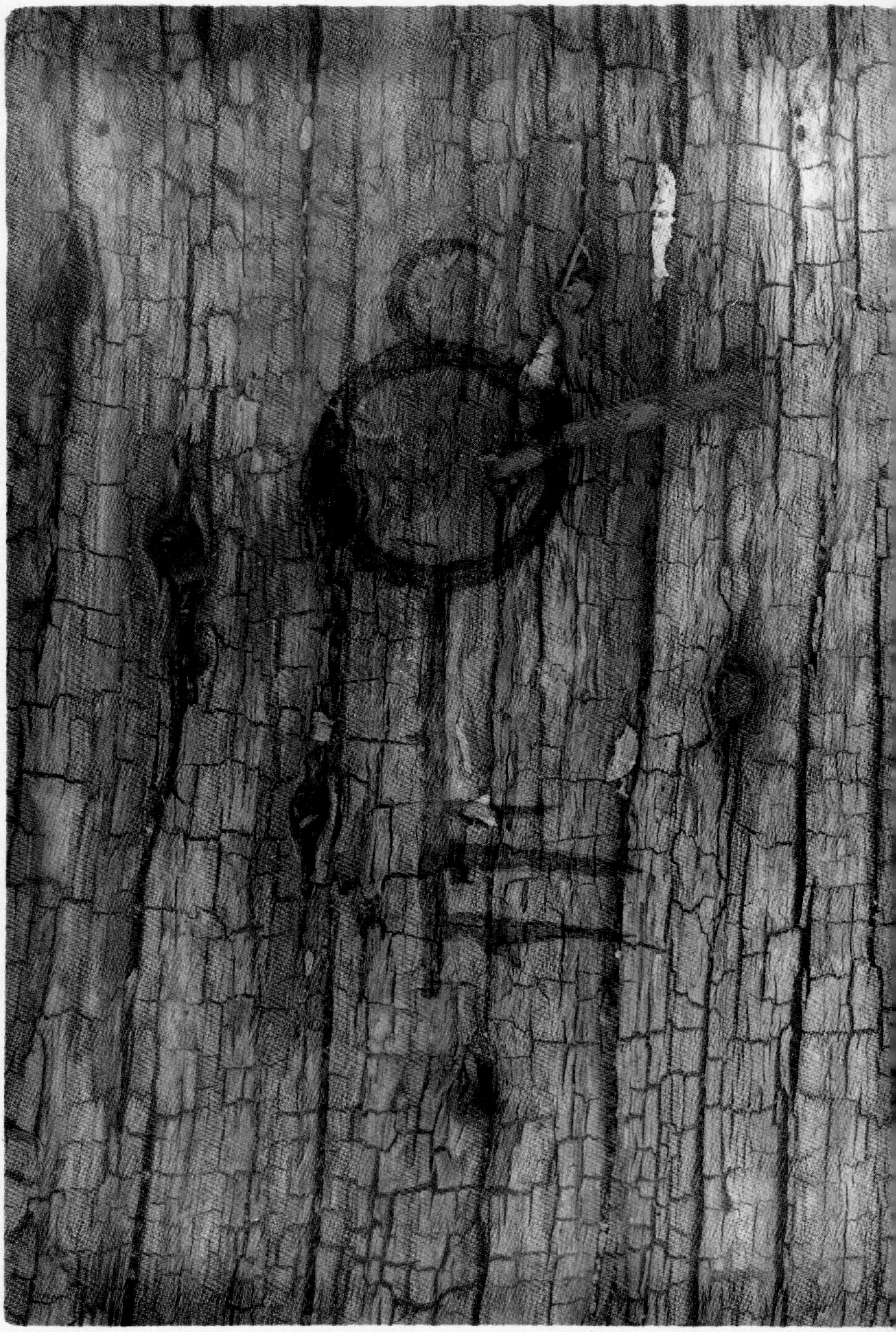

i n t r o d u c t i o n

by HARLAN ELLISON

Possibly the only dismaying aspect of excellence is that it makes living in a world of
diocrity an ongoing prospect of living hell. The subtle distressing perturbation.

Michelangelo wrote: "Trifles make perfection and perfection is no trifle." Hardly a
timent for our times, for a world of assembly lines and buck-passing and litterbugs.

Perfection. Excellence. What a passionate lover. But once having tasted the lips of
ellence, once having given oneself to its perfection, how dreary and burdensome and filled
h anomie are the remainder of one's waking hours trapped in the shackled lock-step of the
rely ordinary, the barely acceptable, the just okay and not a stroke better.

Sadly, most lives are fashioned on that pattern. Settling for what is possible; buying into
cliché because the towering dream is out of stock; learning how to avoid taking the risk of
dizzying leap. Miguel de Unamuno (1864–1936) wrote: "In order to attain the impossible
must attempt the absurd." So the paradigm becomes all the Salieri shadows unable to
ch the Mozart reality, all the respectably-talented but not awesomely-endowed Antonios
ninating with frustration at the occasional Amadeus. Excellence in the untalented and ordi-
y produces pleasure and awe; but in the minimally-talented it produces hatred and envy that
s like sheep fat.

Excellence is its own master, owes no allegiance, bows its head to no regimen. It exists
e and whole like the silver face of the moon. Untouchable, unreachable, exquisite. But
trating because it reminds us of how much mediocrity we put up with, just to get through
week.

The point being: Neil Gaiman's work on *The Sandman*.

In any field of endeavor, in any medium of the arts or sciences, an occasional talent will
nifest itself and, through bare existence, we perceive how mundane has been the effort in
t field or genre, that medium or category. Until Monteverdi, was there higher achievement
n that of Palestrina, Wm. Byrd, Andrea Gabrieli? Before Mark Twain, what were the names
he writers at the pinnacle: Sir Walter Scott, R.D. Blackmore, James Fenimore Cooper?
or to John L. Sullivan, can anyone make a rational comparison of excellence with any of the
neless bare-knuckle champions who spilled their blood in sawdust arenas? There was only
 Machiavelli, only one Chaka Zulu, only one Alexander of Macedon. Name the highest and
ghtest and most accomplished till you get to Fellini or Billie Holiday or George Bernard
w; and compare; and recognize how much higher thereafter is the high water mark.
ldenly, there is more sunlight in the world.

The point being: Neil Gaiman's work on *The Sandman*.

This is remarkable work. Perhaps you know that already. Nonetheless, I tell you. A fact:
with it what you will.

It is not merely that Mr. Gaiman (who is midway between being a frequent acquain-
ce and a close friend of mine, something more than a pal but less than an intimate, and thus
ilable to me as "Neil" rather than "Mr. Gaiman") has committed with these Sandman
ries what is usually known as *macrography*, "huge writing," work that is to be examined with

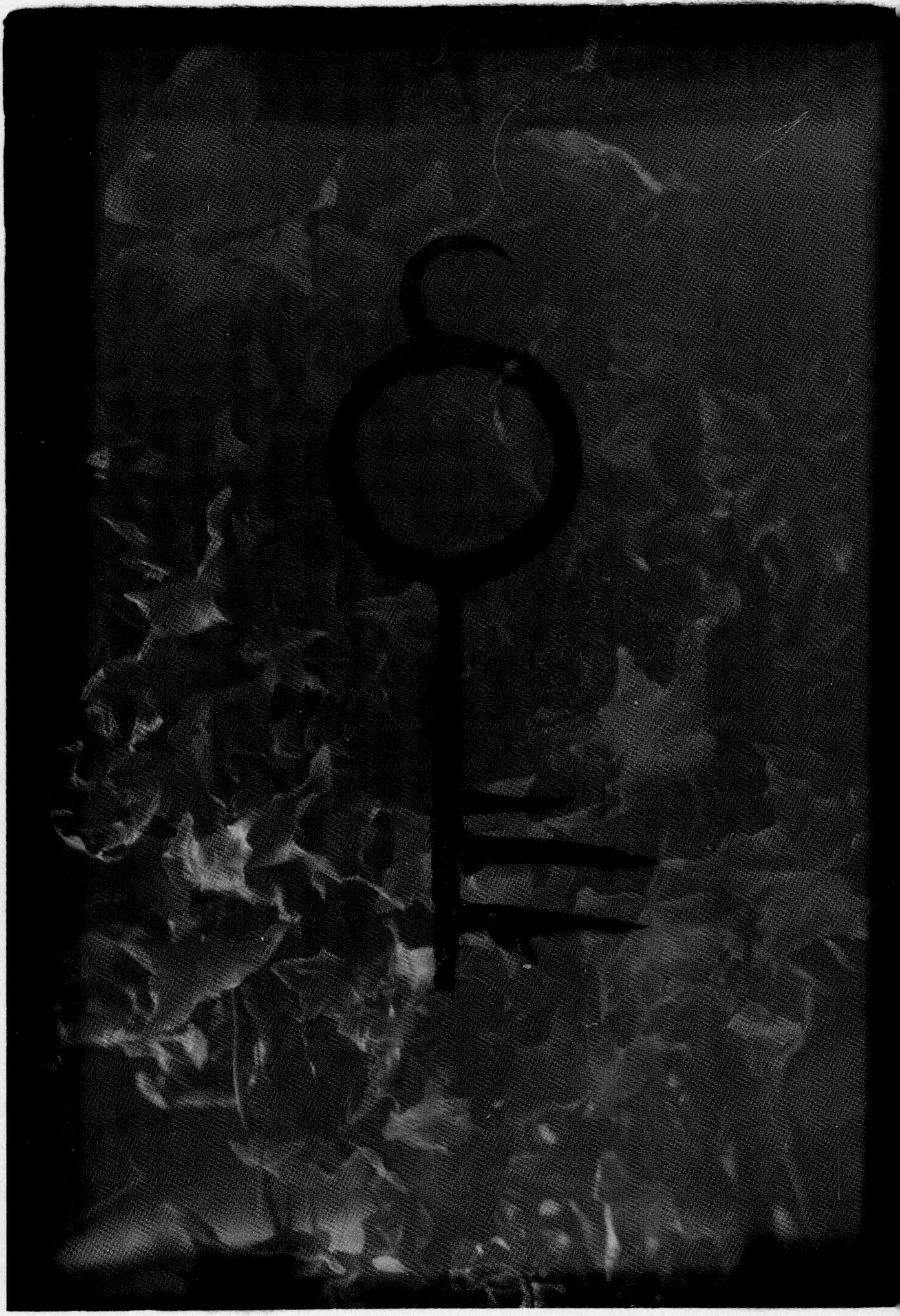

e naked eye, the opposite of *micrography*. Nor is it unique that Neil has created a compelling ternally-consistent universe for these stories: a fully-realized cosmology with a pantheon of ings and godlike non-beings, a non-Aristotelian superimposed pre-continuum, a freshly-inted polytheism as compelling as it is revisionist. Hardly unique, because *every* fantasist ilds a new universe each time s/he creates a new story. It's the way the game of "what-if?" is ayed. Some people do it better than others; and most people can't do it at all (which is why ere are folks who believe actors make up their own lines, that truth is stranger than fiction, at one picture is worth a thousand words, and that we are regularly visited by far-traveling alevolent incredibly intelligent aliens in revolving crockery, who have nothing better to do th their time than snag couch potato humans so they can have unfulfilling sex with them and st for laughs give these lousy sex partners rectal examinations with mechanical appendages e size of oil pipeline caissons); and every once in a while a person does it so splendidly that it ises the high water mark and puts more sunlight into the world.

The point being: Neil Gaiman's work on *The Sandman*.

Notwithstanding the macrography and the new cosmology, the runaway excellence of at Neil has done with this character is wrapped up in the sense one gets, as one reads *The ndman*, that what one is reading is *new*, is of consequence, and isn't as transitory (however tertaining) as most of what is done day-in-and-day-out in comics. If you have been following e progression of Neil as guiding intelligence on *The Sandman* —

(Available for the aficionado in three previous graphic novels — PRELUDES & OCTURNES, THE DOLL'S HOUSE and DREAM COUNTRY — and even as a boxed set of the trio THE WORLD OF THE SANDMAN.)

— you will have been snared by an outstanding intellect given to esoteric amusements d surreal re-viewings of the Natural Order. You will certainly (if you're one of the few sur-ving atavists who still read for the pure pleasure of intellectual invigoration) have been mes-erized by the sneaky wit and puckish nastiness of the Gaiman reformation of the received iverse. I would praise his erudition, his frequent seeding of the stories with arcane facts and erary glyphs, but as it is a truism that it takes a *very* good con artist to con a very good con tist, so it is possible that Neil "Scam Man" Gaiman is no more widely-read and filled with udition than the con artist who writes these words of introduction. And, knowing what a ud *I* am, quoting here and there in Latin and colloquial French just to seem clever, *norantia legis neminem excusat*, like *n'est-ce pas*, I have my suspicions that Neil has as diverse d bellyful a library of references as I maintain just to drop in something obscure to remind e groundlings what a smart cookie I am.

Not to be diverted too long on that preceding point, but let me give you a f'rinstance: Early on in the story of SEASON OF MISTS, when Morpheus sends Cain to deliver e message of his imminent visit to the nether regions, the emissary tells Lucifer what is about transpire, and the fallen angel goes off into one of those wonderful rhapsodic panegyrics all ad scientists, despots, nitwit super-villains and televangelists indulge in for many odd-shaped nels. He culminates his paralogical blather by ranting, "Better to reign in hell, than serve in eav'n."

And just in case the reader hasn't seen the 1941 Warner Bros. adaptation of Jack ondon's THE SEA WOLF, in which Edward G. Robinson as the tyrannical freighter skipper /olf Larsen quotes that quotation repeatedly, Neil bangs us over the head with the information at the aphorism comes from Milton's PARADISE LOST (1667). Leaf ahead to that page and take a ok at it.

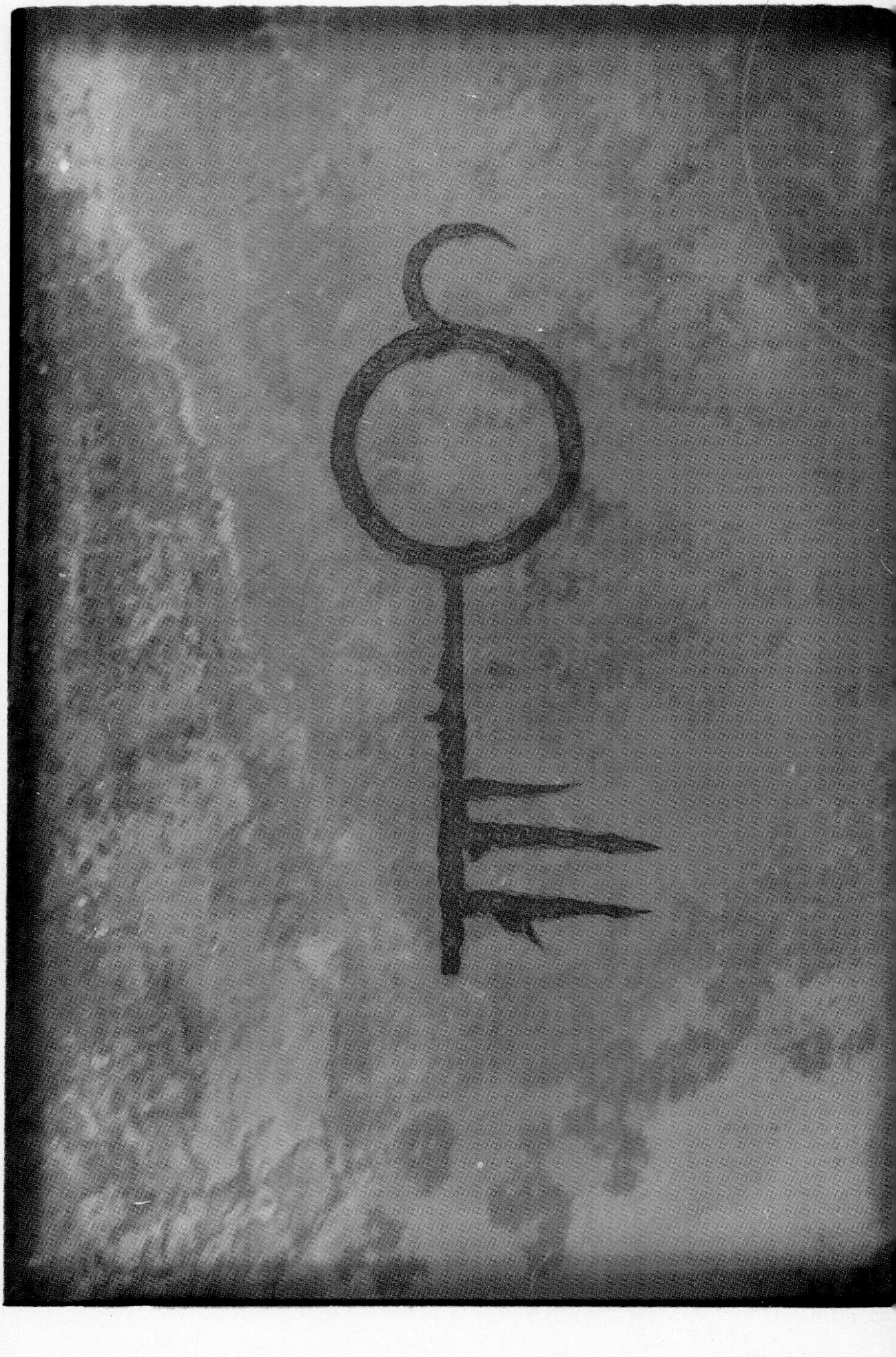

See what I mean? A *really* intellectual guy, secure in his own voluminous erudition, ωuldn't have bothered making sure we know how goddam sharp he is. Now, I'm not saying ᴺil *isn't* as sharp as he wants us to believe he is, I'm merely suggesting that he is so intent on ᵇilding all the buttressing into his fictional structure that he makes certain we perceive of what ᵉllent granite is made the basement slab.

So excellent that one might quote yet again from Milton: "The mind is its own place, ᵈ in itself can make a Heav'n of Hell, a Hell of Heav'n."

The point being: Neil Gaiman's work on *The Sandman* is so excellent, so much a pre-ᵗation of the new high water mark, that we realize as we read, that it is *about something*, that ᵖs not merely an amusing entertainment. (Though it is *that*, of course.)

I'll not reconnoiter the story in this graphic novel … what originally appeared in ⁿnthly comic book format as sections 0 through 7, December 1990–July 1991. The story lies ᵒre you, and I wasn't engaged to restate the obvious. (As critic John Simon wrote in 1981: ᵗ. there is no point in saying less than your predecessors have said." Which is good advice that ᵒuld be taken by all those who write Sherlock Holmes or Sam Spade pastiches.) Nor will I ᵖy the role of the carping bluejay, shrieking that Neil says in the earliest section of the story ᵗ Destiny casts no shadow, but Dringenberg has repeatedly scumbled in shadows only pages ᵉlier. That sort of petty bitching is beneath me, a guy as clever as I am.

I will only repeat the theme of this preamble by reporting that excellence, as contained ᵗ the work of Gaiman's *Sandman*, has made the awareness of the mediocre world extremely ᵖnful for a great many people. I know this to be true, for I sat there at the 13th annual World ᵃntasy Convention in Tucson in 1991 and watched with devilish pleasure as Neil won the ᵍhly-prized FantasyCon "Howard Philips Lovecraft" trophy for the Year's Best Short Story ᵉ an issue of *The Sandman* "comic book." Devilish pleasure, I tell you, because all those artsy-ᵗsy writers and artists and critics sitting there expecting a standard-print short story to win, ᵒked on their little almond cups as this renegade funnybook guy carted off the Diamond as ᵍ as the Ritz. Much snorting through the nose. Much umbrage taken. Many dudgeons ᵉsed to new heights. And screams and cries of foul play at the polls. So infuriated were the ᵃithful at such a choice having been made by a blue ribbon panel of experts who couldn't be ᵇorned or shamed into overlooking excellence, that the Great Gray Eminences who run the ᵃntasyCon from behind their nightshadow veil of secrecy, have rewritten the rules so that, ᵉaven forfend, no "comic book" will ever again be nominated, much less have an opportunity ᵗ kick serious artistic butt.

The point being: Neil Gaiman's work on *The Sandman* brings that perennial DC ᵒmics character, whom I first loved in 1940 in the 96-page 15¢ *New York World's Fair Comics*, ᵗh his green business suit, his orange-colored snapbrim fedora, his fuchsia cape, his World ᵃr I doughboy gas mask and his deadly gas gun, into a refurbished state of rebirth, trans-ᵒgrified for our angst-festooned era, not merely as a marvelous and entertaining myth-figure, ᵗ as the symbol of excellence in a world where mediocrity is our normal prison.

And how do we know that what Gaiman has done is excellence?

We know it because of something critic Susan Sontag wrote. She said, "Real Art has ᵉ capacity to make us nervous."

Nervous. You should've been there at the awards ceremony. Those suckers like as ⁿost laid square bricks.

The point being: isn't this Gaiman just too cute for words!

In which a Family Reunion occasions certain personal recriminations; assorted events are set in motion; and a relationship thought long done with proves to have much relevance today.

EPISODE 0

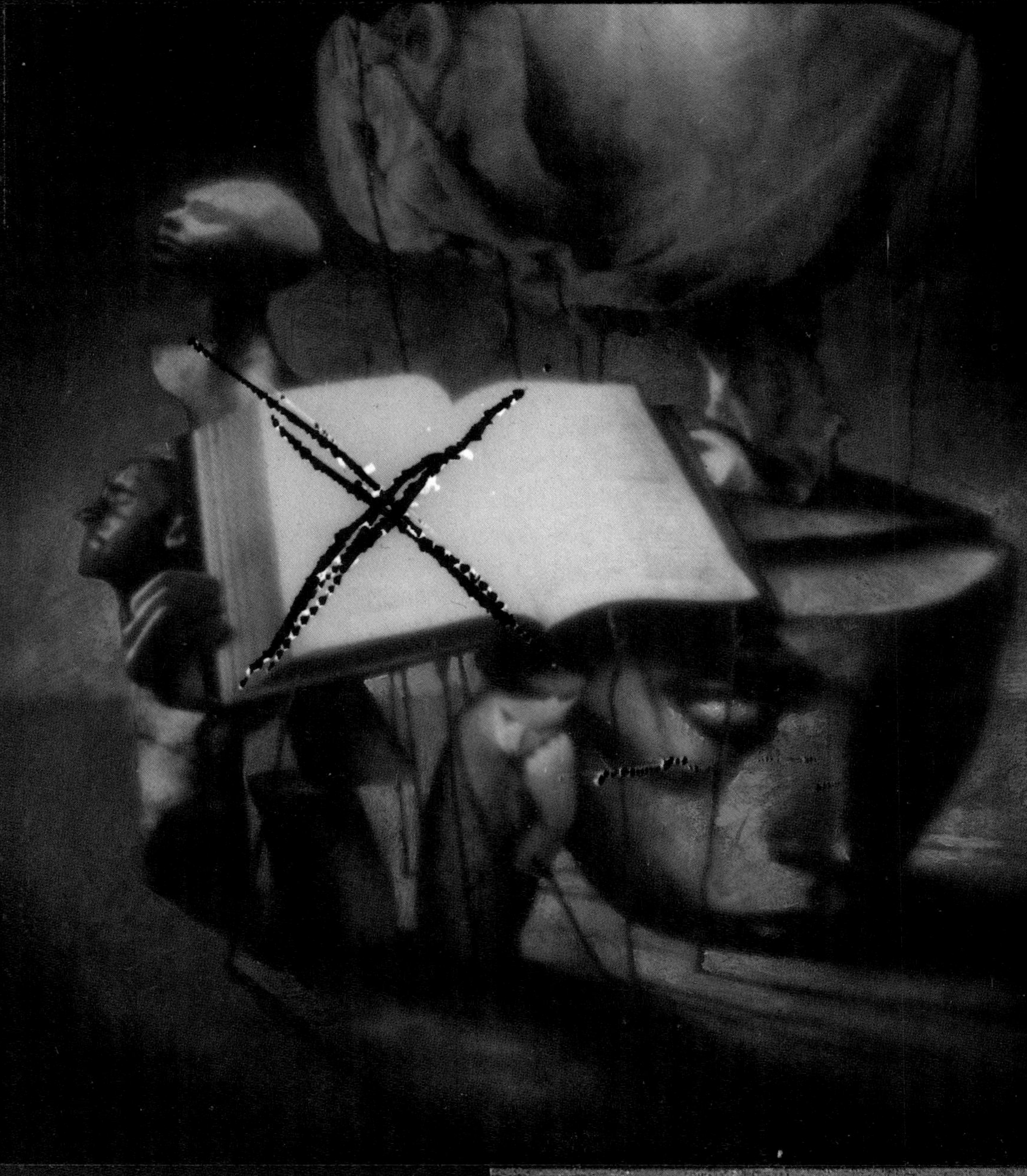

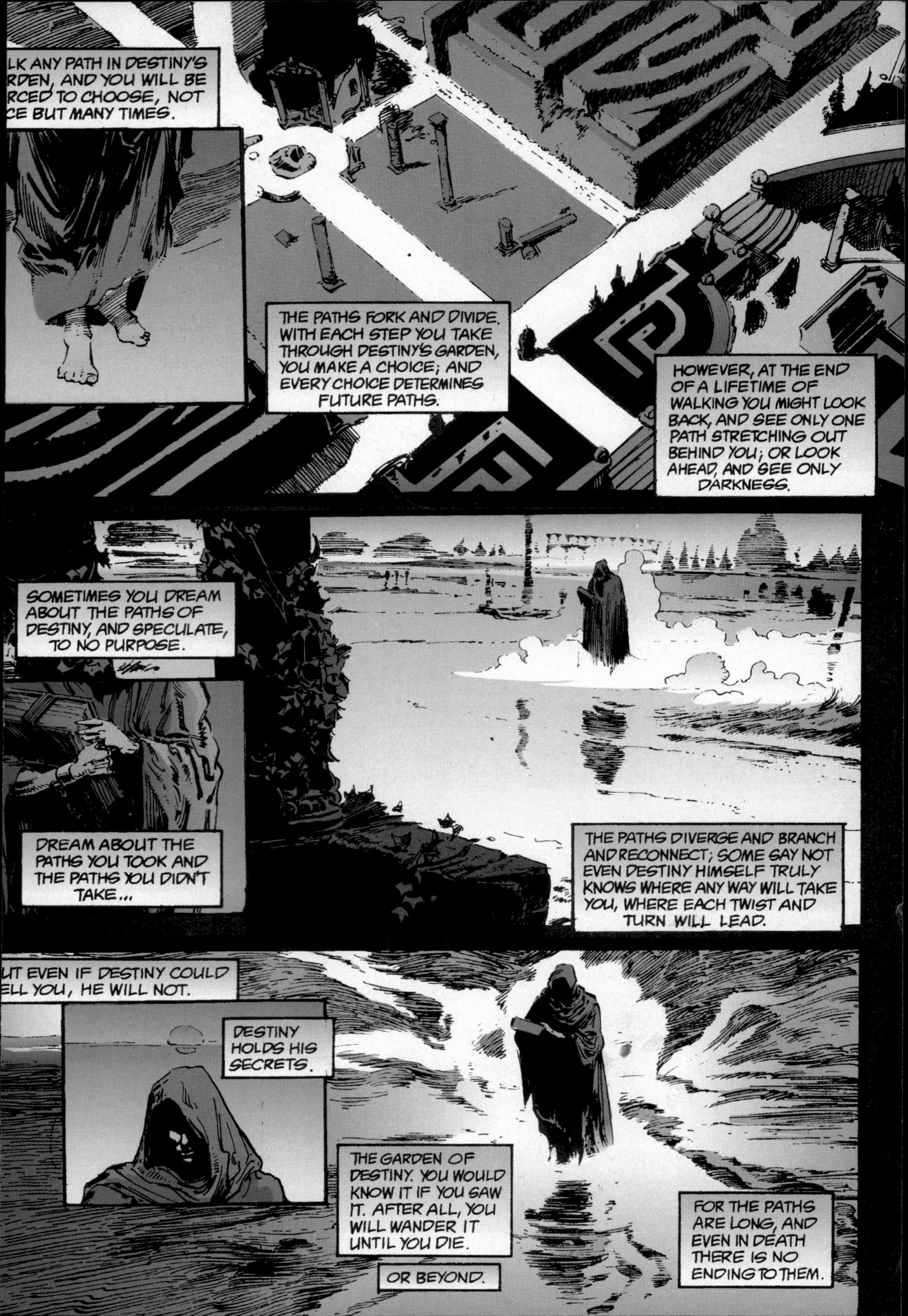

LK ANY PATH IN DESTINY'S RDEN, AND YOU WILL BE RCED TO CHOOSE, NOT CE BUT MANY TIMES.
THE PATHS FORK AND DIVIDE. WITH EACH STEP YOU TAKE THROUGH DESTINY'S GARDEN, YOU MAKE A CHOICE; AND EVERY CHOICE DETERMINES FUTURE PATHS.
HOWEVER, AT THE END OF A LIFETIME OF WALKING YOU MIGHT LOOK BACK, AND SEE ONLY ONE PATH STRETCHING OUT BEHIND YOU; OR LOOK AHEAD, AND SEE ONLY DARKNESS.
SOMETIMES YOU DREAM ABOUT THE PATHS OF DESTINY, AND SPECULATE, TO NO PURPOSE.
DREAM ABOUT THE PATHS YOU TOOK AND THE PATHS YOU DIDN'T TAKE...
THE PATHS DIVERGE AND BRANCH AND RECONNECT; SOME SAY NOT EVEN DESTINY HIMSELF TRULY KNOWS WHERE ANY WAY WILL TAKE YOU, WHERE EACH TWIST AND TURN WILL LEAD.
UT EVEN IF DESTINY COULD ELL YOU, HE WILL NOT.
DESTINY HOLDS HIS SECRETS.
THE GARDEN OF DESTINY. YOU WOULD KNOW IT IF YOU SAW IT. AFTER ALL, YOU WILL WANDER IT UNTIL YOU DIE.
OR BEYOND.
FOR THE PATHS ARE LONG, AND EVEN IN DEATH THERE IS NO ENDING TO THEM.

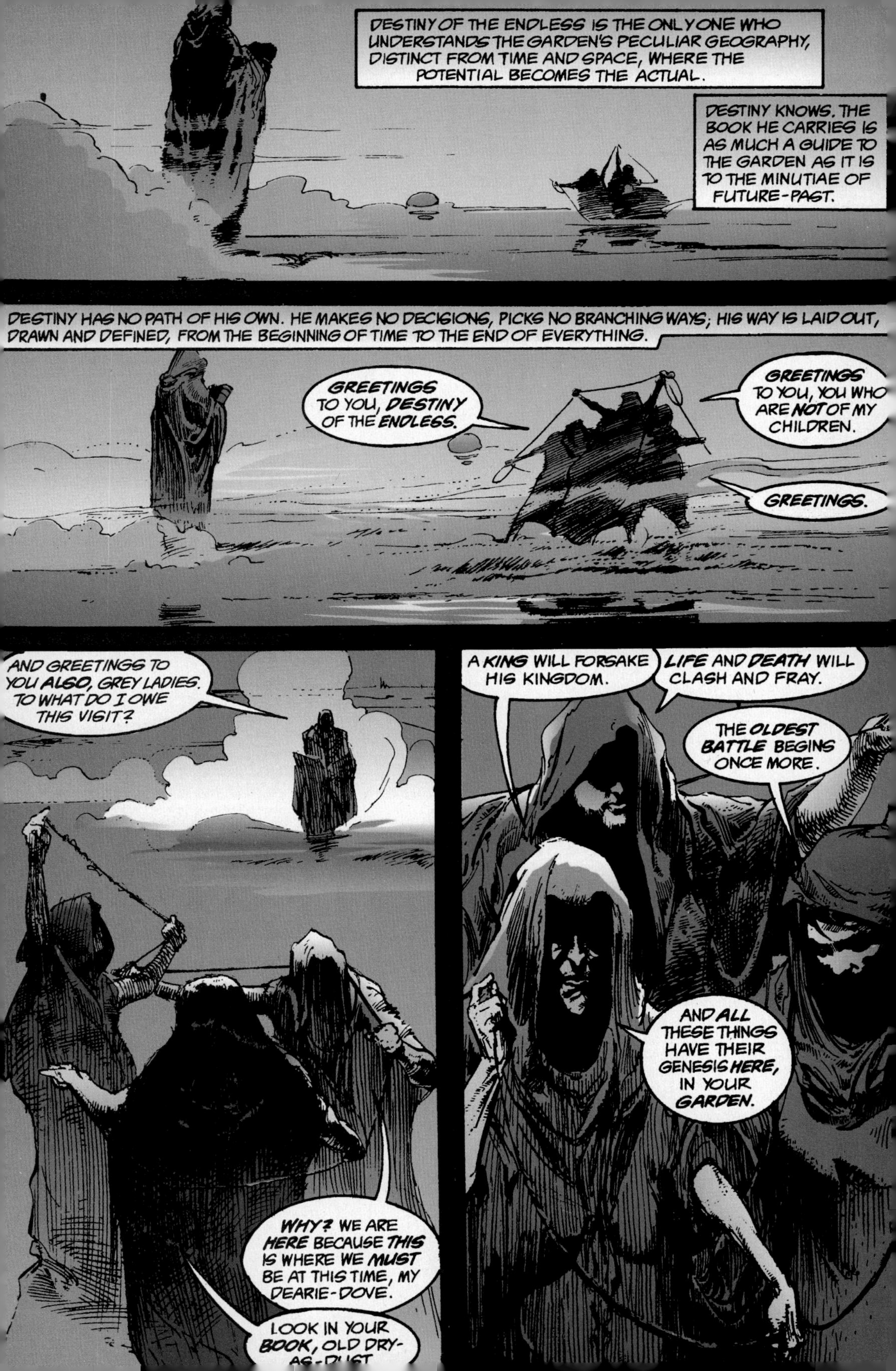
DESTINY OF THE ENDLESS IS THE ONLY ONE WHO UNDERSTANDS THE GARDEN'S PECULIAR GEOGRAPHY, DISTINCT FROM TIME AND SPACE, WHERE THE POTENTIAL BECOMES THE ACTUAL.
DESTINY KNOWS. THE BOOK HE CARRIES IS AS MUCH A GUIDE TO THE GARDEN AS IT IS TO THE MINUTIAE OF FUTURE-PAST.
DESTINY HAS NO PATH OF HIS OWN. HE MAKES NO DECISIONS, PICKS NO BRANCHING WAYS; HIS WAY IS LAID OUT, DRAWN AND DEFINED, FROM THE BEGINNING OF TIME TO THE END OF EVERYTHING.
GREETINGS TO YOU, DESTINY OF THE ENDLESS.
GREETINGS TO YOU, YOU WHO ARE NOT OF MY CHILDREN.
GREETINGS.
AND GREETINGS TO YOU ALSO, GREY LADIES. TO WHAT DO I OWE THIS VISIT?
WHY? WE ARE HERE BECAUSE THIS IS WHERE WE MUST BE AT THIS TIME, MY DEARIE-DOVE.
LOOK IN YOUR BOOK, OLD DRY-
A KING WILL FORSAKE HIS KINGDOM.
LIFE AND DEATH WILL CLASH AND FRAY.
THE OLDEST BATTLE BEGINS ONCE MORE.
AND ALL THESE THINGS HAVE THEIR GENESIS HERE, IN YOUR GARDEN.

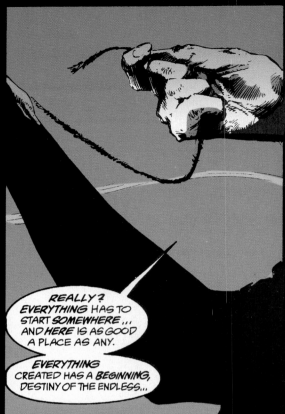

NOTHING BEGINS IN THIS PLACE.

THIS PLACE IS *BEYOND* BEGINNINGS AND ENDINGS, GREY WOMEN.

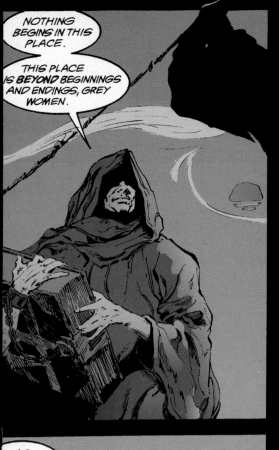

REALLY? *EVERYTHING* HAS TO START *SOMEWHERE* ... AND *HERE* IS AS GOOD A PLACE AS ANY.

EVERYTHING CREATED HAS A *BEGINNING*, DESTINY OF THE ENDLESS...

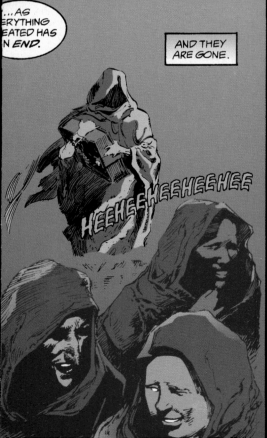

...AS EVERYTHING CREATED HAS AN END.

AND THEY ARE GONE.

HEEHEEHEEHEEHEEHEE

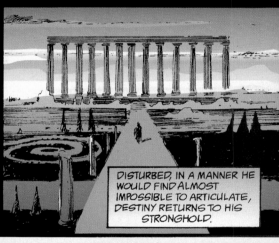

DISTURBED, IN A MANNER HE WOULD FIND ALMOST IMPOSSIBLE TO ARTICULATE, DESTINY RETURNS TO HIS STRONGHOLD.

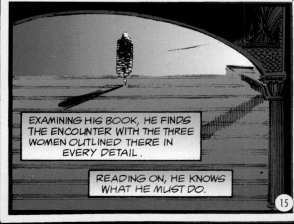

EXAMINING HIS BOOK, HE FINDS THE ENCOUNTER WITH THE THREE WOMEN OUTLINED THERE IN EVERY DETAIL.

READING ON, HE KNOWS WHAT HE MUST DO.

15

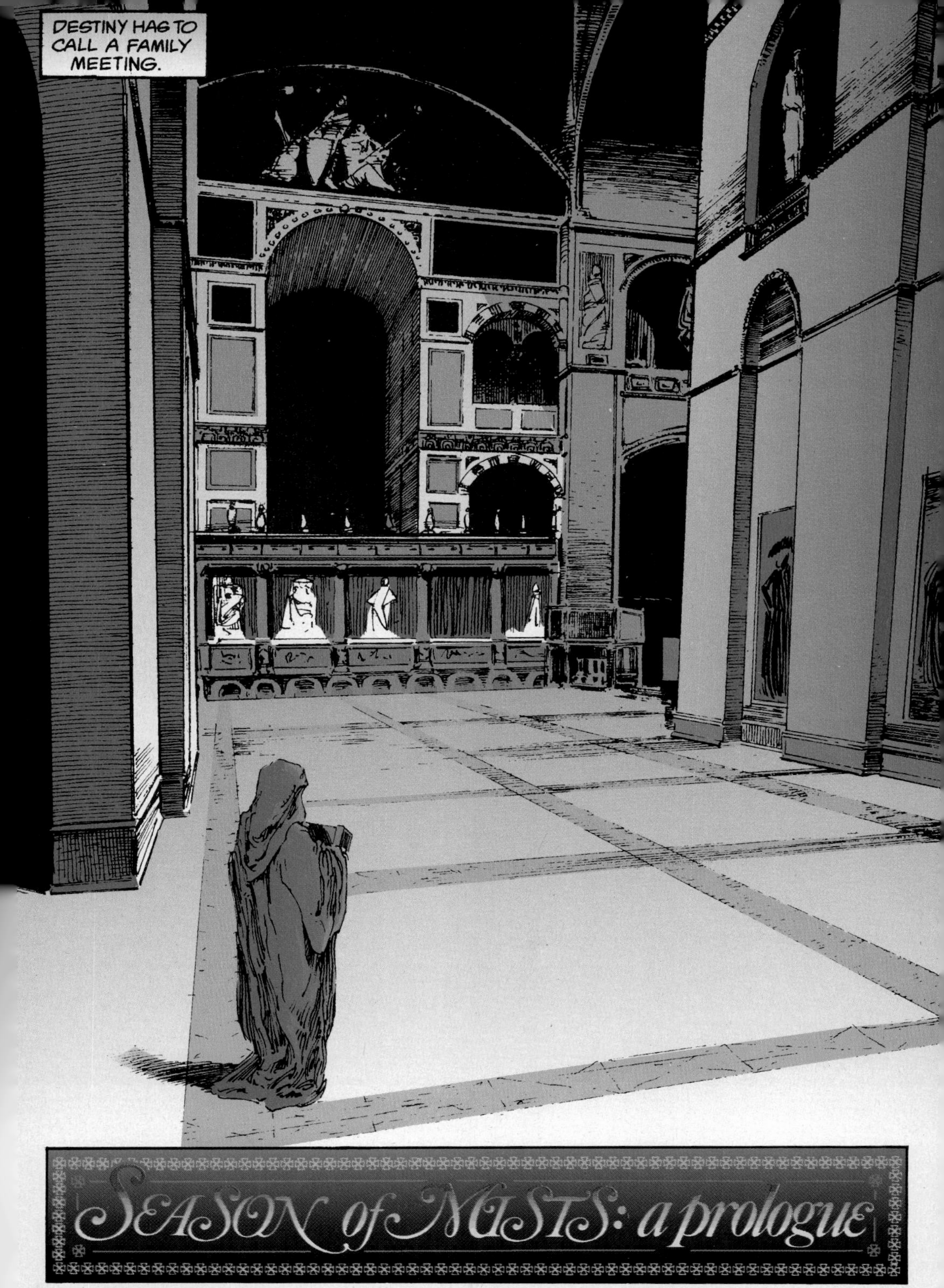
DESTINY HAS TO CALL A FAMILY MEETING.

SEASON of MISTS: a prologue

In which a Family reunion occasions certain personal recriminations; assorted events are set in motion; and a relationship thought long done with proves to have much relevance today.

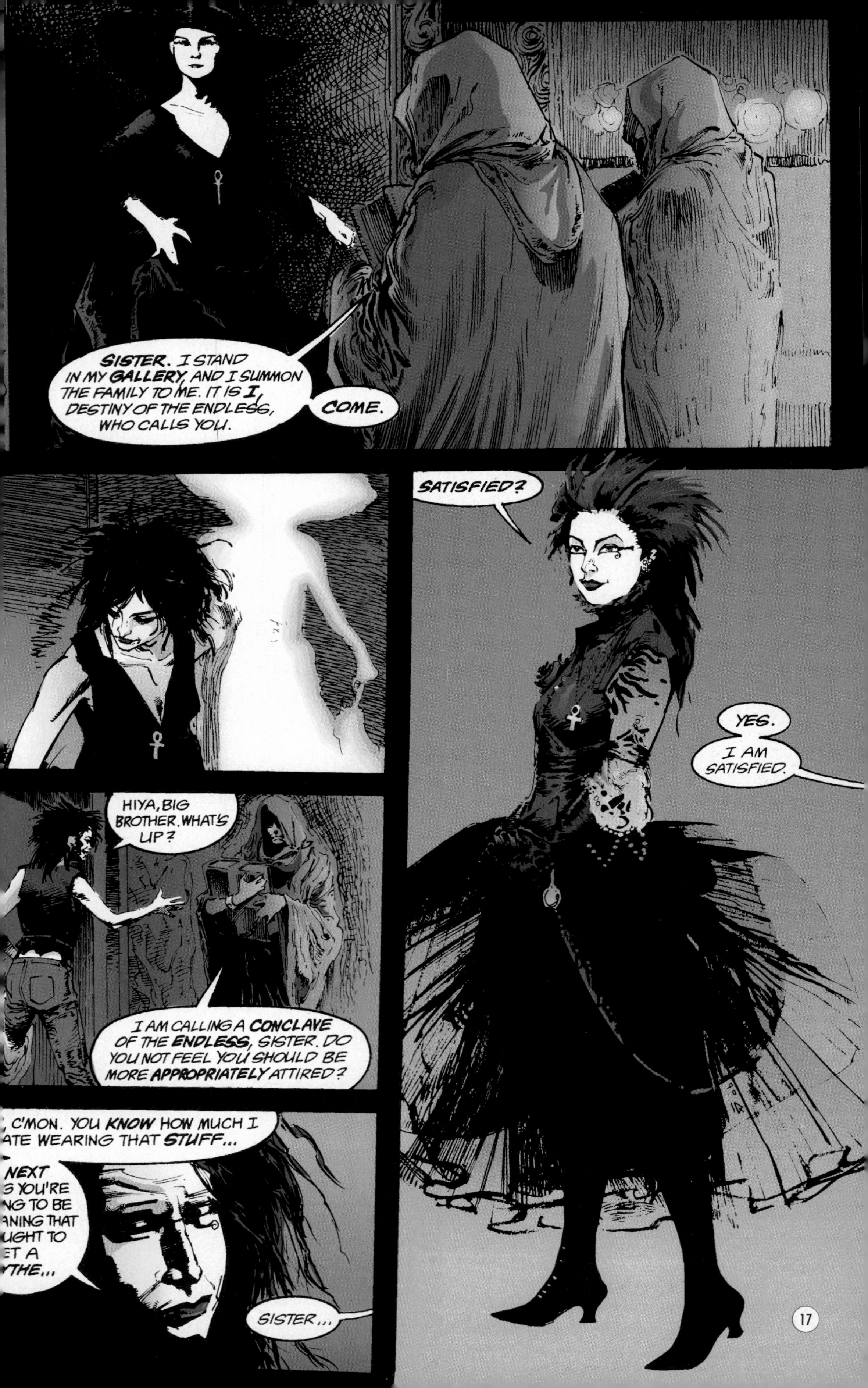

SISTER. I STAND IN MY GALLERY, AND I SUMMON THE FAMILY TO ME. IT IS I, DESTINY OF THE ENDLESS, WHO CALLS YOU.
COME.
HIYA, BIG BROTHER. WHAT'S UP?
I AM CALLING A CONCLAVE OF THE ENDLESS, SISTER. DO YOU NOT FEEL YOU SHOULD BE MORE APPROPRIATELY ATTIRED?
, C'MON. YOU KNOW HOW MUCH I ATE WEARING THAT STUFF...
NEXT S YOU'RE NG TO BE ANING THAT UGHT TO ET A YTHE...
SISTER...
SATISFIED?
YES.
I AM SATISFIED.

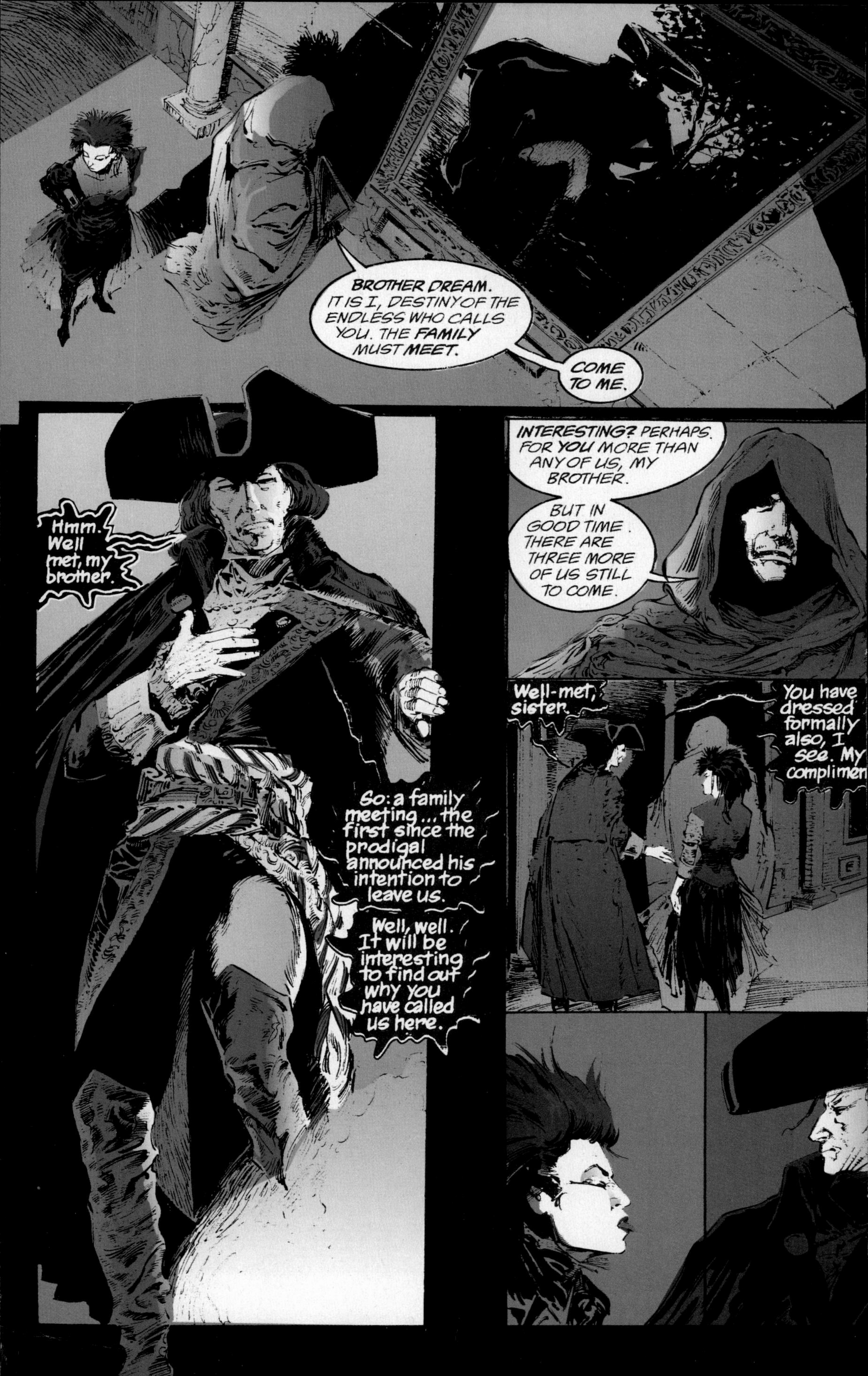
BROTHER DREAM. IT IS I, DESTINY OF THE ENDLESS WHO CALLS YOU. THE FAMILY MUST MEET.
COME TO ME.
Hmm. Well met, my brother.
So: a family meeting ... the first since the prodigal announced his intention to leave us.
Well, well. It will be interesting to find out why you have called us here.
INTERESTING? PERHAPS. FOR YOU MORE THAN ANY OF US, MY BROTHER.
BUT IN GOOD TIME. THERE ARE THREE MORE OF US STILL TO COME.
Well-met, sister.
You have dressed formally also, I see. My complimen

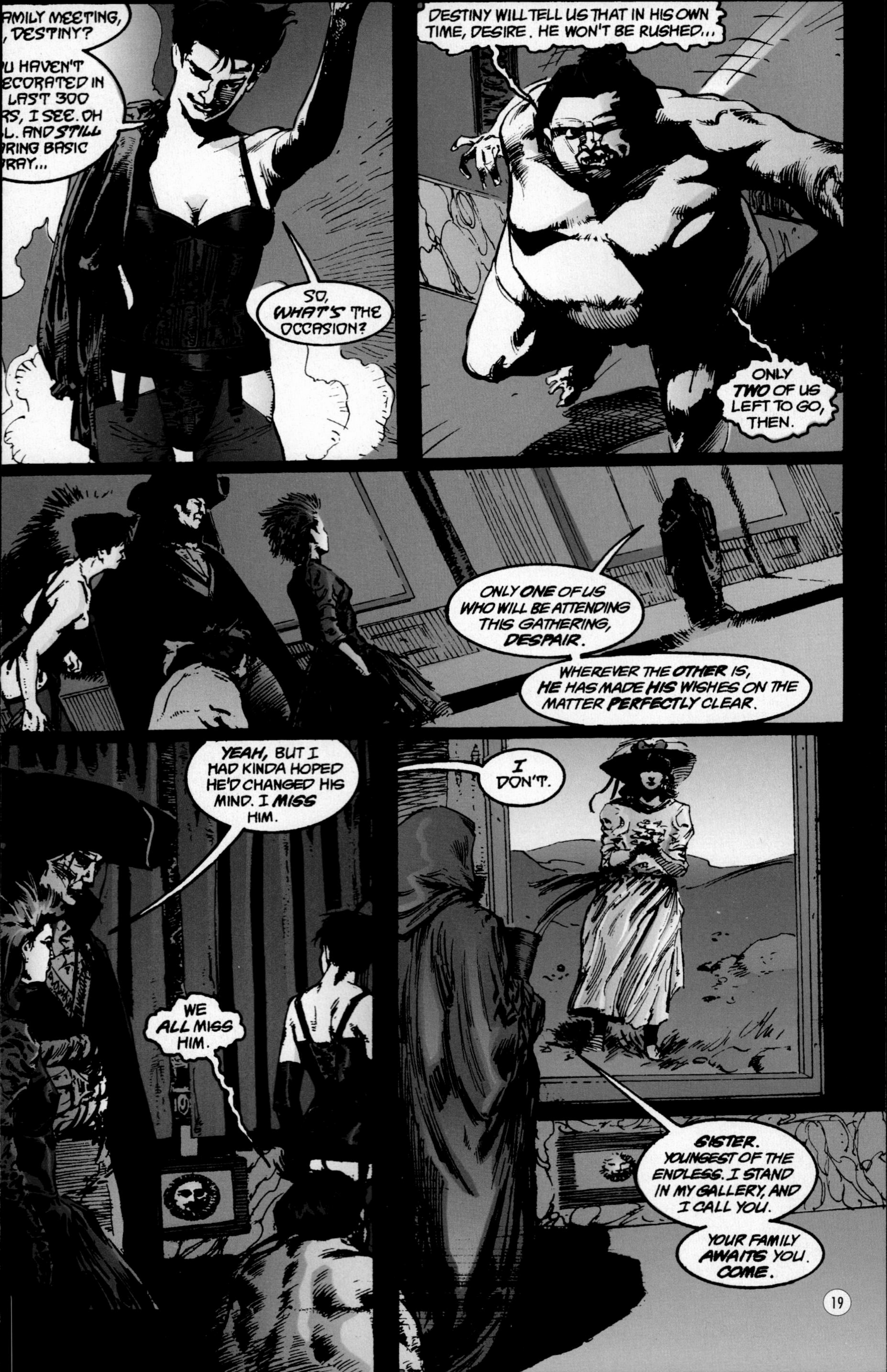
AMILY MEETING, , DESTINY? U HAVEN'T ECORATED IN LAST 300 RS, I SEE. OH L. AND STILL DRING BASIC RRAY...
SO, WHAT'S THE OCCASION?
DESTINY WILL TELL US THAT IN HIS OWN TIME, DESIRE. HE WON'T BE RUSHED...
ONLY TWO OF US LEFT TO GO, THEN.
ONLY ONE OF US WHO WILL BE ATTENDING THIS GATHERING, DESPAIR.
WHEREVER THE OTHER IS, HE HAS MADE HIS WISHES ON THE MATTER PERFECTLY CLEAR.
YEAH, BUT I HAD KINDA HOPED HE'D CHANGED HIS MIND. I MISS HIM.
WE ALL MISS HIM.
I DON'T.
SISTER. YOUNGEST OF THE ENDLESS. I STAND IN MY GALLERY, AND I CALL YOU.
YOUR FAMILY AWAITS YOU. COME.

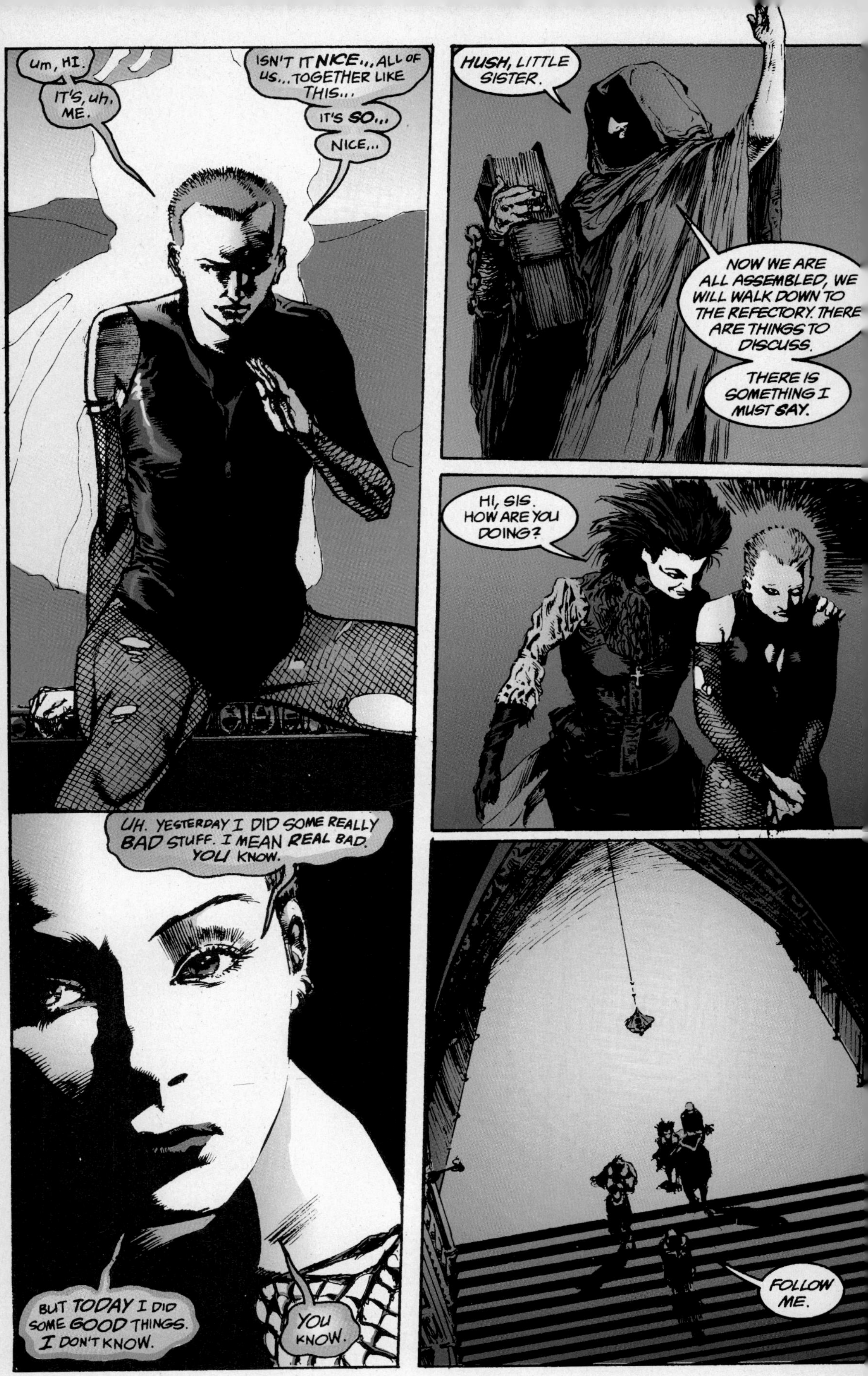
um, HI.
IT'S, uh, ME.
ISN'T IT NICE... ALL OF US... TOGETHER LIKE THIS...
IT'S SO...
NICE...
HUSH, LITTLE SISTER.
NOW WE ARE ALL ASSEMBLED, WE WILL WALK DOWN TO THE REFECTORY. THERE ARE THINGS TO DISCUSS.
THERE IS SOMETHING I MUST SAY.
HI, SIS. HOW ARE YOU DOING?
UH. YESTERDAY I DID SOME REALLY BAD STUFF. I MEAN REAL BAD. YOU KNOW.
BUT TODAY I DID SOME GOOD THINGS. I DON'T KNOW.
YOU KNOW.
FOLLOW ME.

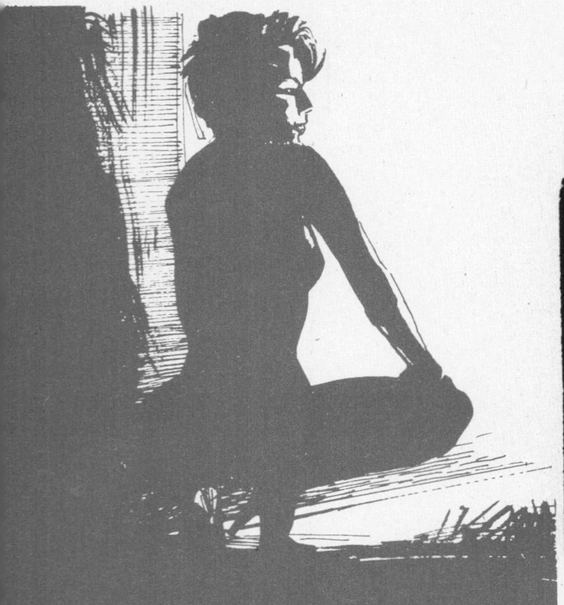

Let us pause for a moment, as they descend the grey steps toward Destiny's banqueting hall, to consider the Endless.

Desire is of medium height. It is unlikely that any portrait will ever do Desire justice, since to see her (or him) is to love him (or her),— passionately, painfully, to the exclusion of all else.

Desire smells almost subliminally of summer peaches, and casts two shadows: one black and sharp-edged, the other translucent and forever wavering, like heat haze.

Desire smiles in brief flashes, like sunlight glinting from a knife-edge. And there is much else that is knife-like about Desire.

Never a possession, always the possessor, with skin as pale as smoke, and eyes tawny and sharp as yellow wine: Desire is everything you have ever wanted. Whoever you are. Whatever you are.

Everything.

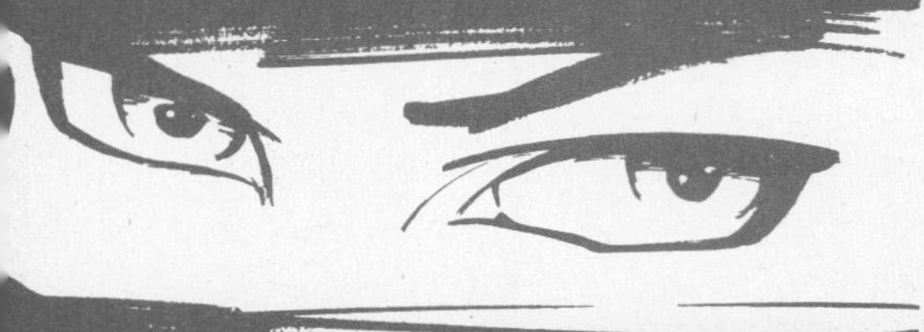

Despair, Desire's sister and twin, is queen of her own bleak bourne. It is said that scattered through Despair's domain are a multitude of tiny windows, hanging in the void. Each window looks out onto a different scene, being, in our world, a mirror. Sometimes you will look into a mirror and feel the eyes of Despair upon you, feel her hook catch and snag on your heart.

Her skin is cold, and clammy; her eyes are the colour of sky, on the grey, wet days that leach the world of colour and meaning; her voice is little more than a whisper; and while she has no odour, her shadow smells musky, and pungent, like the skin of a snake.

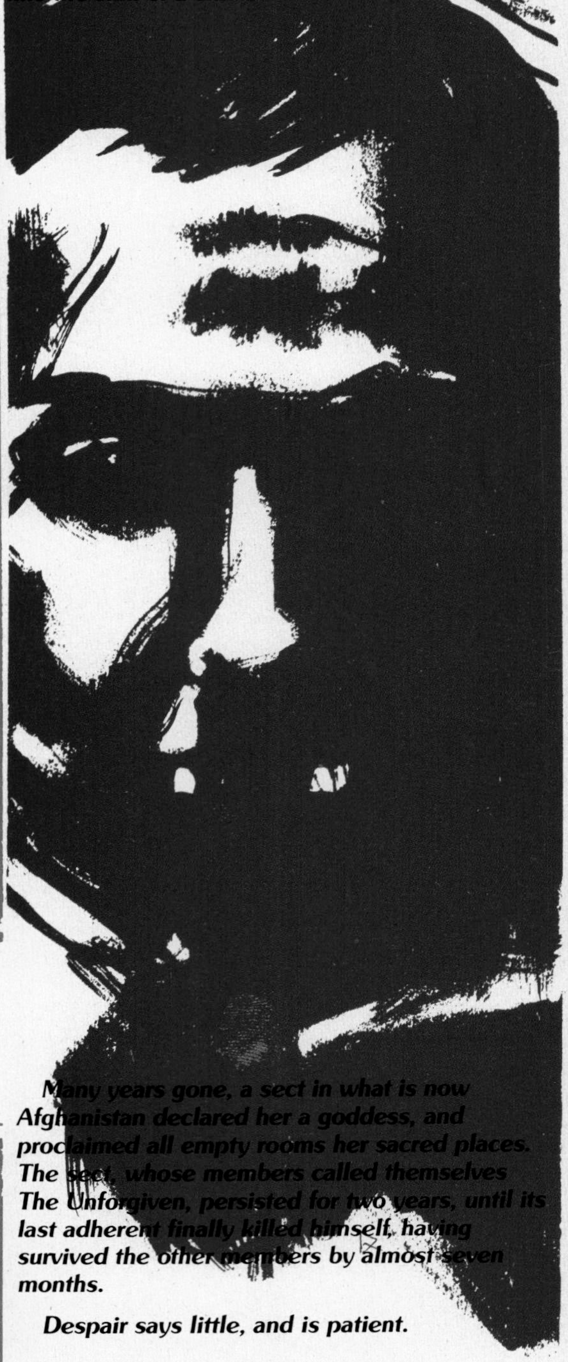

Many years gone, a sect in what is now Afghanistan declared her a goddess, and proclaimed all empty rooms her sacred places. The sect, whose members called themselves The Unforgiven, persisted for two years, until its last adherent finally killed himself, having survived the other members by almost seven months.

Despair says little, and is patient.

Destiny is the oldest of the Endless; in the Beginning was the Word, and it was traced by hand on the first page of his book, before ever it was spoken aloud.

Destiny is also the tallest of the Endless, to mortal eyes.

There are some who believe him to be blind; whilst others, perhaps with more reason, claim that he has travelled far beyond blindness, that indeed, he can do nothing but see: that he sees the fine traceries the galaxies make as they spiral through the void, that he watches the intricate patterns living things make on their journey through time.

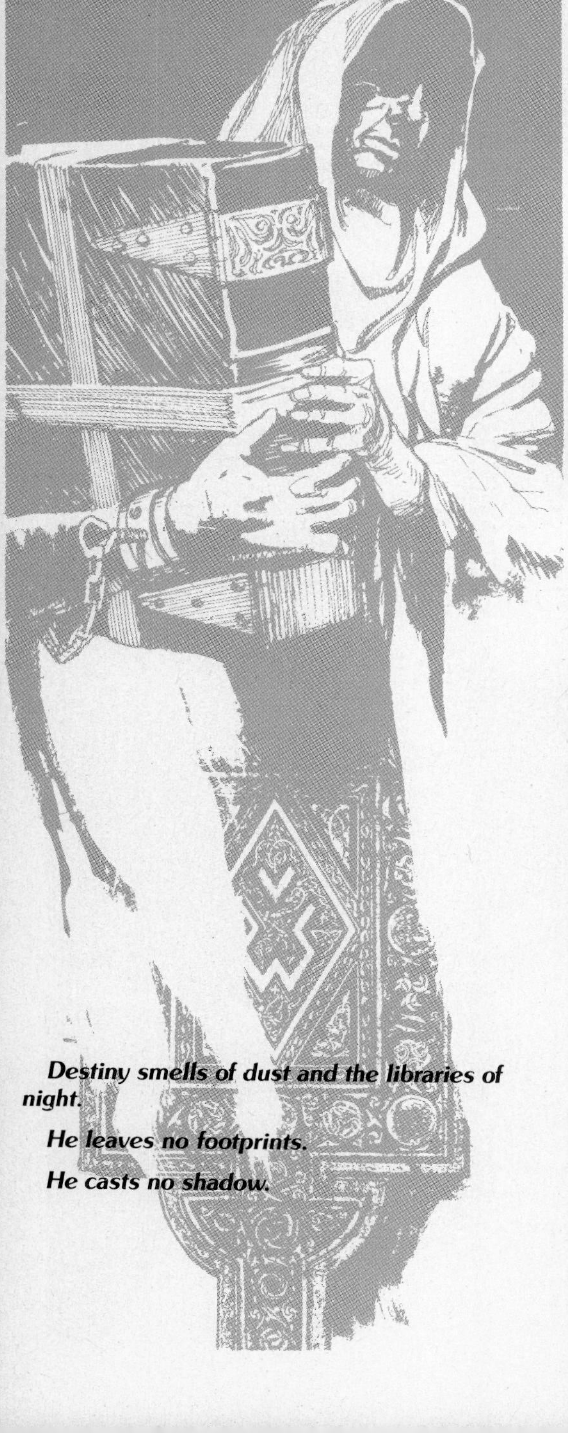

Destiny smells of dust and the libraries of night.

He leaves no footprints.

He casts no shadow.

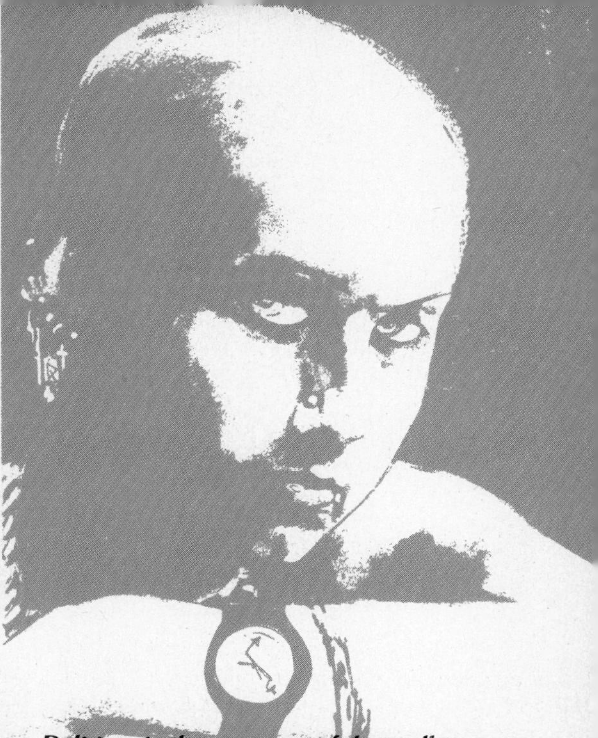

Delirium is the youngest of the endless.

She smells of sweat, sour wines, late nights, old leather.

Her realm is close, and can be visited; however, human minds were not made to comprehend her domain, and those few who have made the journey have been incapable of reporting back more than the tiniest fragments.

The poet Coleridge claimed to have known her intimately, but the man was an inveterate liar, and in this, as in so much, we must doubt his word.

Her appearance is the most variable of all the Endless, who, at best, are ideas cloaked in the semblance of flesh. Her shadow's shape and outline has no relationship to that of any body she wears, and it is tangible, like old velvet.

Some say the tragedy of Delirium is her knowledge that, despite being older than suns, older than gods, she is forever the youngest of the Endless, who do not measure time as we measure time, or see the worlds through mortal eyes.

Others deny this, and say that Delirium has no tragedy, but here they speak without reflection.

For Delirium was once Delight. And although that was long ago now, even today her eyes are badly matched: one eye is a vivid emerald green, spattered with silver flecks that move; her other eye is vein blue.

Who knows what Delirium sees, through her mismatched eyes?

Dream of the Endless: ah, there's a conundrum.

In this aspect (and we perceive but aspects of the Endless, as we see the light glinting from one tiny facet of some huge and flawlessly cut precious stone), he is rake-thin, with skin the color of falling snow.

Dream accumulates names to himself like others make friends; but he permits himself few friends.

If he is closest to anyone, it is to his elder sister, whom he sees but rarely.

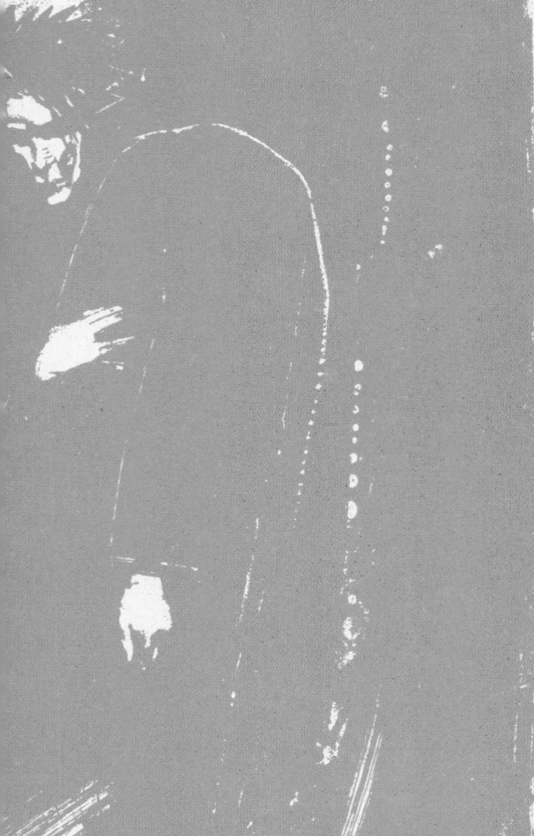

He heard long ago, in a dream, that one day in every century Death takes on mortal flesh, better to comprehend what the lives she takes must feel like, to taste the bitter tang of mortality: that this is the price she must pay for being the divider of the living from all that has gone before, all that must come after.

He broods on this tale, but has never questioned her about its truth. Perhaps he fears that she would answer him.

Of all the Endless, save perhaps Destiny, he is most conscious of his responsibilities, the most meticulous in their execution.

Dream casts a human shadow, when it occurs to him to do so.

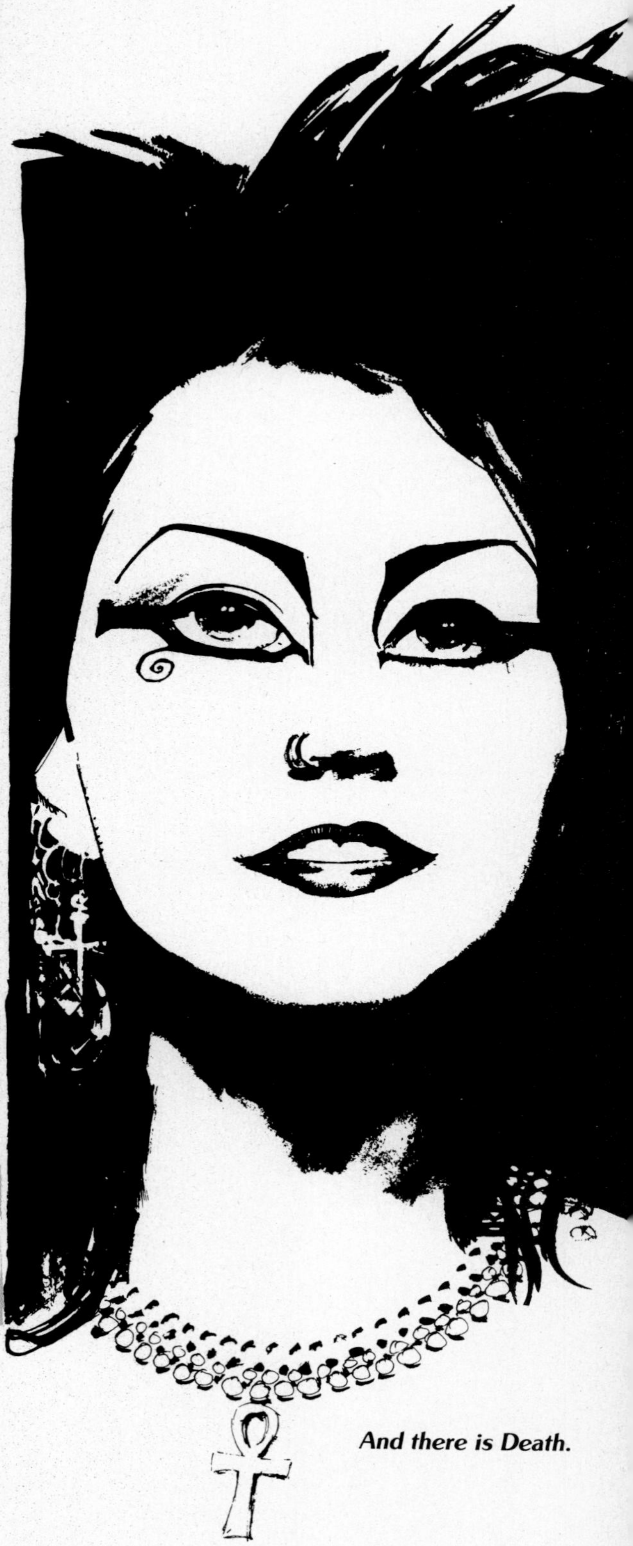

And there is Death.

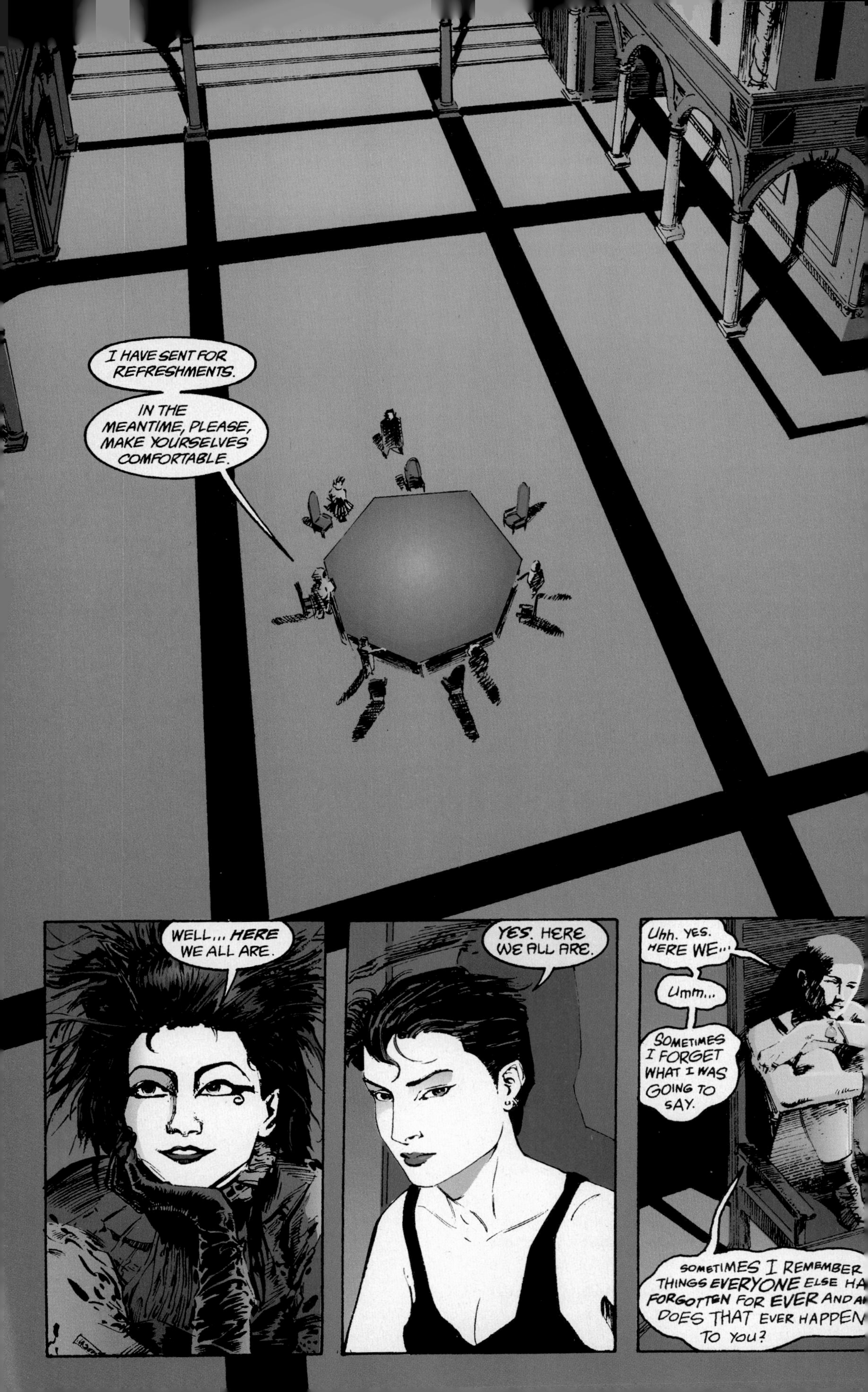
I HAVE SENT FOR REFRESHMENTS.
IN THE MEANTIME, PLEASE, MAKE YOURSELVES COMFORTABLE.
WELL... *HERE* WE ALL ARE.
YES. HERE WE ALL ARE.
Uhh. YES. HERE WE...
Umm...
SOMETIMES I FORGET WHAT I WAS GOING TO SAY.
SOMETIMES I REMEMBER THINGS *EVERYONE* ELSE HA FORGOTTEN FOR *EVER* AND A DOES THAT EVER HAPPEN TO YOU?

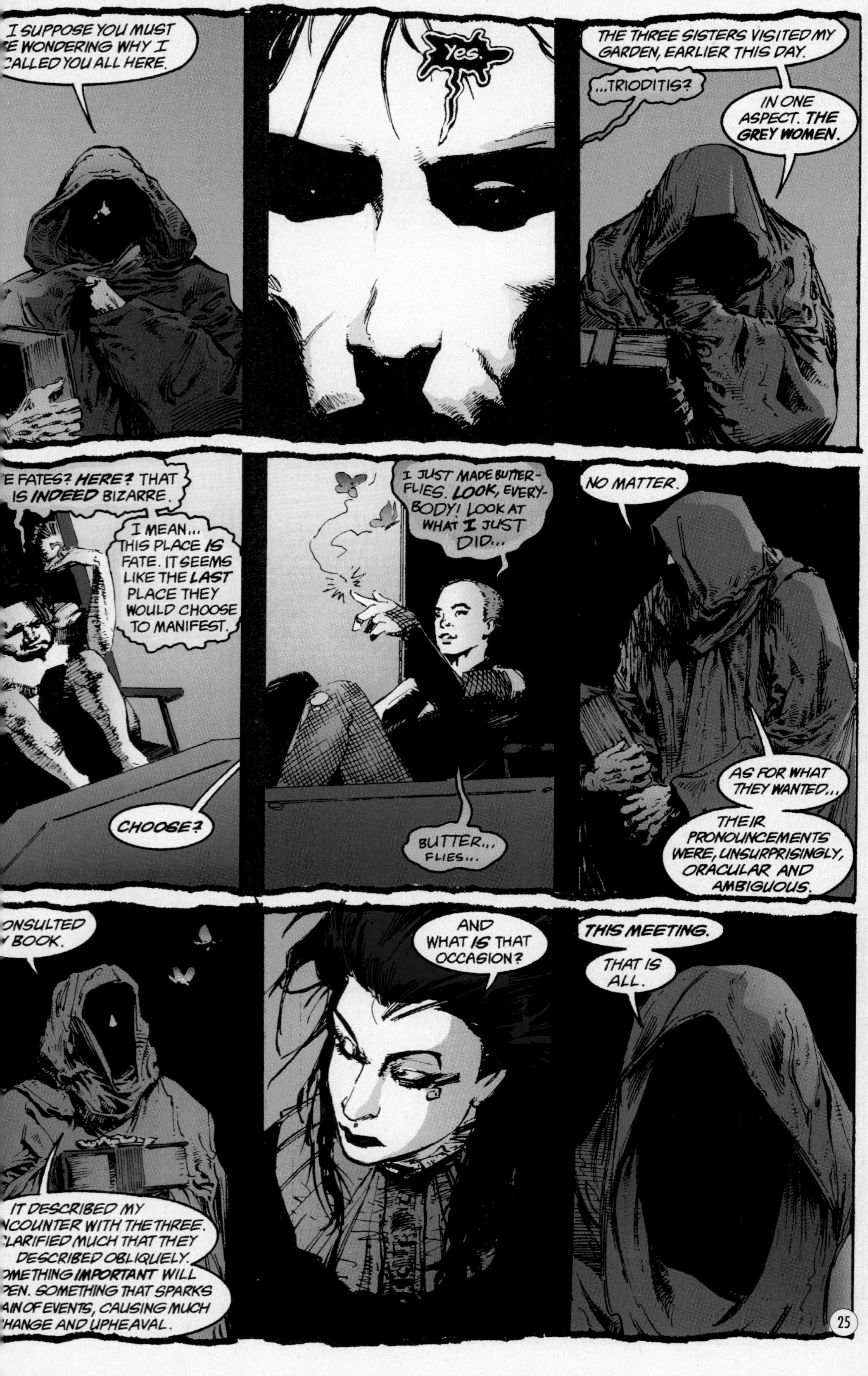
I SUPPOSE YOU MUST
E WONDERING WHY I
CALLED YOU ALL HERE.
Yes.
THE THREE SISTERS VISITED MY GARDEN, EARLIER THIS DAY.
...TRIODITIS?
IN ONE ASPECT. THE GREY WOMEN.
E FATES? HERE? THAT IS INDEED BIZARRE.
I MEAN... THIS PLACE IS FATE. IT SEEMS LIKE THE LAST PLACE THEY WOULD CHOOSE TO MANIFEST.
CHOOSE?
I JUST MADE BUTTER-FLIES. LOOK, EVERY-BODY! LOOK AT WHAT I JUST DID...
BUTTER... FLIES...
NO MATTER.
AS FOR WHAT THEY WANTED...
THEIR PRONOUNCEMENTS WERE, UNSURPRISINGLY, ORACULAR AND AMBIGUOUS.
ONSULTED
BOOK.
IT DESCRIBED MY
NCOUNTER WITH THE THREE.
LARIFIED MUCH THAT THEY
DESCRIBED OBLIQUELY.
OMETHING IMPORTANT WILL
PEN. SOMETHING THAT SPARKS
AIN OF EVENTS, CAUSING MUCH
HANGE AND UPHEAVAL.
AND WHAT IS THAT OCCASION?
THIS MEETING.
THAT IS ALL.

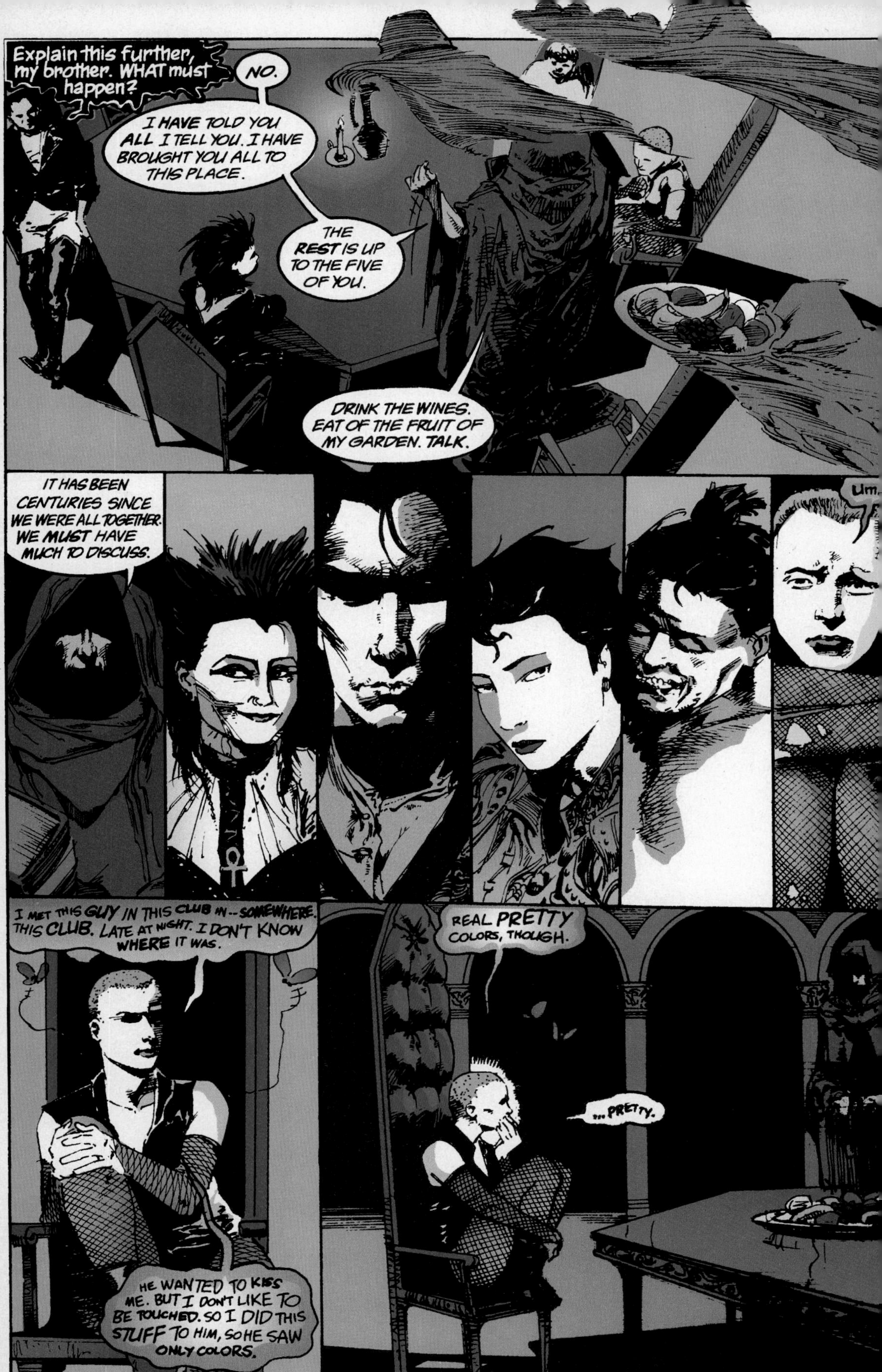

Explain this further, my brother. WHAT must happen?
NO.
I HAVE TOLD YOU ALL I TELL YOU. I HAVE BROUGHT YOU ALL TO THIS PLACE.
THE REST IS UP TO THE FIVE OF YOU.
DRINK THE WINES. EAT OF THE FRUIT OF MY GARDEN. TALK.
IT HAS BEEN CENTURIES SINCE WE WERE ALL TOGETHER. WE MUST HAVE MUCH TO DISCUSS.
Um.
I MET THIS GUY IN THIS CLUB IN -- SOMEWHERE. THIS CLUB. LATE AT NIGHT. I DON'T KNOW WHERE IT WAS.
HE WANTED TO KISS ME. BUT I DON'T LIKE TO BE TOUCHED. SO I DID THIS STUFF TO HIM, SO HE SAW ONLY COLORS.
REAL PRETTY COLORS, THOUGH.
...PRETTY.

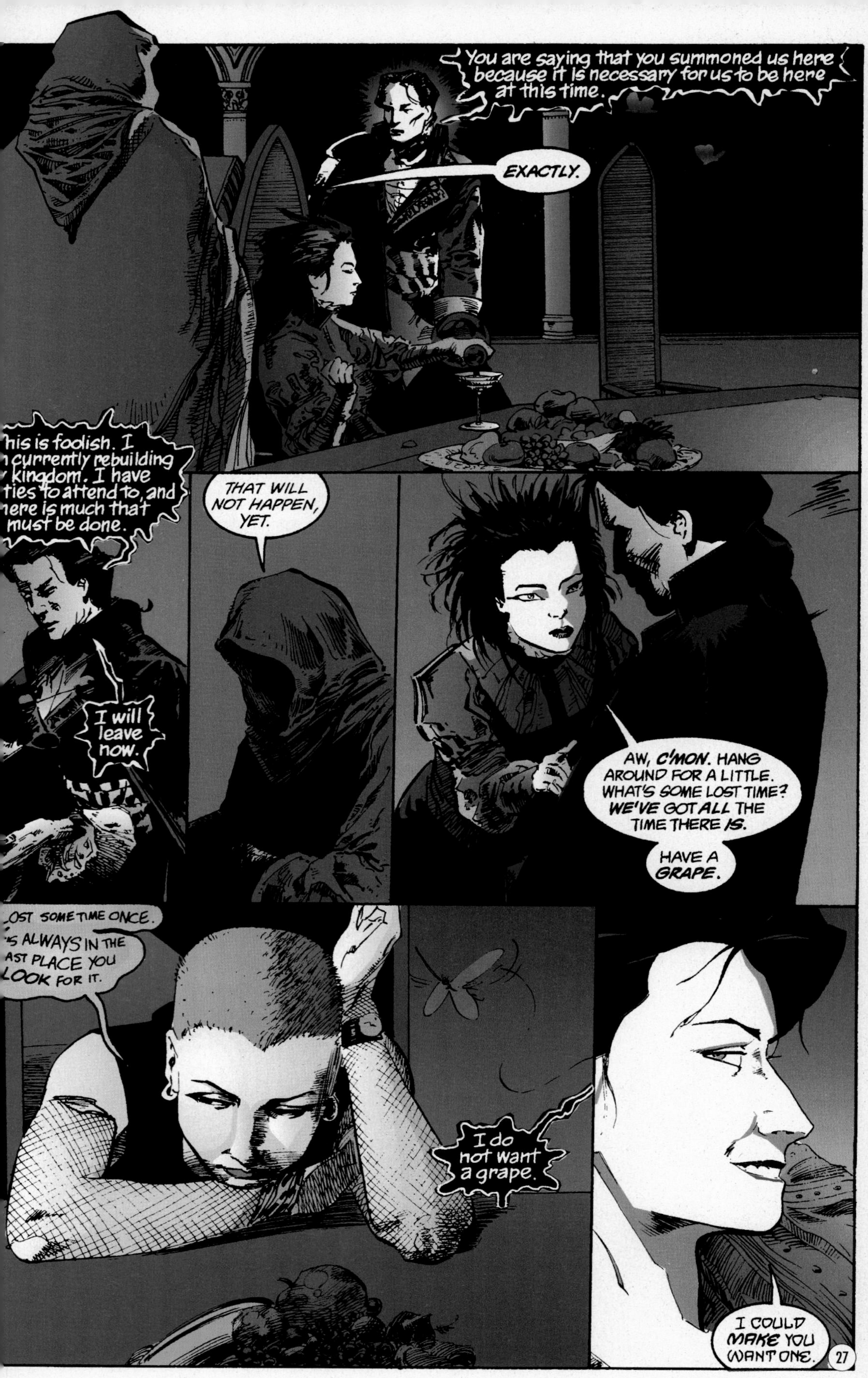

You are saying that you summoned us here because it is necessary for us to be here at this time.
EXACTLY.
his is foolish. I n currently rebuilding kingdom. I have ties to attend to, and here is much that must be done.
THAT WILL NOT HAPPEN, YET.
I will leave now.
AW, C'MON. HANG AROUND FOR A LITTLE. WHAT'S SOME LOST TIME? WE'VE GOT ALL THE TIME THERE IS.
HAVE A GRAPE.
OST SOME TIME ONCE. 'S ALWAYS IN THE AST PLACE YOU LOOK FOR IT.
I do not want a grape.
I COULD MAKE YOU WANT ONE.

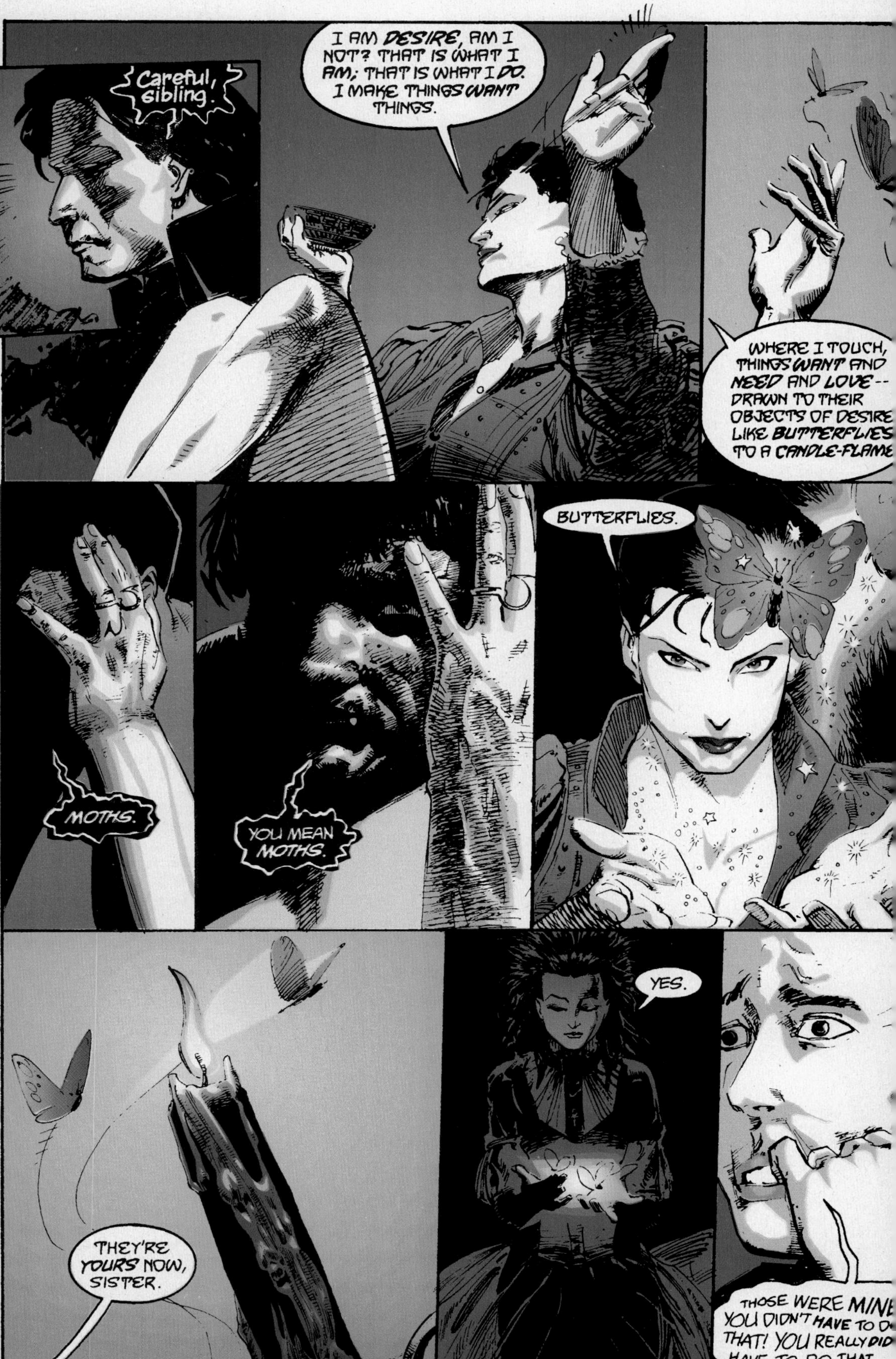
Careful, sibling.
I AM DESIRE, AM I NOT? THAT IS WHAT I AM; THAT IS WHAT I DO. I MAKE THINGS WANT THINGS.
WHERE I TOUCH, THINGS WANT AND NEED AND LOVE-- DRAWN TO THEIR OBJECTS OF DESIRE LIKE BUTTERFLIES TO A CANDLE-FLAME
MOTHS.
YOU MEAN MOTHS.
BUTTERFLIES.
THEY'RE YOURS NOW, SISTER.
YES.
THOSE WERE MINE YOU DIDN'T HAVE TO DO THAT! YOU REALLY DIDN'T HAVE TO DO THAT.

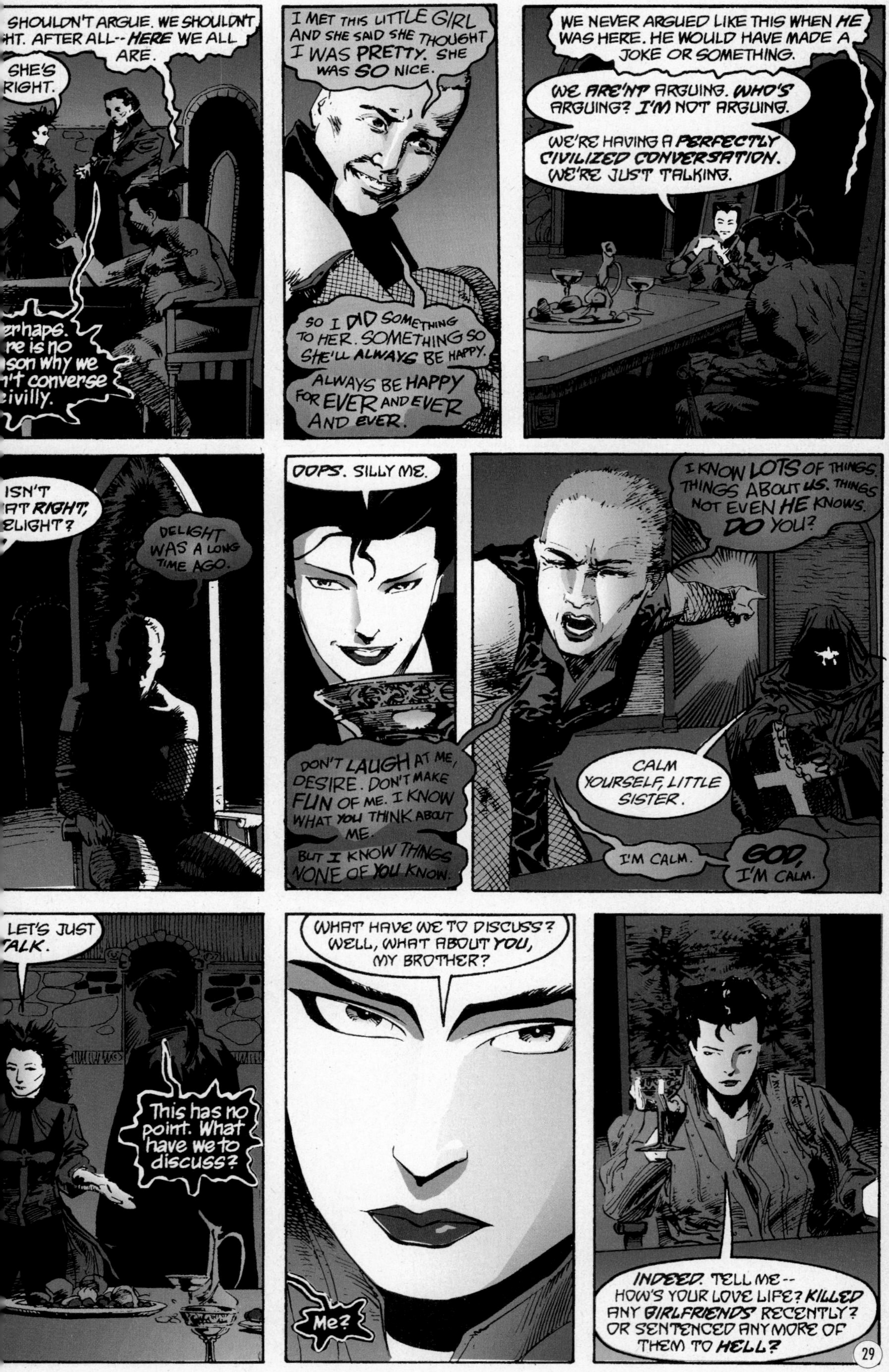
SHOULDN'T ARGUE. WE SHOULDN'T
GHT. AFTER ALL-- HERE WE ALL ARE.
SHE'S RIGHT.
erhaps. re is no son why we n't converse civilly.
I MET THIS LITTLE GIRL AND SHE SAID SHE THOUGHT I WAS PRETTY. SHE WAS SO NICE.
SO I DID SOMETHING TO HER. SOMETHING SO SHE'LL ALWAYS BE HAPPY.
ALWAYS BE HAPPY FOR EVER AND EVER AND EVER.
WE NEVER ARGUED LIKE THIS WHEN HE WAS HERE. HE WOULD HAVE MADE A JOKE OR SOMETHING.
WE AREN'T ARGUING. WHO'S ARGUING? I'M NOT ARGUING.
WE'RE HAVING A PERFECTLY CIVILIZED CONVERSATION. WE'RE JUST TALKING.
ISN'T AT RIGHT, ELIGHT?
DELIGHT WAS A LONG TIME AGO.
OOPS. SILLY ME.
DON'T LAUGH AT ME, DESIRE. DON'T MAKE FUN OF ME. I KNOW WHAT YOU THINK ABOUT ME.
BUT I KNOW THINGS NONE OF YOU KNOW.
I KNOW LOTS OF THINGS. THINGS ABOUT US. THINGS NOT EVEN HE KNOWS. DO YOU?
CALM YOURSELF, LITTLE SISTER.
I'M CALM.
GOD, I'M CALM.
LET'S JUST TALK.
This has no point. What have we to discuss?
WHAT HAVE WE TO DISCUSS? WELL, WHAT ABOUT YOU, MY BROTHER?
Me?
INDEED. TELL ME -- HOW'S YOUR LOVE LIFE? KILLED ANY GIRLFRIENDS RECENTLY? OR SENTENCED ANY MORE OF THEM TO HELL?

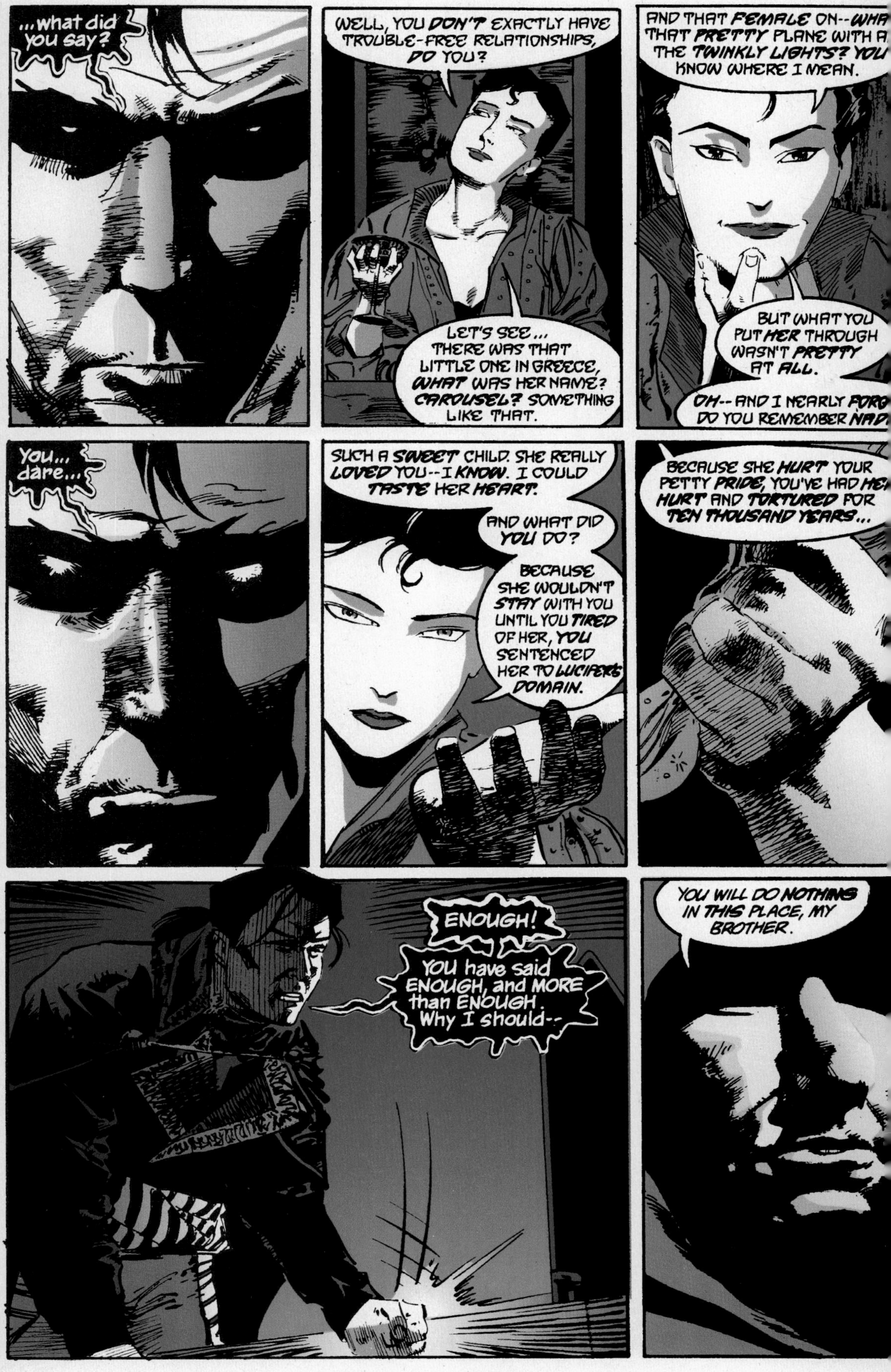
...what did you say?
WELL, YOU DON'T EXACTLY HAVE TROUBLE-FREE RELATIONSHIPS, DO YOU?
LET'S SEE... THERE WAS THAT LITTLE ONE IN GREECE, WHAT WAS HER NAME? CAROUSEL? SOMETHING LIKE THAT.
AND THAT FEMALE ON--WHA THAT PRETTY PLANE WITH A THE TWINKLY LIGHTS? YOU KNOW WHERE I MEAN.
BUT WHAT YOU PUT HER THROUGH WASN'T PRETTY AT ALL.
OH--AND I NEARLY FORG DO YOU REMEMBER NAD
You... dare...
SUCH A SWEET CHILD. SHE REALLY LOVED YOU--I KNOW. I COULD TASTE HER HEART.
AND WHAT DID YOU DO?
BECAUSE SHE WOULDN'T STAY WITH YOU UNTIL YOU TIRED OF HER, YOU SENTENCED HER TO LUCIFER'S DOMAIN.
BECAUSE SHE HURT YOUR PETTY PRIDE, YOU'VE HAD HE HURT AND TORTURED FOR TEN THOUSAND YEARS...
ENOUGH!
YOU have said ENOUGH, and MORE than ENOUGH. Why I should--
YOU WILL DO NOTHING IN THIS PLACE, MY BROTHER.

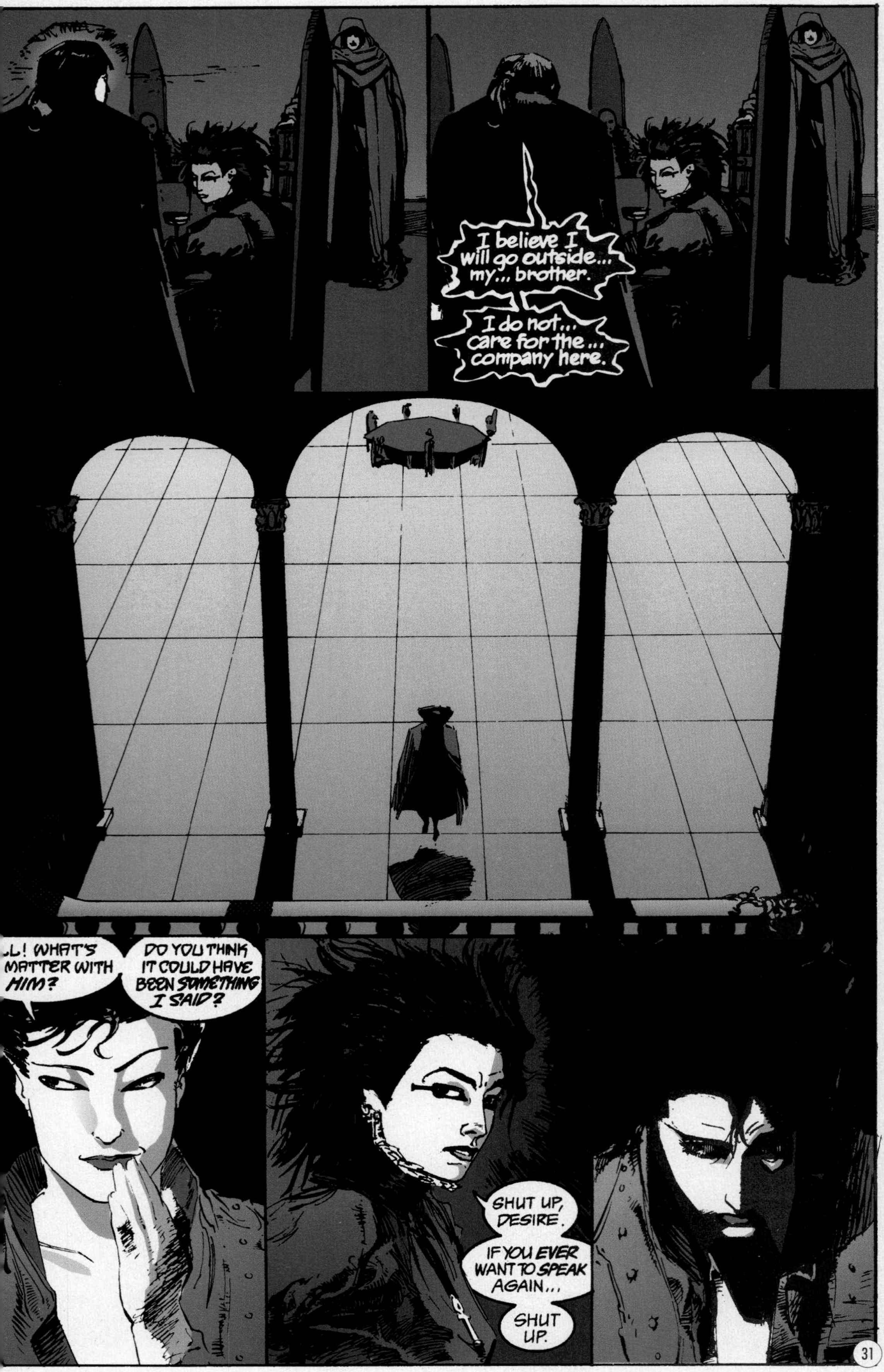
I believe I will go outside... my... brother.
I do not... care for the... company here.
...LL! WHAT'S ...MATTER WITH HIM?
DO YOU THINK IT COULD HAVE BEEN SOMETHING I SAID?
SHUT UP, DESIRE.
IF YOU EVER WANT TO SPEAK AGAIN...
SHUT UP.

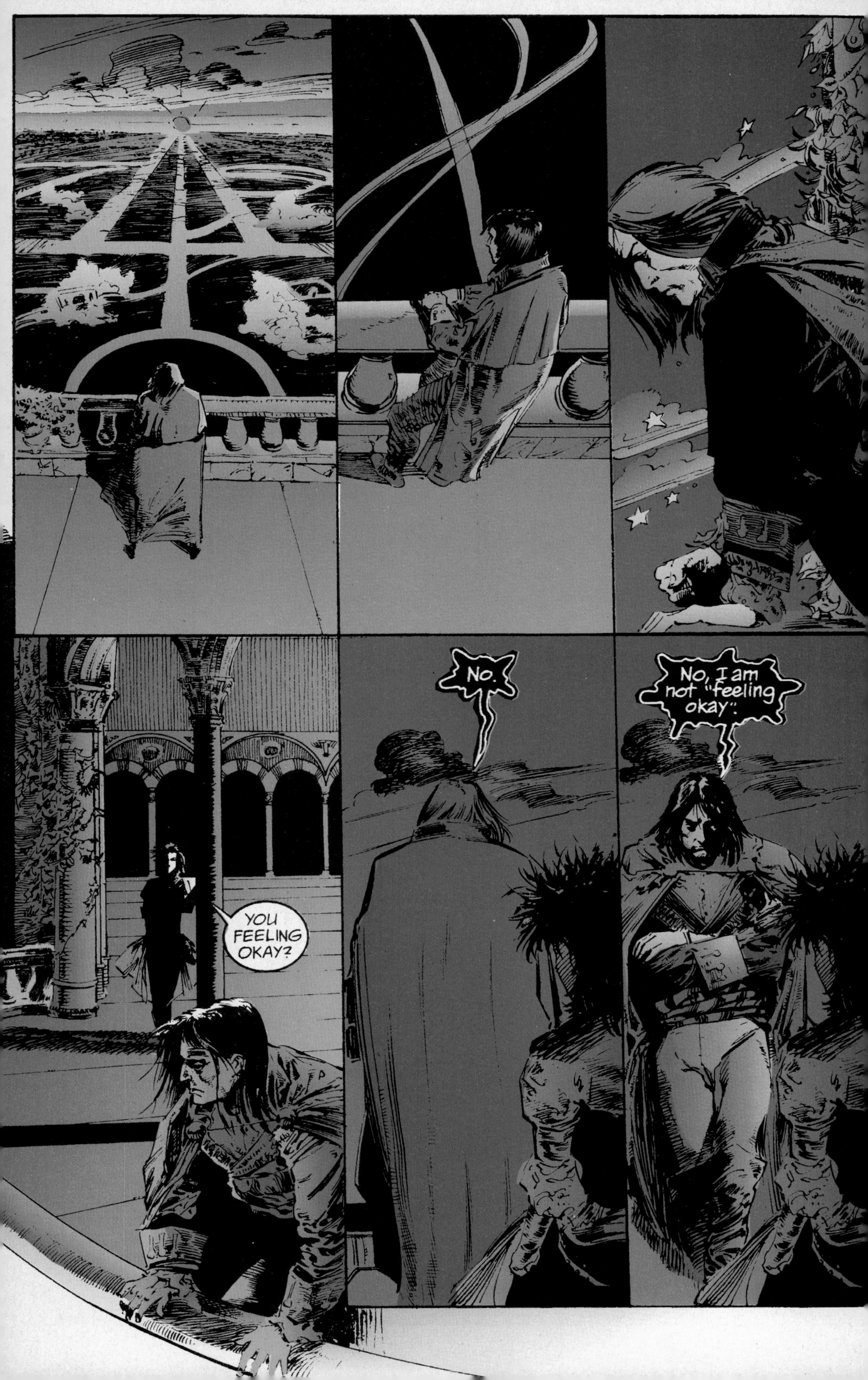
YOU FEELING OKAY?
No.
No, I am not "feeling okay".

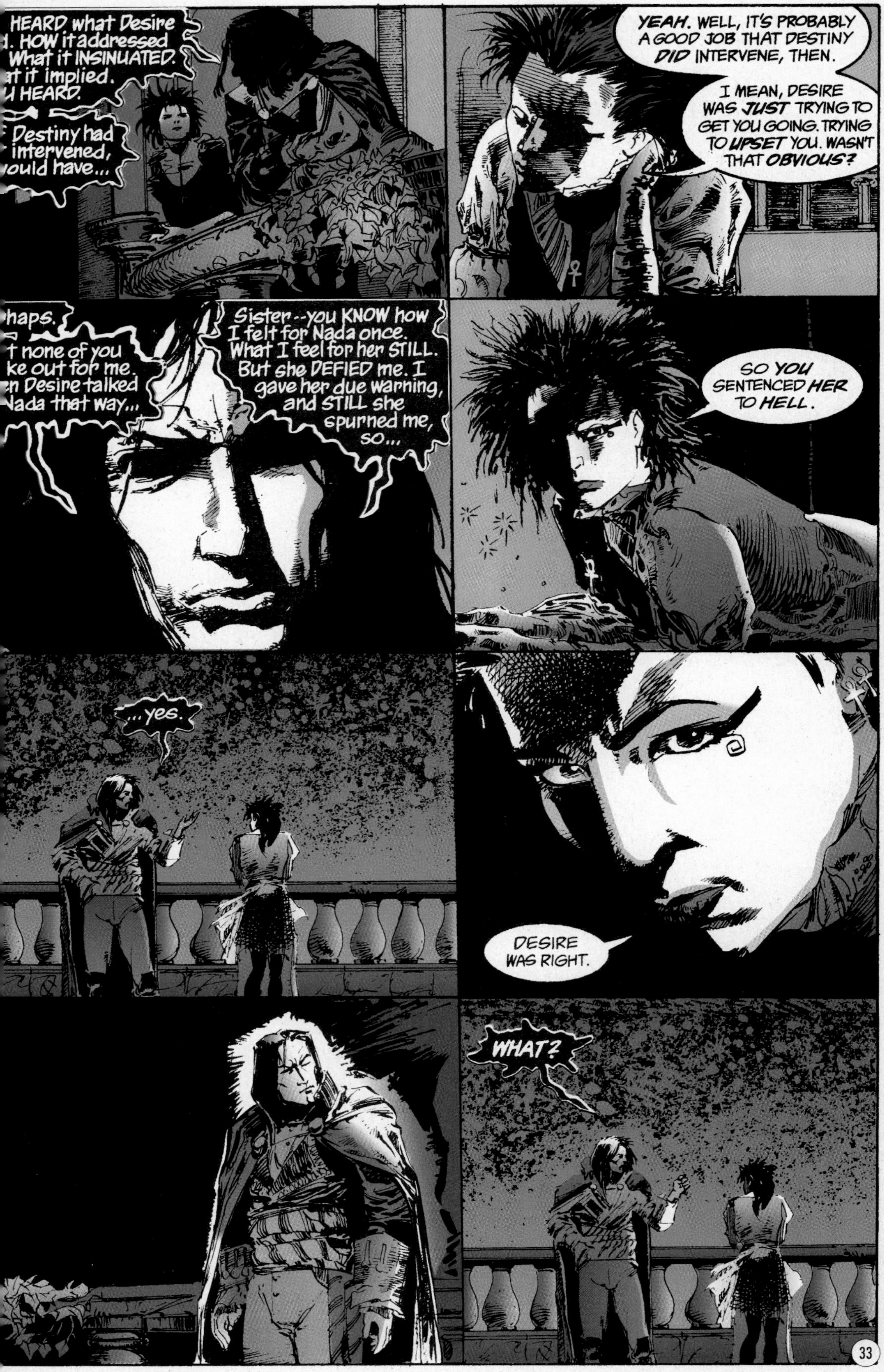
HEARD what Desire d. HOW it addressed What it INSINUATED. at it implied. u HEARD.
Destiny had intervened, ould have...
YEAH. WELL, IT'S PROBABLY A GOOD JOB THAT DESTINY DID INTERVENE, THEN.
I MEAN, DESIRE WAS JUST TRYING TO GET YOU GOING. TRYING TO UPSET YOU. WASN'T THAT OBVIOUS?
haps. t none of you ke out for me. n Desire talked Nada that way...
Sister--you KNOW how I felt for Nada once. What I feel for her STILL. But she DEFIED me. I gave her due warning, and STILL she spurned me, so...
SO YOU SENTENCED HER TO HELL.
...yes.
DESIRE WAS RIGHT.
WHAT?

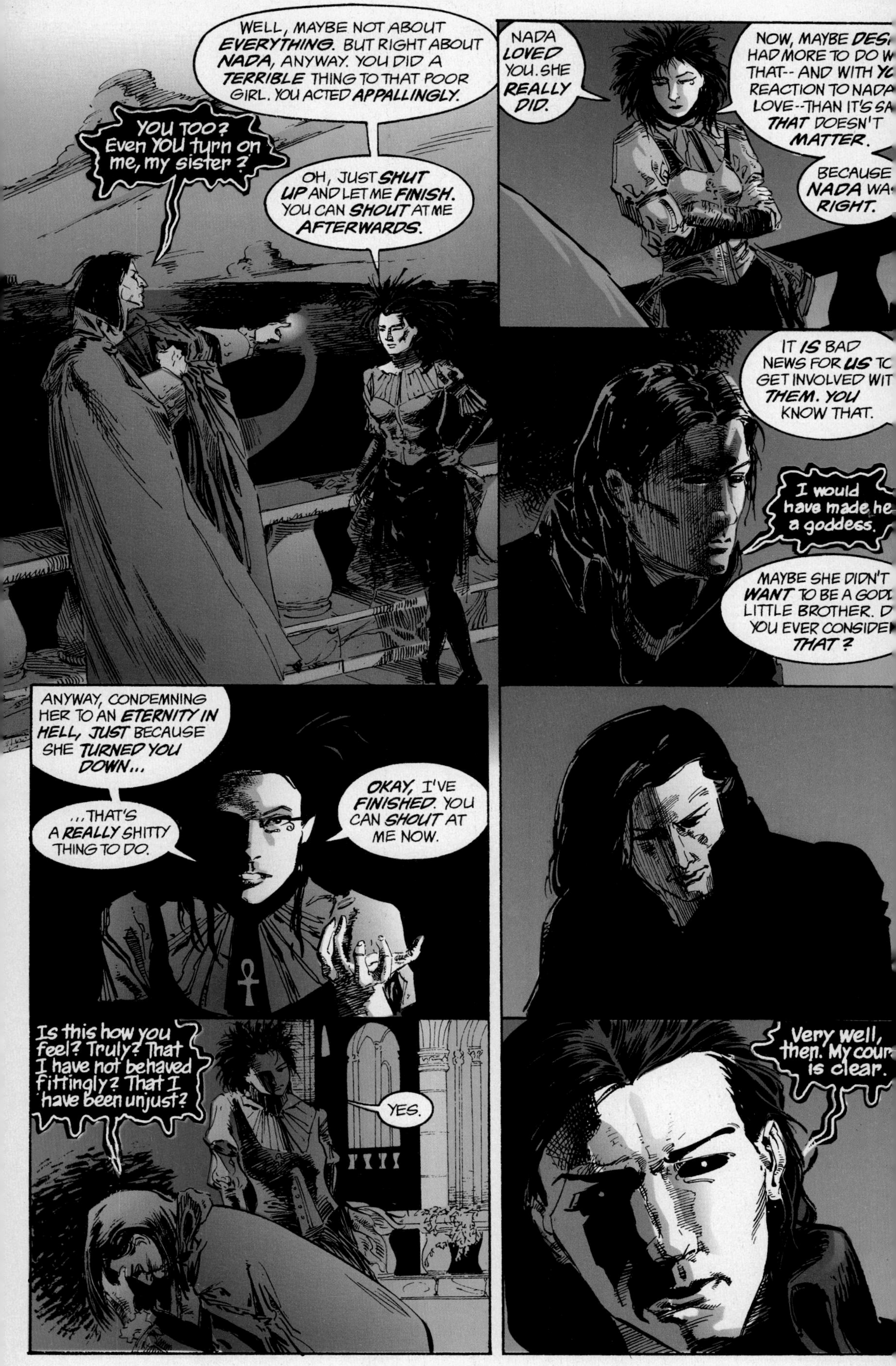
WELL, MAYBE NOT ABOUT EVERYTHING. BUT RIGHT ABOUT NADA, ANYWAY. YOU DID A TERRIBLE THING TO THAT POOR GIRL. YOU ACTED APPALLINGLY.
YOU TOO? Even YOU turn on me, my sister?
OH, JUST SHUT UP AND LET ME FINISH. YOU CAN SHOUT AT ME AFTERWARDS.
NADA LOVED YOU. SHE REALLY DID.
NOW, MAYBE DES
HAD MORE TO DO W
THAT-- AND WITH YO
REACTION TO NADA
LOVE--THAN IT'S SA
THAT DOESN'T
MATTER.
BECAUSE NADA WA RIGHT.
IT IS BAD NEWS FOR US TO GET INVOLVED WIT THEM. YOU KNOW THAT.
I would have made he a goddess.
MAYBE SHE DIDN'T WANT TO BE A GOD LITTLE BROTHER. D YOU EVER CONSIDE THAT?
ANYWAY, CONDEMNING HER TO AN ETERNITY IN HELL, JUST BECAUSE SHE TURNED YOU DOWN...
...THAT'S A REALLY SHITTY THING TO DO.
OKAY, I'VE FINISHED. YOU CAN SHOUT AT ME NOW.
Is this how you feel? Truly? That I have not behaved fittingly? That I have been unjust?
YES.
Very well, then. My cour is clear.

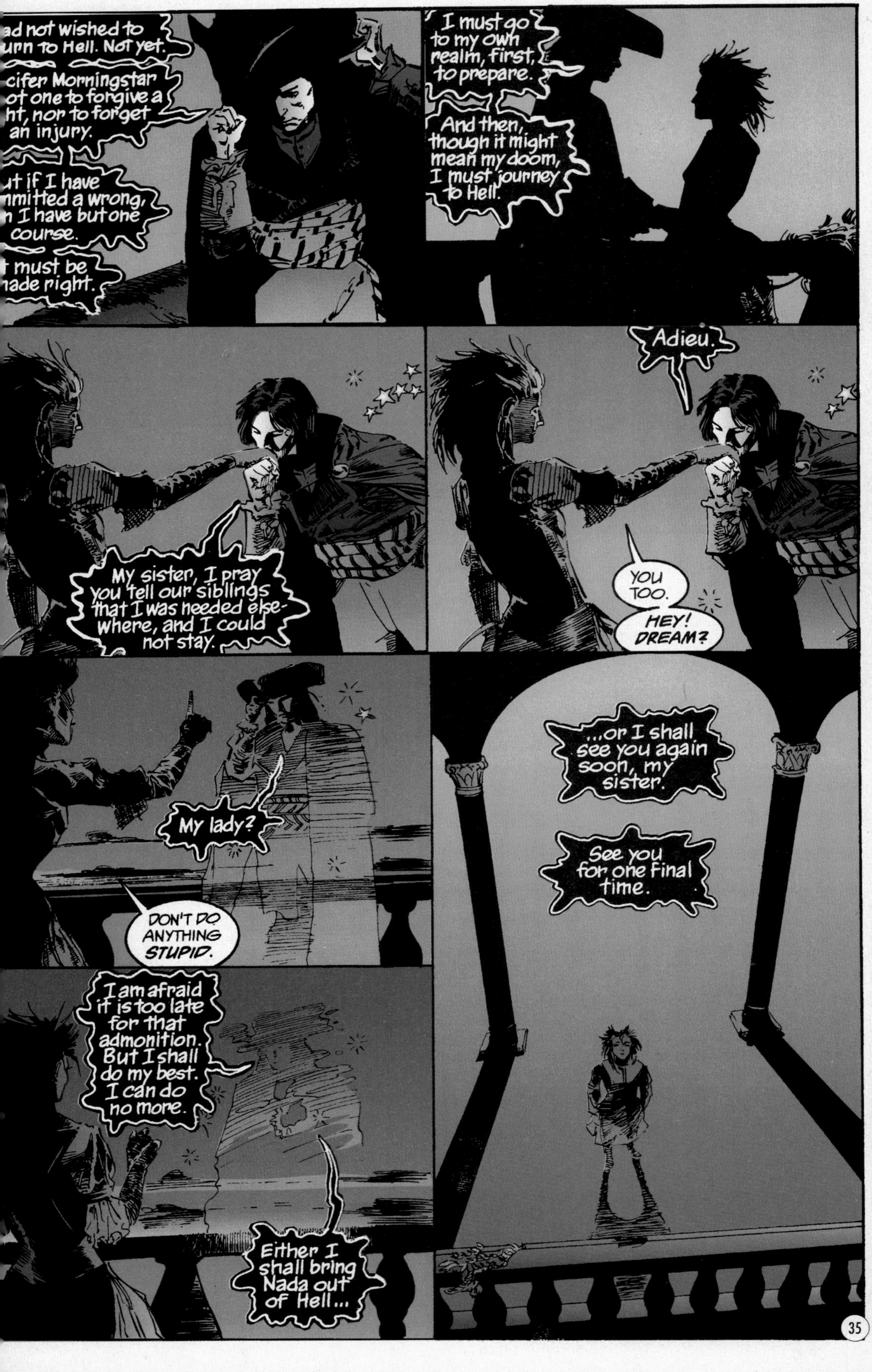
ad not wished to urn to Hell. Not yet.
cifer Morningstar ot one to forgive a ht, nor to forget an injury.
ut if I have nmitted a wrong, n I have but one course.
t must be nade right.
I must go to my own realm, first, to prepare.
And then, though it might mean my doom, I must journey to Hell.
My sister, I pray you tell our siblings that I was needed else-where, and I could not stay.
Adieu.
YOU TOO.
HEY! DREAM?
My lady?
DON'T DO ANYTHING STUPID.
I am afraid it is too late for that admonition. But I shall do my best. I can do no more.
Either I shall bring Nada out of Hell...
...or I shall see you again soon, my sister.
See you for one final time.

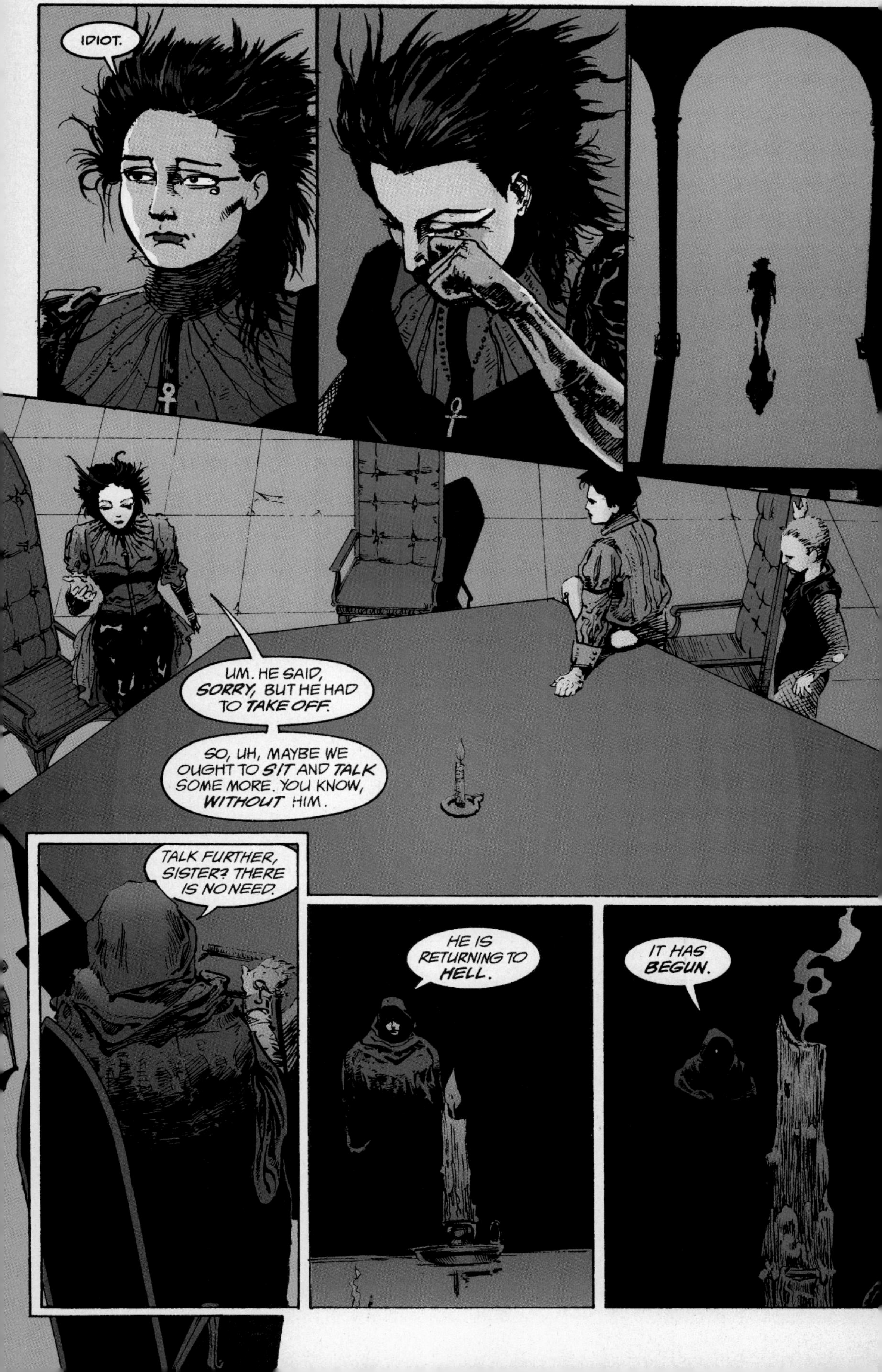
IDIOT.
UM. HE SAID, SORRY, BUT HE HAD TO TAKE OFF.
SO, UH, MAYBE WE OUGHT TO SIT AND TALK SOME MORE. YOU KNOW, WITHOUT HIM.
TALK FURTHER, SISTER? THERE IS NO NEED.
HE IS RETURNING TO HELL.
IT HAS BEGUN.

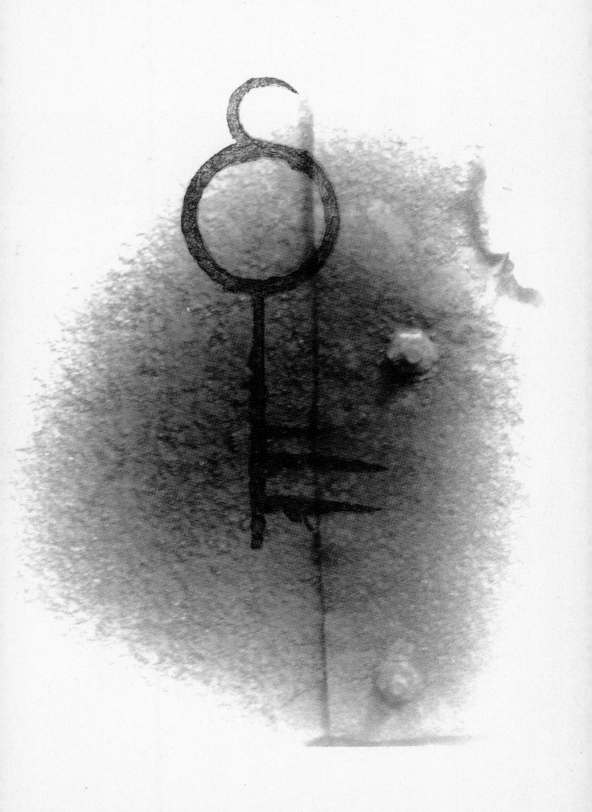

O N WHICH THE LORD OF DREAMS
MAKES PREPARATIONS TO VISIT
THE REALMS INFERNAL;
FAREWELL'S ARE SAID; A TOAST
IS DRUNK; AND IN HELL THE
ADVERSARY MAKES CERTAIN
PREPARATIONS OF HIS OWN.

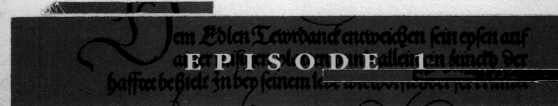

EPISODE 1

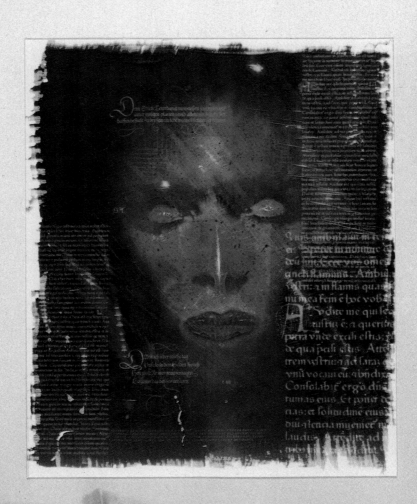

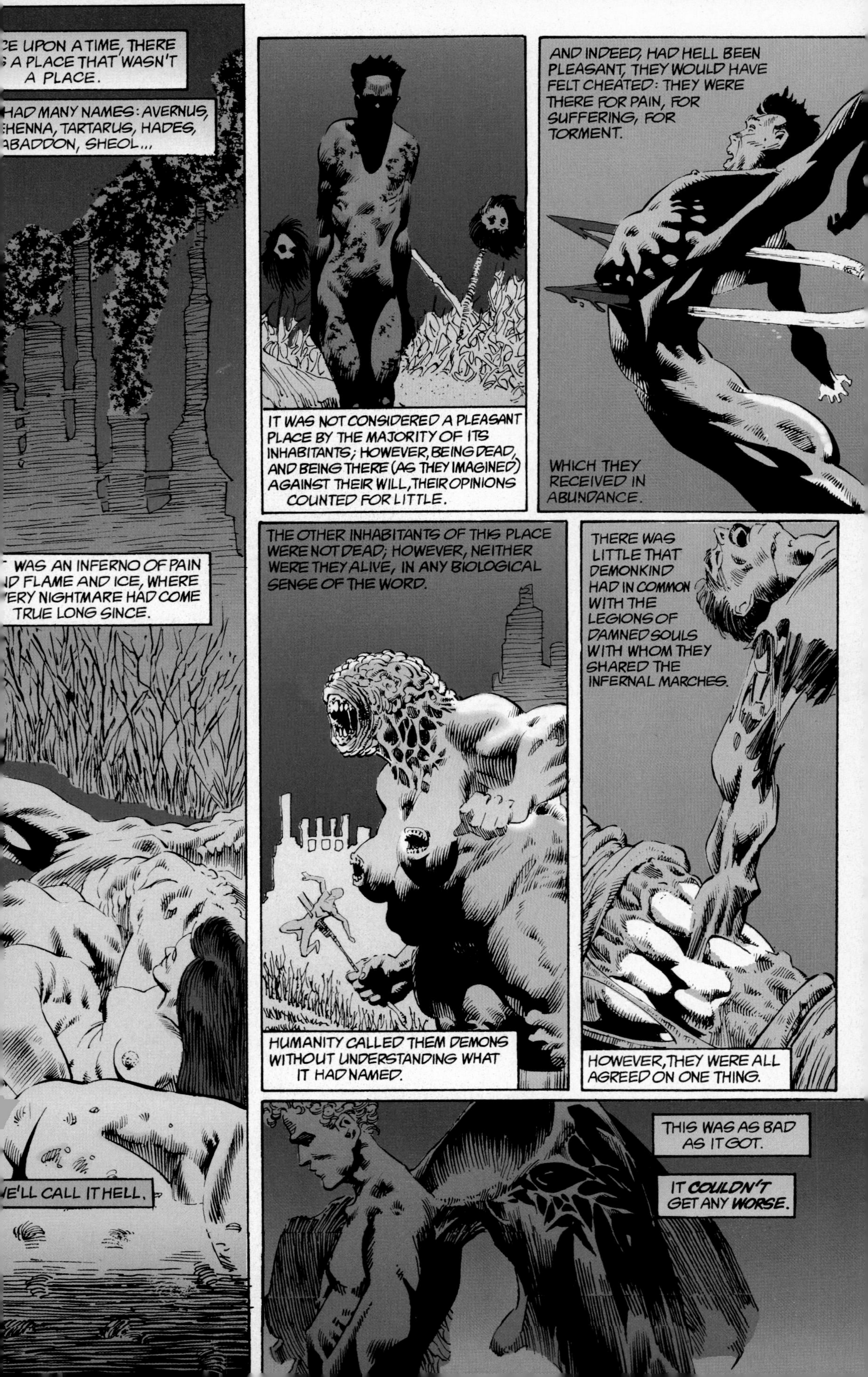
CE UPON A TIME, THERE
S A PLACE THAT WASN'T
A PLACE.
HAD MANY NAMES: AVERNUS,
EHENNA, TARTARUS, HADES,
ABADDON, SHEOL...
WAS AN INFERNO OF PAIN
D FLAME AND ICE, WHERE
ERY NIGHTMARE HAD COME
TRUE LONG SINCE.
E'LL CALL IT HELL.
IT WAS NOT CONSIDERED A PLEASANT PLACE BY THE MAJORITY OF ITS INHABITANTS; HOWEVER, BEING DEAD, AND BEING THERE (AS THEY IMAGINED) AGAINST THEIR WILL, THEIR OPINIONS COUNTED FOR LITTLE.
AND INDEED, HAD HELL BEEN PLEASANT, THEY WOULD HAVE FELT CHEATED: THEY WERE THERE FOR PAIN, FOR SUFFERING, FOR TORMENT.
WHICH THEY RECEIVED IN ABUNDANCE.
THE OTHER INHABITANTS OF THIS PLACE WERE NOT DEAD; HOWEVER, NEITHER WERE THEY ALIVE, IN ANY BIOLOGICAL SENSE OF THE WORD.
HUMANITY CALLED THEM DEMONS WITHOUT UNDERSTANDING WHAT IT HAD NAMED.
THERE WAS LITTLE THAT DEMONKIND HAD IN COMMON WITH THE LEGIONS OF DAMNED SOULS WITH WHOM THEY SHARED THE INFERNAL MARCHES.
HOWEVER, THEY WERE ALL AGREED ON ONE THING.
THIS WAS AS BAD AS IT GOT.
IT *COULDN'T* GET ANY *WORSE*.

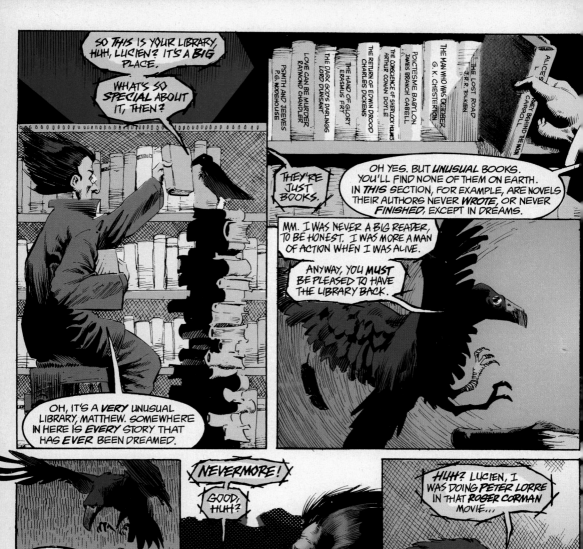
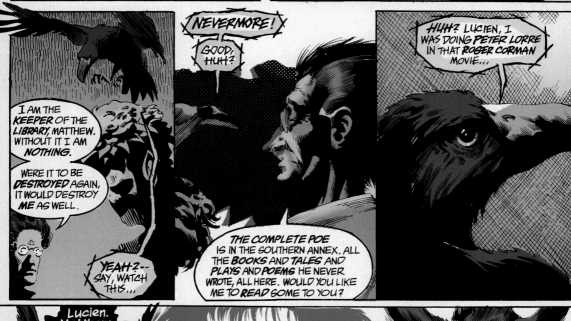
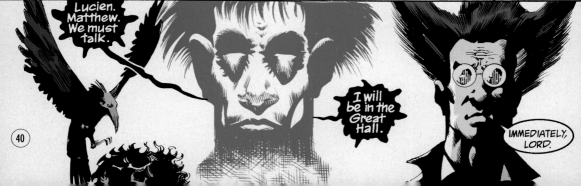

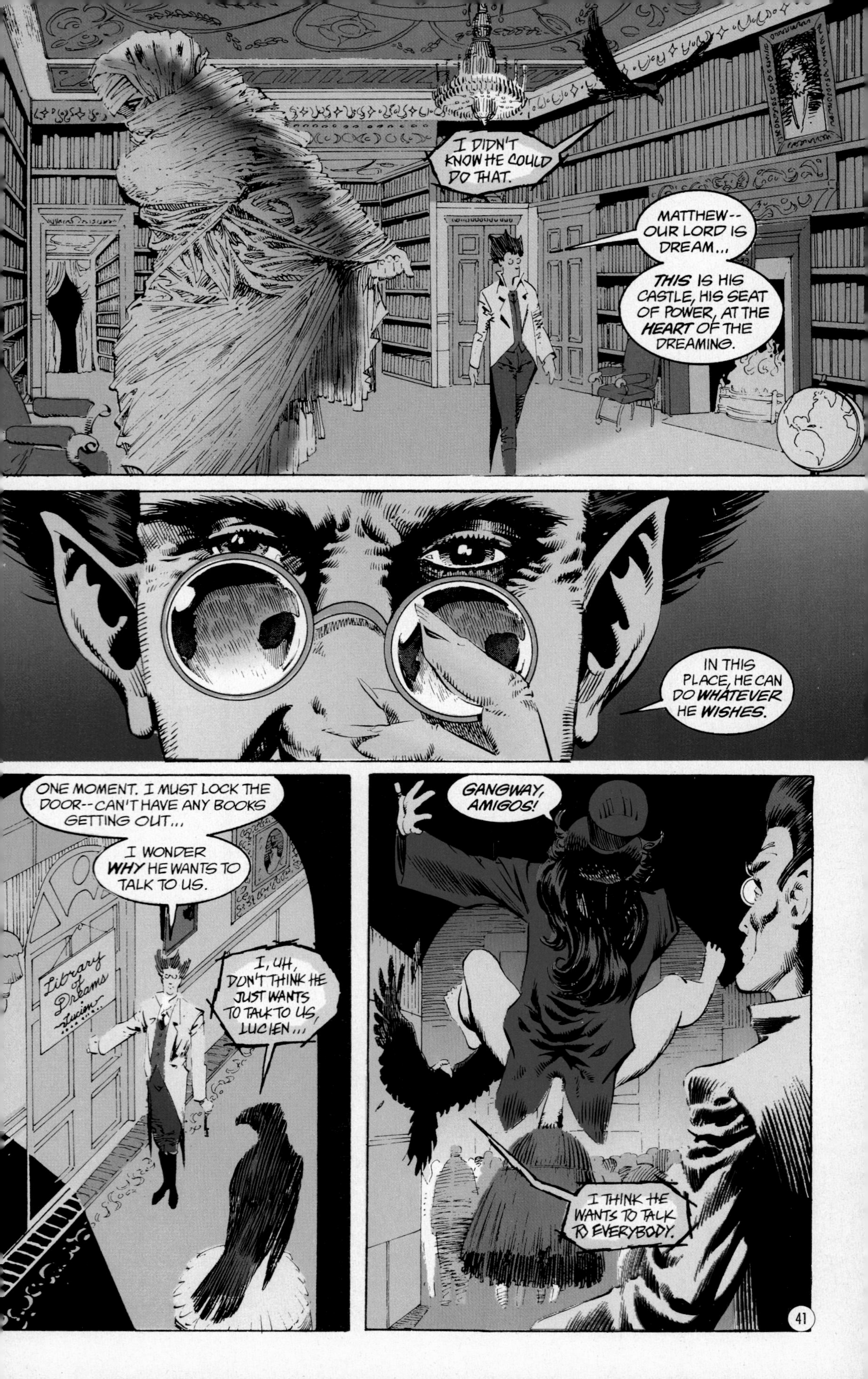

I DIDN'T KNOW HE COULD DO THAT.
MATTHEW-- OUR LORD IS DREAM...
THIS IS HIS CASTLE, HIS SEAT OF POWER, AT THE HEART OF THE DREAMING.
IN THIS PLACE, HE CAN DO WHATEVER HE WISHES.
ONE MOMENT. I MUST LOCK THE DOOR--CAN'T HAVE ANY BOOKS GETTING OUT...
I WONDER WHY HE WANTS TO TALK TO US.
Library of Dreams
Lucien
I, UH, DON'T THINK HE JUST WANTS TO TALK TO US, LUCIEN...
GANGWAY, AMIGOS!
I THINK HE WANTS TO TALK TO EVERYBODY.

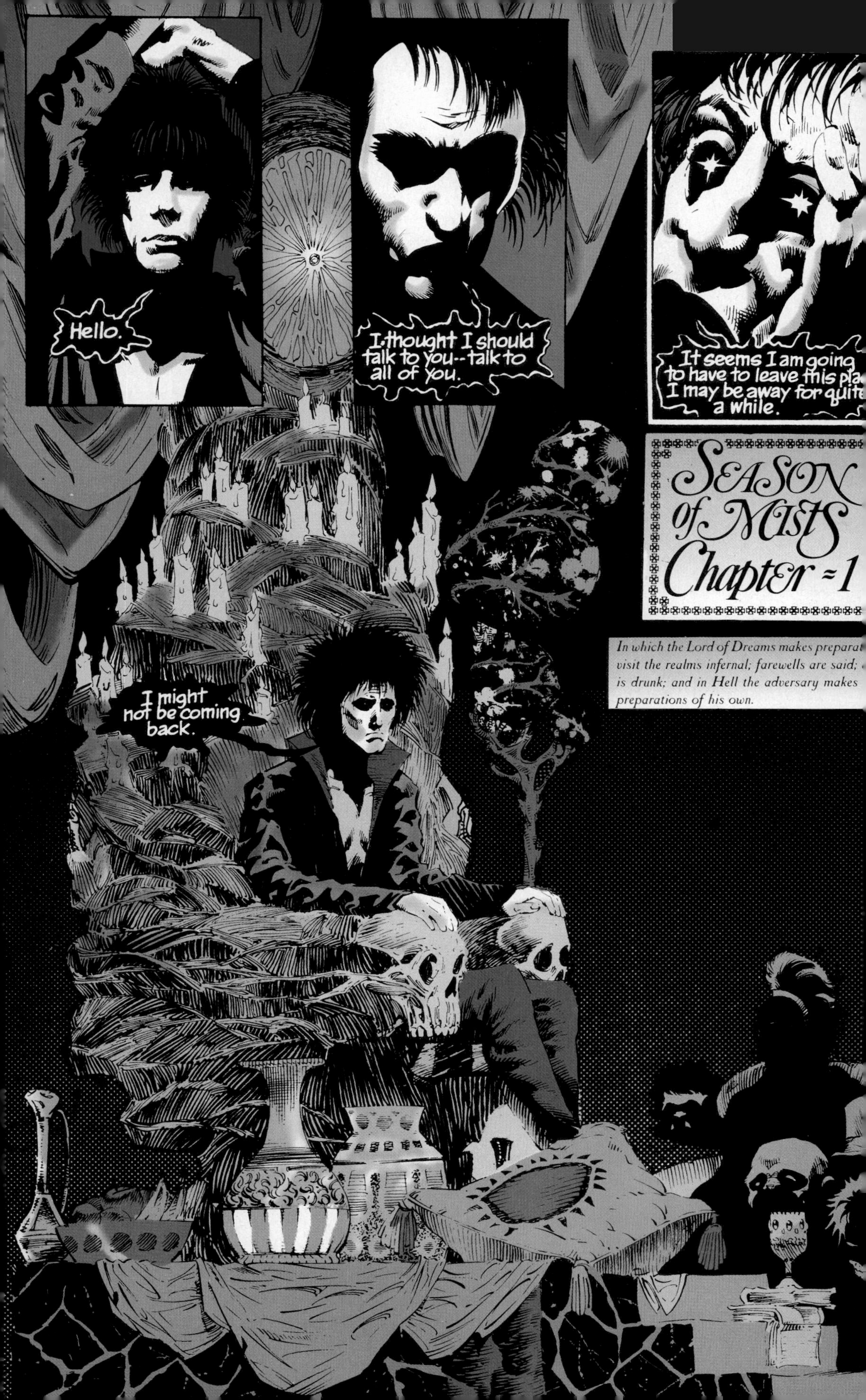

Hello.
I thought I should talk to you--talk to all of you.
It seems I am going to have to leave this pla
I may be away for quit a while.
Season of Mists
Chapter 1
In which the Lord of Dreams makes preparat visit the realms infernal; farewells are said; is drunk; and in Hell the adversary makes preparations of his own.
I might not be coming back.

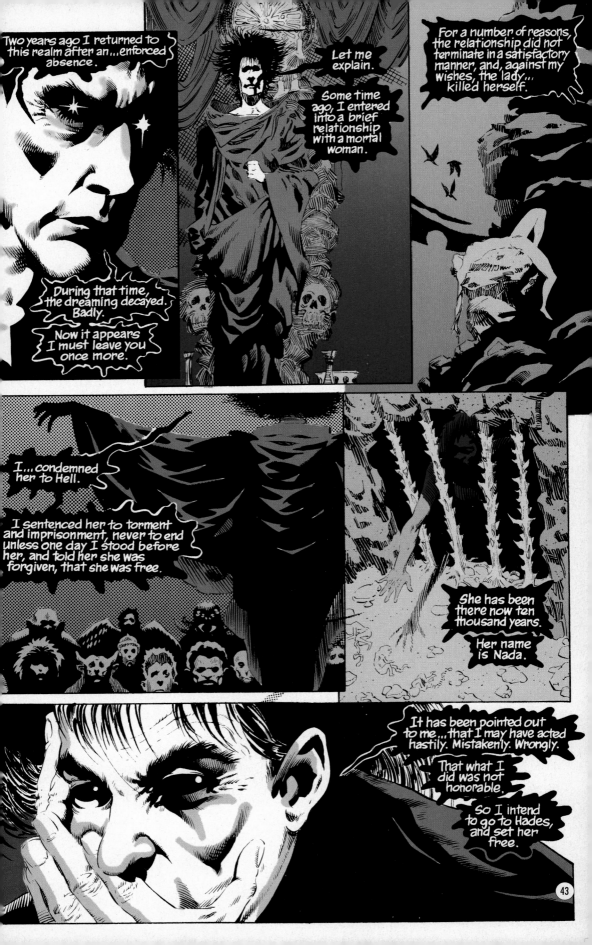

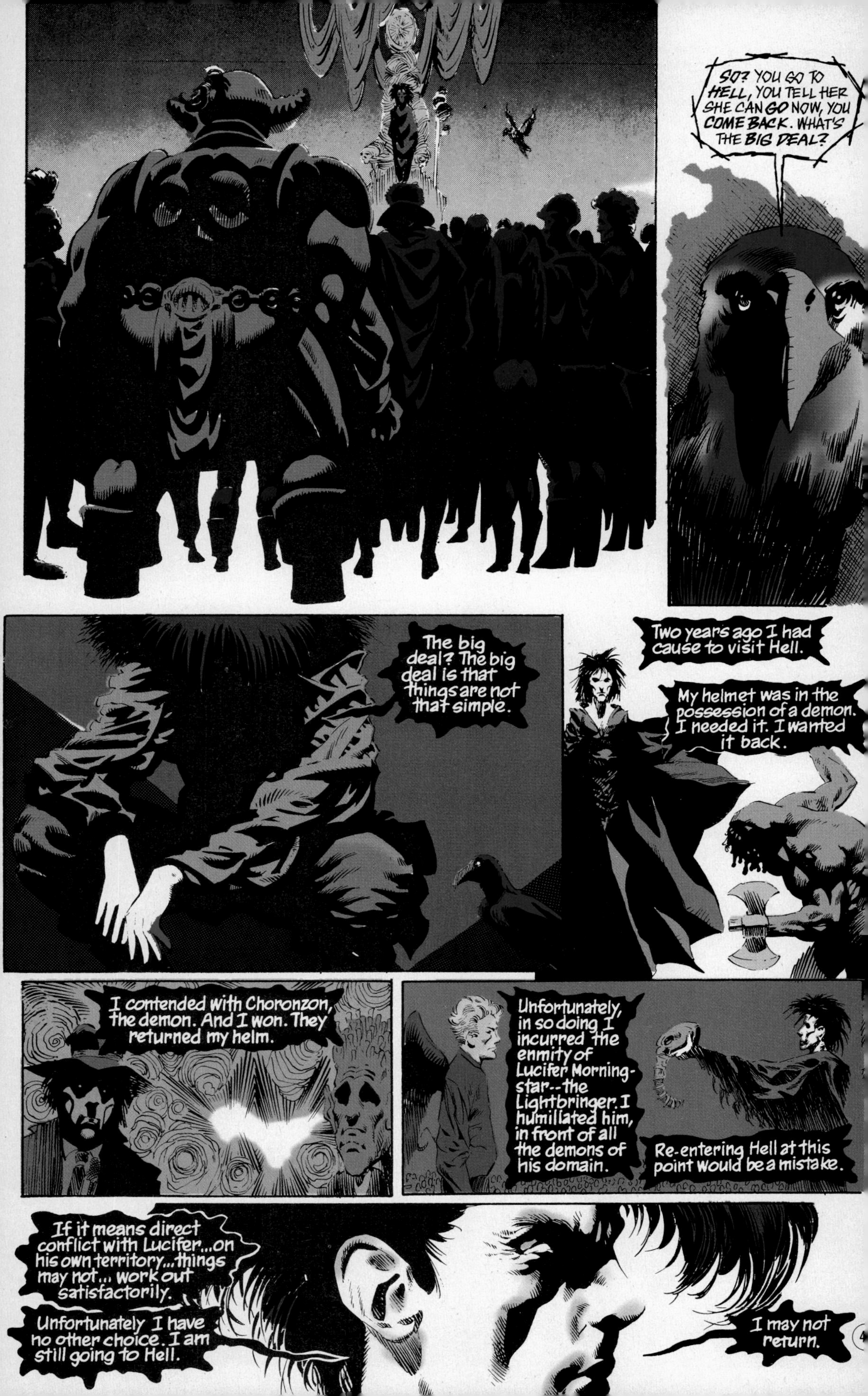
SO? YOU GO TO HELL, YOU TELL HER SHE CAN GO NOW, YOU COME BACK. WHAT'S THE BIG DEAL?
The big deal? The big deal is that things are not that simple.
Two years ago I had cause to visit Hell.
My helmet was in the possession of a demon. I needed it. I wanted it back.
I contended with Choronzon, the demon. And I won. They returned my helm.
Unfortunately, in so doing I incurred the enmity of Lucifer Morningstar--the Lightbringer. I humiliated him, in front of all the demons of his domain.
Re-entering Hell at this point would be a mistake.
If it means direct conflict with Lucifer...on his own territory...things may not... work out satisfactorily.
Unfortunately I have no other choice. I am still going to Hell.
I may not return.

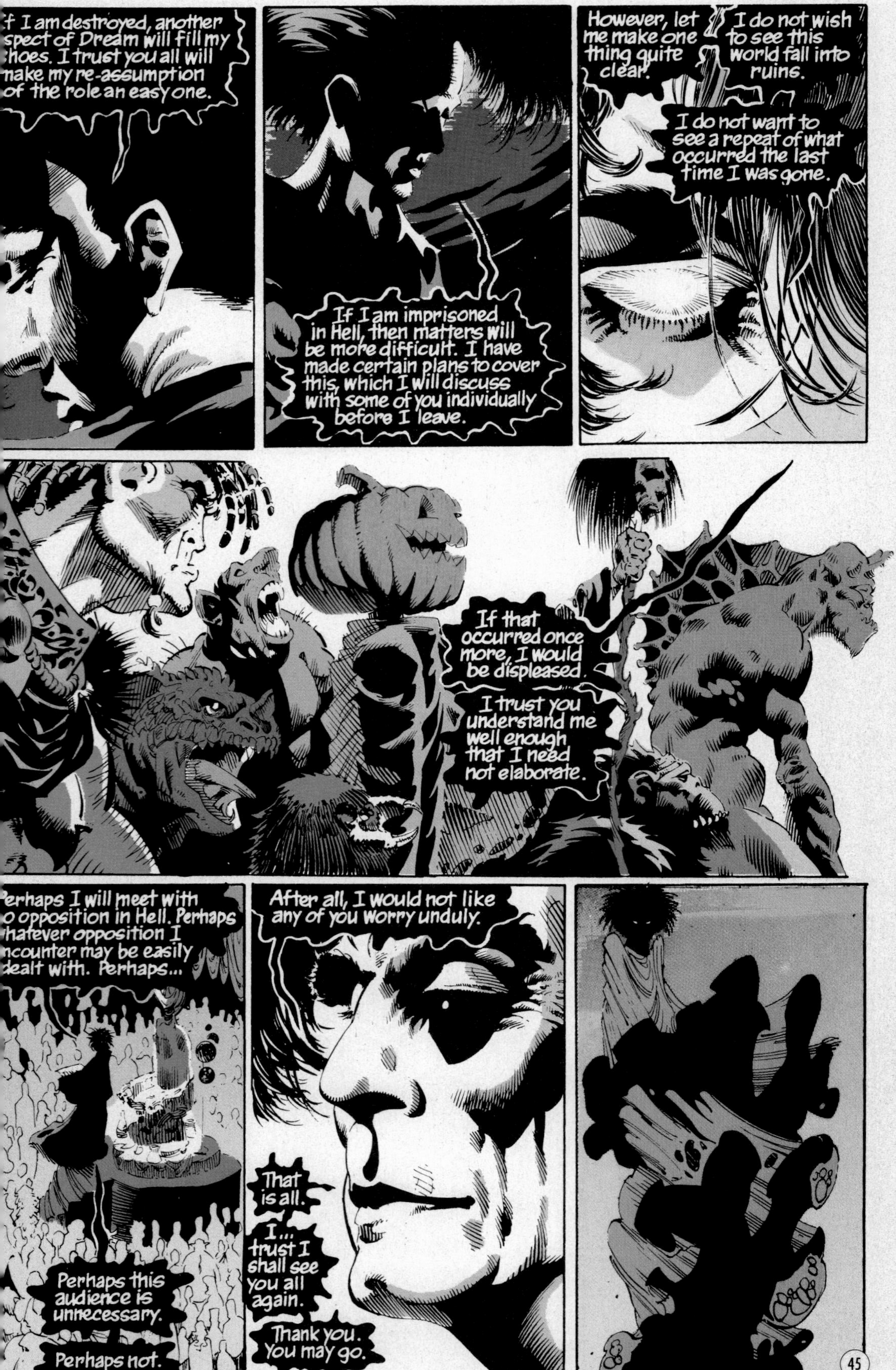

If I am destroyed, another aspect of Dream will fill my shoes. I trust you all will make my re-assumption of the role an easy one.
If I am imprisoned in Hell, then matters will be more difficult. I have made certain plans to cover this, which I will discuss with some of you individually before I leave.
However, let me make one thing quite clear.
I do not wish to see this world fall into ruins.
I do not want to see a repeat of what occurred the last time I was gone.
If that occurred once more, I would be displeased.
I trust you understand me well enough that I need not elaborate.
Perhaps I will meet with no opposition in Hell. Perhaps whatever opposition I encounter may be easily dealt with. Perhaps...
Perhaps this audience is unnecessary.
Perhaps not.
After all, I would not like any of you worry unduly.
That is all.
I... trust I shall see you all again.
Thank you. You may go.

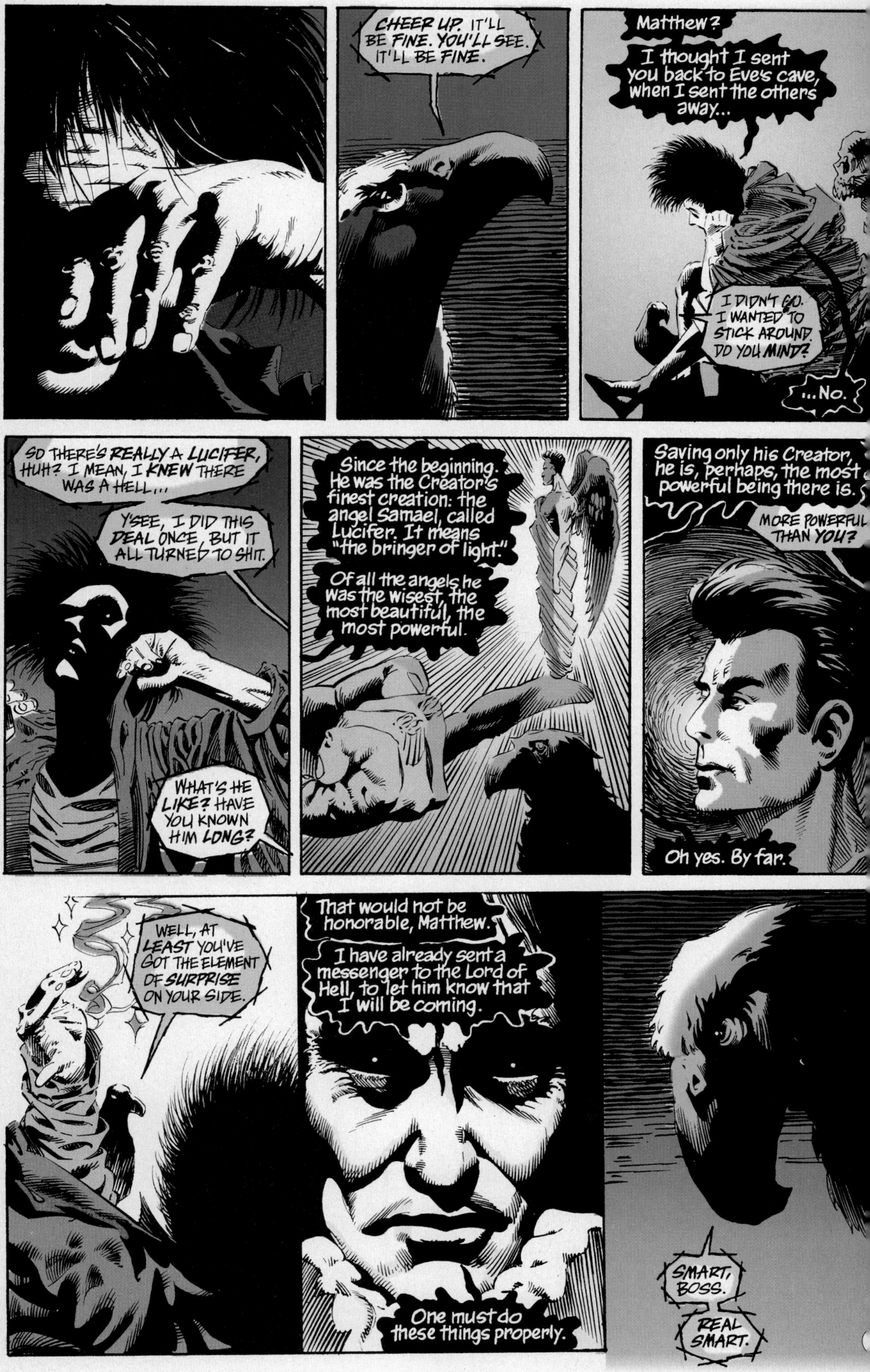

CHEER UP. IT'LL BE FINE. YOU'LL SEE. IT'LL BE FINE.
Matthew?
I thought I sent you back to Eve's cave, when I sent the others away...
I DIDN'T GO. I WANTED TO STICK AROUND. DO YOU MIND?
...No.
SO THERE'S REALLY A LUCIFER, HUH? I MEAN, I KNEW THERE WAS A HELL...
Y'SEE, I DID THIS DEAL ONCE, BUT IT ALL TURNED TO SHIT.
WHAT'S HE LIKE? HAVE YOU KNOWN HIM LONG?
Since the beginning. He was the Creator's finest creation: the angel Samael, called Lucifer. It means "the bringer of light."
Of all the angels he was the wisest, the most beautiful, the most powerful.
Saving only his Creator, he is, perhaps, the most powerful being there is.
MORE POWERFUL THAN YOU?
Oh yes. By far.
WELL, AT LEAST YOU'VE GOT THE ELEMENT OF SURPRISE ON YOUR SIDE.
That would not be honorable, Matthew.
I have already sent a messenger to the Lord of Hell, to let him know that I will be coming.
One must do these things properly.
SMART, BOSS.
REAL SMART.

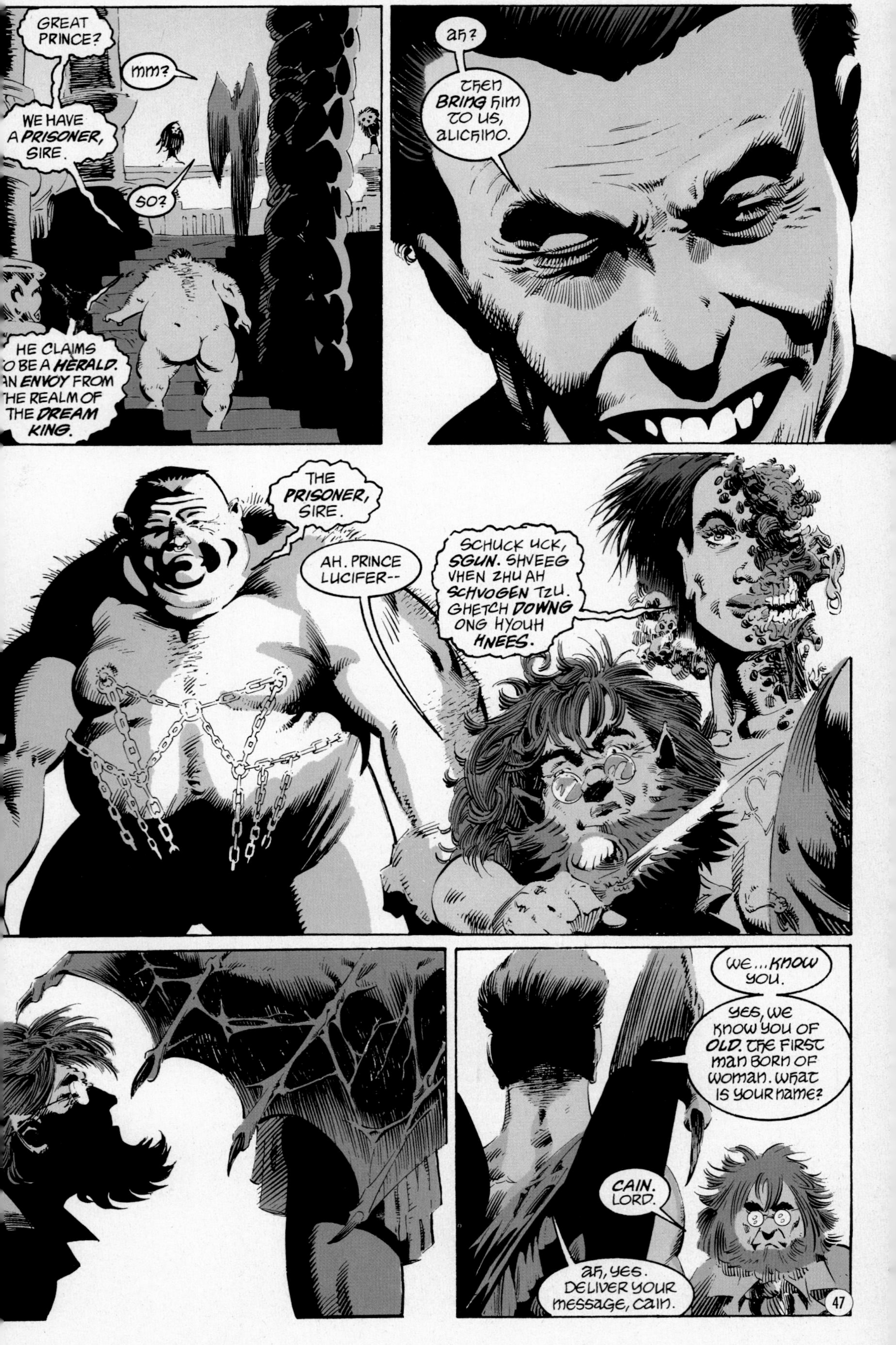
GREAT PRINCE?
mm?
WE HAVE A PRISONER, SIRE.
SO?
HE CLAIMS TO BE A HERALD. AN ENVOY FROM THE REALM OF THE DREAM KING.
ah?
Then BRING him to us, alichino.
THE PRISONER, SIRE.
AH. PRINCE LUCIFER--
SCHUCK UCK, SGUN. SHVEEG VHEN ZHU AH SCHVOGEN TZU. GHETCH DOWNG ONG HYOUH KNEES.
we... know you.
yes, we know you of OLD. the first man born of woman. what is your name?
CAIN. LORD.
ah, yes. deliver your message, cain.

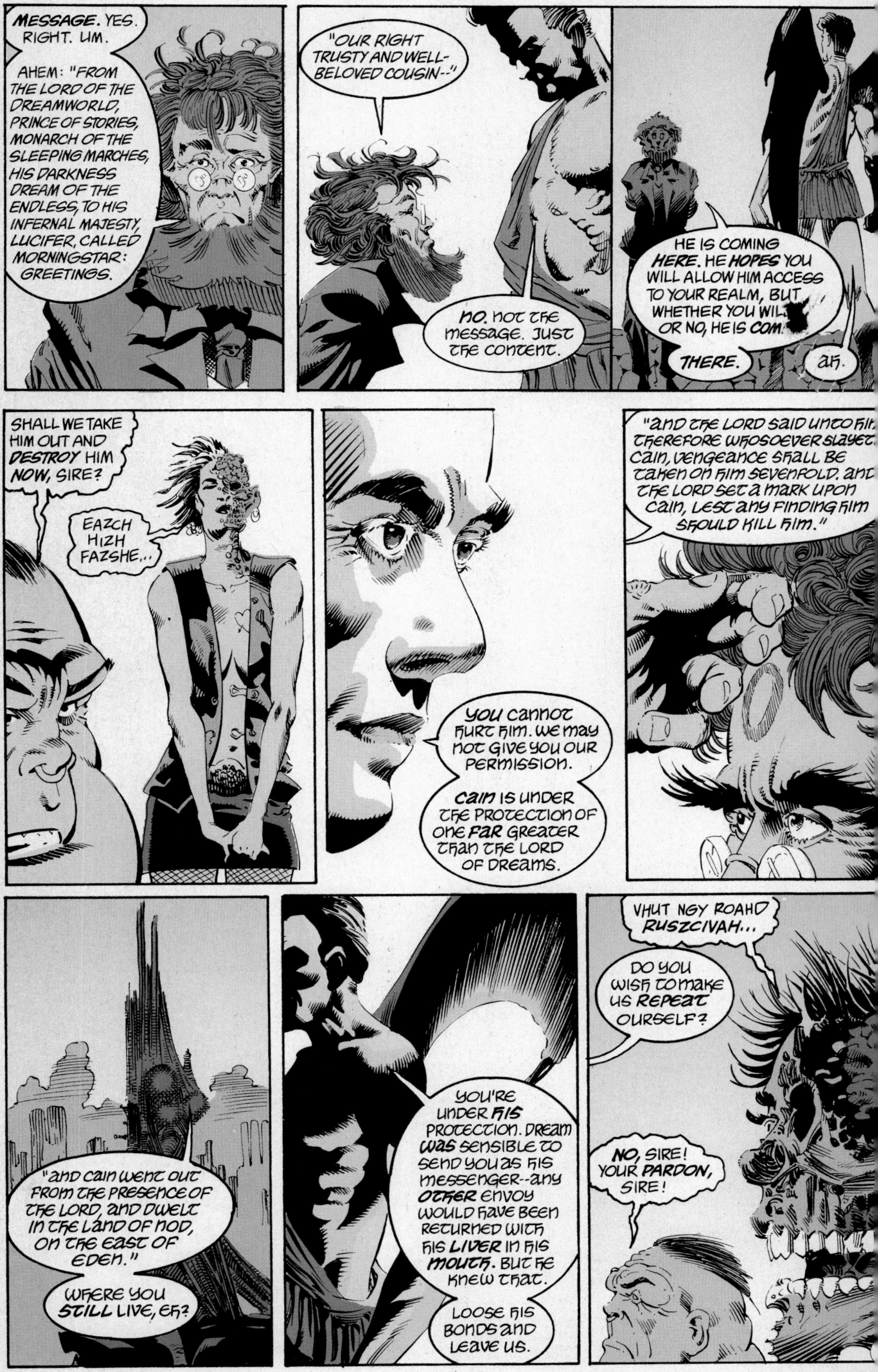
MESSAGE. YES. RIGHT. UM.
AHEM: "FROM THE LORD OF THE DREAMWORLD, PRINCE OF STORIES, MONARCH OF THE SLEEPING MARCHES, HIS DARKNESS DREAM OF THE ENDLESS, TO HIS INFERNAL MAJESTY, LUCIFER, CALLED MORNINGSTAR: GREETINGS.
"OUR RIGHT TRUSTY AND WELL-BELOVED COUSIN--"
NO. NOT THE MESSAGE. JUST THE CONTENT.
HE IS COMING HERE. HE HOPES YOU WILL ALLOW HIM ACCESS TO YOUR REALM, BUT WHETHER YOU WIL OR NO, HE IS COM
THERE.
AH.
SHALL WE TAKE HIM OUT AND DESTROY HIM NOW, SIRE?
EAZCH HIZH FAZSHE...
YOU CANNOT HURT HIM. WE MAY NOT GIVE YOU OUR PERMISSION.
CAIN IS UNDER THE PROTECTION OF ONE FAR GREATER THAN THE LORD OF DREAMS.
"AND THE LORD SAID UNTO HI THEREFORE WHOSOEVER SLAYET CAIN, VENGEANCE SHALL BE TAKEN ON HIM SEVENFOLD. AND THE LORD SET A MARK UPON CAIN, LEST ANY FINDING HIM SHOULD KILL HIM."
"AND CAIN WENT OUT FROM THE PRESENCE OF THE LORD, AND DWELT IN THE LAND OF NOD, ON THE EAST OF EDEN."
WHERE YOU STILL LIVE, EH?
YOU'RE UNDER HIS PROTECTION. DREAM WAS SENSIBLE TO SEND YOU AS HIS MESSENGER--ANY OTHER ENVOY WOULD HAVE BEEN RETURNED WITH HIS LIVER IN HIS MOUTH. BUT HE KNEW THAT.
LOOSE HIS BONDS AND LEAVE US.
VHUT NGY ROAHD RUSZCIVAH...
DO YOU WISH TO MAKE US REPEAT OURSELF?
NO, SIRE! YOUR PARDON, SIRE!

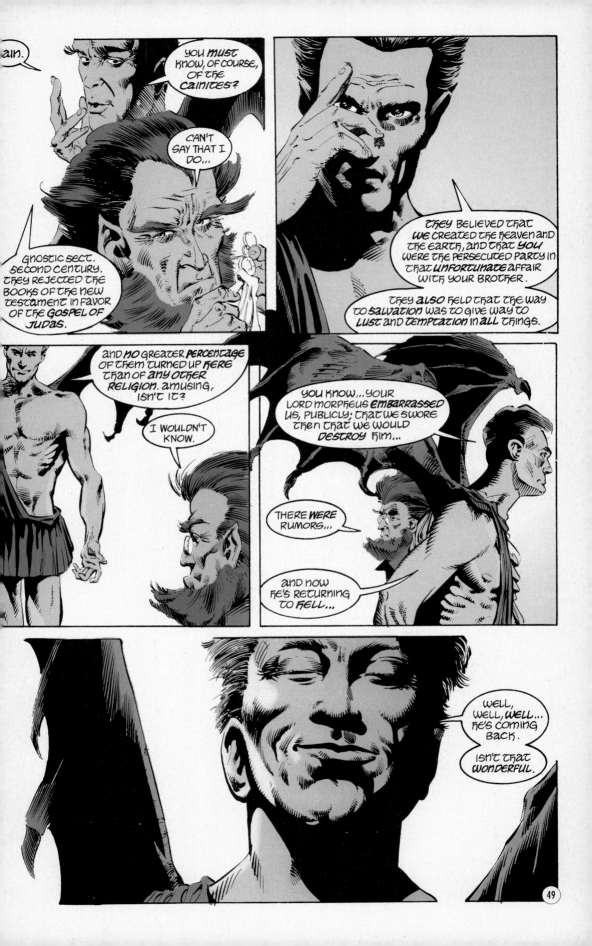

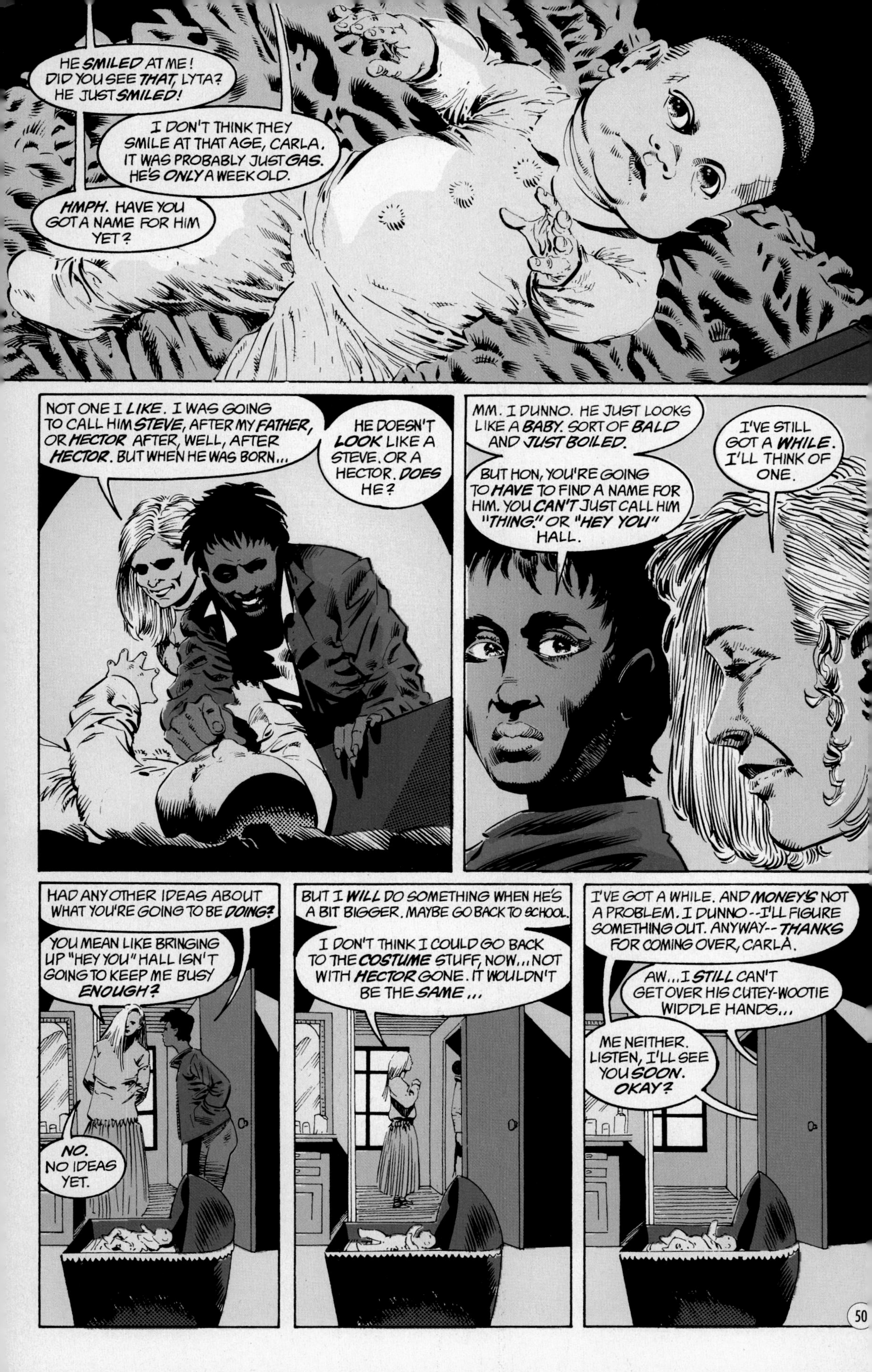

HE SMILED AT ME! DID YOU SEE THAT, LYTA? HE JUST SMILED!
I DON'T THINK THEY SMILE AT THAT AGE, CARLA. IT WAS PROBABLY JUST GAS. HE'S ONLY A WEEK OLD.
HMPH. HAVE YOU GOT A NAME FOR HIM YET?
NOT ONE I LIKE. I WAS GOING TO CALL HIM STEVE, AFTER MY FATHER, OR HECTOR AFTER, WELL, AFTER HECTOR. BUT WHEN HE WAS BORN...
HE DOESN'T LOOK LIKE A STEVE. OR A HECTOR. DOES HE?
MM. I DUNNO. HE JUST LOOKS LIKE A BABY. SORT OF BALD AND JUST BOILED.
BUT HON, YOU'RE GOING TO HAVE TO FIND A NAME FOR HIM. YOU CAN'T JUST CALL HIM "THING." OR "HEY YOU" HALL.
I'VE STILL GOT A WHILE. I'LL THINK OF ONE.
HAD ANY OTHER IDEAS ABOUT WHAT YOU'RE GOING TO BE DOING?
YOU MEAN LIKE BRINGING UP "HEY YOU" HALL ISN'T GOING TO KEEP ME BUSY ENOUGH?
NO. NO IDEAS YET.
BUT I WILL DO SOMETHING WHEN HE'S A BIT BIGGER. MAYBE GO BACK TO SCHOOL.
I DON'T THINK I COULD GO BACK TO THE COSTUME STUFF, NOW... NOT WITH HECTOR GONE. IT WOULDN'T BE THE SAME...
I'VE GOT A WHILE. AND MONEY'S NOT A PROBLEM. I DUNNO--I'LL FIGURE SOMETHING OUT. ANYWAY--THANKS FOR COMING OVER, CARLA.
AW... I STILL CAN'T GET OVER HIS CUTEY-WOOTIE WIDDLE HANDS...
ME NEITHER. LISTEN, I'LL SEE YOU SOON. OKAY?

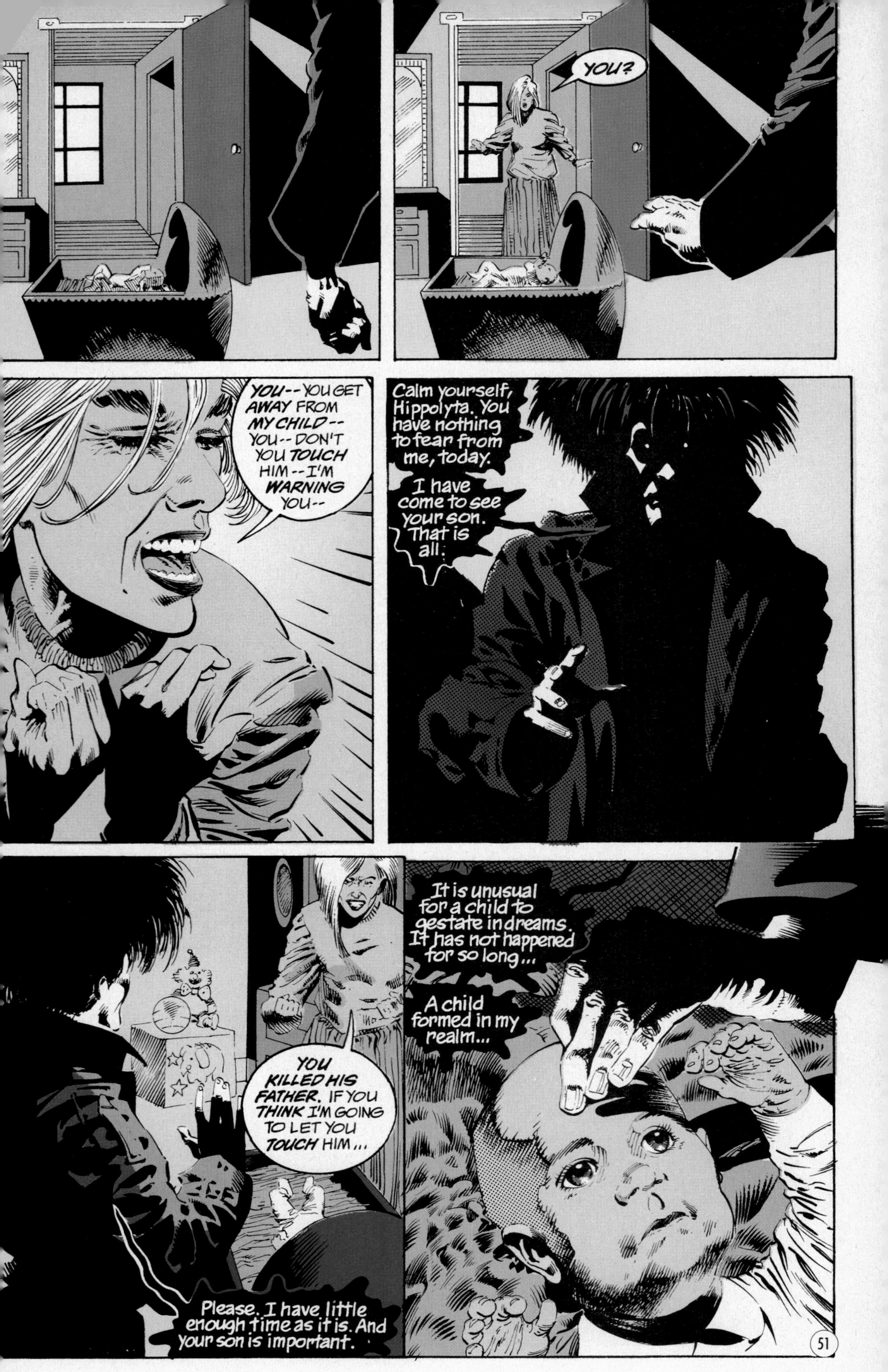

YOU?
YOU--YOU GET AWAY FROM MY CHILD--YOU--DON'T YOU TOUCH HIM--I'M WARNING YOU--
Calm yourself, Hippolyta. You have nothing to fear from me, today.
I have come to see your son. That is all.
YOU KILLED HIS FATHER. IF YOU THINK I'M GOING TO LET YOU TOUCH HIM...
Please. I have little enough time as it is. And your son is important.
It is unusual for a child to gestate in dreams. It has not happened for so long...
A child formed in my realm...

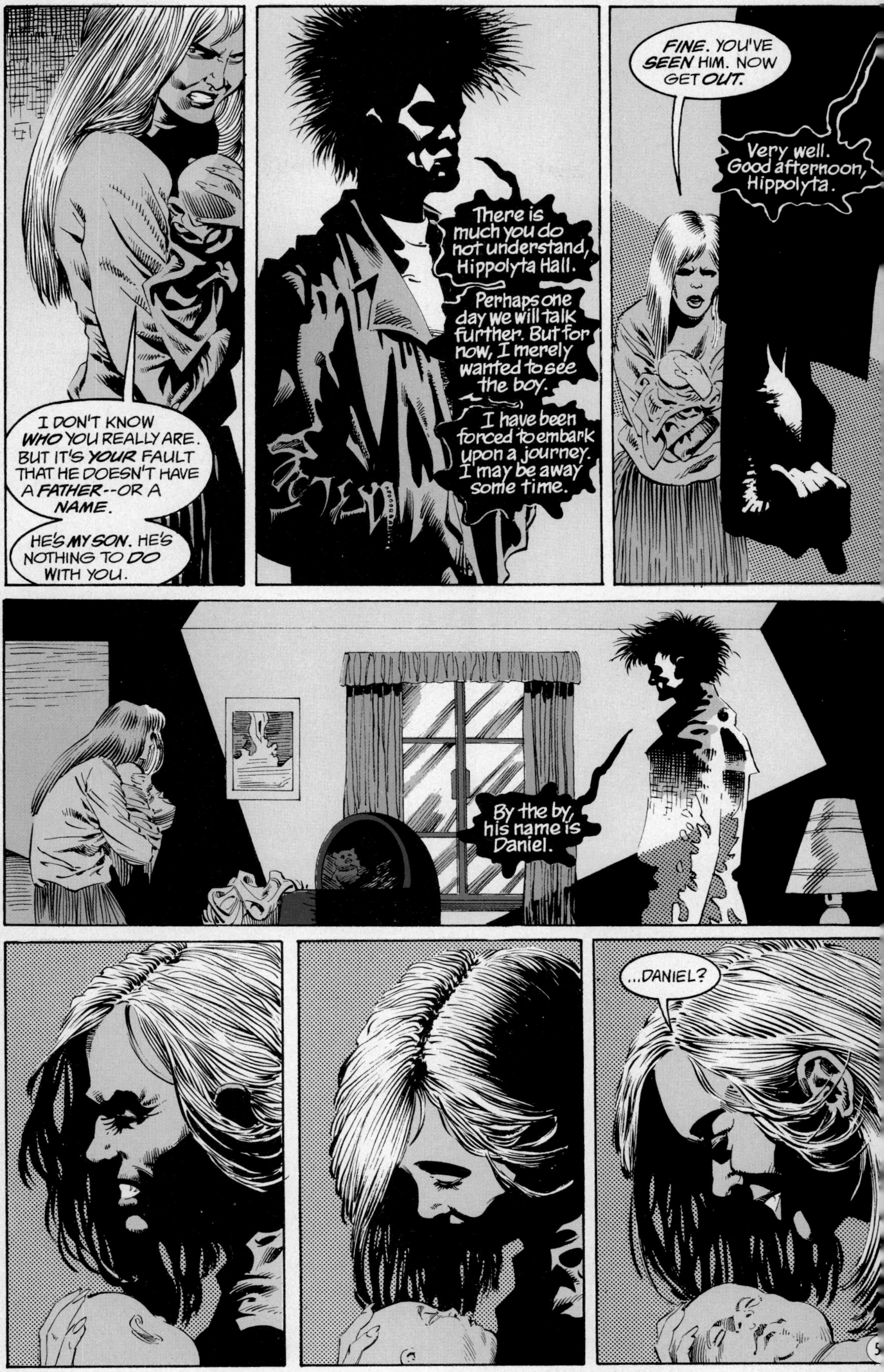
I DON'T KNOW *WHO* YOU REALLY ARE. BUT IT'S *YOUR* FAULT THAT HE DOESN'T HAVE A *FATHER*--OR A *NAME*.
HE'S *MY SON*. HE'S NOTHING TO *DO* WITH YOU.
There is much you do not understand, Hippolyta Hall.
Perhaps one day we will talk further. But for now, I merely wanted to see the boy.
I have been forced to embark upon a journey. I may be away some time.
FINE. YOU'VE *SEEN* HIM. NOW GET *OUT*.
Very well. Good afternoon, Hippolyta.
By the by, his name is Daniel.
...DANIEL?

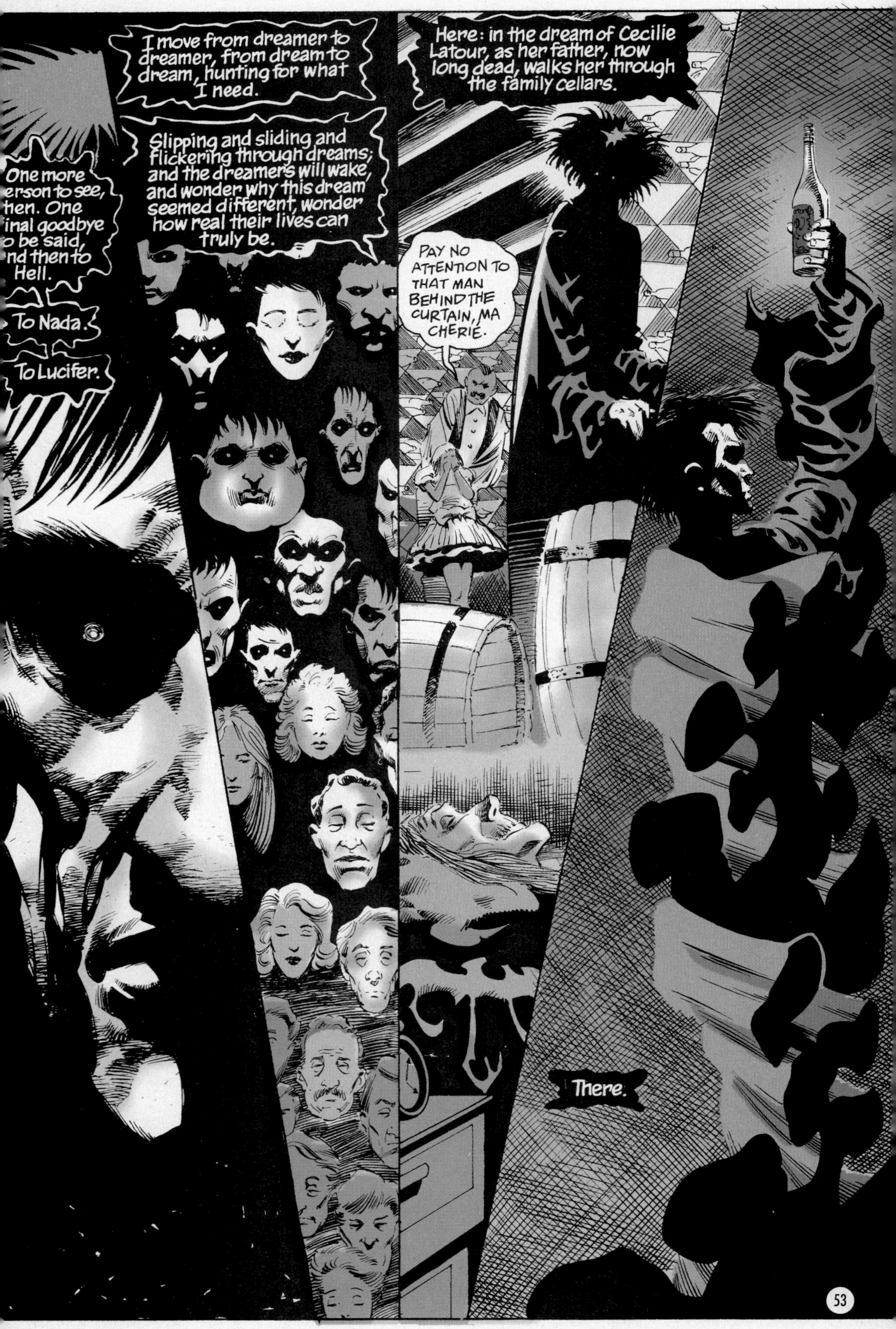
One more erson to see, hen. One inal goodbye o be said, nd then to Hell.
To Nada.
To Lucifer.
I move from dreamer to dreamer, from dream to dream, hunting for what I need.
Slipping and sliding and flickering through dreams; and the dreamers will wake, and wonder why this dream seemed different, wonder how real their lives can truly be.
Here: in the dream of Cecilie Latour, as her father, now long dead, walks her through the family cellars.
PAY NO ATTENTION TO THAT MAN BEHIND THE CURTAIN, MA CHERIE.
There.

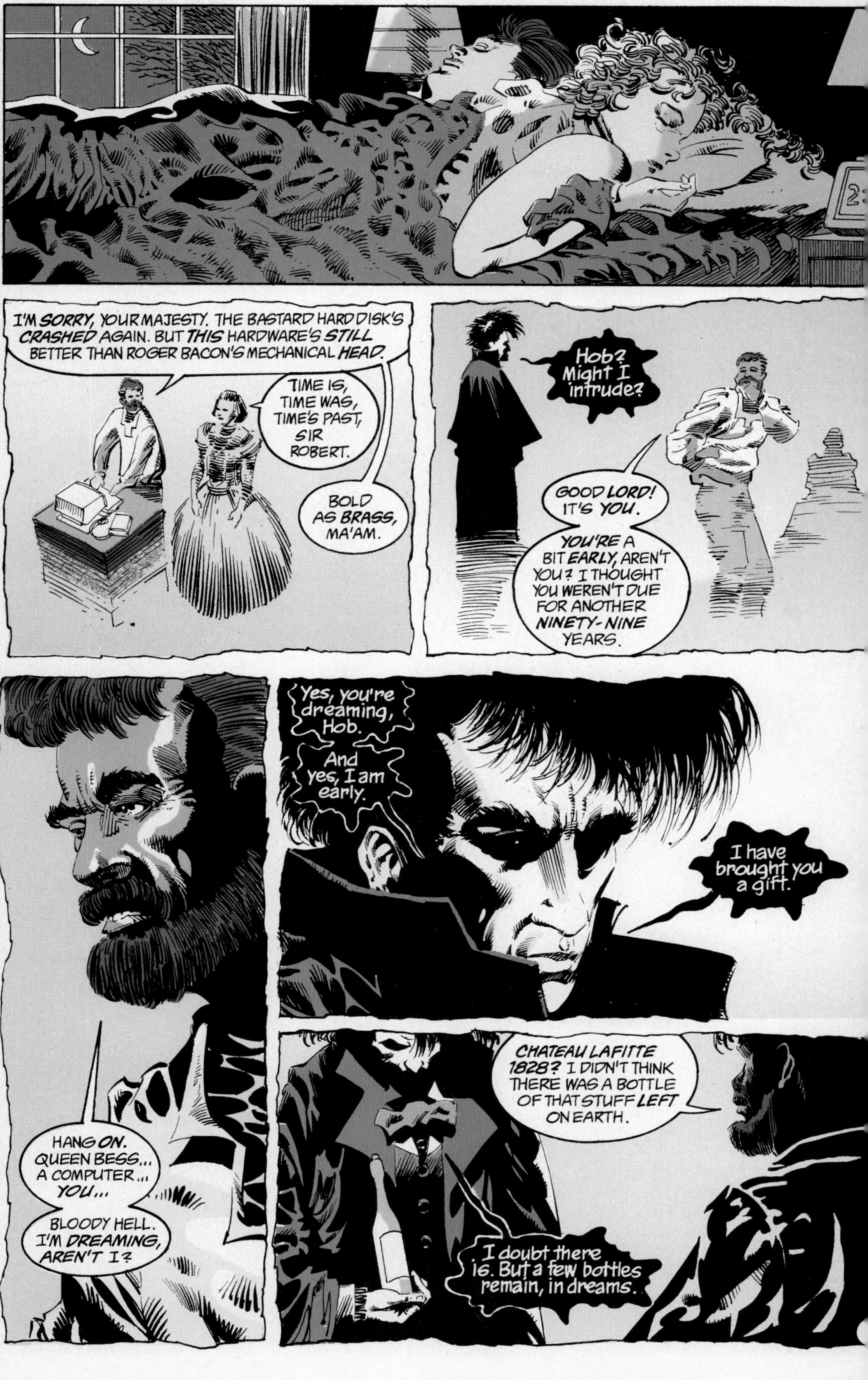
I'M SORRY, YOUR MAJESTY. THE BASTARD HARD DISK'S CRASHED AGAIN. BUT THIS HARDWARE'S STILL BETTER THAN ROGER BACON'S MECHANICAL HEAD.
TIME IS, TIME WAS, TIME'S PAST, SIR ROBERT.
BOLD AS BRASS, MA'AM.
Hob? Might I intrude?
GOOD LORD! IT'S YOU.
YOU'RE A BIT EARLY, AREN'T YOU? I THOUGHT YOU WEREN'T DUE FOR ANOTHER NINETY-NINE YEARS.
HANG ON. QUEEN BESS... A COMPUTER... YOU...
BLOODY HELL. I'M DREAMING, AREN'T I?
Yes, you're dreaming, Hob.
And yes, I am early.
I have brought you a gift.
CHATEAU LAFITTE 1828? I DIDN'T THINK THERE WAS A BOTTLE OF THAT STUFF LEFT ON EARTH.
I doubt there is. But a few bottles remain, in dreams.

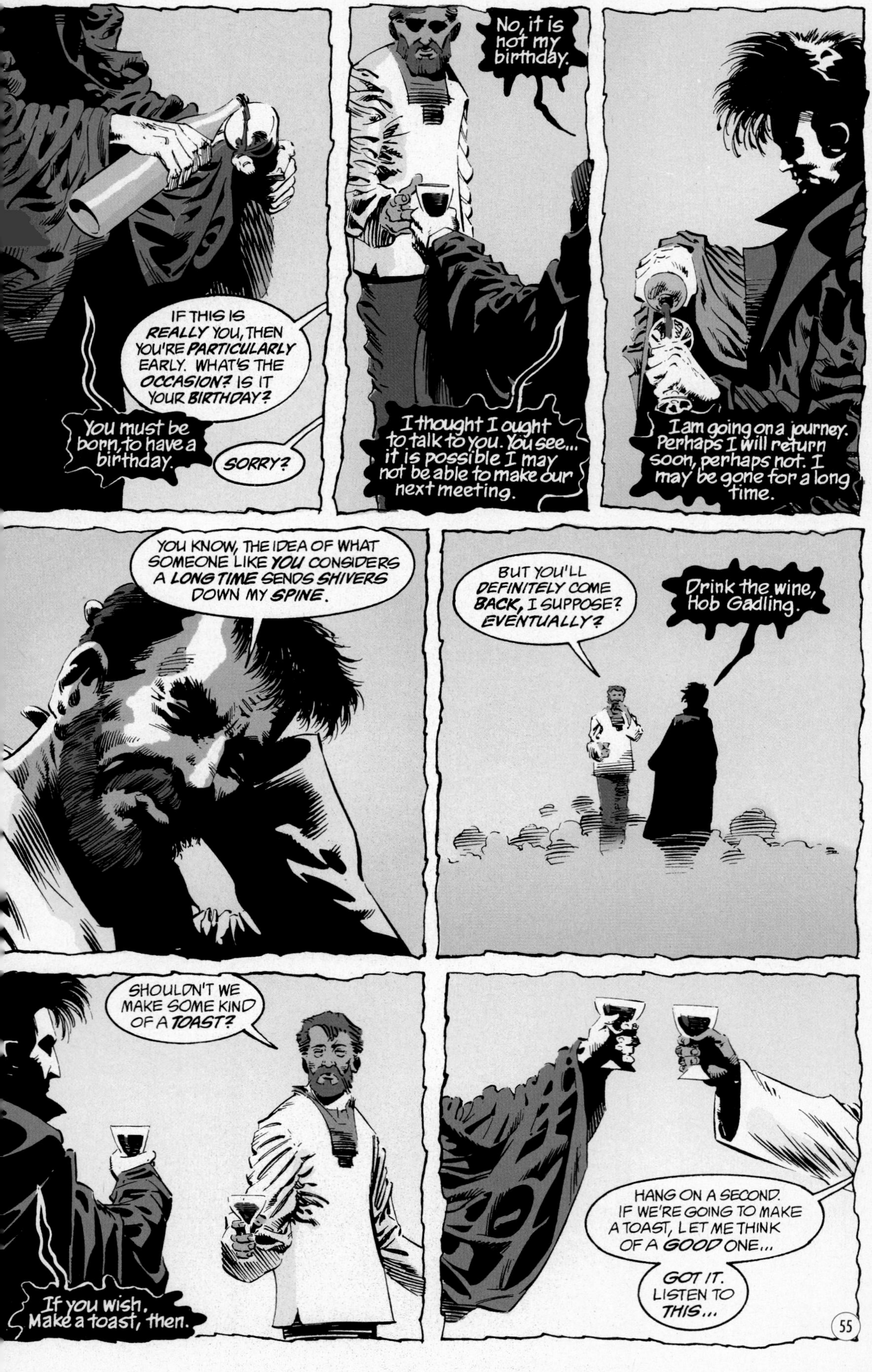
IF THIS IS REALLY YOU, THEN YOU'RE PARTICULARLY EARLY. WHAT'S THE OCCASION? IS IT YOUR BIRTHDAY?
You must be born, to have a birthday.
SORRY?
No, it is not my birthday.
I thought I ought to talk to you. You see... it is possible I may not be able to make our next meeting.
I am going on a journey. Perhaps I will return soon, perhaps not. I may be gone for a long time.
YOU KNOW, THE IDEA OF WHAT SOMEONE LIKE YOU CONSIDERS A LONG TIME SENDS SHIVERS DOWN MY SPINE.
BUT YOU'LL DEFINITELY COME BACK, I SUPPOSE? EVENTUALLY?
Drink the wine, Hob Gadling.
SHOULDN'T WE MAKE SOME KIND OF A TOAST?
If you wish. Make a toast, then.
HANG ON A SECOND. IF WE'RE GOING TO MAKE A TOAST, LET ME THINK OF A GOOD ONE...
GOT IT. LISTEN TO THIS...

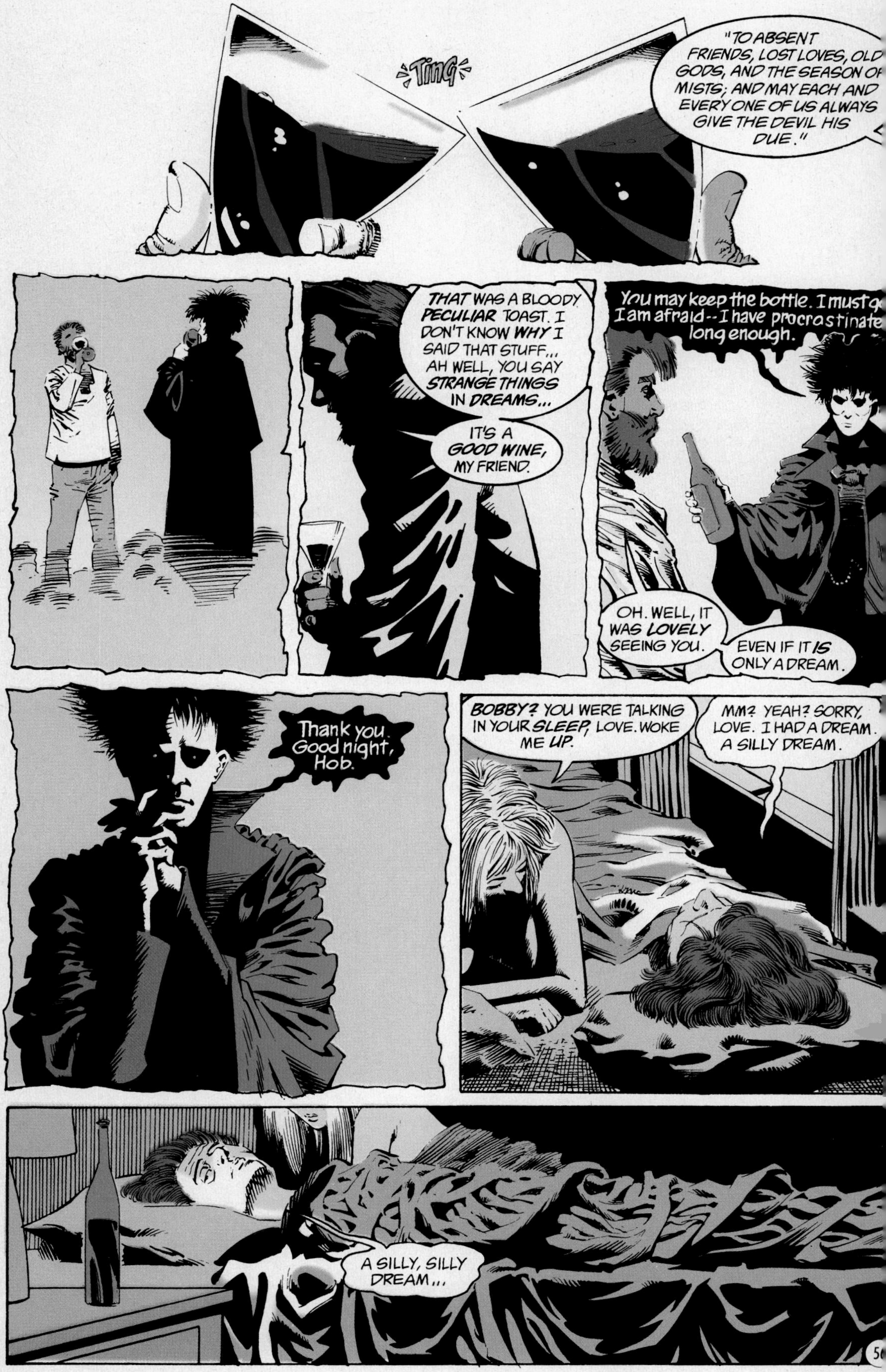
TING
"TO ABSENT FRIENDS, LOST LOVES, OLD GODS, AND THE SEASON OF MISTS; AND MAY EACH AND EVERY ONE OF US ALWAYS GIVE THE DEVIL HIS DUE."
THAT WAS A BLOODY PECULIAR TOAST. I DON'T KNOW WHY I SAID THAT STUFF... AH WELL, YOU SAY STRANGE THINGS IN DREAMS...
IT'S A GOOD WINE, MY FRIEND.
You may keep the bottle. I must go I am afraid--I have procrastinated long enough.
OH. WELL, IT WAS LOVELY SEEING YOU.
EVEN IF IT IS ONLY A DREAM.
Thank you. Good night, Hob.
BOBBY? YOU WERE TALKING IN YOUR SLEEP, LOVE. WOKE ME UP.
MM? YEAH? SORRY, LOVE. I HAD A DREAM. A SILLY DREAM.
A SILLY, SILLY DREAM...

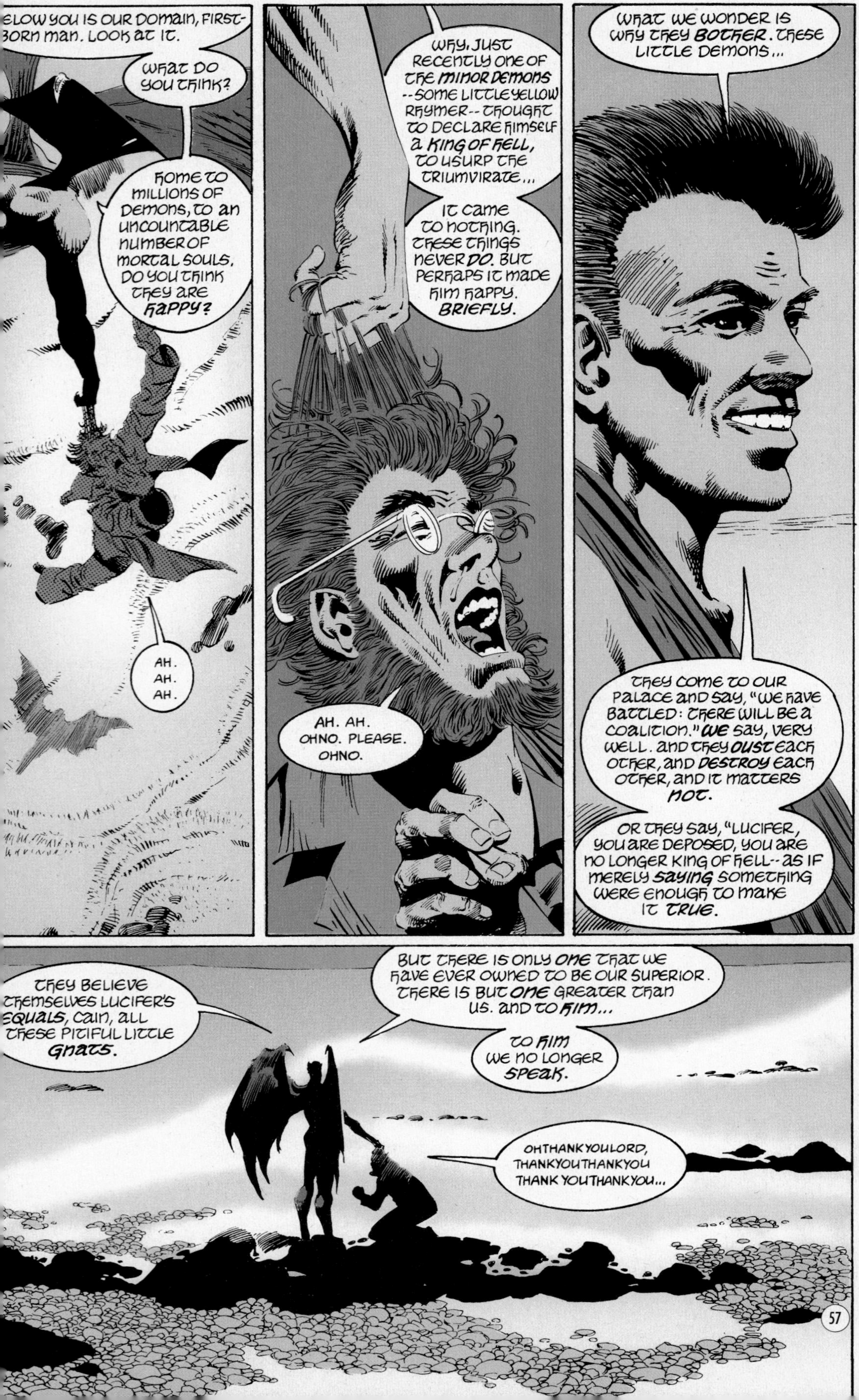
ELOW YOU IS OUR DOMAIN, FIRST-BORN MAN. LOOK AT IT.
WHAT DO YOU THINK?
HOME TO MILLIONS OF DEMONS, TO AN UNCOUNTABLE NUMBER OF MORTAL SOULS. DO YOU THINK THEY ARE HAPPY?
AH. AH. AH.
WHY, JUST RECENTLY ONE OF THE MINOR DEMONS --SOME LITTLE YELLOW RHYMER-- THOUGHT TO DECLARE HIMSELF A KING OF HELL, TO USURP THE TRIUMVIRATE...
IT CAME TO NOTHING. THESE THINGS NEVER DO. BUT PERHAPS IT MADE HIM HAPPY. BRIEFLY.
AH. AH. OHNO. PLEASE. OHNO.
WHAT WE WONDER IS WHY THEY BOTHER. THESE LITTLE DEMONS...
THEY COME TO OUR PALACE AND SAY, "WE HAVE BATTLED: THERE WILL BE A COALITION." WE SAY, VERY WELL. AND THEY OUST EACH OTHER, AND DESTROY EACH OTHER, AND IT MATTERS NOT.
OR THEY SAY, "LUCIFER, YOU ARE DEPOSED, YOU ARE NO LONGER KING OF HELL-- AS IF MERELY SAYING SOMETHING WERE ENOUGH TO MAKE IT TRUE.
THEY BELIEVE THEMSELVES LUCIFER'S EQUALS, CAIN, ALL THESE PITIFUL LITTLE GNATS.
BUT THERE IS ONLY ONE THAT WE HAVE EVER OWNED TO BE OUR SUPERIOR. THERE IS BUT ONE GREATER THAN US. AND TO HIM...
TO HIM WE NO LONGER SPEAK.
OHTHANKYOULORD, THANKYOUTHANKYOU THANK YOUTHANKYOU...

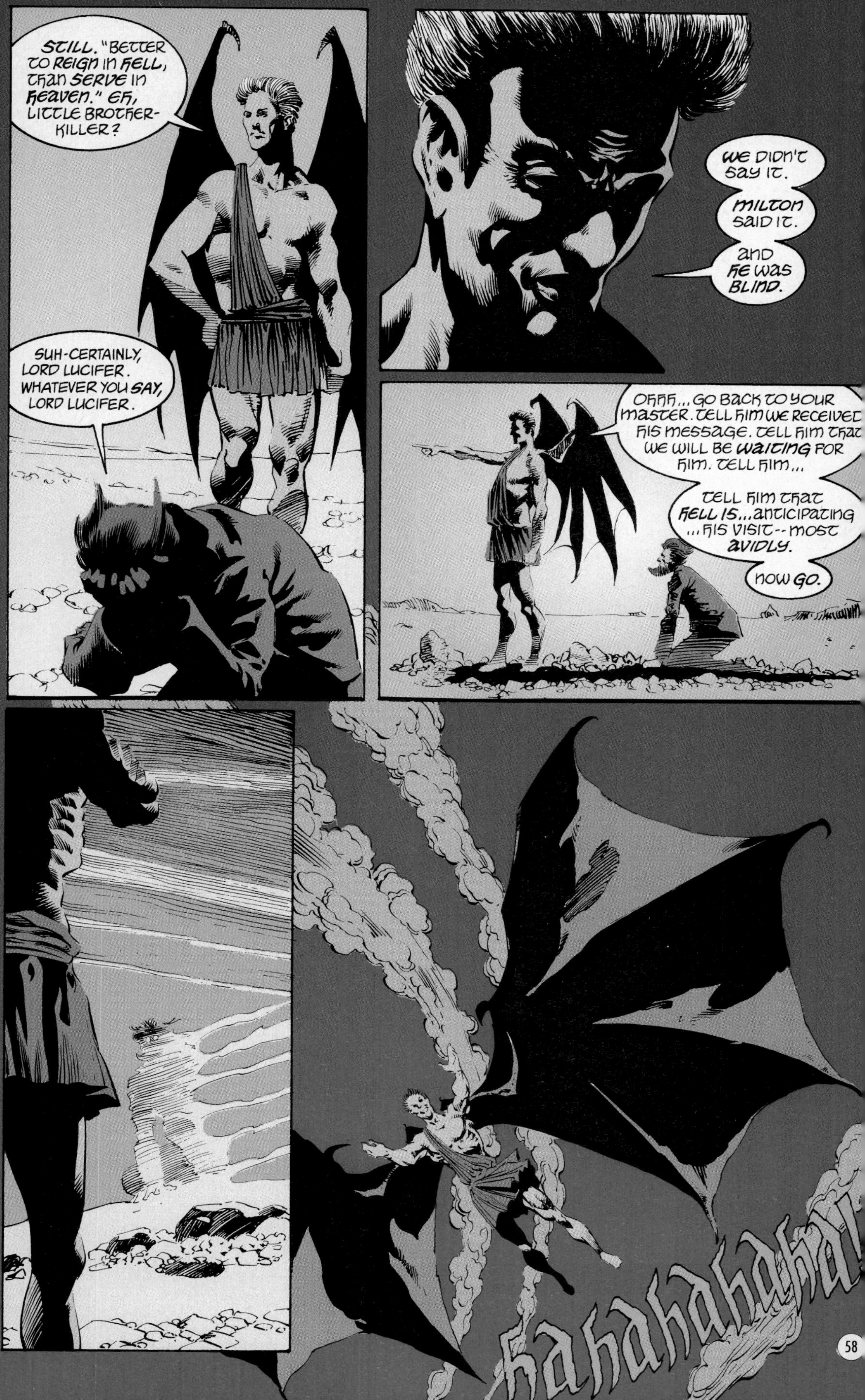
STILL. "BETTER TO REIGN IN HELL, THAN SERVE IN HEAVEN." EH, LITTLE BROTHER-KILLER?
SUH-CERTAINLY, LORD LUCIFER. WHATEVER YOU SAY, LORD LUCIFER.
WE DIDN'T SAY IT.
MILTON SAID IT.
AND HE WAS BLIND.
OHHH... GO BACK TO YOUR MASTER. TELL HIM WE RECEIVED HIS MESSAGE. TELL HIM THAT WE WILL BE WAITING FOR HIM. TELL HIM...
TELL HIM THAT HELL IS...ANTICIPATING ...HIS VISIT--MOST AVIDLY.
NOW GO.
HAHAHAHAHA!

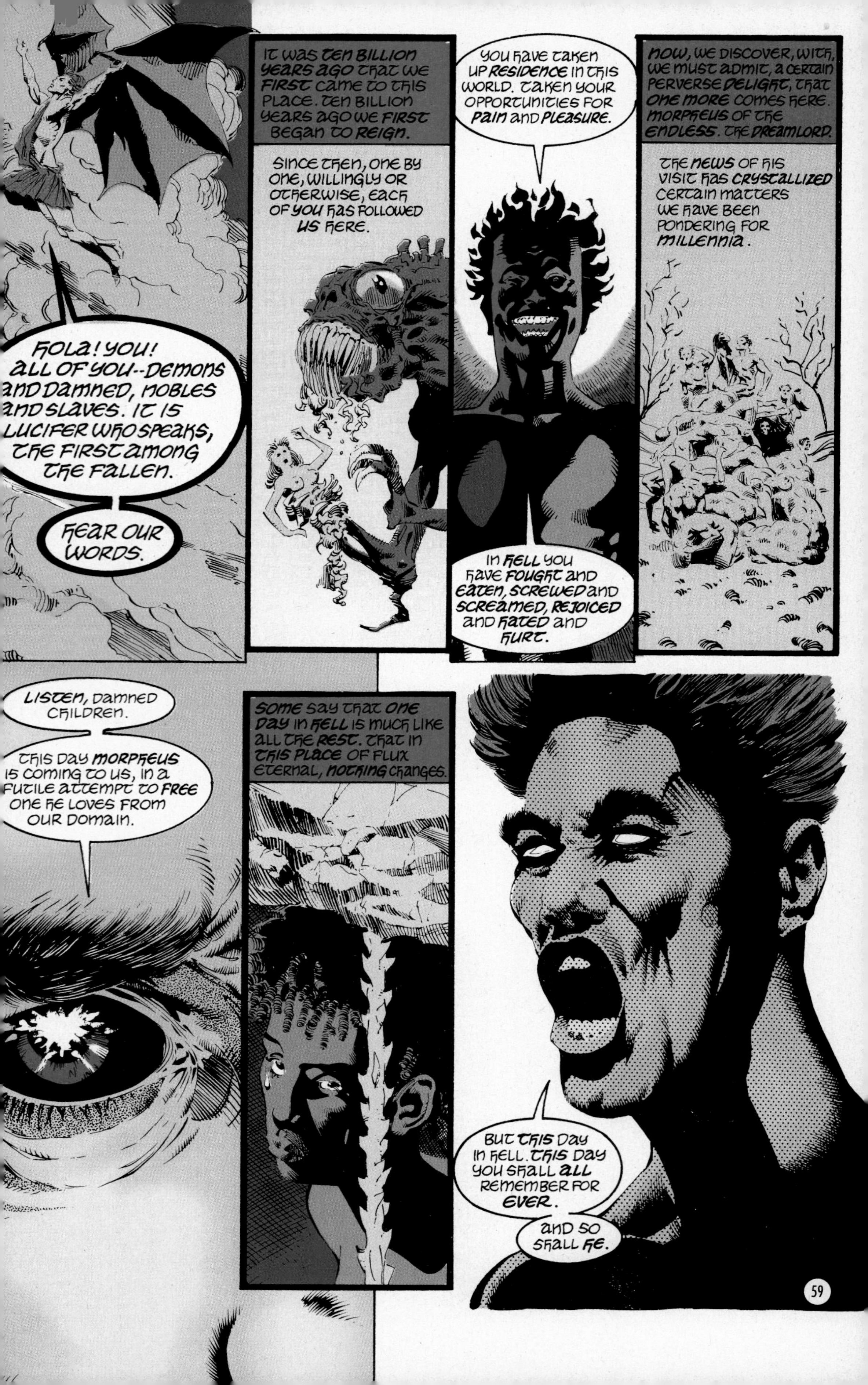
HOLA! YOU! ALL OF YOU--DEMONS AND DAMNED, NOBLES AND SLAVES. IT IS LUCIFER WHO SPEAKS, THE FIRST AMONG THE FALLEN.
HEAR OUR WORDS.
IT WAS TEN BILLION YEARS AGO THAT WE FIRST CAME TO THIS PLACE. TEN BILLION YEARS AGO WE FIRST BEGAN TO REIGN.
SINCE THEN, ONE BY ONE, WILLINGLY OR OTHERWISE, EACH OF YOU HAS FOLLOWED US HERE.
YOU HAVE TAKEN UP RESIDENCE IN THIS WORLD. TAKEN YOUR OPPORTUNITIES FOR PAIN AND PLEASURE.
IN HELL YOU HAVE FOUGHT AND EATEN, SCREWED AND SCREAMED, REJOICED AND HATED AND HURT.
NOW, WE DISCOVER, WITH, WE MUST ADMIT, A CERTAIN PERVERSE DELIGHT, THAT ONE MORE COMES HERE. MORPHEUS OF THE ENDLESS. THE DREAMLORD.
THE NEWS OF HIS VISIT HAS CRYSTALLIZED CERTAIN MATTERS WE HAVE BEEN PONDERING FOR MILLENNIA.
LISTEN, DAMNED CHILDREN.
THIS DAY MORPHEUS IS COMING TO US, IN A FUTILE ATTEMPT TO FREE ONE HE LOVES FROM OUR DOMAIN.
SOME SAY THAT ONE DAY IN HELL IS MUCH LIKE ALL THE REST. THAT IN THIS PLACE OF FLUX ETERNAL, NOTHING CHANGES.
BUT THIS DAY IN HELL. THIS DAY YOU SHALL ALL REMEMBER FOR EVER.
AND SO SHALL HE.

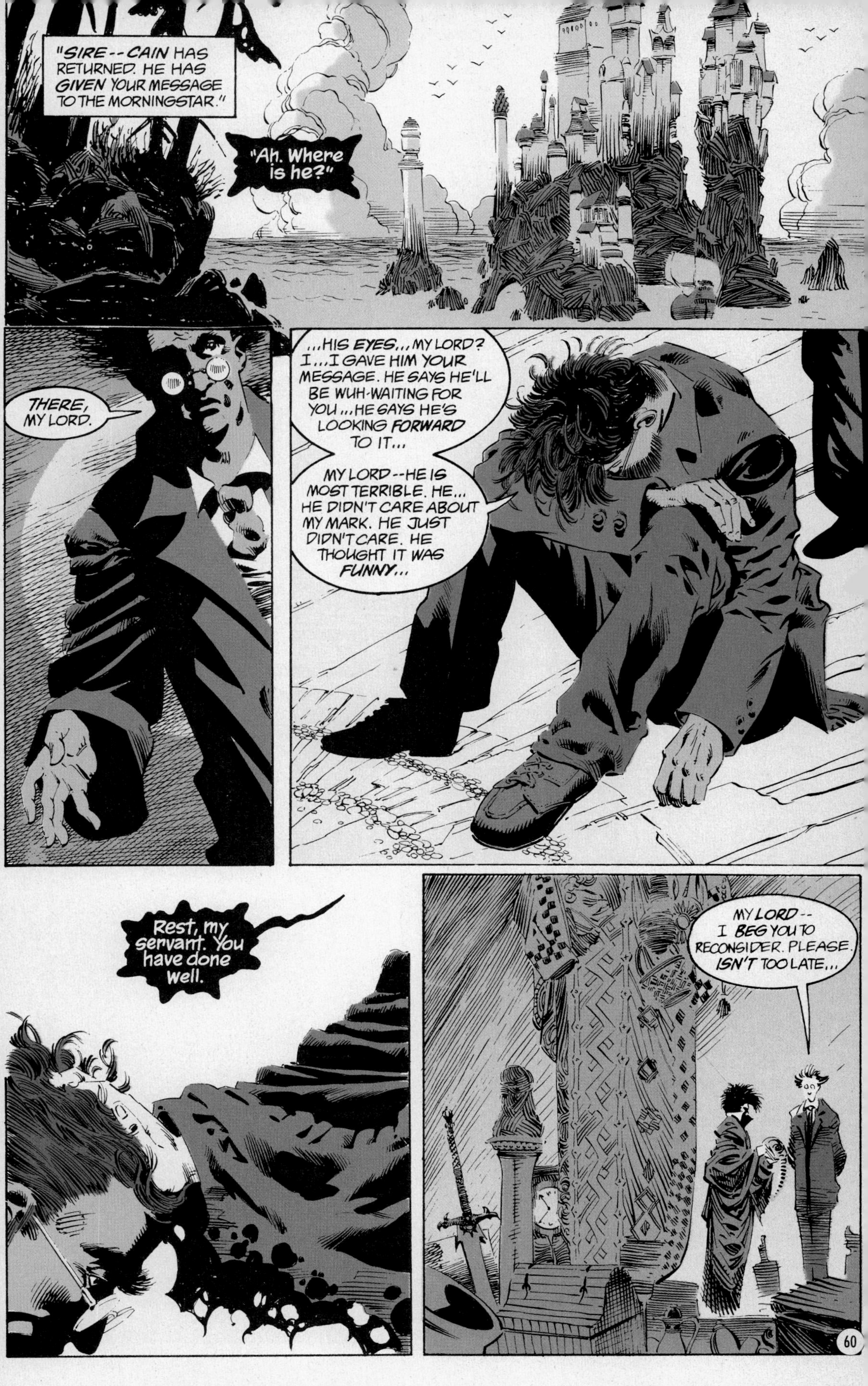
"SIRE--CAIN HAS RETURNED. HE HAS GIVEN YOUR MESSAGE TO THE MORNINGSTAR."
"Ah. Where is he?"
THERE, MY LORD.
...HIS EYES... MY LORD? I...I GAVE HIM YOUR MESSAGE. HE SAYS HE'LL BE WUH-WAITING FOR YOU...HE SAYS HE'S LOOKING FORWARD TO IT...
MY LORD--HE IS MOST TERRIBLE. HE... HE DIDN'T CARE ABOUT MY MARK. HE JUST DIDN'T CARE. HE THOUGHT IT WAS FUNNY...
Rest, my servant. You have done well.
MY LORD-- I BEG YOU TO RECONSIDER. PLEASE. ISN'T TOO LATE...

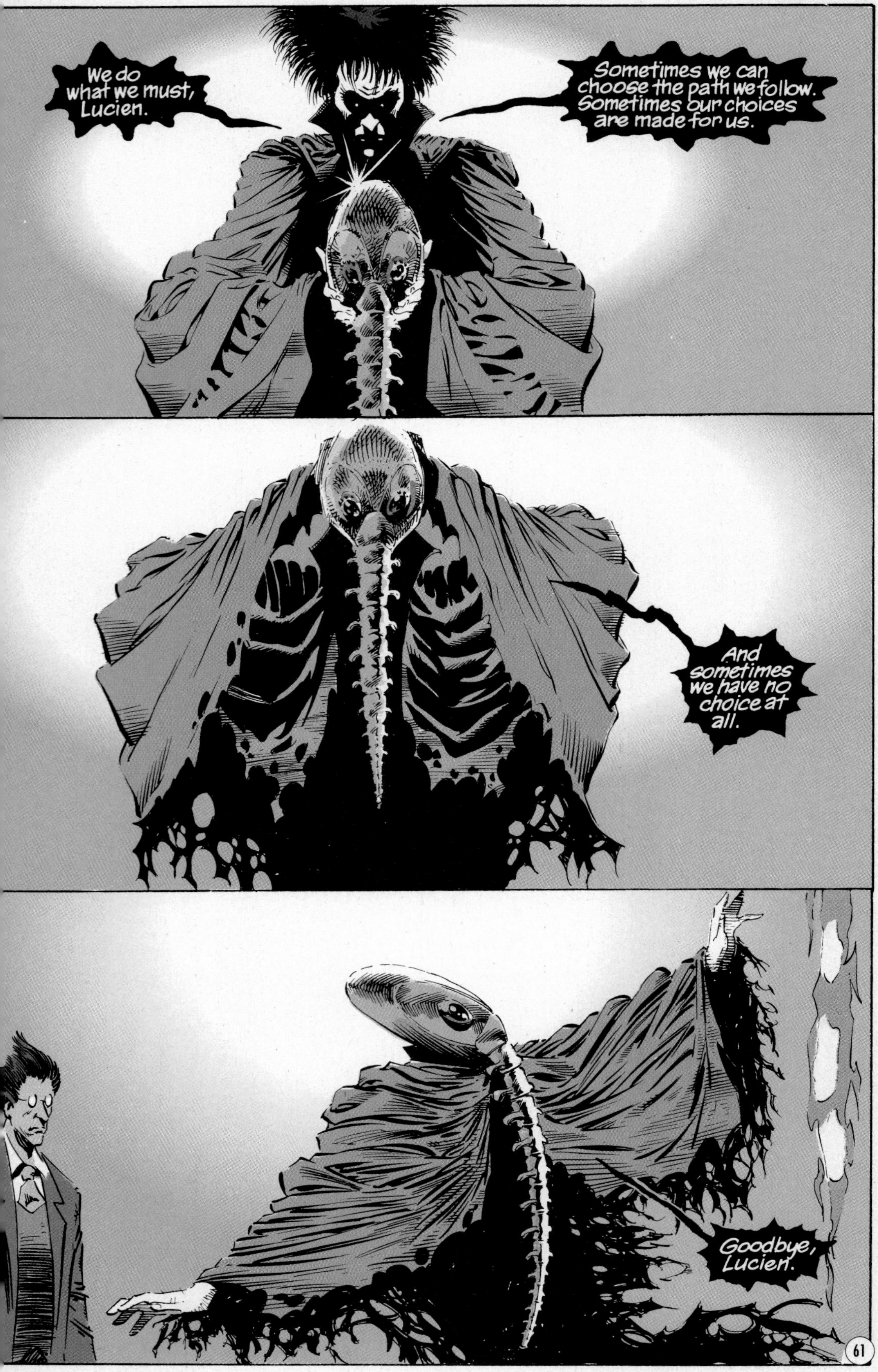
We do what we must, Lucien.
Sometimes we can choose the path we follow. Sometimes our choices are made for us.
And sometimes we have no choice at all.
Goodbye, Lucien.

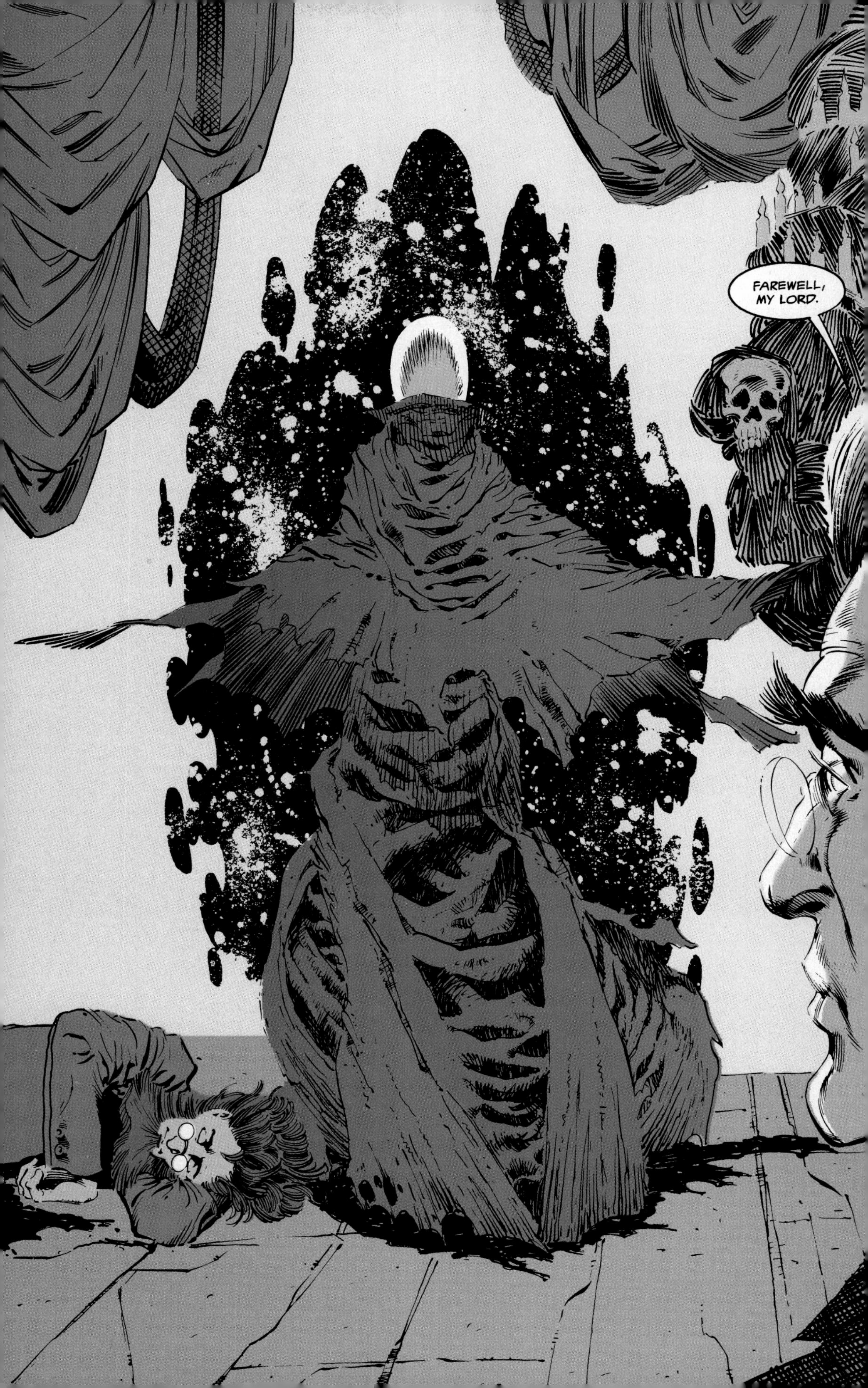
FAREWELL, MY LORD.

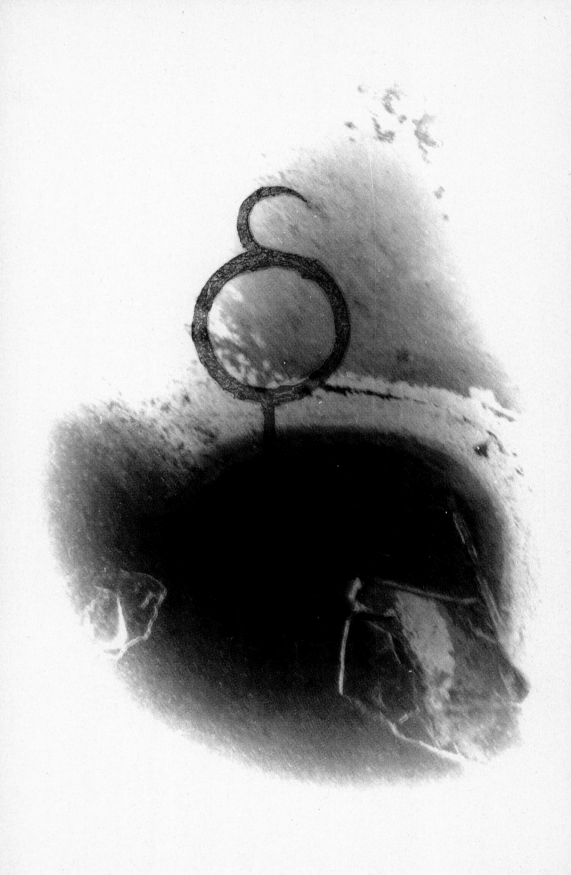

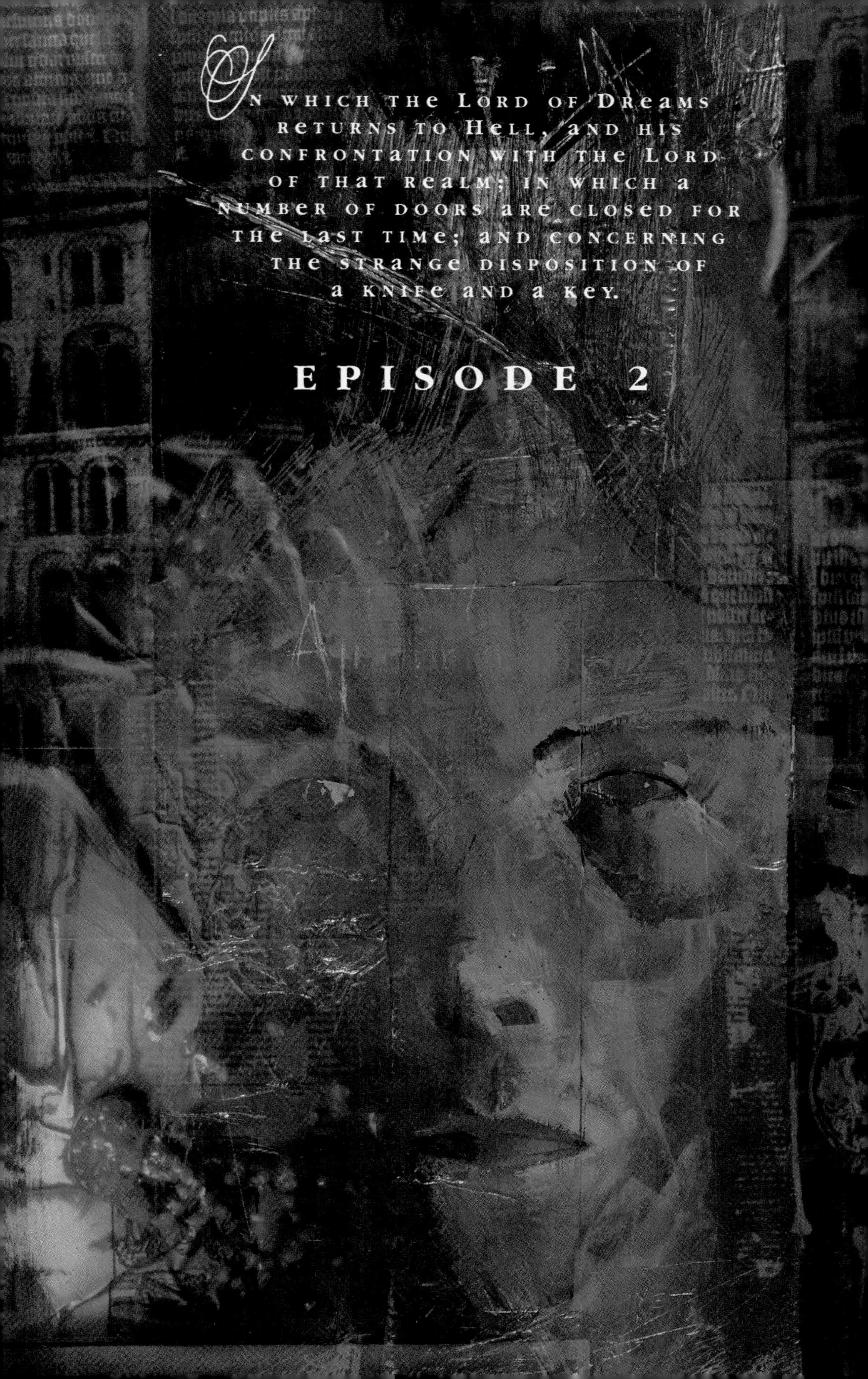

In which the Lord of Dreams returns to Hell, and his confrontation with the Lord of that realm; in which a number of doors are closed for the last time; and concerning the strange disposition of a knife and a key.

EPISODE 2

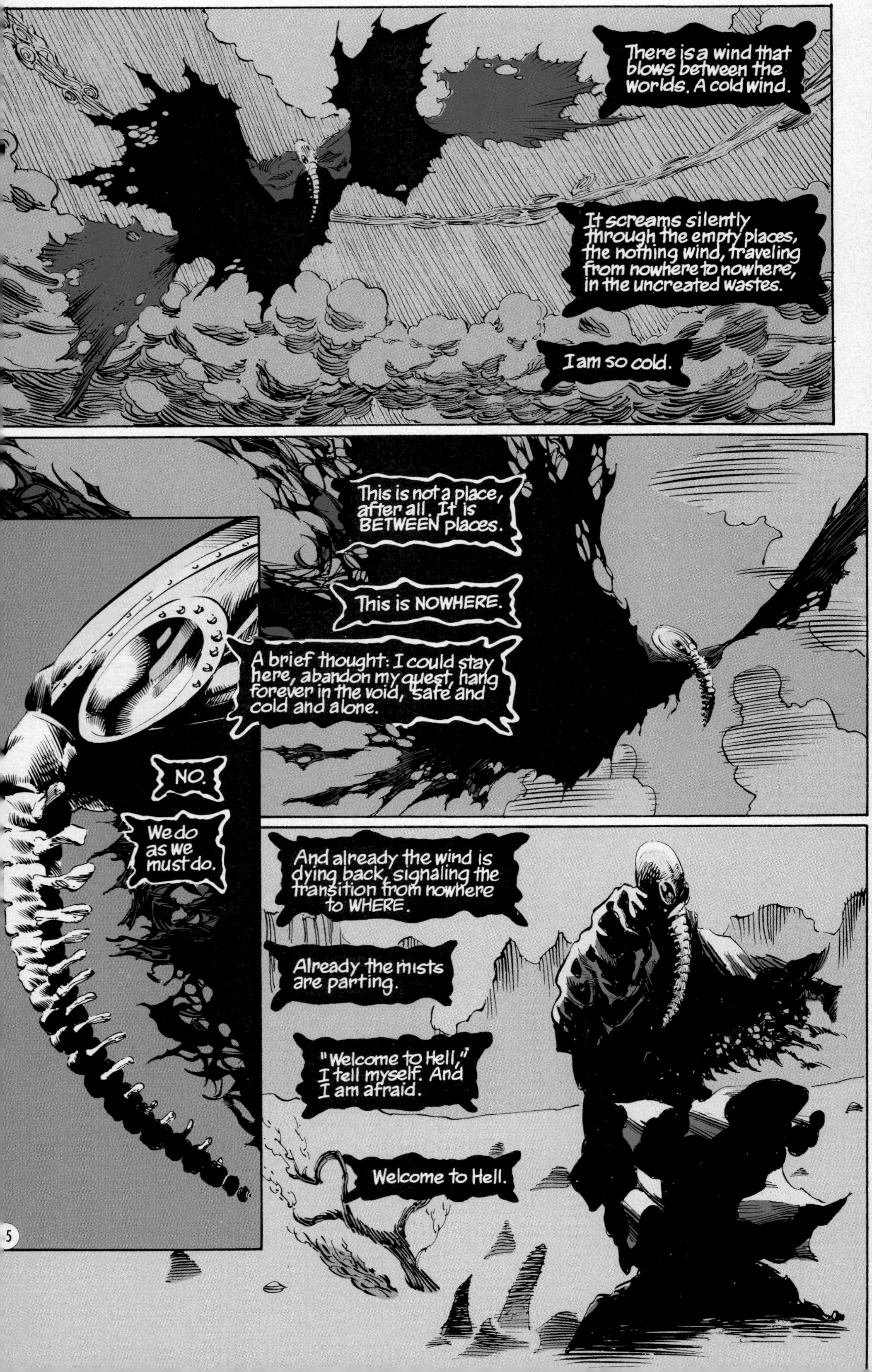
There is a wind that blows between the worlds. A cold wind.
It screams silently through the empty places, the nothing wind, traveling from nowhere to nowhere, in the uncreated wastes.
I am so cold.
This is not a place, after all. It is BETWEEN places.
This is NOWHERE.
A brief thought: I could stay here, abandon my quest, hang forever in the void, safe and cold and alone.
NO.
We do as we must do.
And already the wind is dying back, signaling the transition from nowhere to WHERE.
Already the mists are parting.
"Welcome to Hell," I tell myself. And I am afraid.
Welcome to Hell.

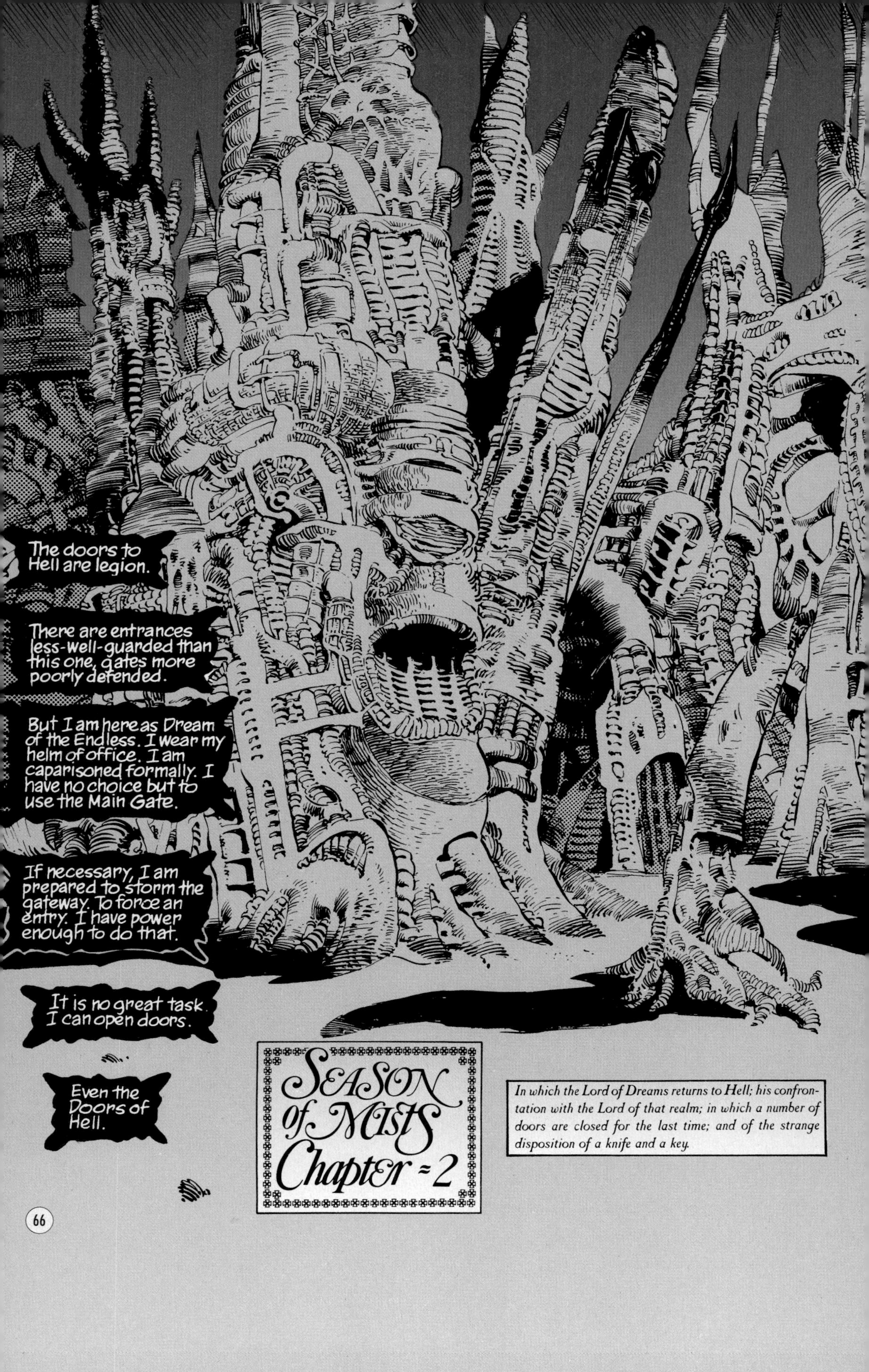
The doors to Hell are legion.
There are entrances less-well-guarded than this one, gates more poorly defended.
But I am here as Dream of the Endless. I wear my helm of office. I am caparisoned formally. I have no choice but to use the Main Gate.
If necessary, I am prepared to storm the gateway. To force an entry. I have power enough to do that.
It is no great task. I can open doors.
Even the Doors of Hell.

Season of Mists Chapter 2

In which the Lord of Dreams returns to Hell; his confrontation with the Lord of that realm; in which a number of doors are closed for the last time; and of the strange disposition of a knife and a key.

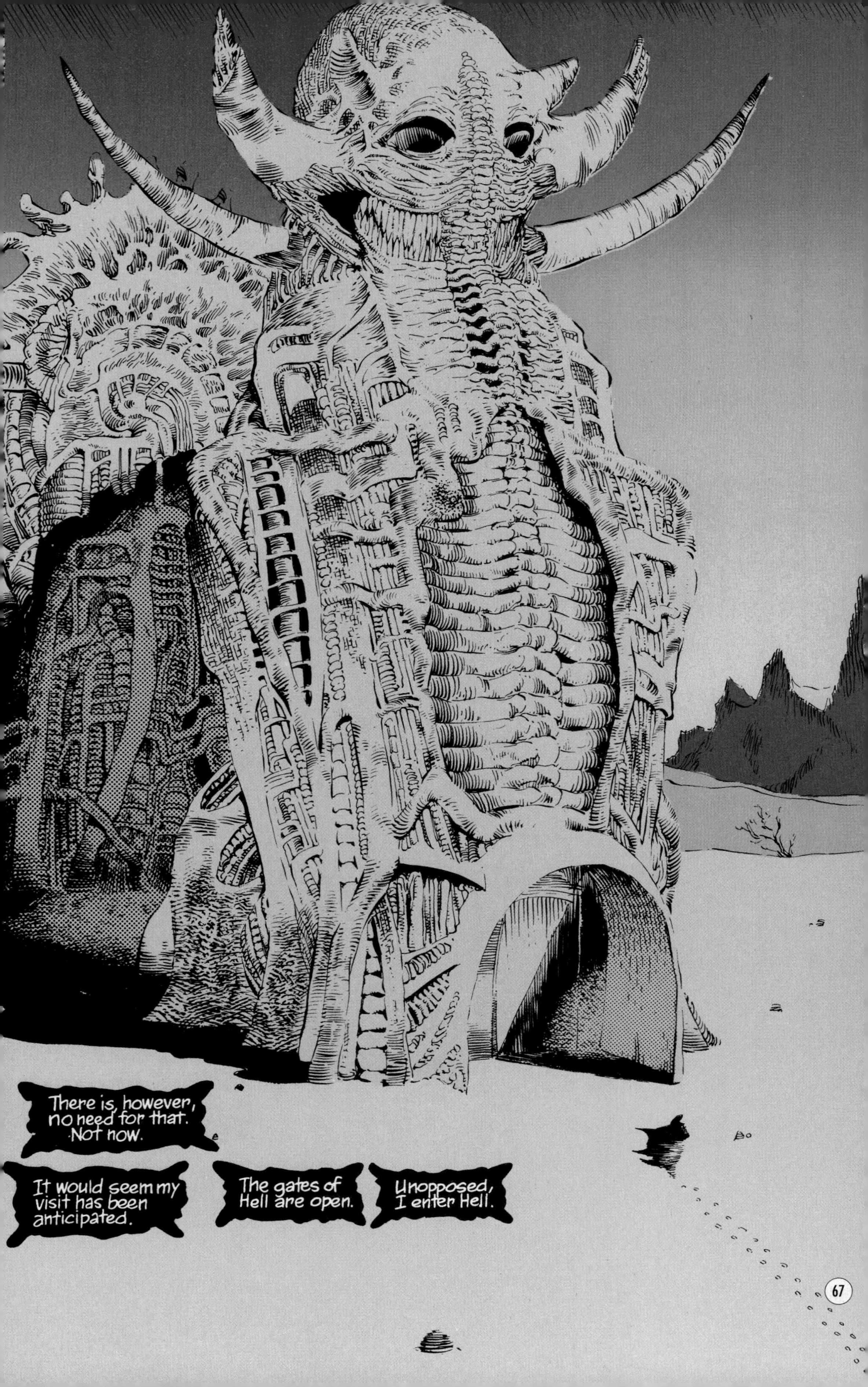
There is, however, no need for that. Not now.
It would seem my visit has been anticipated.
The gates of Hell are open.
Unopposed, I enter Hell.

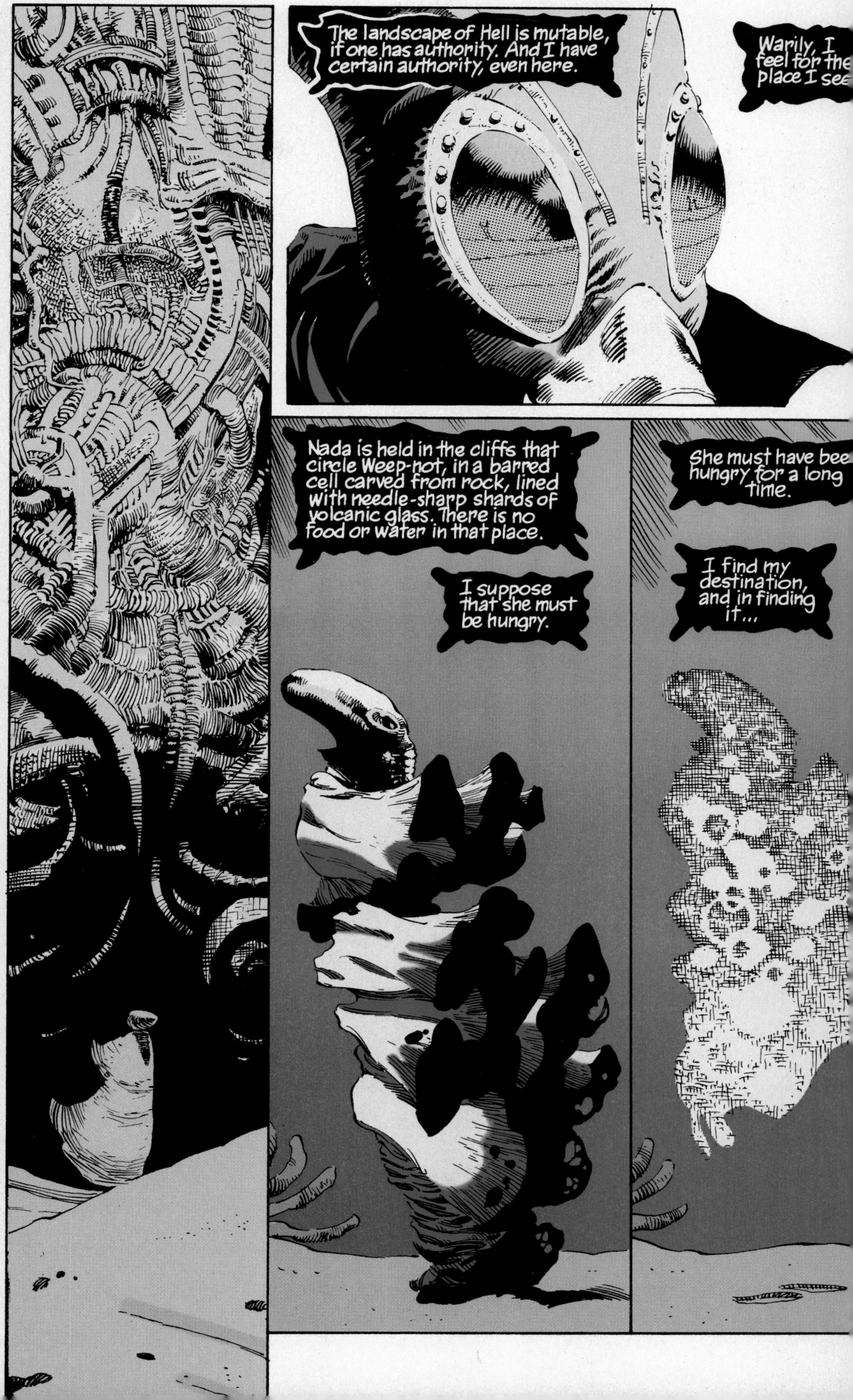

The landscape of Hell is mutable, if one has authority. And I have certain authority, even here.
Warily, I feel for the place I see
Nada is held in the cliffs that circle Weep-not, in a barred cell carved from rock, lined with needle-sharp shards of volcanic glass. There is no food or water in that place.
I suppose that she must be hungry.
She must have bee hungry for a long time.
I find my destination, and in finding it...

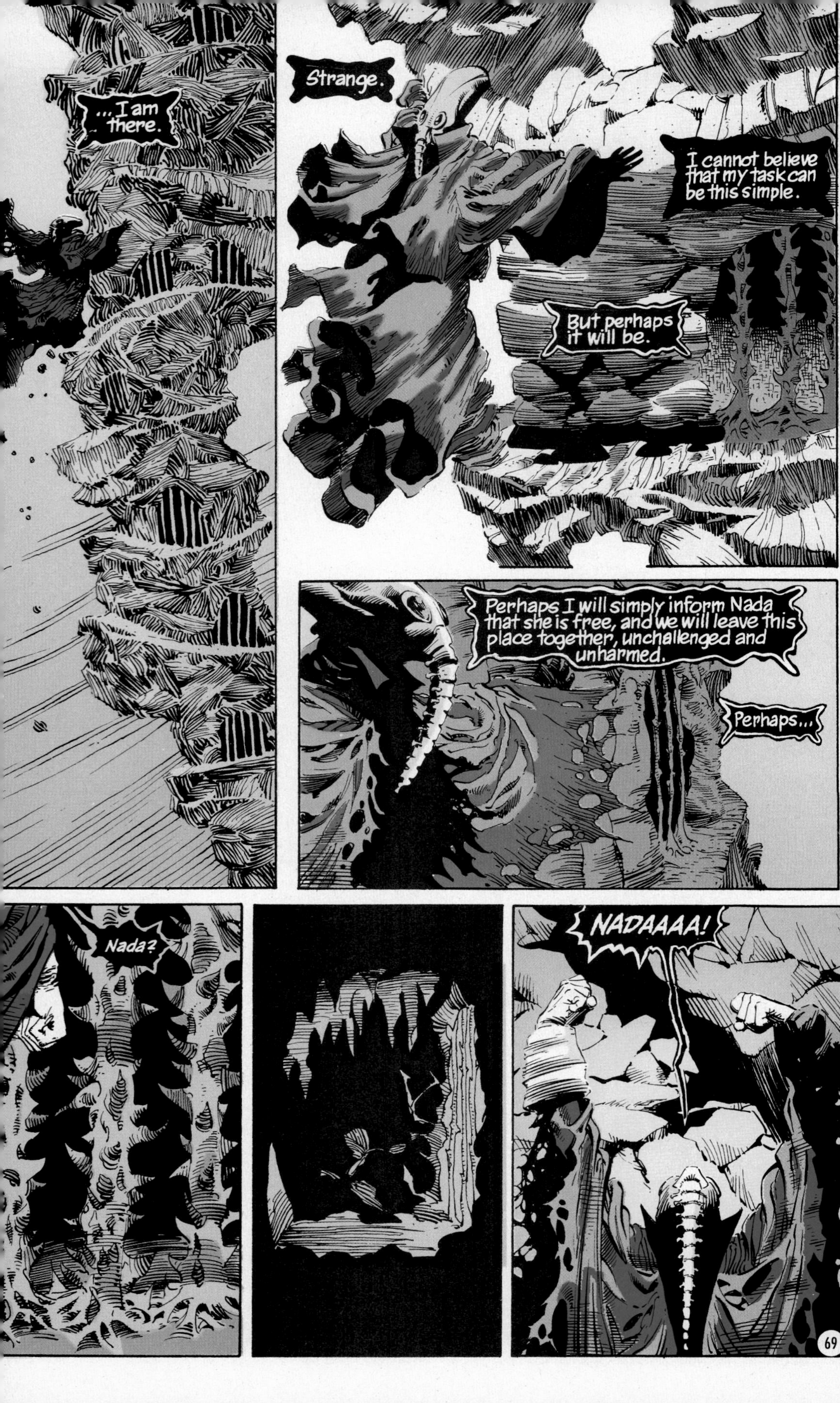
...I am there.
Strange.
I cannot believe that my task can be this simple.
But perhaps it will be.
Perhaps I will simply inform Nada that she is free, and we will leave this place together, unchallenged and unharmed.
Perhaps...
Nada?
NADAAAA!

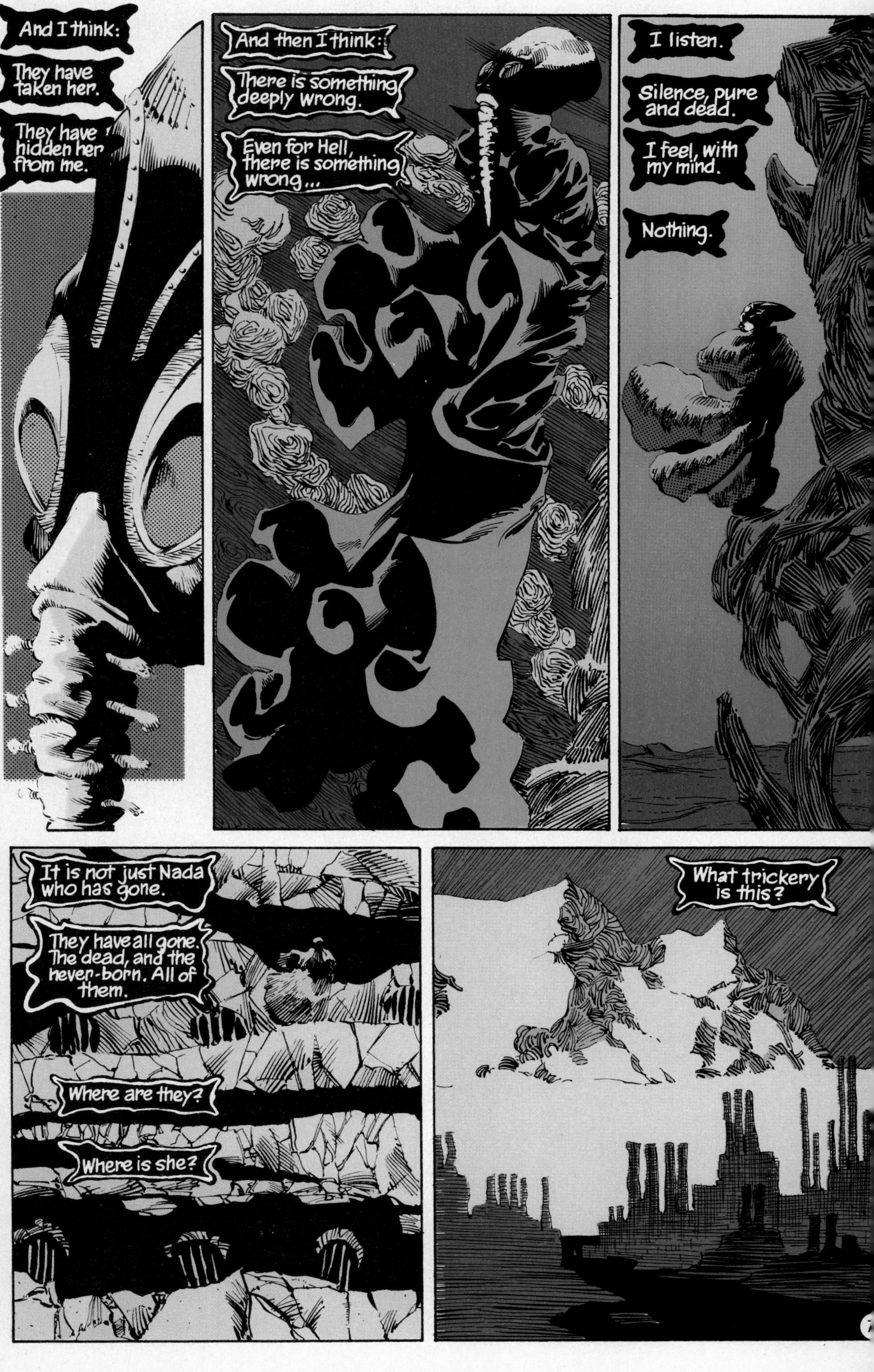

And I think:
They have taken her.
They have hidden her from me.
And then I think:
There is something deeply wrong.
Even for Hell, there is something wrong...
I listen.
Silence, pure and dead.
I feel, with my mind.
Nothing.
It is not just Nada who has gone.
They have all gone. The dead, and the never-born. All of them.
Where are they?
Where is she?
What trickery is this?

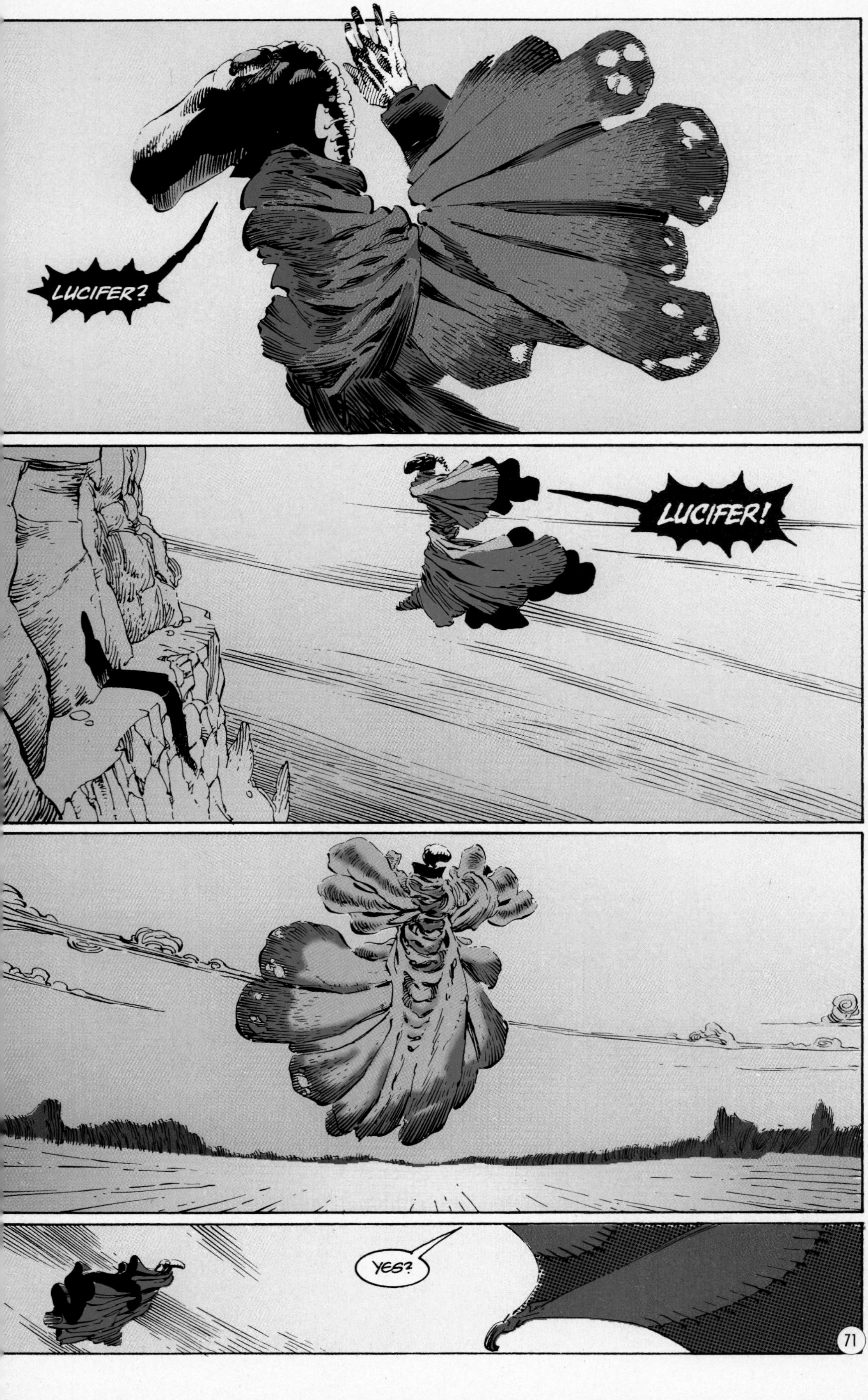
LUCIFER?
LUCIFER!
YES?

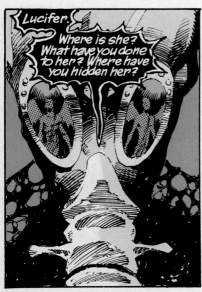

Lucifer. Where is she? What have you done to her? Where have you hidden her?

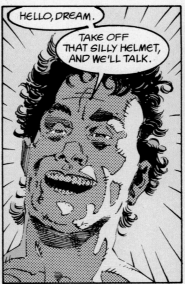

HELLO, DREAM.

TAKE OFF THAT SILLY HELMET, AND WE'LL TALK.

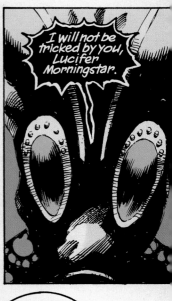

I will not be tricked by you, Lucifer Morningstar.

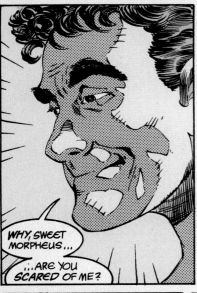

WHY, SWEET MORPHEUS...

...ARE YOU *SCARED* OF ME?

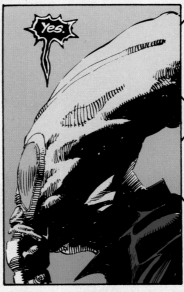

Yes.

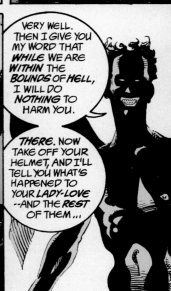

VERY WELL. THEN I GIVE YOU MY WORD THAT *WHILE* WE ARE *WITHIN* THE *BOUNDS* OF HELL, I WILL DO *NOTHING* TO HARM YOU.

THERE. NOW TAKE OFF YOUR HELMET, AND I'LL TELL YOU WHAT'S HAPPENED TO YOUR *LADY-LOVE* --AND THE *REST* OF THEM ...

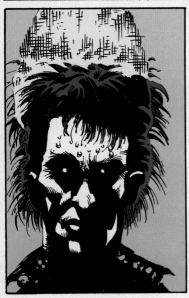

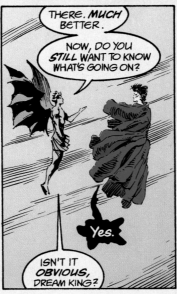

THERE. *MUCH* BETTER.

NOW, DO YOU *STILL* WANT TO KNOW WHAT'S GOING ON?

Yes.

ISN'T IT *OBVIOUS,* DREAM KING?

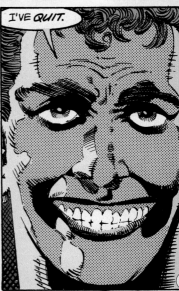

I'VE *QUIT.*

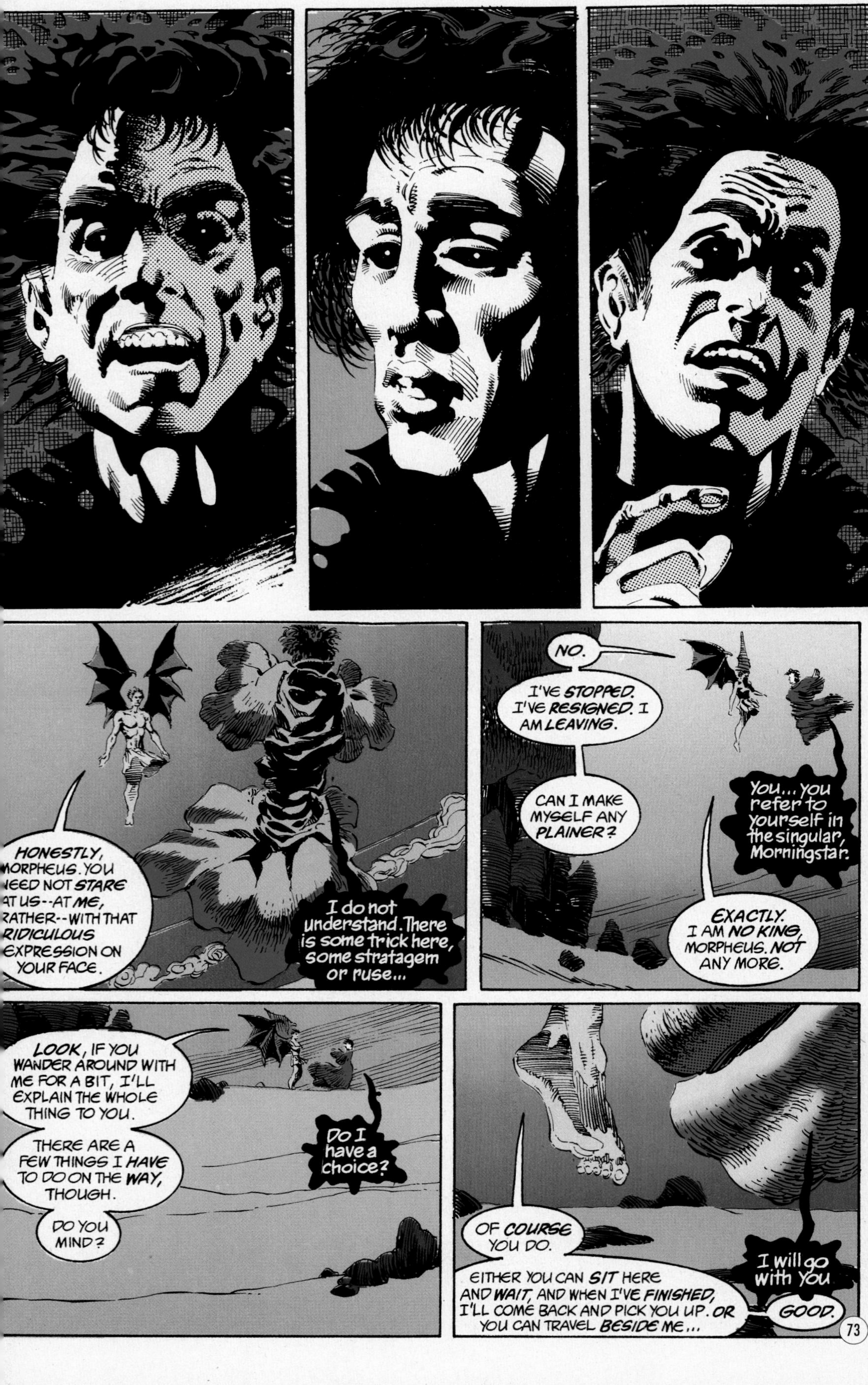
HONESTLY, MORPHEUS. YOU NEED NOT STARE AT US--AT ME, RATHER--WITH THAT RIDICULOUS EXPRESSION ON YOUR FACE.
I do not understand. There is some trick here, some stratagem or ruse...
NO.
I'VE STOPPED. I'VE RESIGNED. I AM LEAVING.
CAN I MAKE MYSELF ANY PLAINER?
You... you refer to yourself in the singular, Morningstar.
EXACTLY. I AM NO KING, MORPHEUS. NOT ANY MORE.
LOOK, IF YOU WANDER AROUND WITH ME FOR A BIT, I'LL EXPLAIN THE WHOLE THING TO YOU.
THERE ARE A FEW THINGS I HAVE TO DO ON THE WAY, THOUGH.
DO YOU MIND?
Do I have a choice?
OF COURSE YOU DO.
EITHER YOU CAN SIT HERE AND WAIT, AND WHEN I'VE FINISHED, I'LL COME BACK AND PICK YOU UP. OR YOU CAN TRAVEL BESIDE ME...
I will go with you
GOOD.

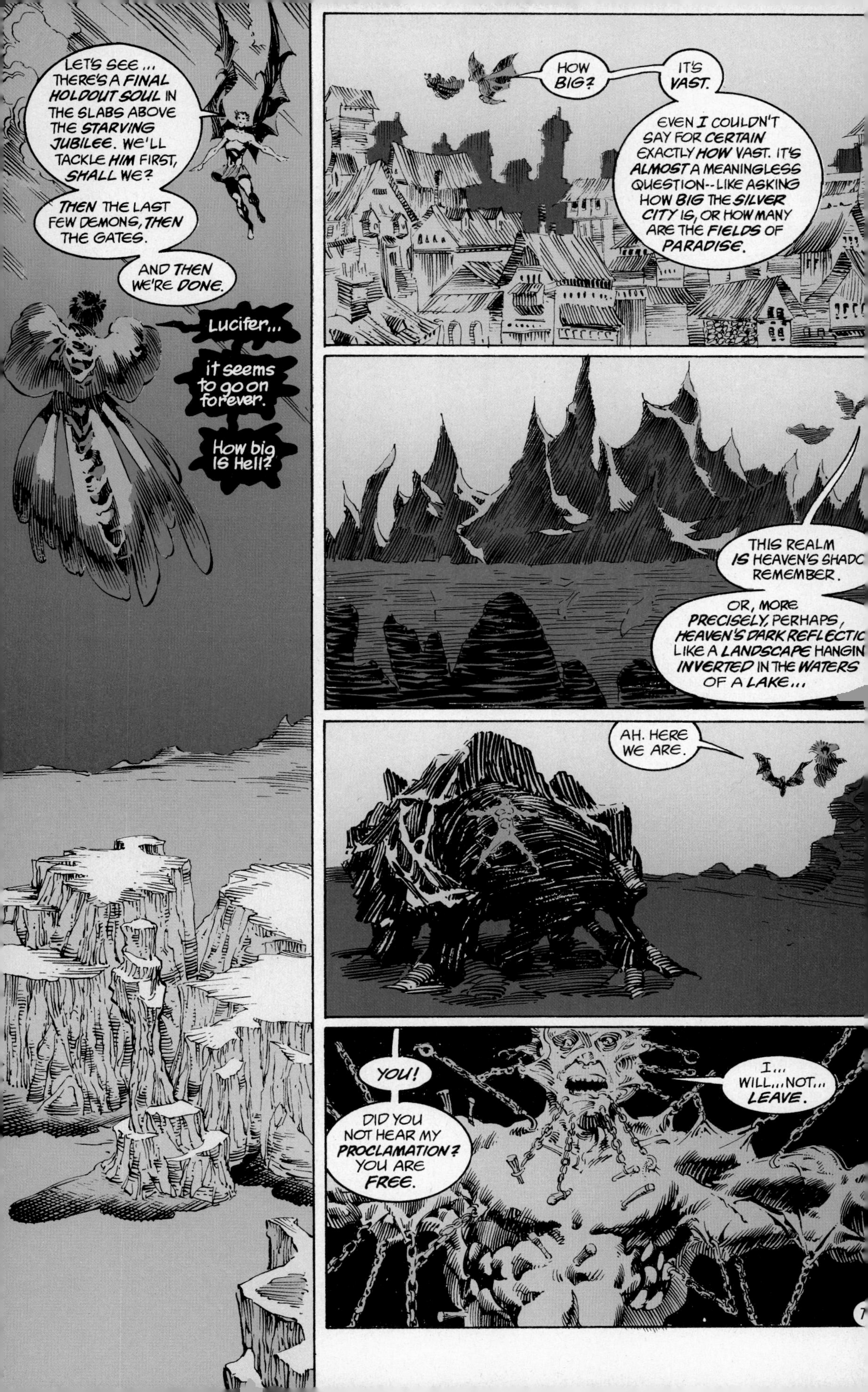

LET'S SEE ... THERE'S A FINAL HOLDOUT SOUL IN THE SLABS ABOVE THE STARVING JUBILEE. WE'LL TACKLE HIM FIRST, SHALL WE?
THEN THE LAST FEW DEMONS, THEN THE GATES.
AND THEN WE'RE DONE.
Lucifer,..
it seems to go on forever.
How big IS Hell?
HOW BIG?
IT'S VAST.
EVEN I COULDN'T SAY FOR CERTAIN EXACTLY HOW VAST. IT'S ALMOST A MEANINGLESS QUESTION--LIKE ASKING HOW BIG THE SILVER CITY IS, OR HOW MANY ARE THE FIELDS OF PARADISE.
THIS REALM IS HEAVEN'S SHADC REMEMBER.
OR, MORE PRECISELY, PERHAPS, HEAVEN'S DARK REFLECTIC LIKE A LANDSCAPE HANGIN INVERTED IN THE WATERS OF A LAKE...
AH. HERE WE ARE.
YOU!
DID YOU NOT HEAR MY PROCLAMATION? YOU ARE FREE.
I... WILL... NOT... LEAVE.

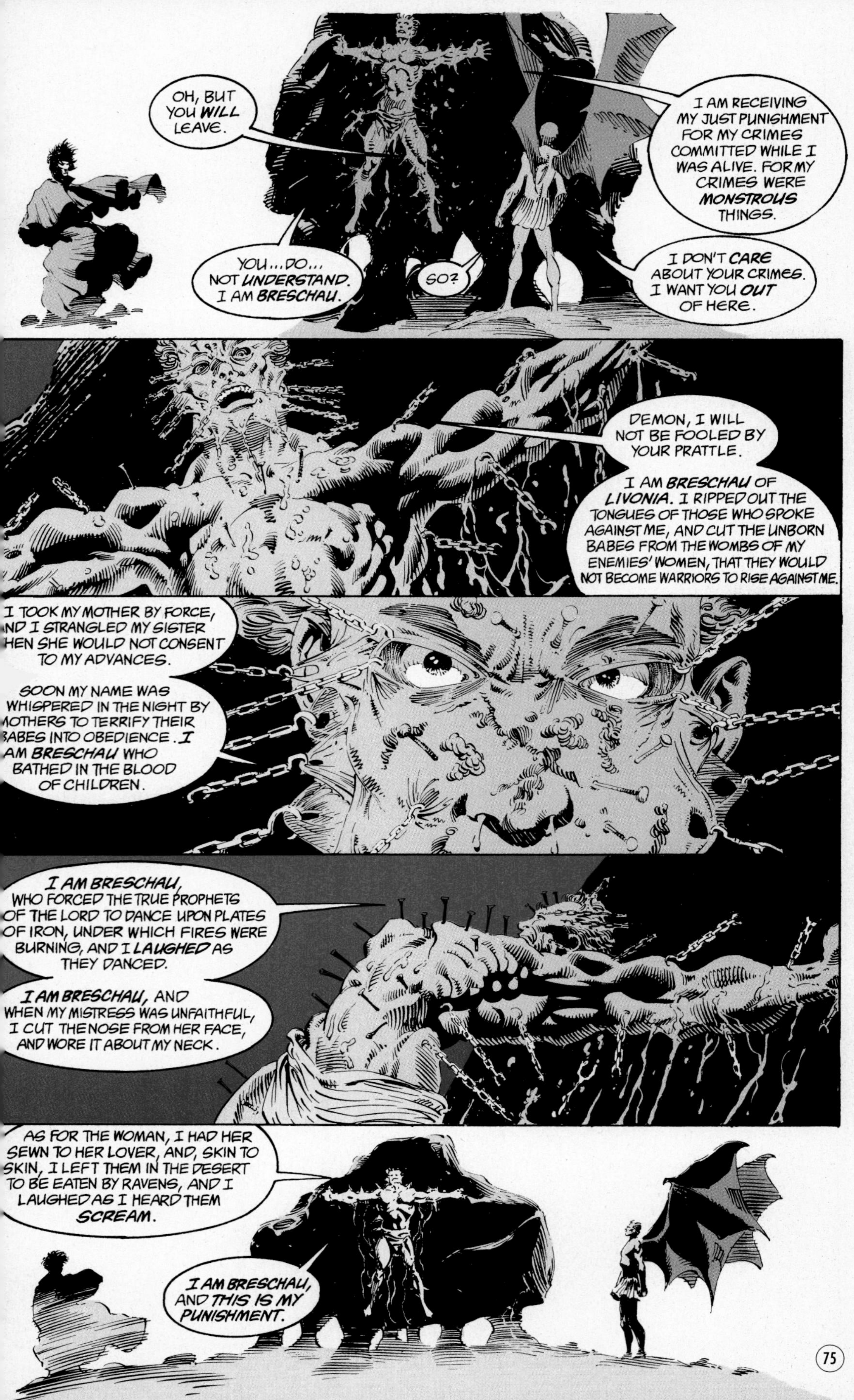
OH, BUT YOU WILL LEAVE.
I AM RECEIVING MY JUST PUNISHMENT FOR MY CRIMES COMMITTED WHILE I WAS ALIVE. FOR MY CRIMES WERE MONSTROUS THINGS.
YOU... DO... NOT UNDERSTAND. I AM BRESCHAU.
SO?
I DON'T CARE ABOUT YOUR CRIMES. I WANT YOU OUT OF HERE.
DEMON, I WILL NOT BE FOOLED BY YOUR PRATTLE.
I AM BRESCHAU OF LIVONIA. I RIPPED OUT THE TONGUES OF THOSE WHO SPOKE AGAINST ME, AND CUT THE UNBORN BABES FROM THE WOMBS OF MY ENEMIES' WOMEN, THAT THEY WOULD NOT BECOME WARRIORS TO RISE AGAINST ME.
I TOOK MY MOTHER BY FORCE, ND I STRANGLED MY SISTER HEN SHE WOULD NOT CONSENT TO MY ADVANCES.
SOON MY NAME WAS WHISPERED IN THE NIGHT BY MOTHERS TO TERRIFY THEIR BABES INTO OBEDIENCE. I AM BRESCHAU WHO BATHED IN THE BLOOD OF CHILDREN.
I AM BRESCHAU, WHO FORCED THE TRUE PROPHETS OF THE LORD TO DANCE UPON PLATES OF IRON, UNDER WHICH FIRES WERE BURNING, AND I LAUGHED AS THEY DANCED.
I AM BRESCHAU, AND WHEN MY MISTRESS WAS UNFAITHFUL, I CUT THE NOSE FROM HER FACE, AND WORE IT ABOUT MY NECK.
AS FOR THE WOMAN, I HAD HER SEWN TO HER LOVER, AND, SKIN TO SKIN, I LEFT THEM IN THE DESERT TO BE EATEN BY RAVENS, AND I LAUGHED AS I HEARD THEM SCREAM.
I AM BRESCHAU, AND THIS IS MY PUNISHMENT.

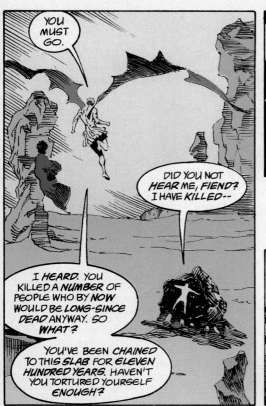

YOU MUST GO.

DID YOU NOT HEAR ME, FIEND? I HAVE KILLED--

I HEARD. YOU KILLED A NUMBER OF PEOPLE WHO BY NOW WOULD BE LONG-SINCE DEAD ANYWAY. SO WHAT?

YOU'VE BEEN CHAINED TO THIS SLAB FOR ELEVEN HUNDRED YEARS. HAVEN'T YOU TORTURED YOURSELF ENOUGH?

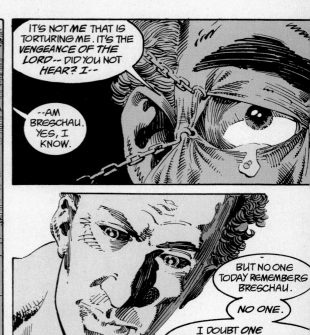

IT'S NOT ME THAT IS TORTURING ME. IT'S THE VENGEANCE OF THE LORD -- DID YOU NOT HEAR? I--

--AM BRESCHAU. YES, I KNOW.

BUT NO ONE TODAY REMEMBERS BRESCHAU.

NO ONE.

I DOUBT ONE LIVING MORTAL IN A HUNDRED THOUSAND COULD EVEN POINT TO WHERE LIVONIA USED TO BE, ON A MAP.

THE WORLD HAS FORGOTTEN YOU.

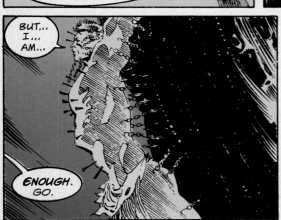

BUT... I.... AM...

ENOUGH. GO.

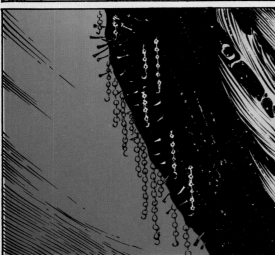

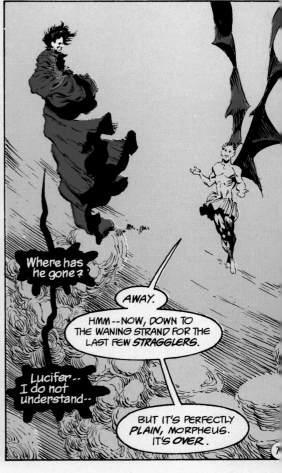

Where has he gone?

AWAY.

HMM--NOW, DOWN TO THE WANING STRAND FOR THE LAST FEW STRAGGLERS.

Lucifer-- I do not understand--

BUT IT'S PERFECTLY PLAIN, MORPHEUS. IT'S OVER.

7

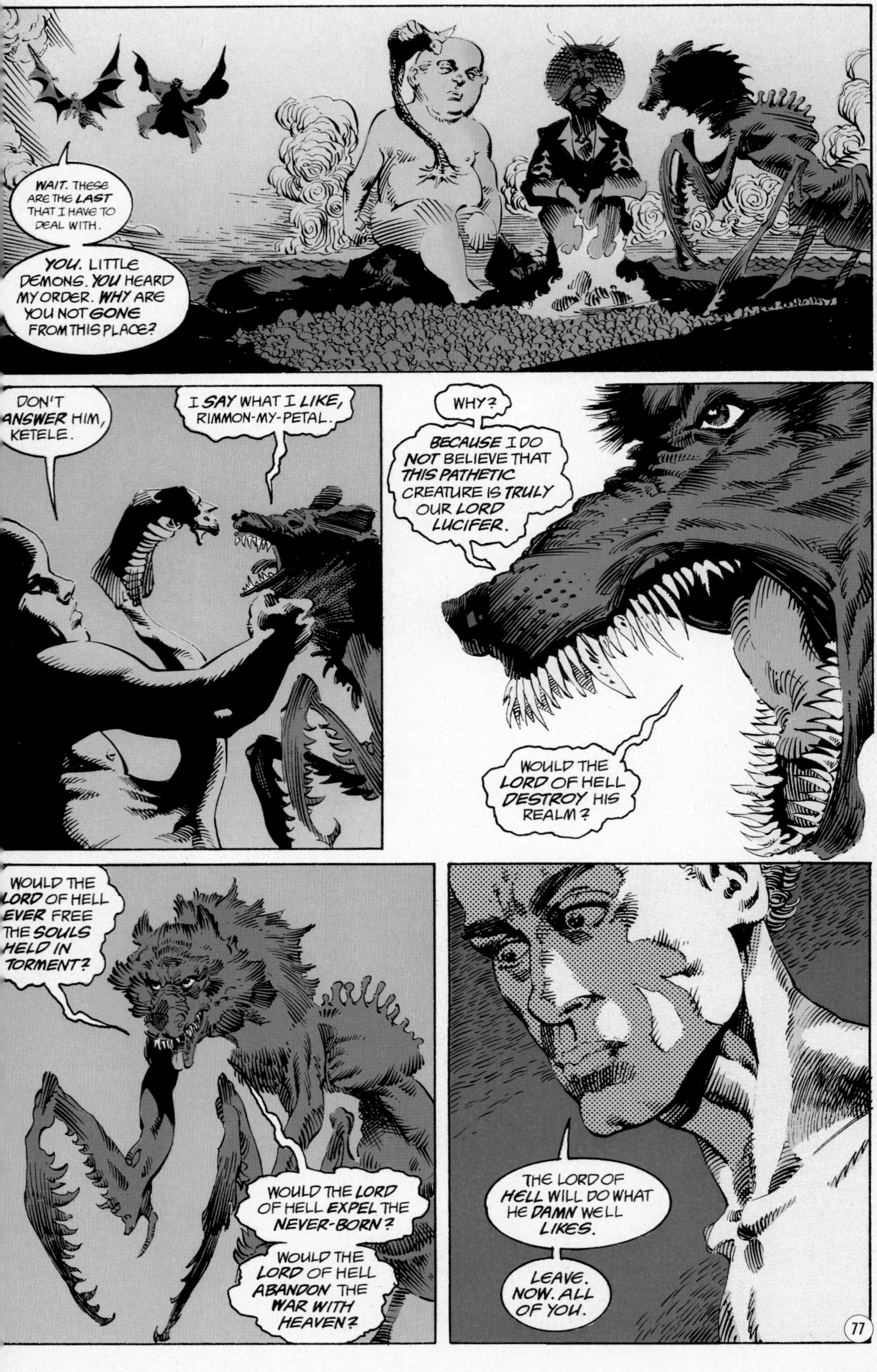
WAIT. THESE ARE THE LAST THAT I HAVE TO DEAL WITH.
YOU. LITTLE DEMONS. YOU HEARD MY ORDER. WHY ARE YOU NOT GONE FROM THIS PLACE?
DON'T ANSWER HIM, KETELE.
I SAY WHAT I LIKE, RIMMON-MY-PETAL.
WHY?
BECAUSE I DO NOT BELIEVE THAT THIS PATHETIC CREATURE IS TRULY OUR LORD LUCIFER.
WOULD THE LORD OF HELL DESTROY HIS REALM?
WOULD THE LORD OF HELL EVER FREE THE SOULS HELD IN TORMENT?
WOULD THE LORD OF HELL EXPEL THE NEVER-BORN?
WOULD THE LORD OF HELL ABANDON THE WAR WITH HEAVEN?
THE LORD OF HELL WILL DO WHAT HE DAMN WELL LIKES.
LEAVE. NOW. ALL OF YOU.

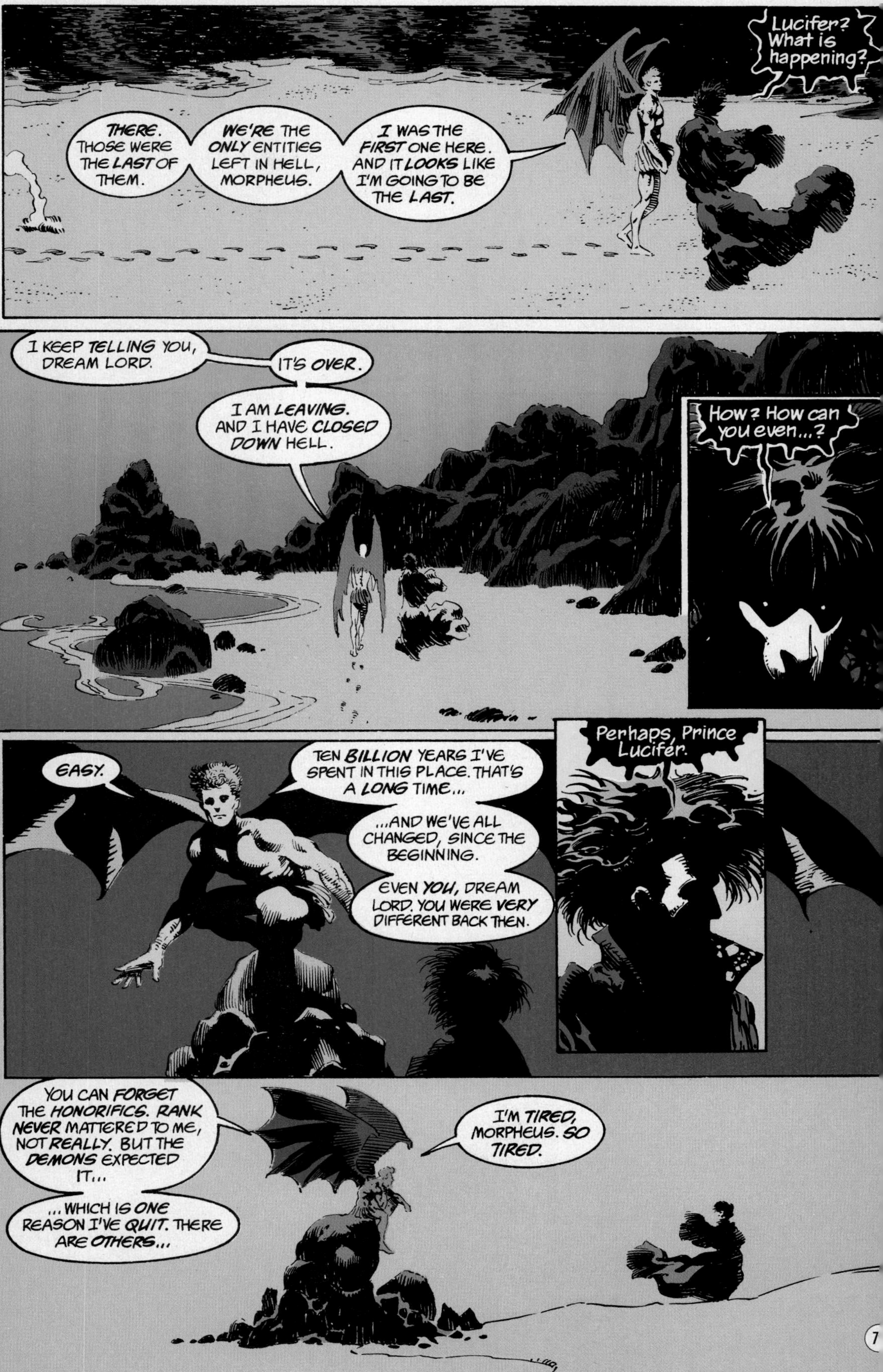

Lucifer? What is happening?
THERE. THOSE WERE THE LAST OF THEM.
WE'RE THE ONLY ENTITIES LEFT IN HELL, MORPHEUS.
I WAS THE FIRST ONE HERE. AND IT LOOKS LIKE I'M GOING TO BE THE LAST.
I KEEP TELLING YOU, DREAM LORD.
IT'S OVER.
I AM LEAVING. AND I HAVE CLOSED DOWN HELL.
How? How can you even...?
EASY.
TEN BILLION YEARS I'VE SPENT IN THIS PLACE. THAT'S A LONG TIME...
...AND WE'VE ALL CHANGED, SINCE THE BEGINNING.
EVEN YOU, DREAM LORD. YOU WERE VERY DIFFERENT BACK THEN.
Perhaps, Prince Lucifer.
YOU CAN FORGET THE HONORIFICS. RANK NEVER MATTERED TO ME, NOT REALLY. BUT THE DEMONS EXPECTED IT...
...WHICH IS ONE REASON I'VE QUIT. THERE ARE OTHERS...
I'M TIRED, MORPHEUS. SO TIRED.

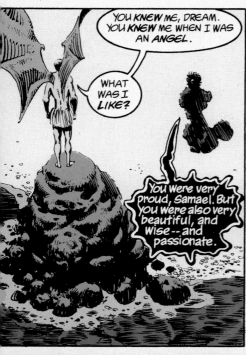
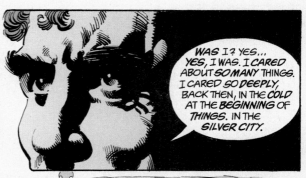
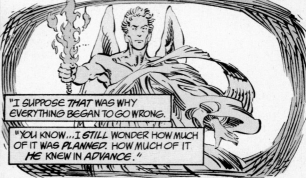
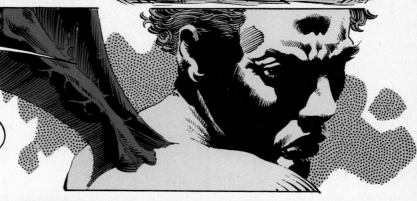
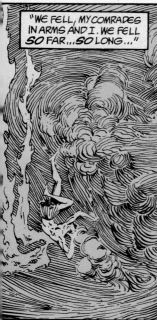
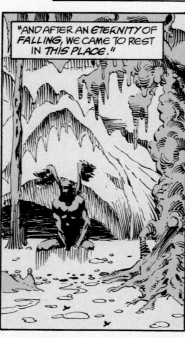
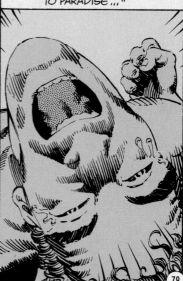

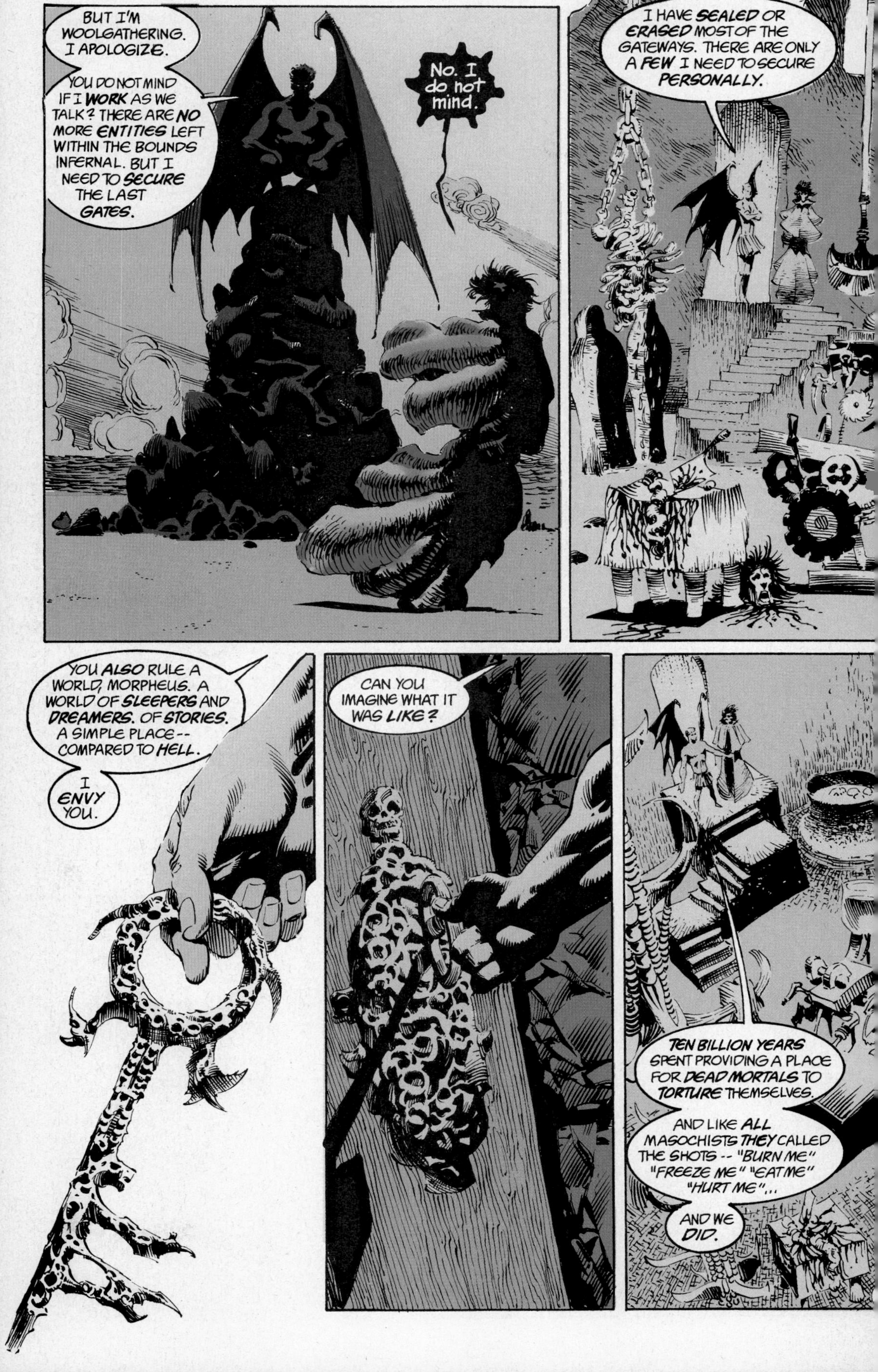
BUT I'M WOOLGATHERING. I APOLOGIZE.
YOU DO NOT MIND IF I WORK AS WE TALK? THERE ARE NO MORE ENTITIES LEFT WITHIN THE BOUNDS INFERNAL. BUT I NEED TO SECURE THE LAST GATES.
No. I do not mind.
I HAVE SEALED OR ERASED MOST OF THE GATEWAYS. THERE ARE ONLY A FEW I NEED TO SECURE PERSONALLY.
YOU ALSO RULE A WORLD, MORPHEUS. A WORLD OF SLEEPERS AND DREAMERS. OF STORIES. A SIMPLE PLACE-- COMPARED TO HELL.
I ENVY YOU.
CAN YOU IMAGINE WHAT IT WAS LIKE?
TEN BILLION YEARS SPENT PROVIDING A PLACE FOR DEAD MORTALS TO TORTURE THEMSELVES.
AND LIKE ALL MASOCHISTS THEY CALLED THE SHOTS -- "BURN ME" "FREEZE ME" "EAT ME" "HURT ME"...
AND WE DID.

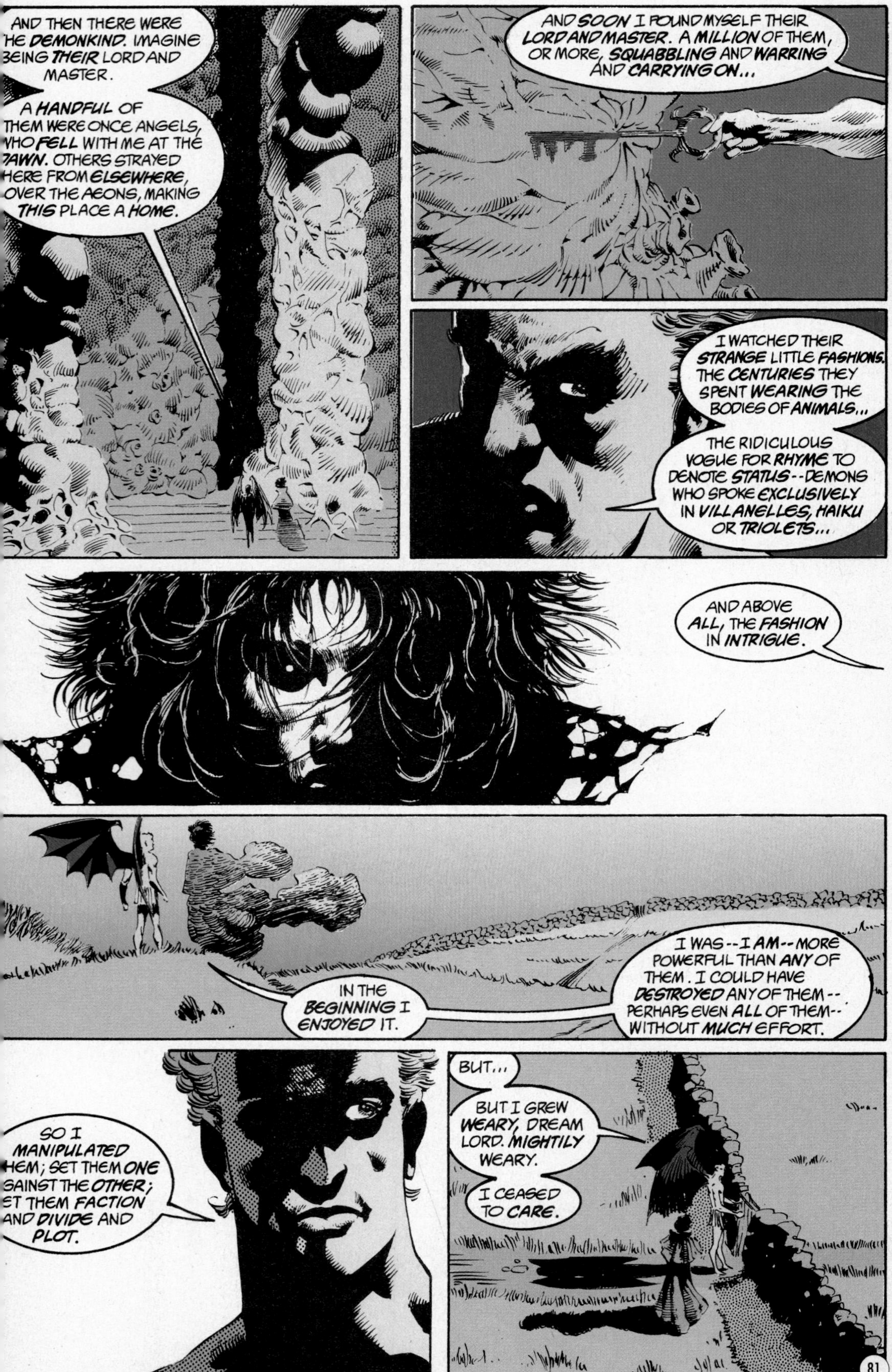
AND THEN THERE WERE THE DEMONKIND. IMAGINE BEING THEIR LORD AND MASTER.
A HANDFUL OF THEM WERE ONCE ANGELS, WHO FELL WITH ME AT THE DAWN. OTHERS STRAYED HERE FROM ELSEWHERE, OVER THE AEONS, MAKING THIS PLACE A HOME.
AND SOON I FOUND MYSELF THEIR LORD AND MASTER. A MILLION OF THEM, OR MORE, SQUABBLING AND WARRING AND CARRYING ON...
I WATCHED THEIR STRANGE LITTLE FASHIONS. THE CENTURIES THEY SPENT WEARING THE BODIES OF ANIMALS...
THE RIDICULOUS VOGUE FOR RHYME TO DENOTE STATUS--DEMONS WHO SPOKE EXCLUSIVELY IN VILLANELLES, HAIKU OR TRIOLETS...
AND ABOVE ALL, THE FASHION IN INTRIGUE.
IN THE BEGINNING I ENJOYED IT.
I WAS--I AM--MORE POWERFUL THAN ANY OF THEM. I COULD HAVE DESTROYED ANY OF THEM--PERHAPS EVEN ALL OF THEM--WITHOUT MUCH EFFORT.
SO I MANIPULATED THEM; SET THEM ONE AGAINST THE OTHER; LET THEM FACTION AND DIVIDE AND PLOT.
BUT...
BUT I GREW WEARY, DREAM LORD. MIGHTILY WEARY.
I CEASED TO CARE.

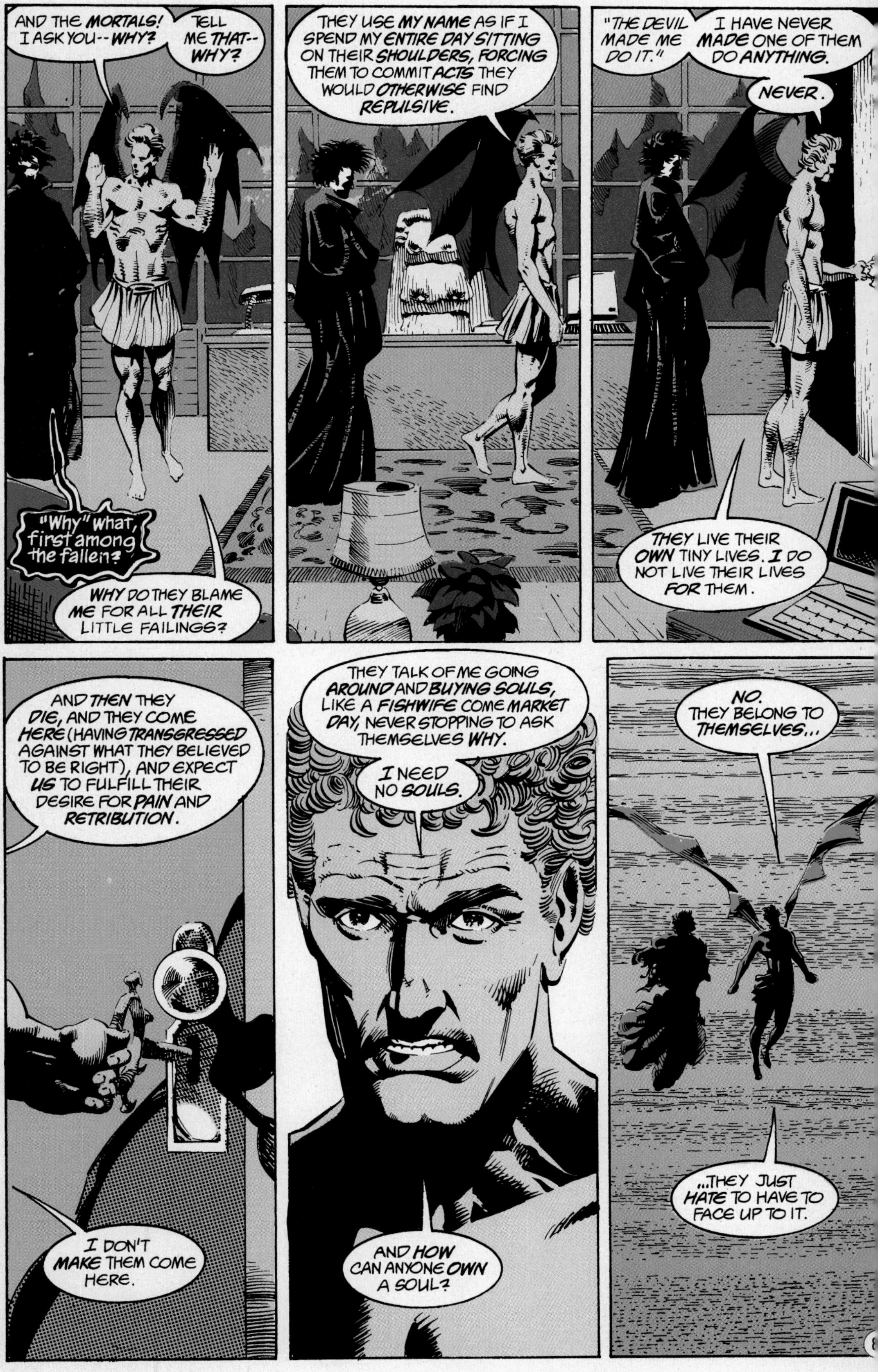
AND THE MORTALS! I ASK YOU--WHY?
TELL ME THAT-- WHY?
"Why" what, first among the fallen?
WHY DO THEY BLAME ME FOR ALL THEIR LITTLE FAILINGS?
THEY USE MY NAME AS IF I SPEND MY ENTIRE DAY SITTING ON THEIR SHOULDERS, FORCING THEM TO COMMIT ACTS THEY WOULD OTHERWISE FIND REPULSIVE.
"THE DEVIL MADE ME DO IT."
I HAVE NEVER MADE ONE OF THEM DO ANYTHING.
NEVER.
THEY LIVE THEIR OWN TINY LIVES. I DO NOT LIVE THEIR LIVES FOR THEM.
AND THEN THEY DIE, AND THEY COME HERE (HAVING TRANSGRESSED AGAINST WHAT THEY BELIEVED TO BE RIGHT), AND EXPECT US TO FULFILL THEIR DESIRE FOR PAIN AND RETRIBUTION.
I DON'T MAKE THEM COME HERE.
THEY TALK OF ME GOING AROUND AND BUYING SOULS, LIKE A FISHWIFE COME MARKET DAY, NEVER STOPPING TO ASK THEMSELVES WHY.
I NEED NO SOULS.
AND HOW CAN ANYONE OWN A SOUL?
NO. THEY BELONG TO THEMSELVES...
...THEY JUST HATE TO HAVE TO FACE UP TO IT.

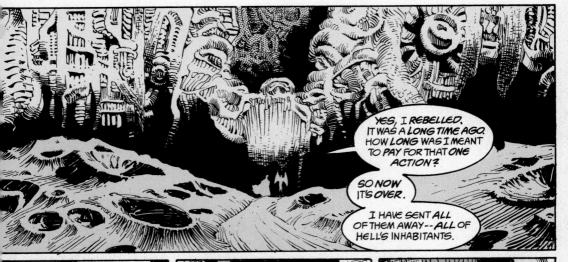

YES, I REBELLED. IT WAS A *LONG* TIME AGO. HOW *LONG* WAS I MEANT TO *PAY* FOR THAT *ONE* ACTION?

SO NOW IT'S *OVER*.

I HAVE SENT *ALL* OF THEM AWAY-- ALL OF HELL'S INHABITANTS.

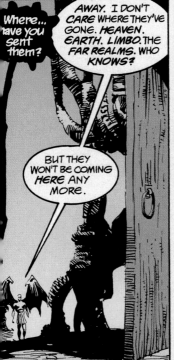

WHERE... HAVE YOU SENT THEM?

AWAY. I DON'T *CARE* WHERE THEY'VE GONE. HEAVEN. EARTH. LIMBO. THE FAR REALMS. WHO *KNOWS*?

BUT THEY WON'T BE COMING *HERE* ANY MORE.

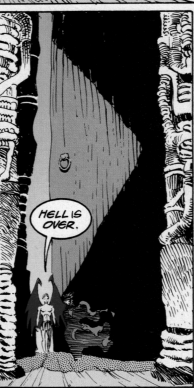

HELL IS *OVER*.

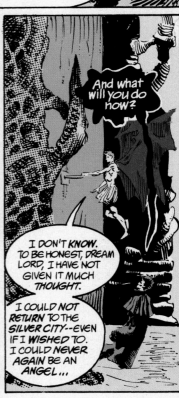

And what will you do *now*?

I DON'T *KNOW*. TO BE HONEST, DREAM LORD, I HAVE NOT GIVEN IT MUCH *THOUGHT*.

I COULD NOT *RETURN* TO THE *SILVER CITY*--EVEN IF I *WISHED* TO. I COULD NEVER AGAIN BE AN *ANGEL*...

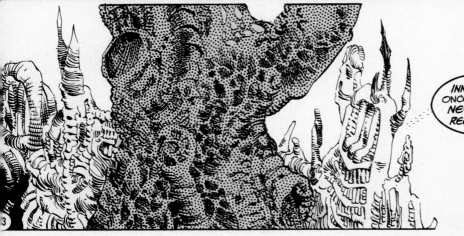

INNOCENCE, ONCE *LOST*, CAN NEVER BE REGAINED.

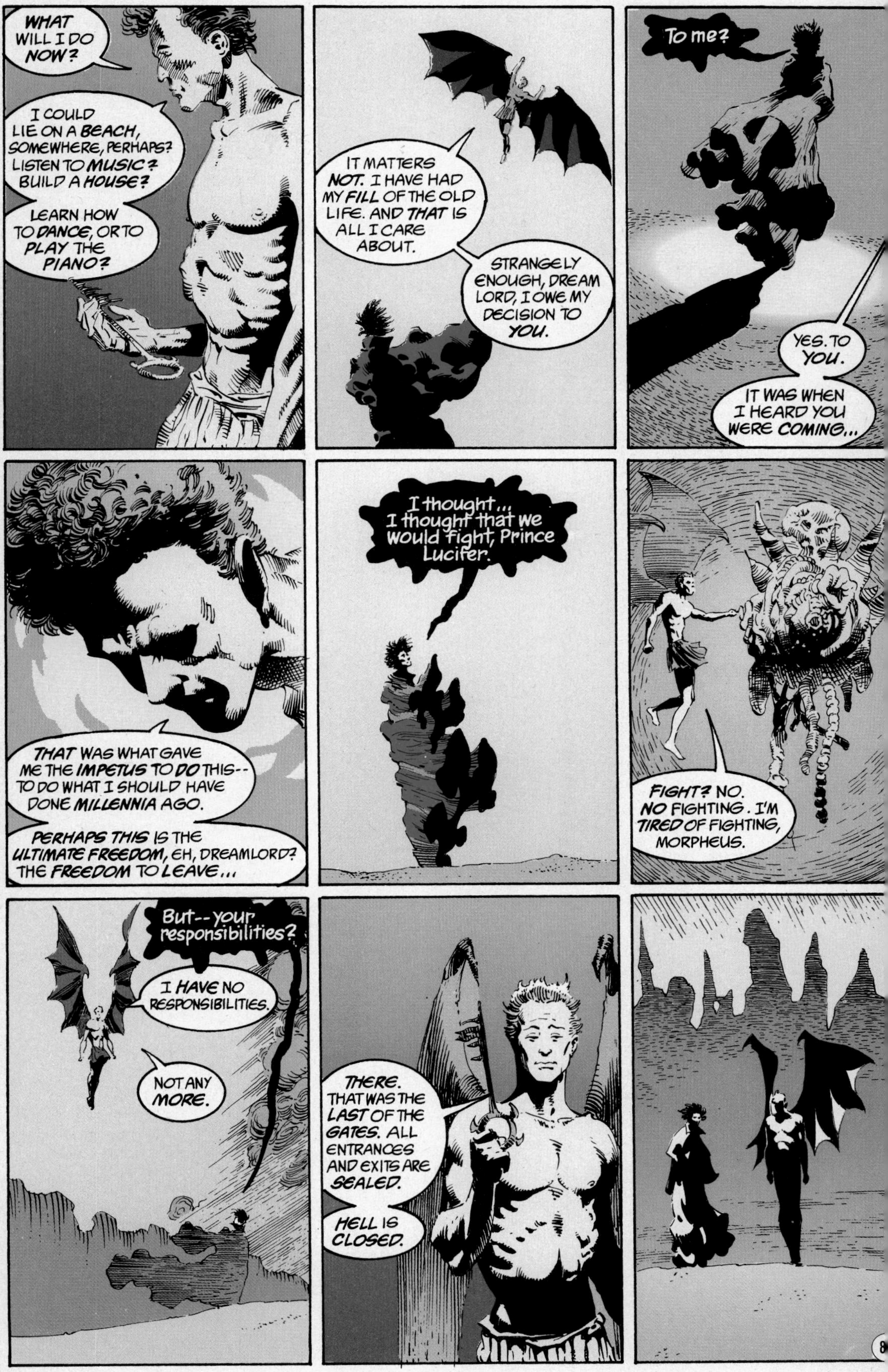
WHAT WILL I DO NOW?
I COULD LIE ON A BEACH, SOMEWHERE, PERHAPS? LISTEN TO MUSIC? BUILD A HOUSE?
LEARN HOW TO DANCE, OR TO PLAY THE PIANO?
IT MATTERS NOT. I HAVE HAD MY FILL OF THE OLD LIFE. AND THAT IS ALL I CARE ABOUT.
STRANGELY ENOUGH, DREAM LORD, I OWE MY DECISION TO YOU.
To me?
YES. TO YOU.
IT WAS WHEN I HEARD YOU WERE COMING...
THAT WAS WHAT GAVE ME THE IMPETUS TO DO THIS-- TO DO WHAT I SHOULD HAVE DONE MILLENNIA AGO.
PERHAPS THIS IS THE ULTIMATE FREEDOM, EH, DREAMLORD? THE FREEDOM TO LEAVE...
I thought... I thought that we would fight, Prince Lucifer.
FIGHT? NO. NO FIGHTING. I'M TIRED OF FIGHTING, MORPHEUS.
But--your responsibilities?
I HAVE NO RESPONSIBILITIES.
NOT ANY MORE.
THERE. THAT WAS THE LAST OF THE GATES. ALL ENTRANCES AND EXITS ARE SEALED.
HELL IS CLOSED.

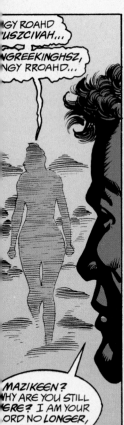

NGY ROAHD 'USZCIVAH...

NGREEKINGHSZ, NGY RROAHD...

MAZIKEEN? WHY ARE YOU STILL HERE? I AM YOUR LORD NO *LONGER*, CHILD.

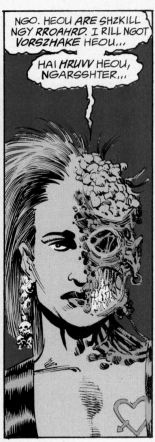

NGO. HEOU *ARE* SHZKILL NGY RROAHRD. I RILL NGOT *VORSZHAKE* HEOU...

HAI *HRUVV* HEOU, NGARSSHTER...

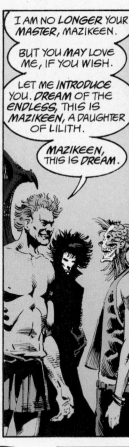

I AM NO *LONGER* YOUR *MASTER*, MAZIKEEN.

BUT YOU MAY LOVE ME, IF YOU WISH.

LET ME *INTRODUCE* YOU. *DREAM* OF THE *ENDLESS*, THIS IS *MAZIKEEN*, A DAUGHTER OF *LILITH*.

MAZIKEEN, THIS IS *DREAM*.

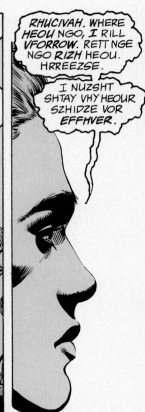

RHUCIVAH. WHERE *HEOU* NGO, I RILL *VFORROW*. RETT NGE NGO *RIZH* HEOU. *HRREEZSE*.

I NUZSHT SHTAY VHY HEOUR SZHIDZE VOR *EFFHVER*.

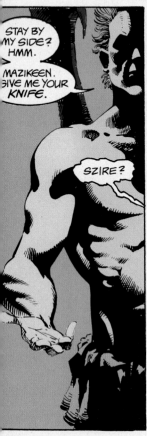

STAY BY MY SIDE? HMM.

MAZIKEEN. GIVE ME YOUR KNIFE.

SZIRE?

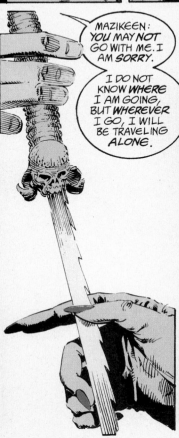

MAZIKEEN: *YOU* MAY *NOT* GO WITH ME. I AM *SORRY*.

I DO NOT KNOW *WHERE* I AM GOING, BUT *WHEREVER* I GO, I WILL BE TRAVELING *ALONE*.

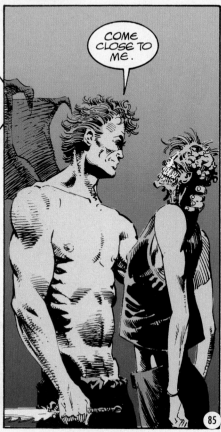

COME CLOSE TO ME.

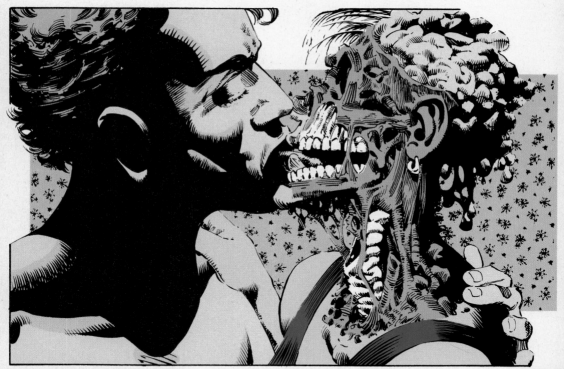

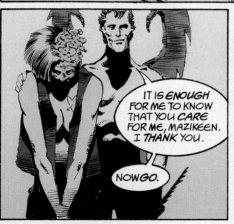

IT IS *ENOUGH* FOR ME TO KNOW THAT YOU *CARE* FOR ME, MAZIKEEN. I *THANK* YOU.

NOW GO.

GOODBYE, MAZIKEEN.

YOU ARE VERY BEAUTIFUL.

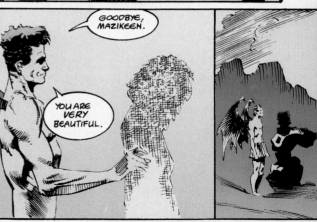

MORPHEUS. YOU MUST CUT OFF MY *WINGS.*

IT IS THE *LAST* THING THAT NEEDS DOING.

PLEASE, DO THIS THING FOR ME.

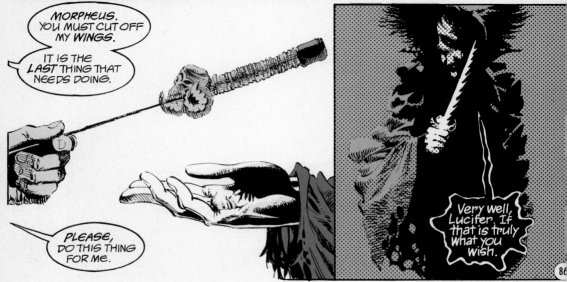

Very well, Lucifer. If that is truly what you wish.

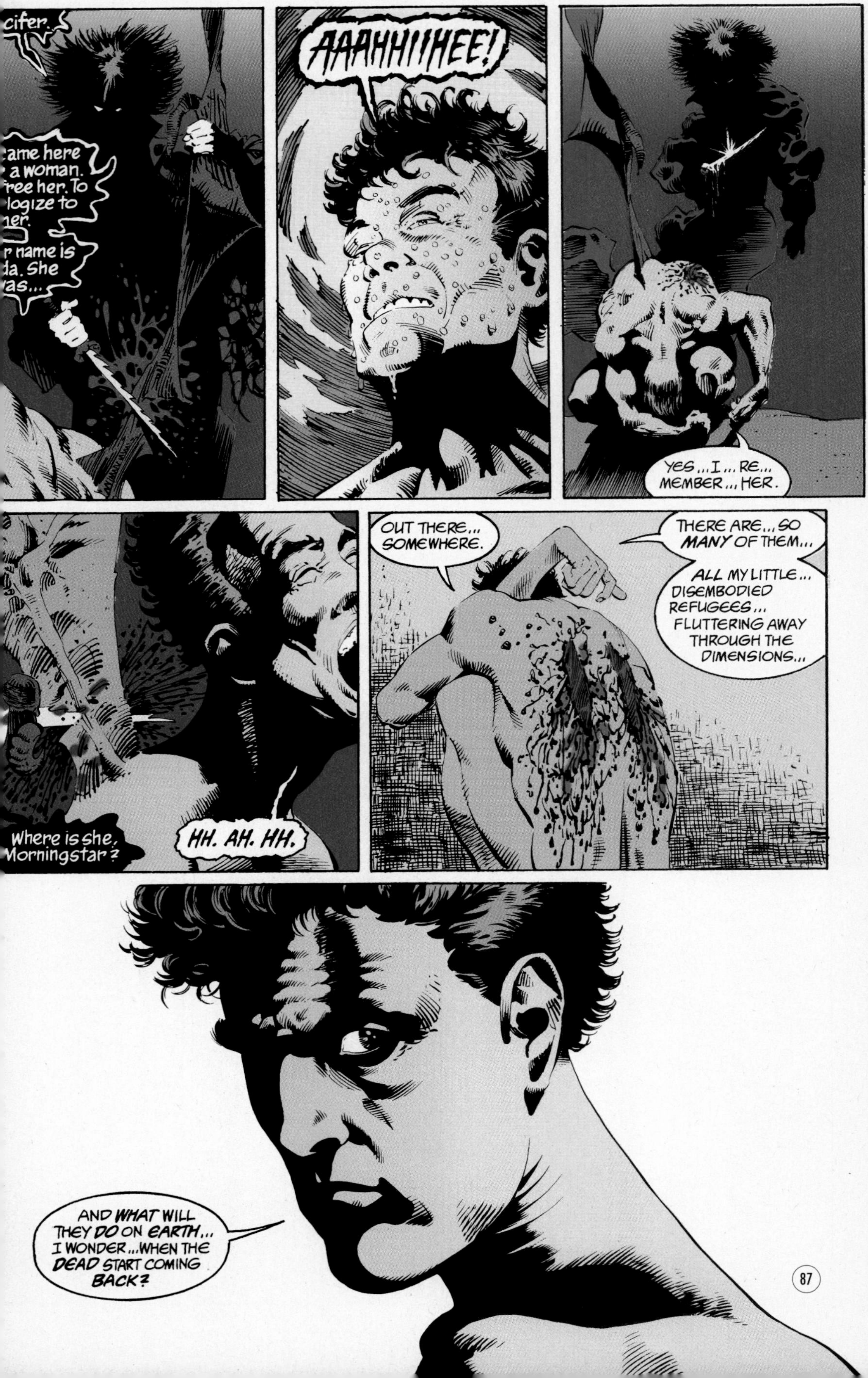
cifer.
ame here
a woman.
ree her. To
logize to
ner.
r name is
da. She
as...
AAAHHIIIHEE!
YES...I...RE...
MEMBER...HER.
Where is she,
Morningstar?
HH. AH. HH.
OUT THERE...
SOMEWHERE.
THERE ARE...SO
MANY OF THEM...
ALL MY LITTLE...
DISEMBODIED
REFUGEES...
FLUTTERING AWAY
THROUGH THE
DIMENSIONS...
AND WHAT WILL
THEY DO ON EARTH...
I WONDER...WHEN THE
DEAD START COMING
BACK?

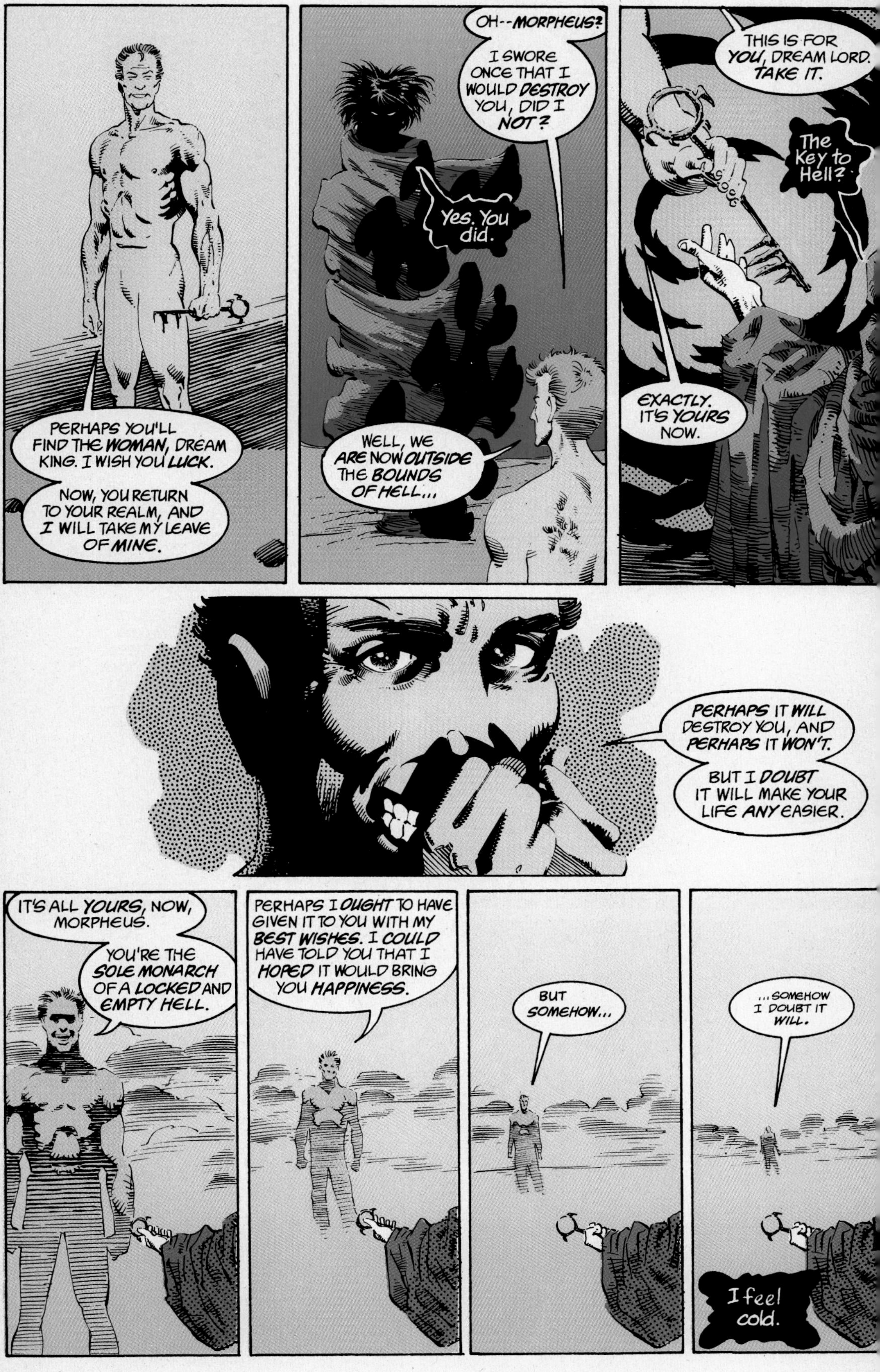
PERHAPS YOU'LL FIND THE WOMAN, DREAM KING. I WISH YOU LUCK.
NOW, YOU RETURN TO YOUR REALM, AND I WILL TAKE MY LEAVE OF MINE.
OH--MORPHEUS?
I SWORE ONCE THAT I WOULD DESTROY YOU, DID I NOT?
Yes. You did.
WELL, WE ARE NOW OUTSIDE THE BOUNDS OF HELL...
THIS IS FOR YOU, DREAM LORD. TAKE IT.
The Key to Hell?
EXACTLY. IT'S YOURS NOW.
PERHAPS IT WILL DESTROY YOU, AND PERHAPS IT WON'T.
BUT I DOUBT IT WILL MAKE YOUR LIFE ANY EASIER.
IT'S ALL YOURS, NOW, MORPHEUS.
YOU'RE THE SOLE MONARCH OF A LOCKED AND EMPTY HELL.
PERHAPS I OUGHT TO HAVE GIVEN IT TO YOU WITH MY BEST WISHES. I COULD HAVE TOLD YOU THAT I HOPED IT WOULD BRING YOU HAPPINESS.
BUT SOMEHOW...
...SOMEHOW I DOUBT IT WILL.
I feel cold.

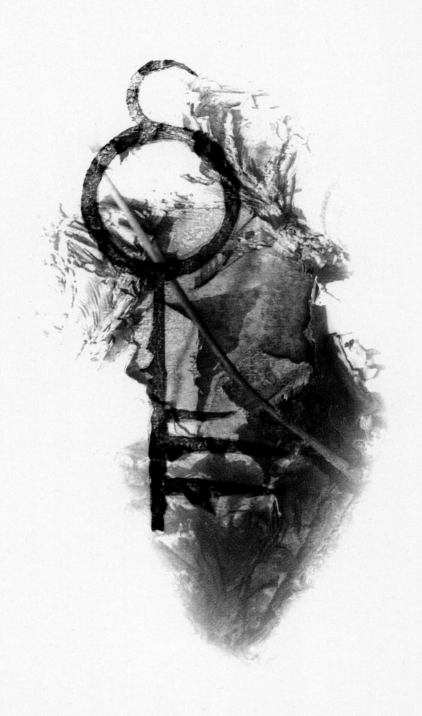

ON WHICH LUCIFER'S PARTING
GIFT ATTRACTS UNWANTED
ATTENTION; AND THE DREAM
LORD RECEIVES UNWELCOME
VISITORS.

EPISODE 3

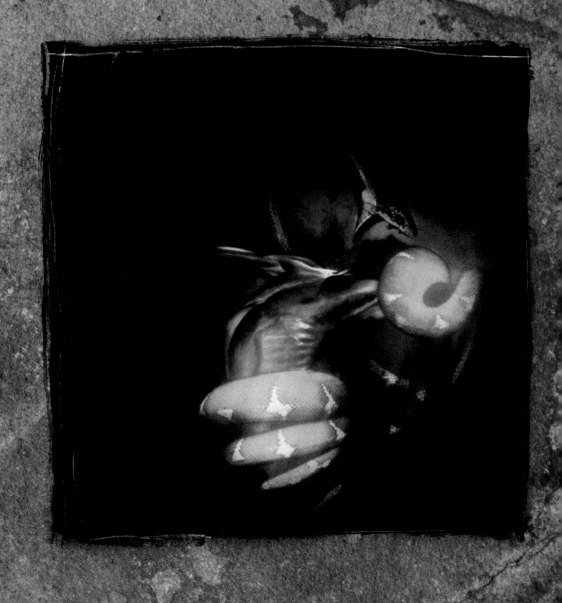

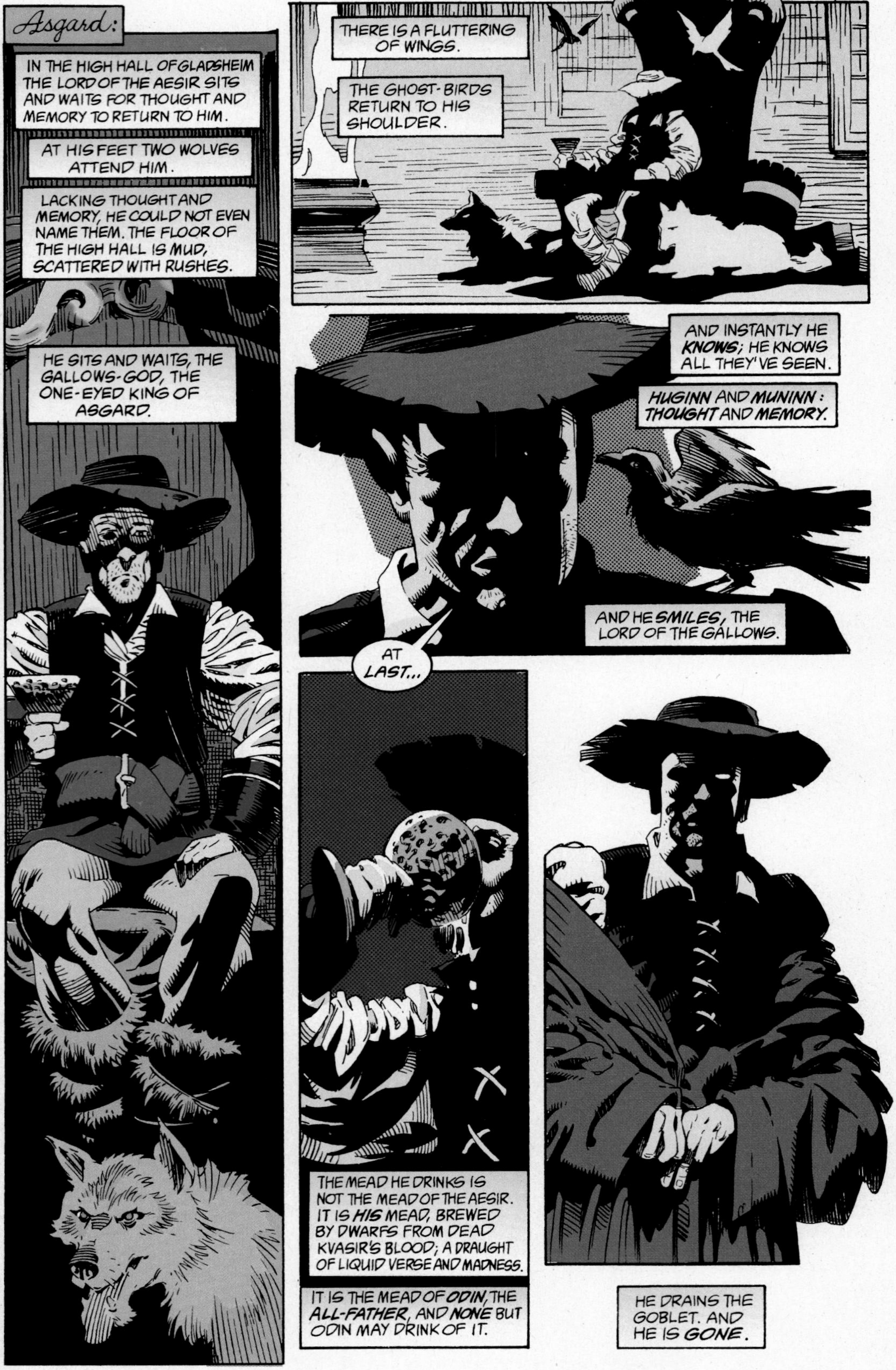
Asgard:
IN THE HIGH HALL OF GLADSHEIM THE LORD OF THE AESIR SITS AND WAITS FOR THOUGHT AND MEMORY TO RETURN TO HIM.
AT HIS FEET TWO WOLVES ATTEND HIM.
LACKING THOUGHT AND MEMORY, HE COULD NOT EVEN NAME THEM. THE FLOOR OF THE HIGH HALL IS MUD, SCATTERED WITH RUSHES.
HE SITS AND WAITS, THE GALLOWS-GOD, THE ONE-EYED KING OF ASGARD.
THERE IS A FLUTTERING OF WINGS.
THE GHOST-BIRDS RETURN TO HIS SHOULDER.
AND INSTANTLY HE ***KNOWS;*** HE KNOWS ALL THEY'VE SEEN.
HUGINN AND ***MUNINN***: ***THOUGHT*** AND ***MEMORY.***
AND HE ***SMILES,*** THE LORD OF THE GALLOWS.
AT ***LAST...***
THE MEAD HE DRINKS IS NOT THE MEAD OF THE AESIR. IT IS ***HIS*** MEAD, BREWED BY DWARFS FROM DEAD KVASIR'S BLOOD; A DRAUGHT OF LIQUID VERSE AND MADNESS.
IT IS THE MEAD OF ***ODIN,*** THE ***ALL-FATHER,*** AND ***NONE*** BUT ODIN MAY DRINK OF IT.
HE DRAINS THE GOBLET. AND HE IS ***GONE.***

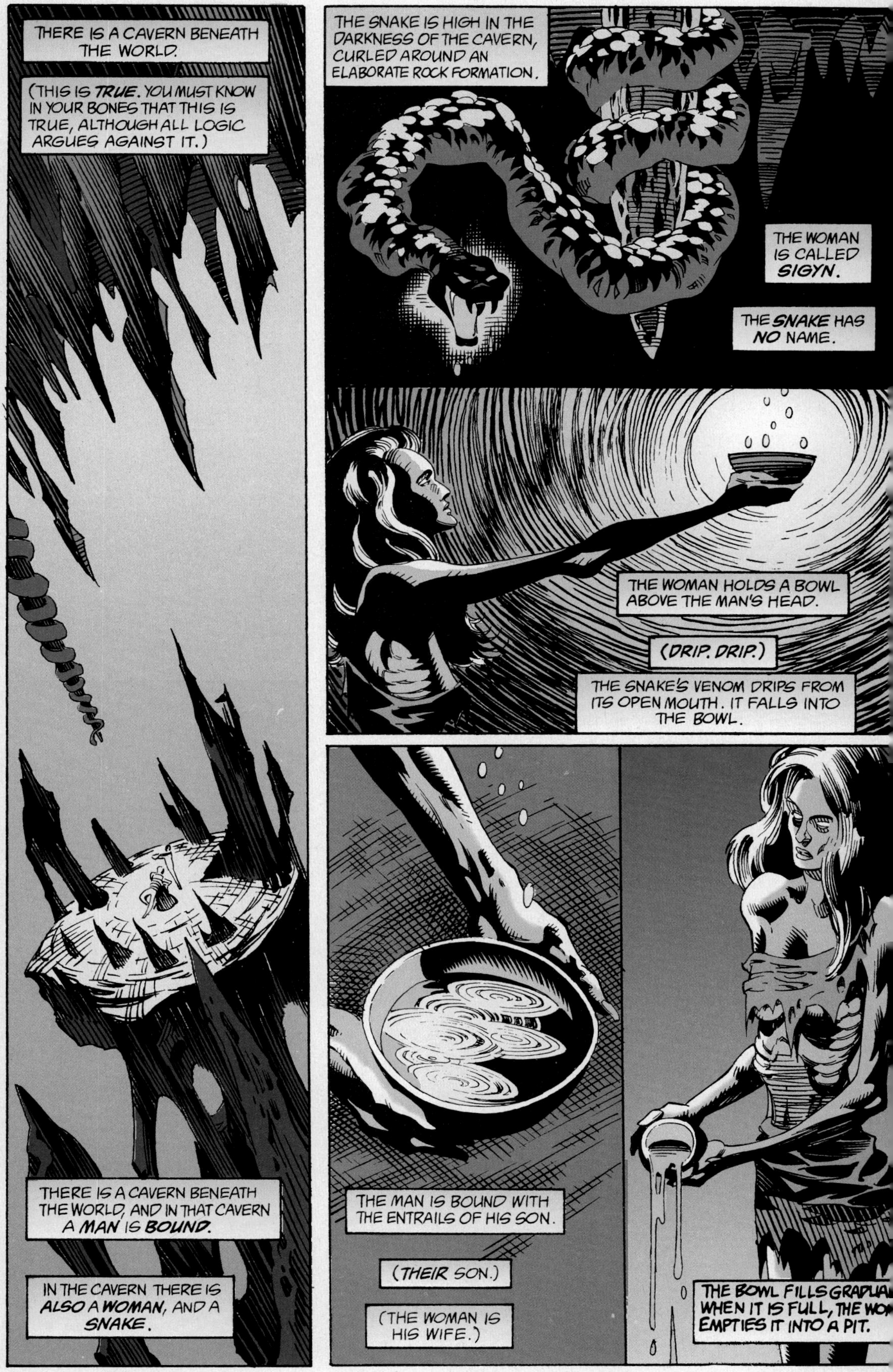
THERE IS A CAVERN BENEATH THE WORLD.
(THIS IS TRUE. YOU MUST KNOW IN YOUR BONES THAT THIS IS TRUE, ALTHOUGH ALL LOGIC ARGUES AGAINST IT.)
THERE IS A CAVERN BENEATH THE WORLD, AND IN THAT CAVERN A MAN IS BOUND.
IN THE CAVERN THERE IS ALSO A WOMAN, AND A SNAKE.
THE SNAKE IS HIGH IN THE DARKNESS OF THE CAVERN, CURLED AROUND AN ELABORATE ROCK FORMATION.
THE WOMAN IS CALLED SIGYN.
THE SNAKE HAS NO NAME.
THE WOMAN HOLDS A BOWL ABOVE THE MAN'S HEAD.
(DRIP. DRIP.)
THE SNAKE'S VENOM DRIPS FROM ITS OPEN MOUTH. IT FALLS INTO THE BOWL.
THE MAN IS BOUND WITH THE ENTRAILS OF HIS SON.
(THEIR SON.)
(THE WOMAN IS HIS WIFE.)
THE BOWL FILLS GRADUA
WHEN IT IS FULL, THE WO
EMPTIES IT INTO A PIT.

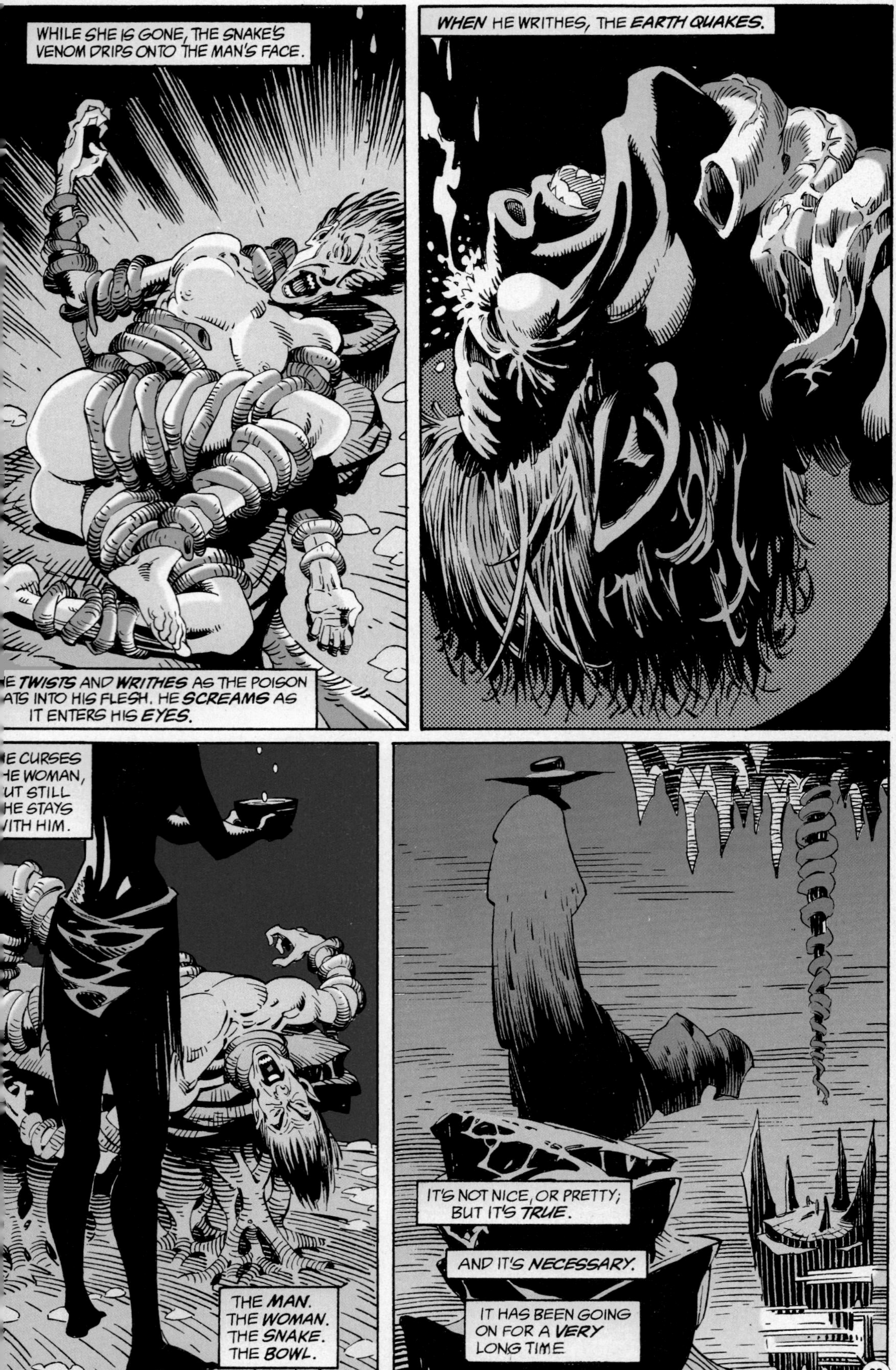
WHILE SHE IS GONE, THE SNAKE'S VENOM DRIPS ONTO THE MAN'S FACE.
E TWISTS AND WRITHES AS THE POISON ATS INTO HIS FLESH. HE SCREAMS AS IT ENTERS HIS EYES.
WHEN HE WRITHES, THE EARTH QUAKES.
E CURSES HE WOMAN, UT STILL HE STAYS VITH HIM.
THE MAN. THE WOMAN. THE SNAKE. THE BOWL.
IT'S NOT NICE, OR PRETTY; BUT IT'S TRUE.
AND IT'S NECESSARY.
IT HAS BEEN GOING ON FOR A VERY LONG TIME

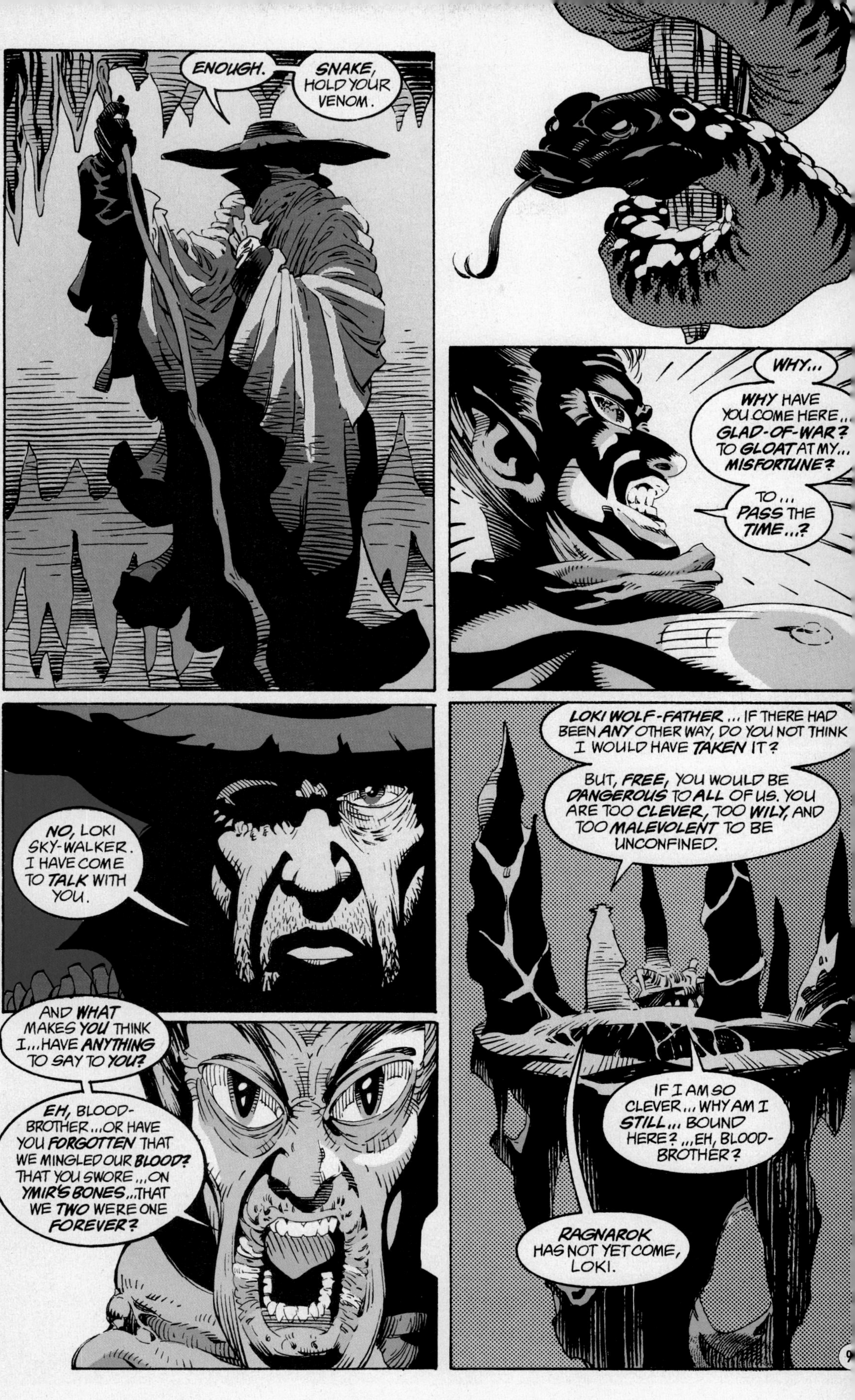
ENOUGH.
SNAKE, HOLD YOUR VENOM.
WHY...
WHY HAVE YOU COME HERE... GLAD-OF-WAR? TO GLOAT AT MY... MISFORTUNE?
TO... PASS THE TIME...?
NO, LOKI SKY-WALKER. I HAVE COME TO TALK WITH YOU.
AND WHAT MAKES YOU THINK I... HAVE ANYTHING TO SAY TO YOU?
EH, BLOOD-BROTHER... OR HAVE YOU FORGOTTEN THAT WE MINGLED OUR BLOOD? THAT YOU SWORE... ON YMIR'S BONES... THAT WE TWO WERE ONE FOREVER?
LOKI WOLF-FATHER... IF THERE HAD BEEN ANY OTHER WAY, DO YOU NOT THINK I WOULD HAVE TAKEN IT?
BUT, FREE, YOU WOULD BE DANGEROUS TO ALL OF US. YOU ARE TOO CLEVER, TOO WILY, AND TOO MALEVOLENT TO BE UNCONFINED.
IF I AM SO CLEVER... WHY AM I STILL... BOUND HERE? ...EH, BLOOD-BROTHER?
RAGNAROK HAS NOT YET COME, LOKI.

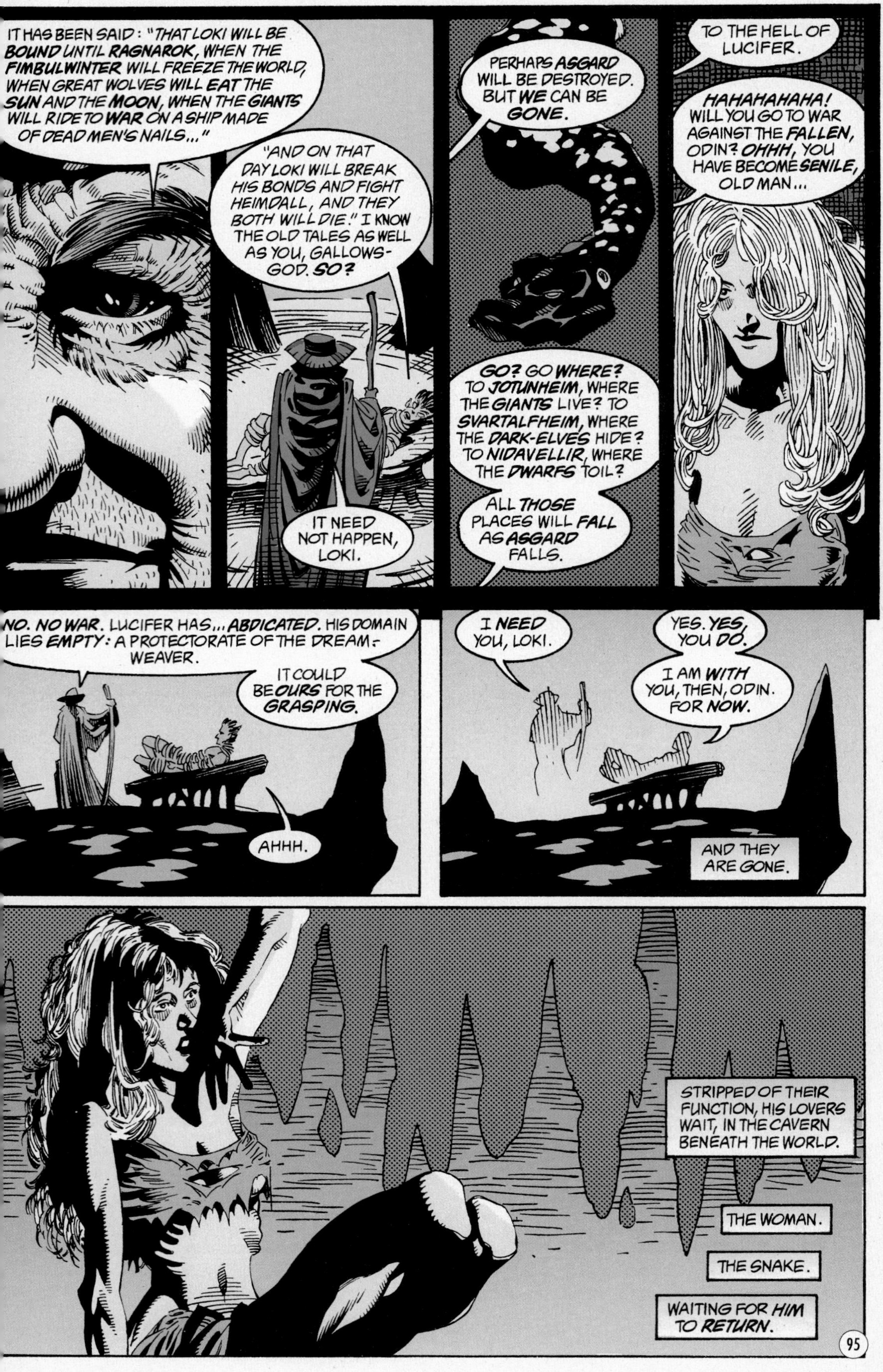
IT HAS BEEN SAID: "THAT LOKI WILL BE BOUND UNTIL RAGNAROK, WHEN THE FIMBULWINTER WILL FREEZE THE WORLD, WHEN GREAT WOLVES WILL EAT THE SUN AND THE MOON, WHEN THE GIANTS WILL RIDE TO WAR ON A SHIP MADE OF DEAD MEN'S NAILS..."
"AND ON THAT DAY LOKI WILL BREAK HIS BONDS AND FIGHT HEIMDALL, AND THEY BOTH WILL DIE." I KNOW THE OLD TALES AS WELL AS YOU, GALLOWS-GOD. SO?
IT NEED NOT HAPPEN, LOKI.
PERHAPS ASGARD WILL BE DESTROYED. BUT WE CAN BE GONE.
GO? GO WHERE? TO JOTUNHEIM, WHERE THE GIANTS LIVE? TO SVARTALFHEIM, WHERE THE DARK-ELVES HIDE? TO NIDAVELLIR, WHERE THE DWARFS TOIL?
ALL THOSE PLACES WILL FALL AS ASGARD FALLS.
TO THE HELL OF LUCIFER.
HAHAHAHAHA! WILL YOU GO TO WAR AGAINST THE FALLEN, ODIN? OHHH, YOU HAVE BECOME SENILE, OLD MAN...
NO. NO WAR. LUCIFER HAS... ABDICATED. HIS DOMAIN LIES EMPTY: A PROTECTORATE OF THE DREAM-WEAVER.
IT COULD BE OURS FOR THE GRASPING.
AHHH.
I NEED YOU, LOKI.
YES. YES, YOU DO.
I AM WITH YOU, THEN, ODIN. FOR NOW.
AND THEY ARE GONE.
STRIPPED OF THEIR FUNCTION, HIS LOVERS WAIT, IN THE CAVERN BENEATH THE WORLD.
THE WOMAN.
THE SNAKE.
WAITING FOR HIM TO RETURN.

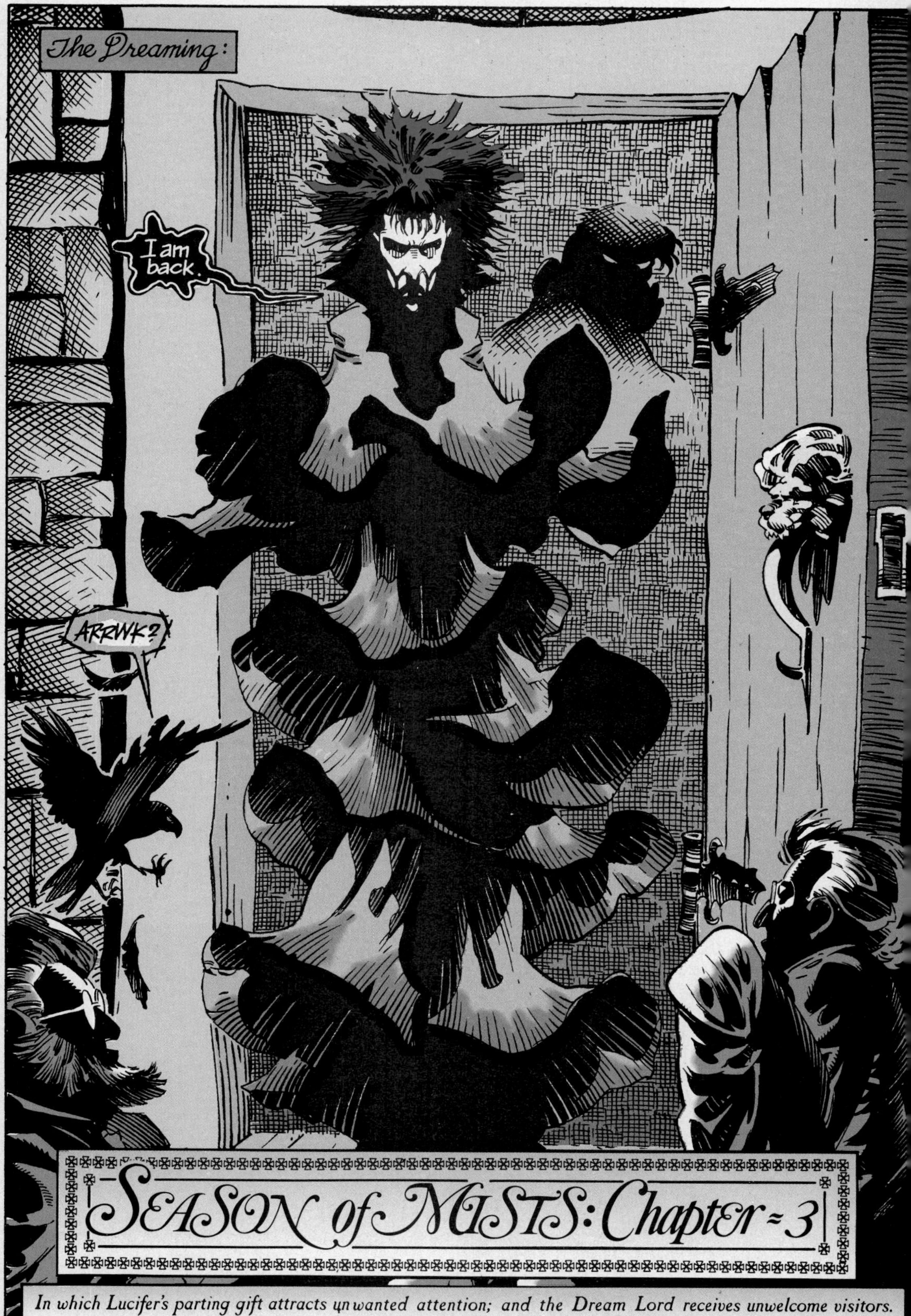

The Dreaming:
I am back.
ARRWK?
SEASON of MISTS: Chapter 3
In which Lucifer's parting gift attracts unwanted attention; and the Dream Lord receives unwelcome visitors.

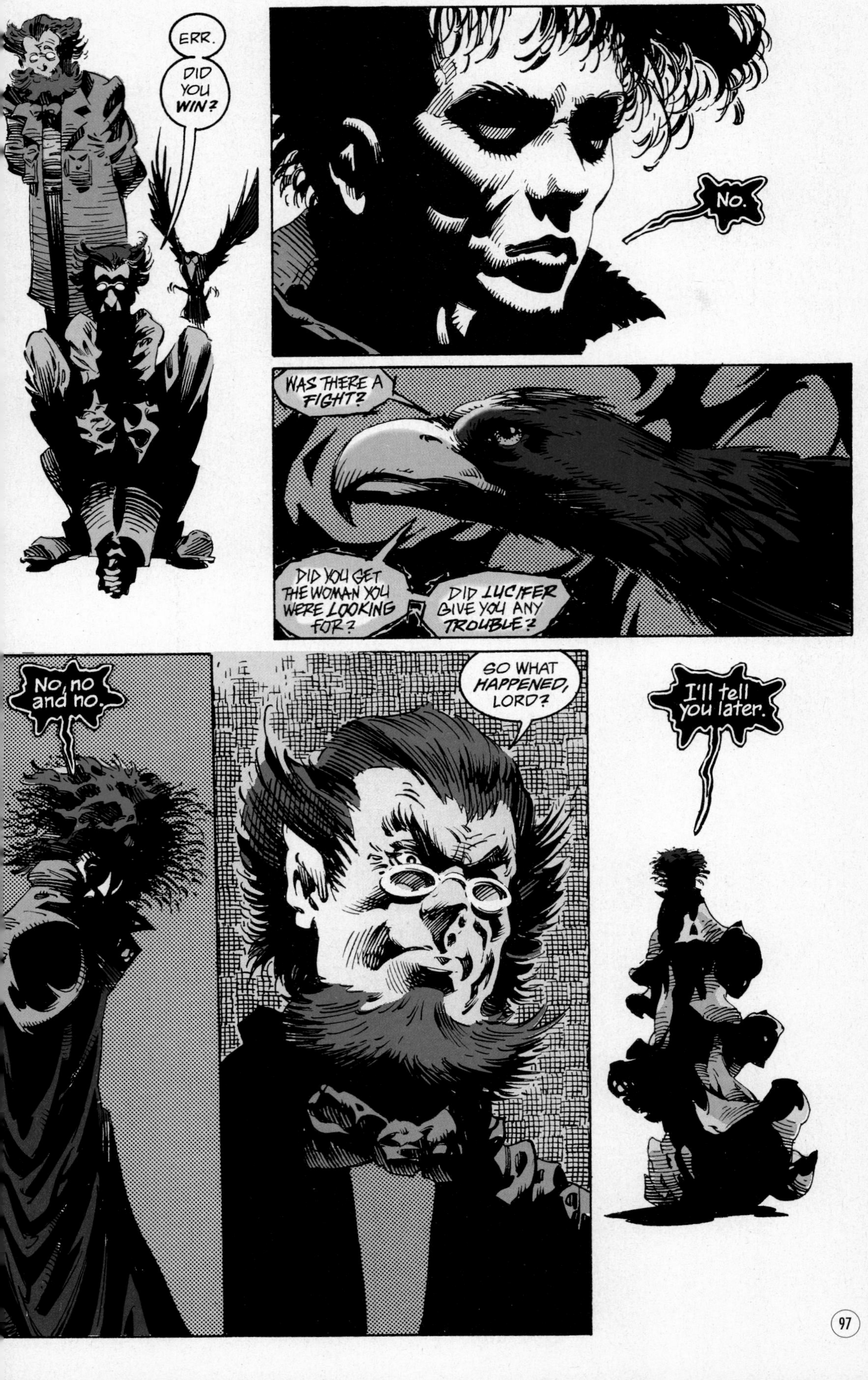

ERR.
DID YOU WIN?
NO.
WAS THERE A FIGHT?
DID YOU GET THE WOMAN YOU WERE LOOKING FOR?
DID LUCIFER GIVE YOU ANY TROUBLE?
No, no and no.
SO WHAT HAPPENED, LORD?
I'll tell you later.

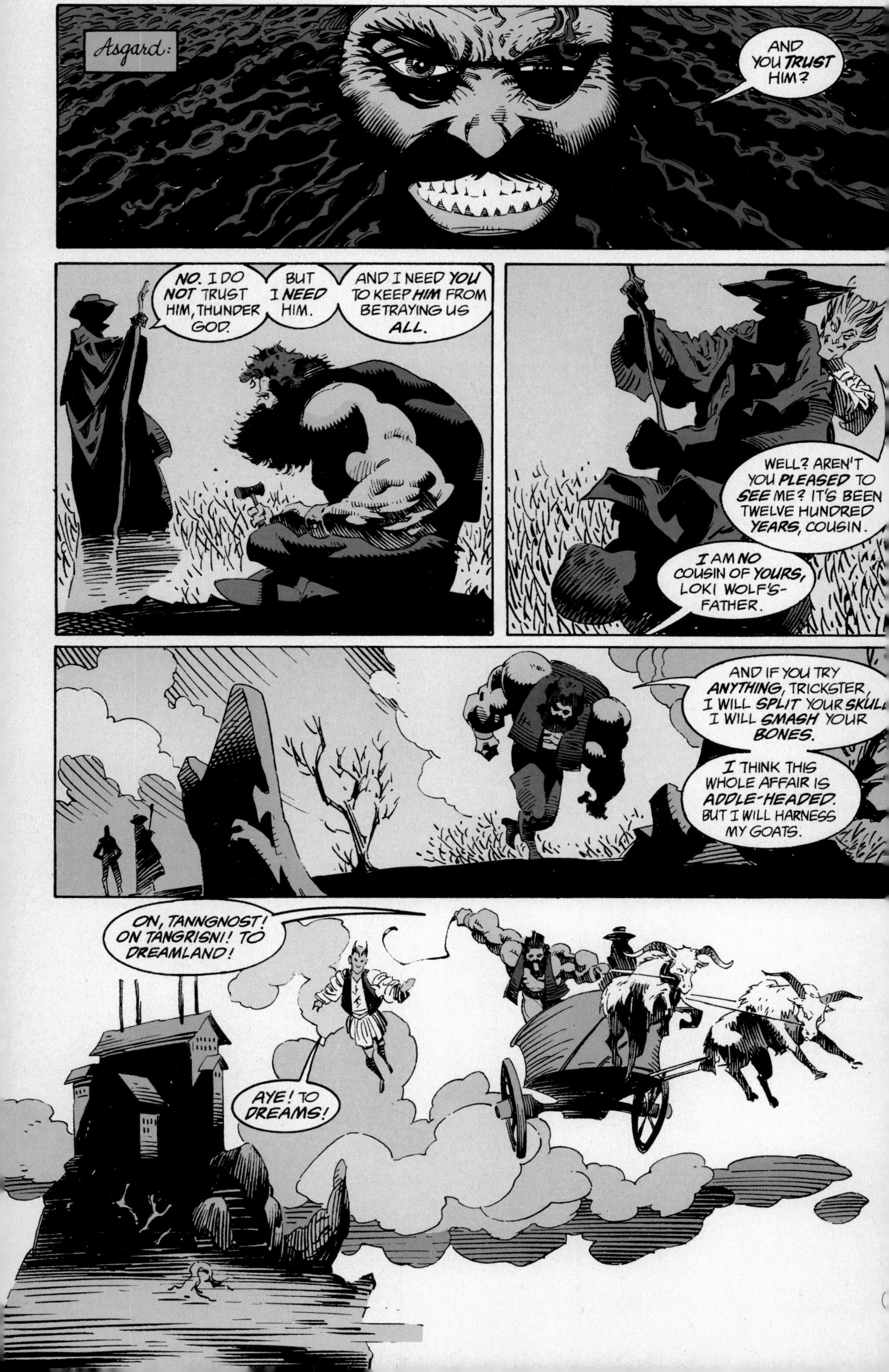

Asgard:
AND YOU TRUST HIM?
NO. I DO NOT TRUST HIM, THUNDER GOD.
BUT I NEED HIM.
AND I NEED YOU TO KEEP HIM FROM BETRAYING US ALL.
WELL? AREN'T YOU PLEASED TO SEE ME? IT'S BEEN TWELVE HUNDRED YEARS, COUSIN.
I AM NO COUSIN OF YOURS, LOKI WOLF'S-FATHER.
AND IF YOU TRY ANYTHING, TRICKSTER, I WILL SPLIT YOUR SKUL I WILL SMASH YOUR BONES.
I THINK THIS WHOLE AFFAIR IS ADDLE-HEADED. BUT I WILL HARNESS MY GOATS.
ON, TANNGNOST! ON TANGRISNI! TO DREAMLAND!
AYE! TO DREAMS!

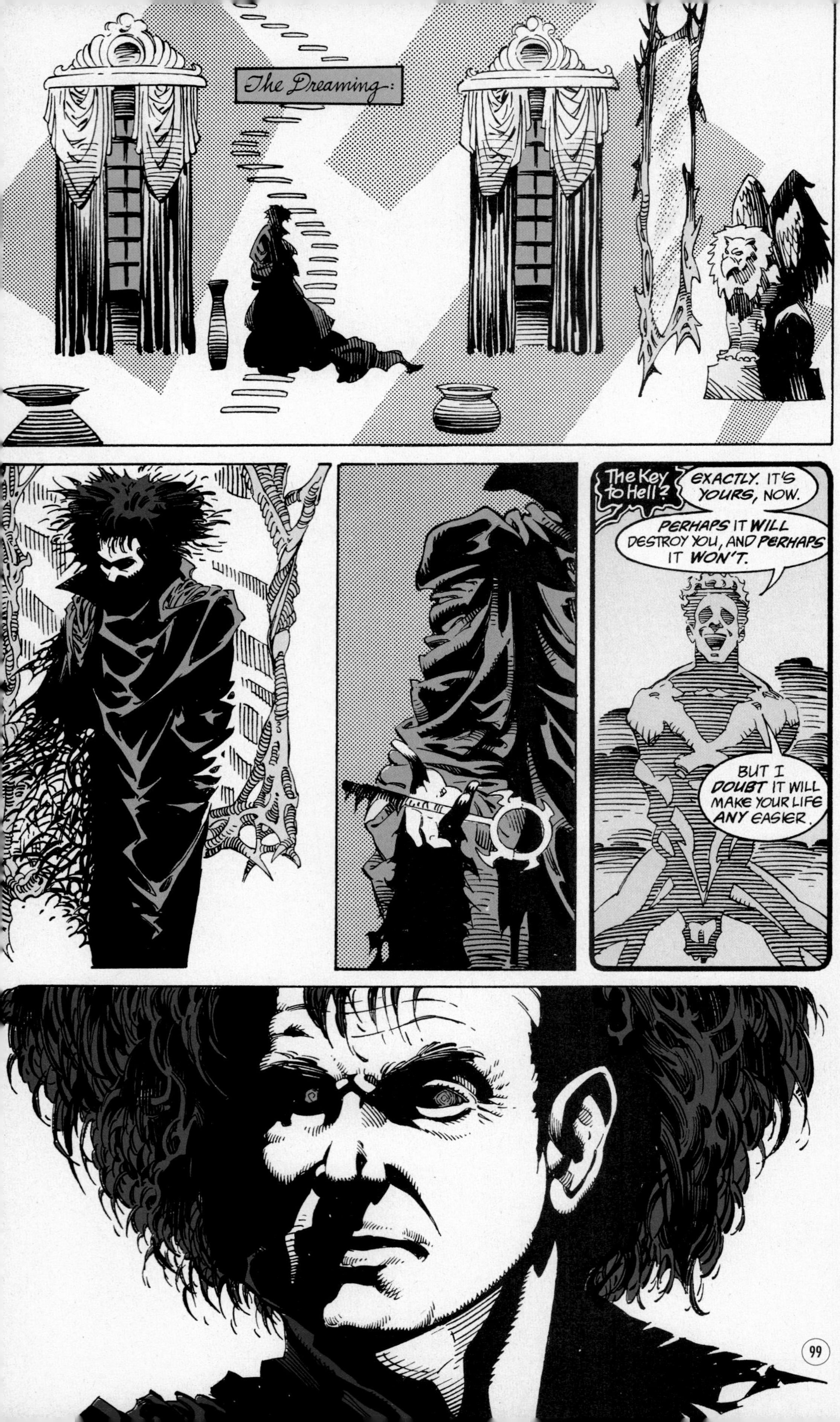
The Dreaming:
The Key to Hell?
EXACTLY. IT'S YOURS, NOW.
PERHAPS IT WILL DESTROY YOU, AND PERHAPS IT WON'T.
BUT I DOUBT IT WILL MAKE YOUR LIFE ANY EASIER.

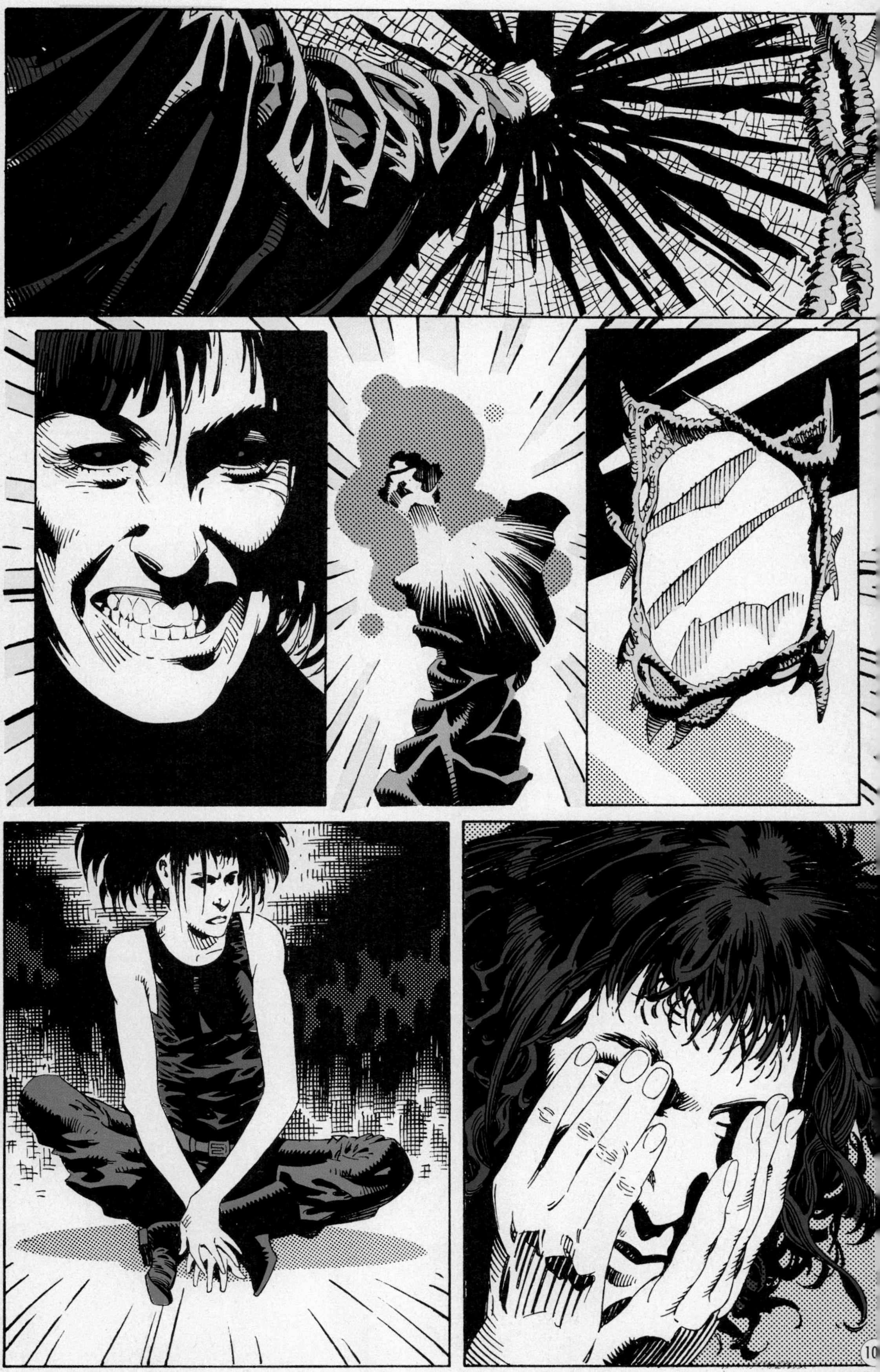

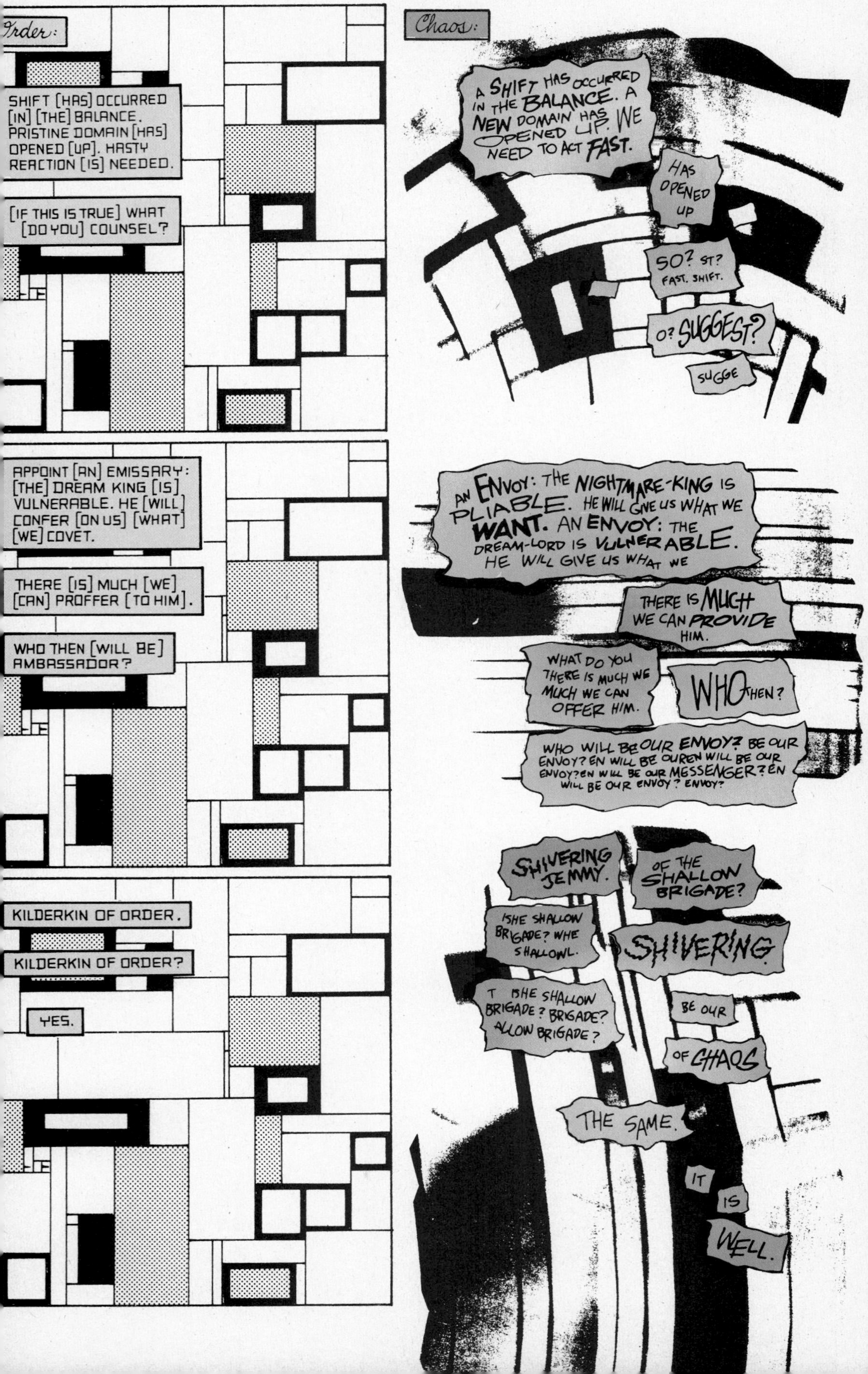
Order:
SHIFT [HAS] OCCURRED [IN] [THE] BALANCE. PRISTINE DOMAIN [HAS] OPENED [UP]. HASTY REACTION [IS] NEEDED.
[IF THIS IS TRUE] WHAT [DO YOU] COUNSEL?
APPOINT [AN] EMISSARY: [THE] DREAM KING [IS] VULNERABLE. HE [WILL] CONFER [ON US] [WHAT] [WE] COVET.
THERE [IS] MUCH [WE] [CAN] PROFFER [TO HIM].
WHO THEN [WILL BE] AMBASSADOR?
KILDERKIN OF ORDER.
KILDERKIN OF ORDER?
YES.
Chaos:
A SHIFT HAS OCCURRED IN THE BALANCE. A NEW DOMAIN HAS OPENED UP. WE NEED TO ACT FAST.
HAS OPENED UP
SO? ST? FAST. SHIFT.
O? SUGGEST?
SUGGE
AN ENVOY: THE NIGHTMARE-KING IS PLIABLE. HE WILL GIVE US WHAT WE WANT. AN ENVOY: THE DREAM-LORD IS VULNERABLE. HE WILL GIVE US WHAT WE
THERE IS MUCH WE CAN PROVIDE HIM.
WHAT DO YOU THERE IS MUCH WE MUCH WE CAN OFFER HIM.
WHO THEN?
WHO WILL BE OUR ENVOY? BE OUR ENVOY? EN WILL BE OUREN WILL BE OUR ENVOY?EN WILL BE OUR MESSENGER?EN WILL BE OUR ENVOY? ENVOY?
SHIVERING JEMMY.
OF THE SHALLOW BRIGADE?
ISHE SHALLOW BRIGADE? WHE SHALLOWL.
SHIVERING.
T ISHE SHALLOW BRIGADE? BRIGADE? ALLOW BRIGADE?
BE OUR
OF CHAOS
THE SAME.
IT
IS
WELL.

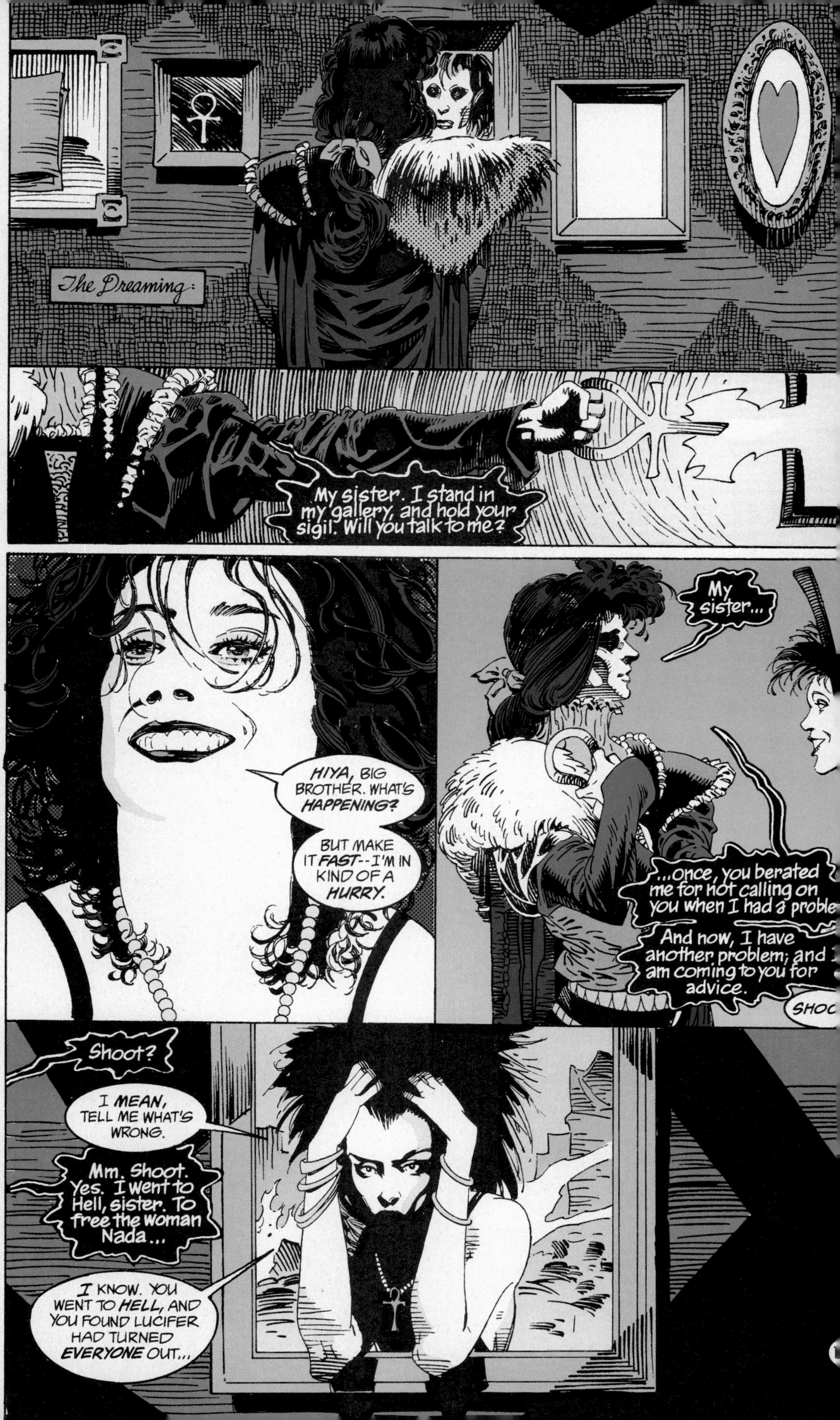
The Dreaming:
My sister. I stand in my gallery, and hold your sigil. Will you talk to me?
HIYA, BIG BROTHER. WHAT'S HAPPENING?
BUT MAKE IT FAST--I'M IN KIND OF A HURRY.
My sister...
...once, you berated me for not calling on you when I had a proble
And now, I have another problem; and I am coming to you for advice.
SHOO
Shoot?
I MEAN, TELL ME WHAT'S WRONG.
Mm. Shoot. Yes. I went to Hell, sister. To free the woman Nada...
I KNOW. YOU WENT TO HELL, AND YOU FOUND LUCIFER HAD TURNED EVERYONE OUT...

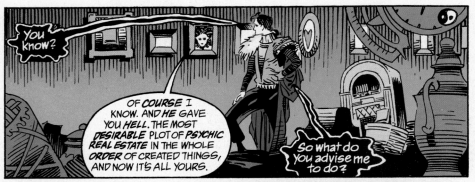

YOU KNOW?

OF COURSE I KNOW. AND HE GAVE YOU HELL. THE MOST DESIRABLE PLOT OF PSYCHIC REAL ESTATE IN THE WHOLE ORDER OF CREATED THINGS, AND NOW IT'S ALL YOURS.

So what do you advise me to do?

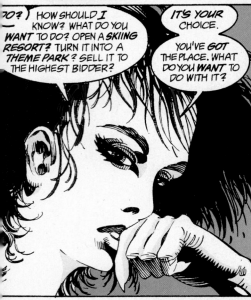

TO? HOW SHOULD I KNOW? WHAT DO YOU WANT TO DO? OPEN A SKIING RESORT? TURN IT INTO A THEME PARK? SELL IT TO THE HIGHEST BIDDER?

IT'S YOUR CHOICE.

YOU'VE GOT THE PLACE. WHAT DO YOU WANT TO DO WITH IT?

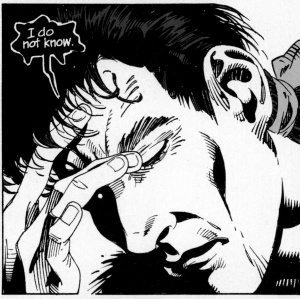

I do not know.

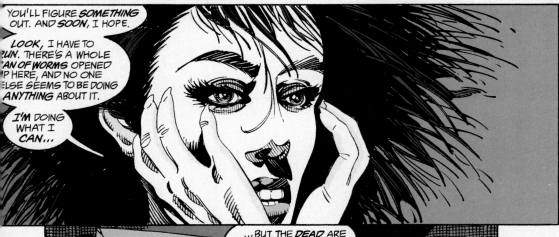

YOU'LL FIGURE SOMETHING OUT. AND SOON, I HOPE.

LOOK, I HAVE TO RUN. THERE'S A WHOLE CAN OF WORMS OPENED UP HERE, AND NO ONE ELSE SEEMS TO BE DOING ANYTHING ABOUT IT.

I'M DOING WHAT I CAN...

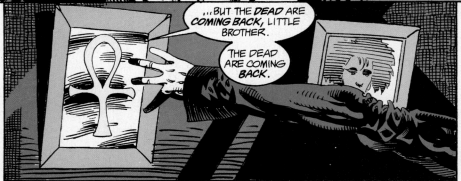

...BUT THE DEAD ARE COMING BACK, LITTLE BROTHER.

THE DEAD ARE COMING BACK.

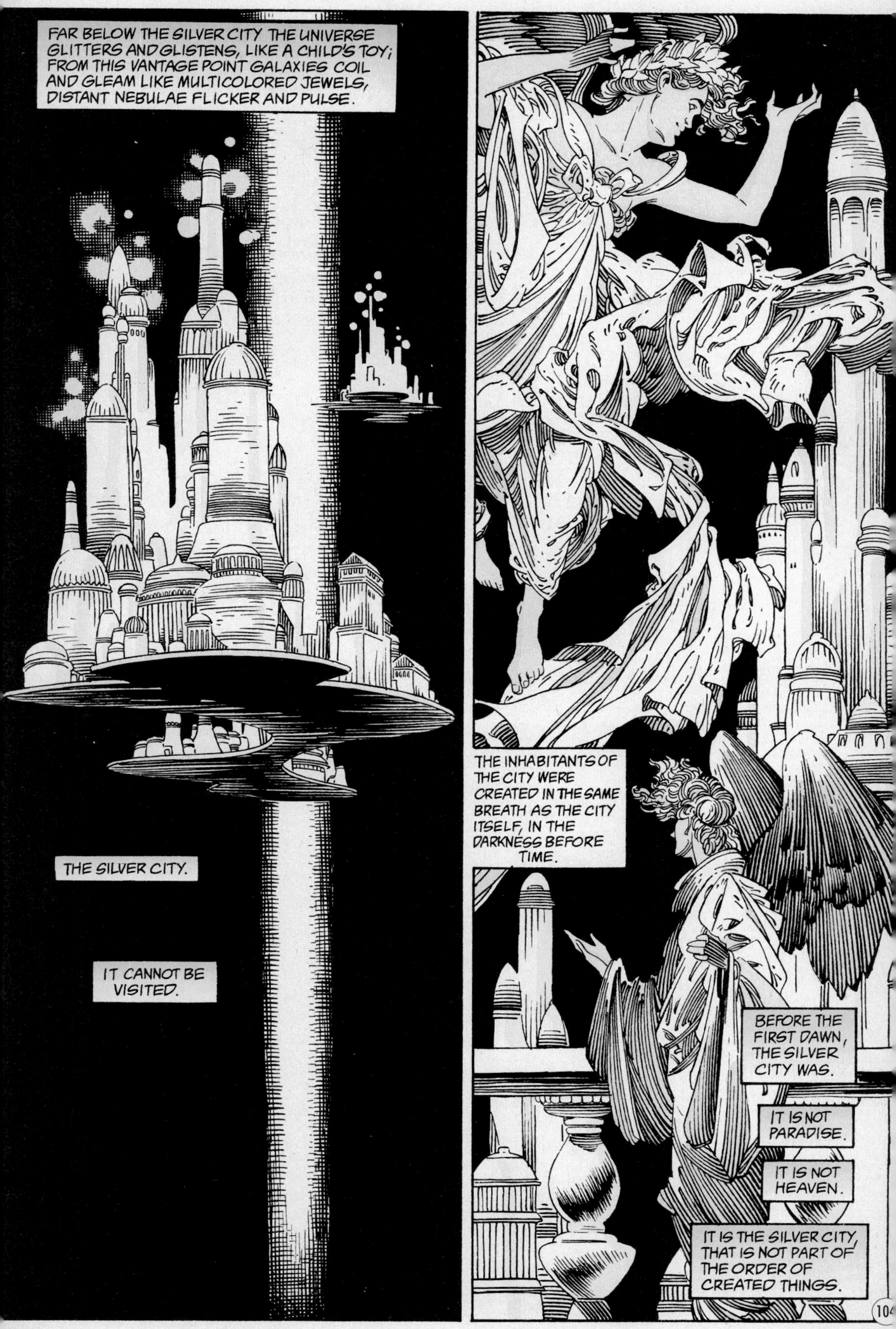
FAR BELOW THE SILVER CITY THE UNIVERSE GLITTERS AND GLISTENS, LIKE A CHILD'S TOY; FROM THIS VANTAGE POINT GALAXIES COIL AND GLEAM LIKE MULTICOLORED JEWELS, DISTANT NEBULAE FLICKER AND PULSE.
THE SILVER CITY.
IT CANNOT BE VISITED.
THE INHABITANTS OF THE CITY WERE CREATED IN THE SAME BREATH AS THE CITY ITSELF, IN THE DARKNESS BEFORE TIME.
BEFORE THE FIRST DAWN, THE SILVER CITY WAS.
IT IS NOT PARADISE.
IT IS NOT HEAVEN.
IT IS THE SILVER CITY, THAT IS NOT PART OF THE ORDER OF CREATED THINGS.

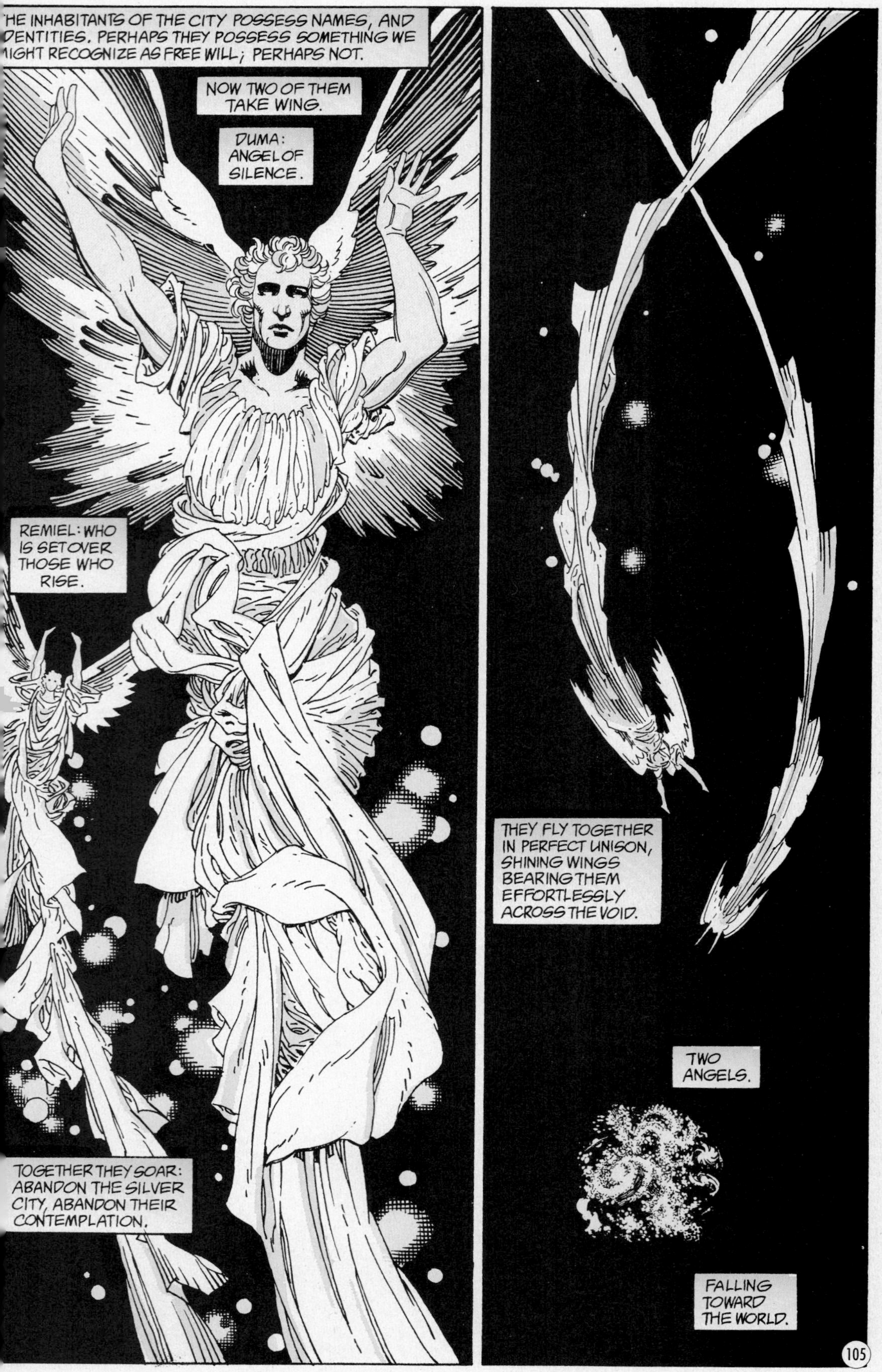
THE INHABITANTS OF THE CITY POSSESS NAMES, AND IDENTITIES. PERHAPS THEY POSSESS SOMETHING WE MIGHT RECOGNIZE AS FREE WILL; PERHAPS NOT.
NOW TWO OF THEM TAKE WING.
DUMA: ANGEL OF SILENCE.
REMIEL: WHO IS SET OVER THOSE WHO RISE.
TOGETHER THEY SOAR: ABANDON THE SILVER CITY, ABANDON THEIR CONTEMPLATION.
THEY FLY TOGETHER IN PERFECT UNISON, SHINING WINGS BEARING THEM EFFORTLESSLY ACROSS THE VOID.
TWO ANGELS.
FALLING TOWARD THE WORLD.

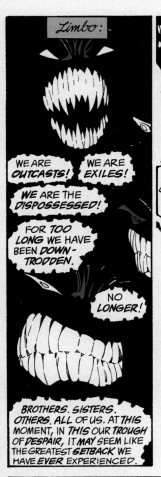

Limbo:

WE ARE *OUTCASTS!*

WE ARE *EXILES!*

WE ARE THE *DISPOSSESSED!*

FOR *TOO LONG* WE HAVE BEEN *DOWN-TRODDEN.*

NO *LONGER!*

BROTHERS. SISTERS. *OTHERS.* ALL OF US. AT *THIS* MOMENT, IN *THIS* OUR *TROUGH* OF *DESPAIR,* IT MAY SEEM LIKE THE GREATEST *SETBACK* WE HAVE *EVER* EXPERIENCED.

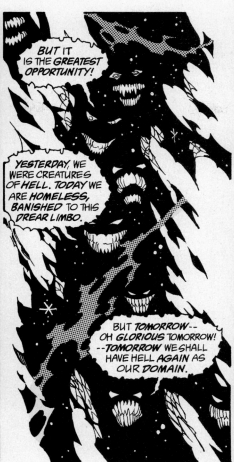

BUT IT IS THE *GREATEST OPPORTUNITY!*

YESTERDAY, WE WERE CREATURES OF HELL. *TODAY* WE ARE HOMELESS, BANISHED TO THIS *DREAR LIMBO.*

BUT *TOMORROW*-- OH *GLORIOUS* TOMORROW! --*TOMORROW* WE SHALL HAVE HELL *AGAIN* AS OUR *DOMAIN.*

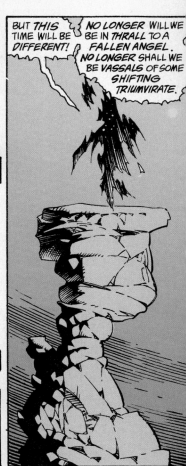

BUT *THIS* TIME WILL BE *DIFFERENT!*

NO *LONGER* WILL WE BE IN *THRALL* TO A *FALLEN* ANGEL. NO *LONGER* SHALL WE BE VASSALS OF SOME *SHIFTING TRIUMVIRATE.*

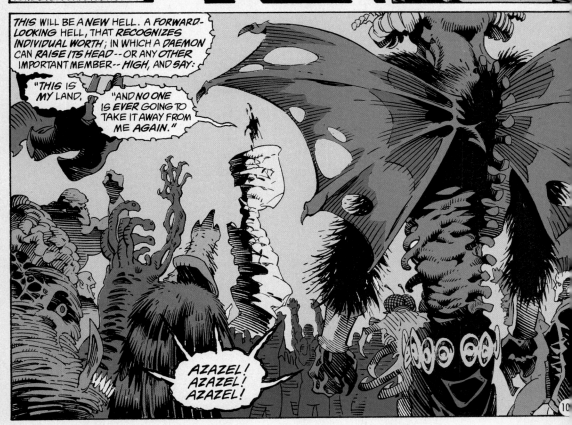

THIS WILL BE A *NEW* HELL. A FORWARD-LOOKING HELL, THAT *RECOGNIZES* INDIVIDUAL WORTH; IN WHICH A *DAEMON* CAN *RAISE ITS HEAD*-- OR ANY *OTHER* IMPORTANT MEMBER-- *HIGH,* AND SAY:

"*THIS* IS *MY* LAND,

"AND *NO ONE* IS *EVER* GOING TO TAKE IT AWAY FROM ME *AGAIN.*"

AZAZEL! AZAZEL! AZAZEL!

10

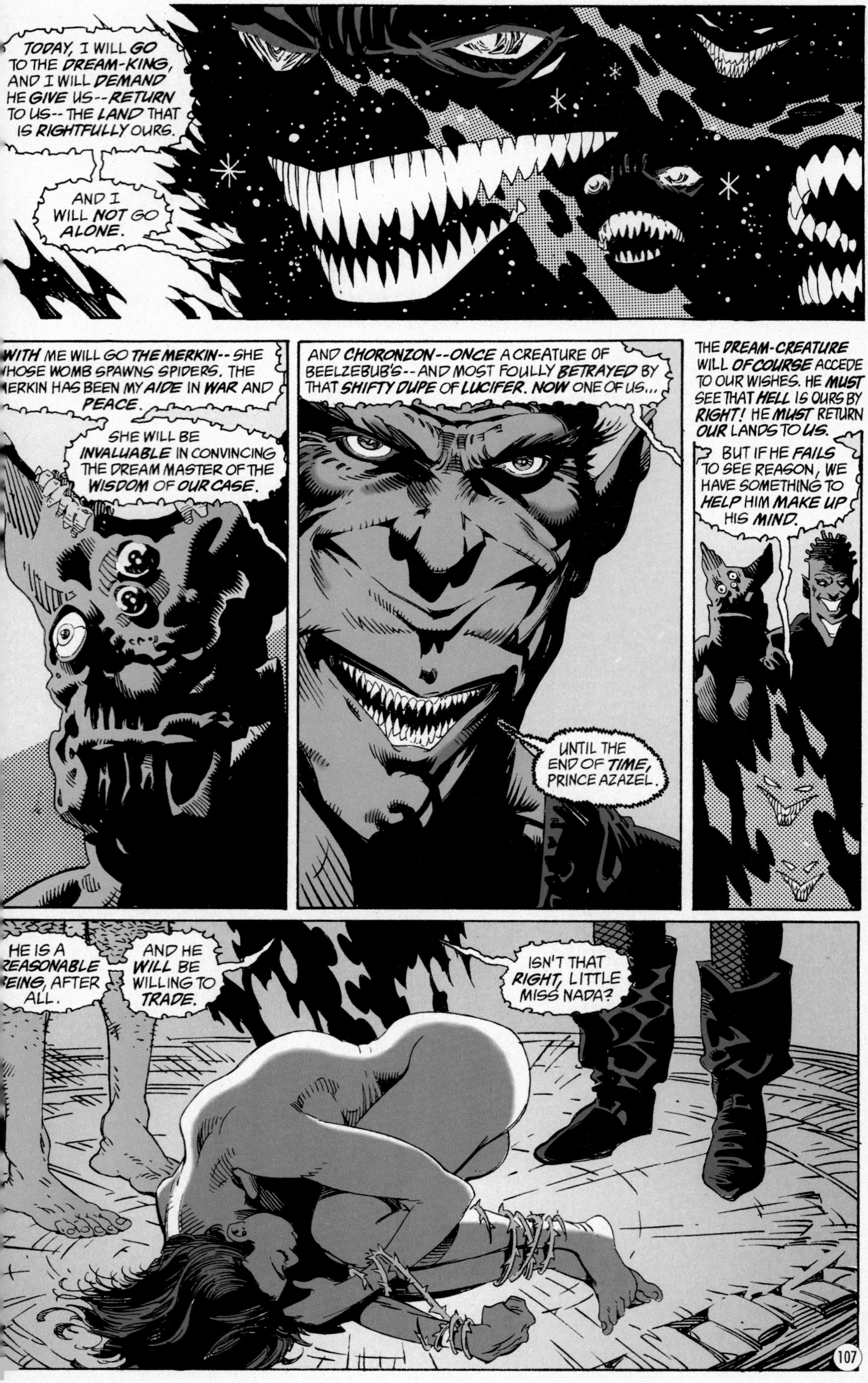
TODAY, I WILL GO TO THE DREAM-KING, AND I WILL DEMAND HE GIVE US--RETURN TO US-- THE LAND THAT IS RIGHTFULLY OURS.
AND I WILL NOT GO ALONE.
WITH ME WILL GO THE MERKIN-- SHE WHOSE WOMB SPAWNS SPIDERS. THE MERKIN HAS BEEN MY AIDE IN WAR AND PEACE.
SHE WILL BE INVALUABLE IN CONVINCING THE DREAM MASTER OF THE WISDOM OF OUR CASE.
AND CHORONZON--ONCE A CREATURE OF BEELZEBUB'S--AND MOST FOULLY BETRAYED BY THAT SHIFTY DUPE OF LUCIFER. NOW ONE OF US...
UNTIL THE END OF TIME, PRINCE AZAZEL.
THE DREAM-CREATURE WILL OF COURSE ACCEDE TO OUR WISHES. HE MUST SEE THAT HELL IS OURS BY RIGHT! HE MUST RETURN OUR LANDS TO US.
BUT IF HE FAILS TO SEE REASON, WE HAVE SOMETHING TO HELP HIM MAKE UP HIS MIND.
HE IS A REASONABLE BEING, AFTER ALL.
AND HE WILL BE WILLING TO TRADE.
ISN'T THAT RIGHT, LITTLE MISS NADA?

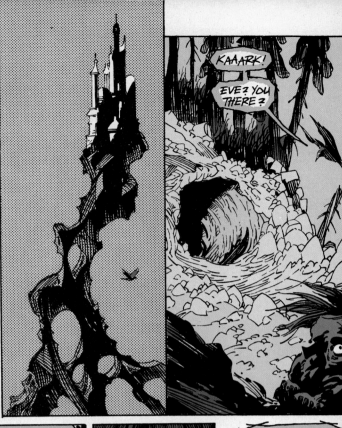

The Dreaming.

KAAARK!

EVE? YOU THERE?

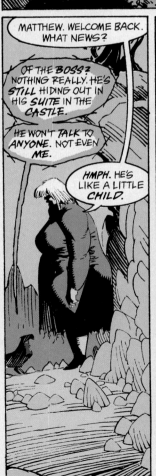

MATTHEW. WELCOME BACK. WHAT NEWS?

OF THE *BOSS?* NOTHING REALLY. HE'S *STILL* HIDING OUT IN HIS *SUITE* IN THE *CASTLE.*

HE WON'T *TALK* TO *ANYONE.* NOT EVEN *ME.*

HMPH. HE'S LIKE A LITTLE *CHILD.*

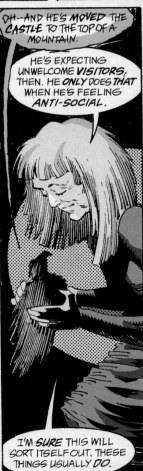

OH--AND HE'S *MOVED* THE *CASTLE* TO THE TOP OF A *MOUNTAIN.*

HE'S EXPECTING UNWELCOME *VISITORS,* THEN. HE *ONLY DOES THAT* WHEN HE'S FEELING *ANTI-SOCIAL.*

I'M *SURE* THIS WILL SORT ITSELF OUT. THESE THINGS USUALLY *DO.*

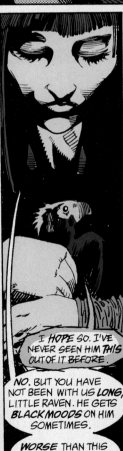

I HOPE SO. I'VE NEVER SEEN HIM *THIS* OUT OF IT BEFORE.

NO. BUT YOU HAVE NOT BEEN WITH US *LONG,* LITTLE RAVEN. HE GETS *BLACK MOODS* ON HIM SOMETIMES.

WORSE THAN THIS ONE SOUNDS. *MUCH* WORSE.

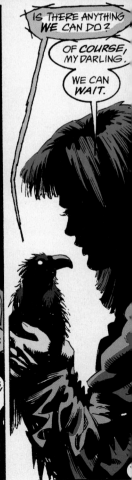

IS THERE ANYTHING *WE CAN* DO?

OF *COURSE,* MY DARLING.

WE CAN *WAIT.*

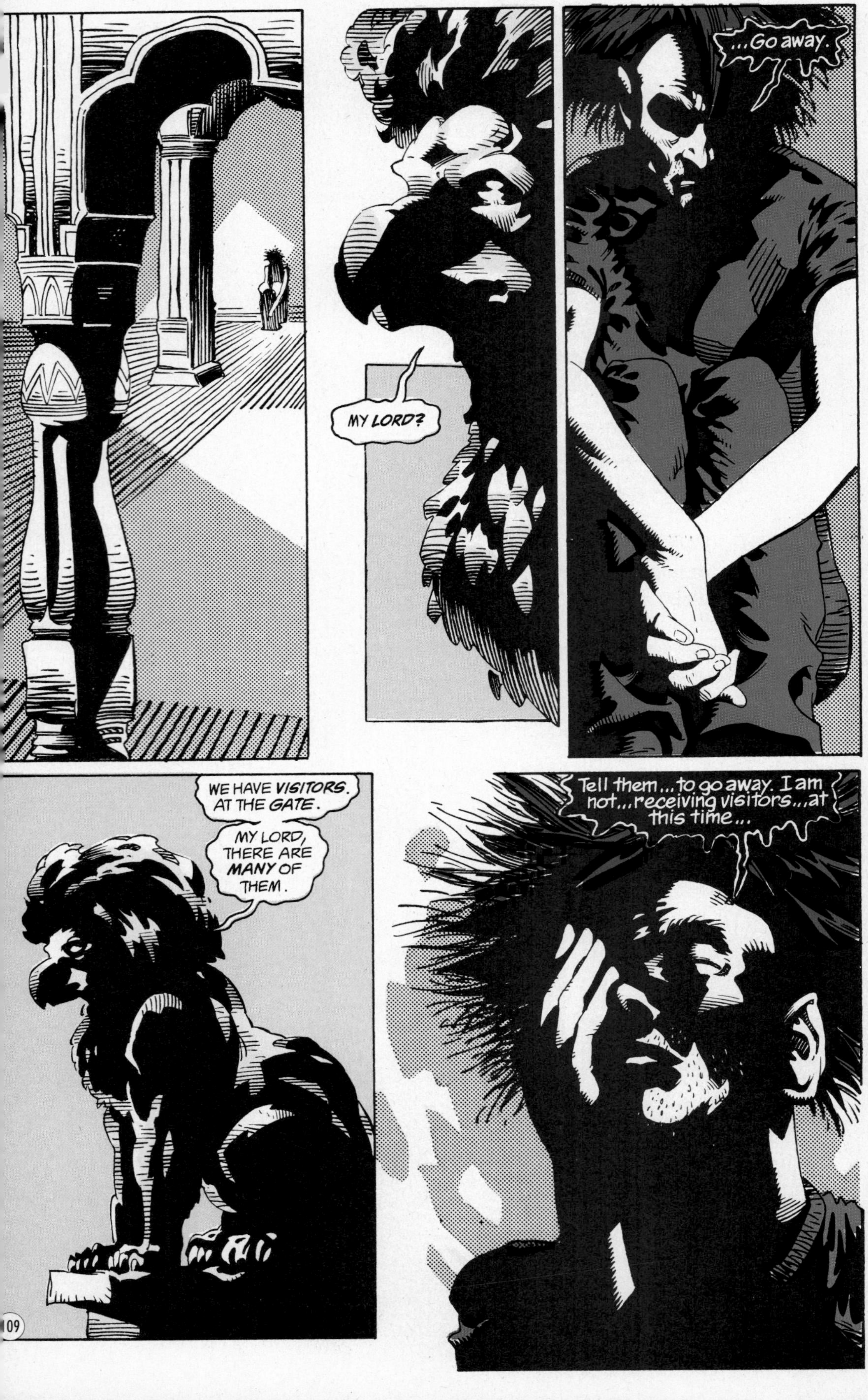
MY LORD?
...Go away.
WE HAVE VISITORS. AT THE GATE.
MY LORD, THERE ARE MANY OF THEM.
Tell them... to go away. I am not... receiving visitors... at this time...

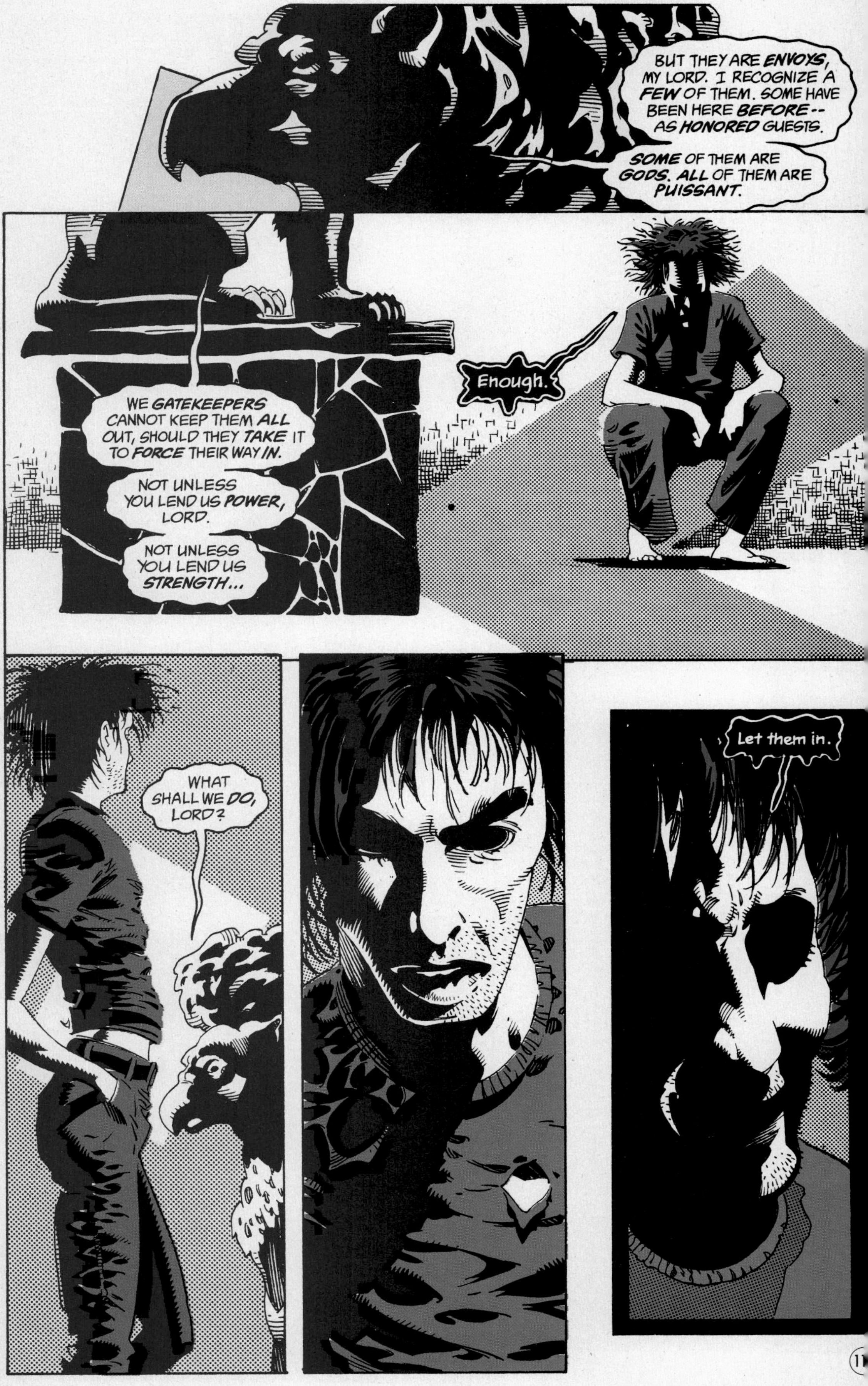
BUT THEY ARE ENVOYS, MY LORD. I RECOGNIZE A FEW OF THEM. SOME HAVE BEEN HERE BEFORE-- AS HONORED GUESTS.
SOME OF THEM ARE GODS. ALL OF THEM ARE PUISSANT.
WE GATEKEEPERS CANNOT KEEP THEM ALL OUT, SHOULD THEY TAKE IT TO FORCE THEIR WAY IN.
NOT UNLESS YOU LEND US POWER, LORD.
NOT UNLESS YOU LEND US STRENGTH...
Enough.
WHAT SHALL WE DO, LORD?
Let them in.

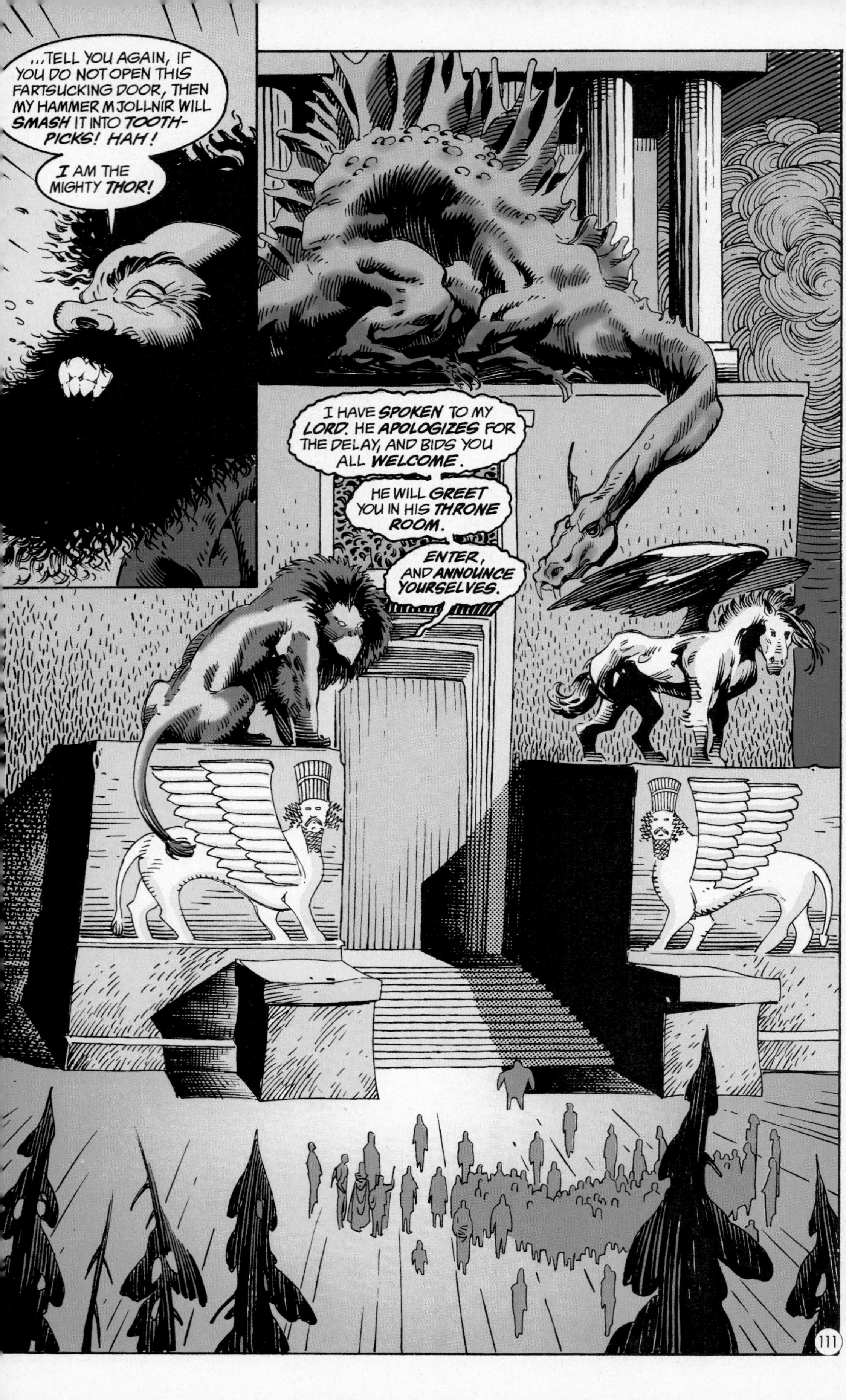
...TELL YOU AGAIN, IF YOU DO NOT OPEN THIS FARTSUCKING DOOR, THEN MY HAMMER MJOLLNIR WILL SMASH IT INTO TOOTH-PICKS! HAH!
I AM THE MIGHTY THOR!
I HAVE SPOKEN TO MY LORD. HE APOLOGIZES FOR THE DELAY, AND BIDS YOU ALL WELCOME.
HE WILL GREET YOU IN HIS THRONE ROOM.
ENTER, AND ANNOUNCE YOURSELVES.

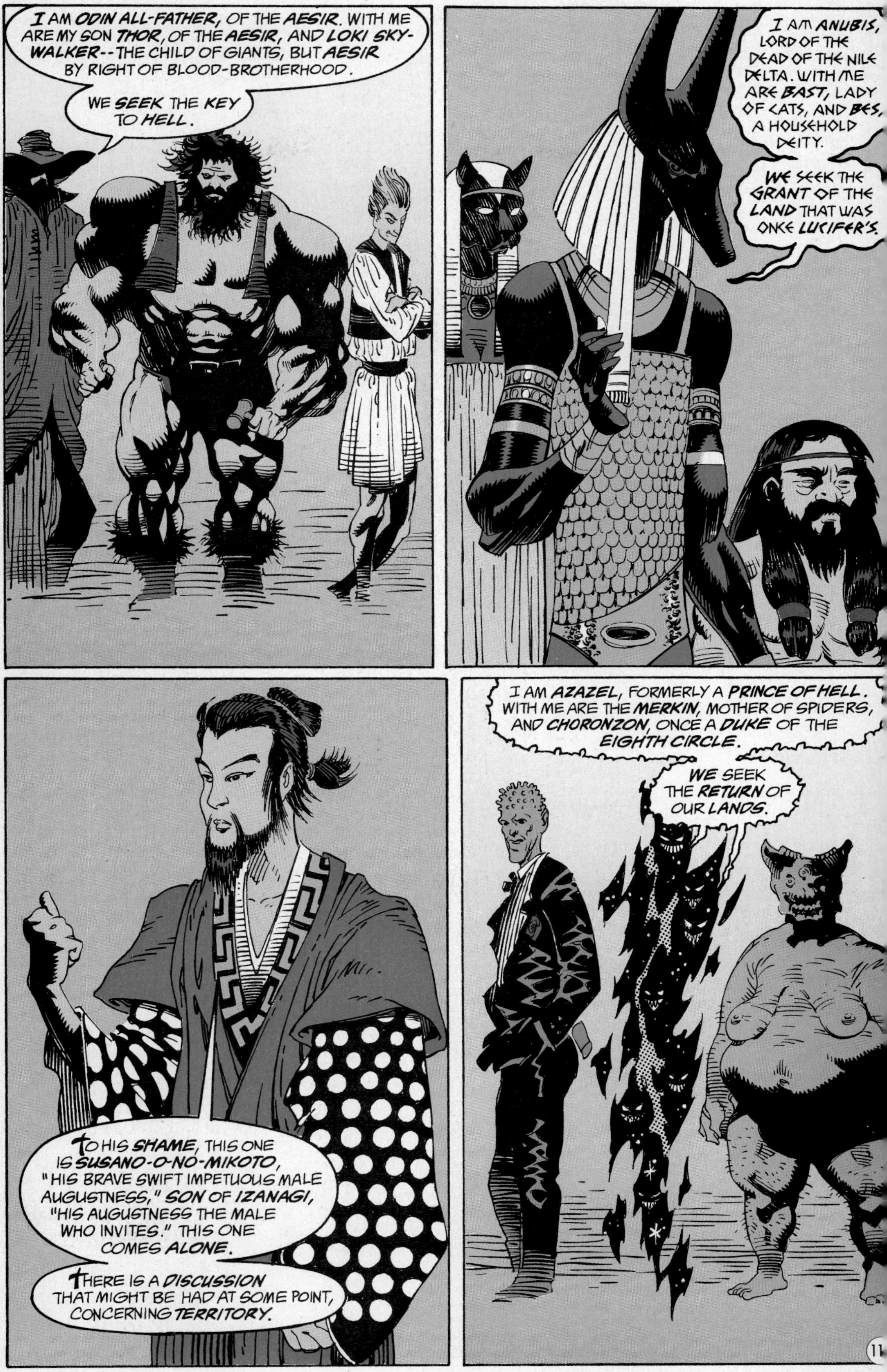
I AM ODIN ALL-FATHER, OF THE AESIR. WITH ME ARE MY SON THOR, OF THE AESIR, AND LOKI SKY-WALKER--THE CHILD OF GIANTS, BUT AESIR BY RIGHT OF BLOOD-BROTHERHOOD.
WE SEEK THE KEY TO HELL.
I AM ANUBIS, LORD OF THE DEAD OF THE NILE DELTA. WITH ME ARE BAST, LADY OF CATS, AND BES, A HOUSEHOLD DEITY.
WE SEEK THE GRANT OF THE LAND THAT WAS ONCE LUCIFER'S.
TO HIS SHAME, THIS ONE IS SUSANO-O-NO-MIKOTO, "HIS BRAVE SWIFT IMPETUOUS MALE AUGUSTNESS," SON OF IZANAGI, "HIS AUGUSTNESS THE MALE WHO INVITES." THIS ONE COMES ALONE.
THERE IS A DISCUSSION THAT MIGHT BE HAD AT SOME POINT, CONCERNING TERRITORY.
I AM AZAZEL, FORMERLY A PRINCE OF HELL. WITH ME ARE THE MERKIN, MOTHER OF SPIDERS, AND CHORONZON, ONCE A DUKE OF THE EIGHTH CIRCLE.
WE SEEK THE RETURN OF OUR LANDS.

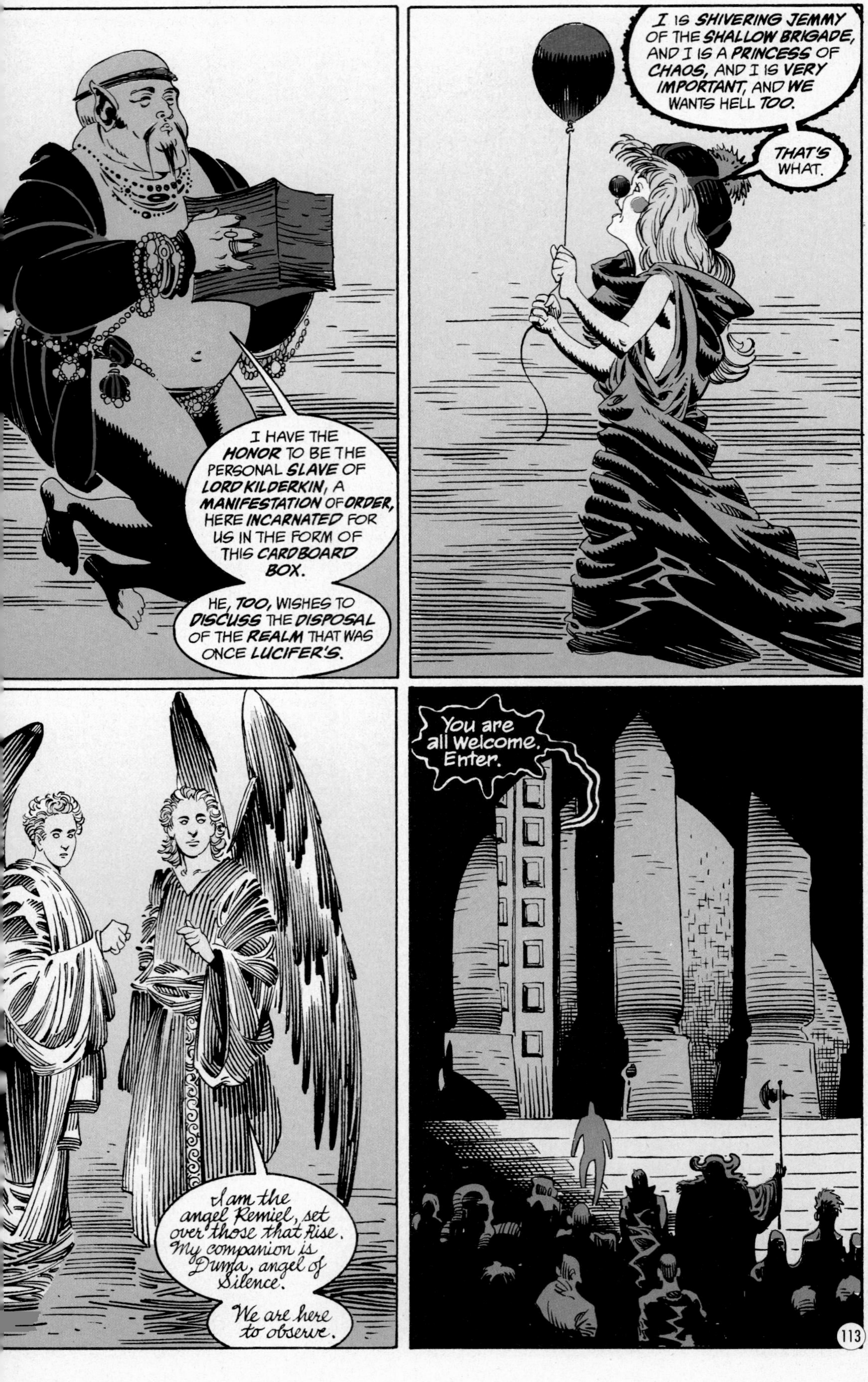
I HAVE THE HONOR TO BE THE PERSONAL SLAVE OF LORD KILDERKIN, A MANIFESTATION OF ORDER, HERE INCARNATED FOR US IN THE FORM OF THIS CARDBOARD BOX.
HE, TOO, WISHES TO DISCUSS THE DISPOSAL OF THE REALM THAT WAS ONCE LUCIFER'S.
I IS SHIVERING JEMMY OF THE SHALLOW BRIGADE, AND I IS A PRINCESS OF CHAOS, AND I IS VERY IMPORTANT, AND WE WANTS HELL TOO.
THAT'S WHAT.
I am the angel Remiel, set over those that Rise. My companion is Duma, angel of Silence.
We are here to observe.
You are all welcome. Enter.

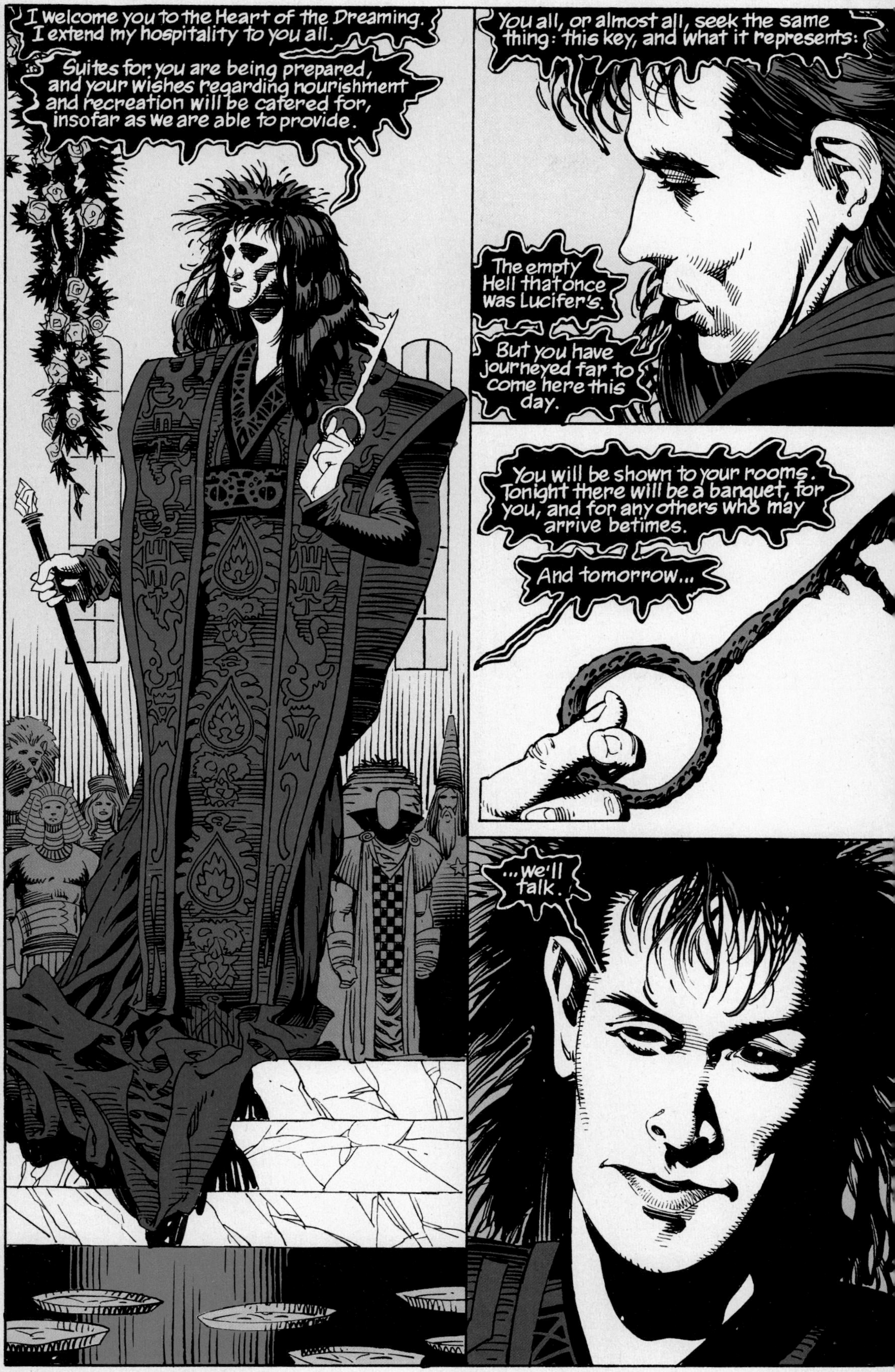
I welcome you to the Heart of the Dreaming. I extend my hospitality to you all.
Suites for you are being prepared, and your wishes regarding nourishment and recreation will be catered for, insofar as we are able to provide.
You all, or almost all, seek the same thing: this key, and what it represents:
The empty Hell that once was Lucifer's.
But you have journeyed far to come here this day.
You will be shown to your rooms. Tonight there will be a banquet, for you, and for any others who may arrive betimes.
And tomorrow...
...we'll talk.

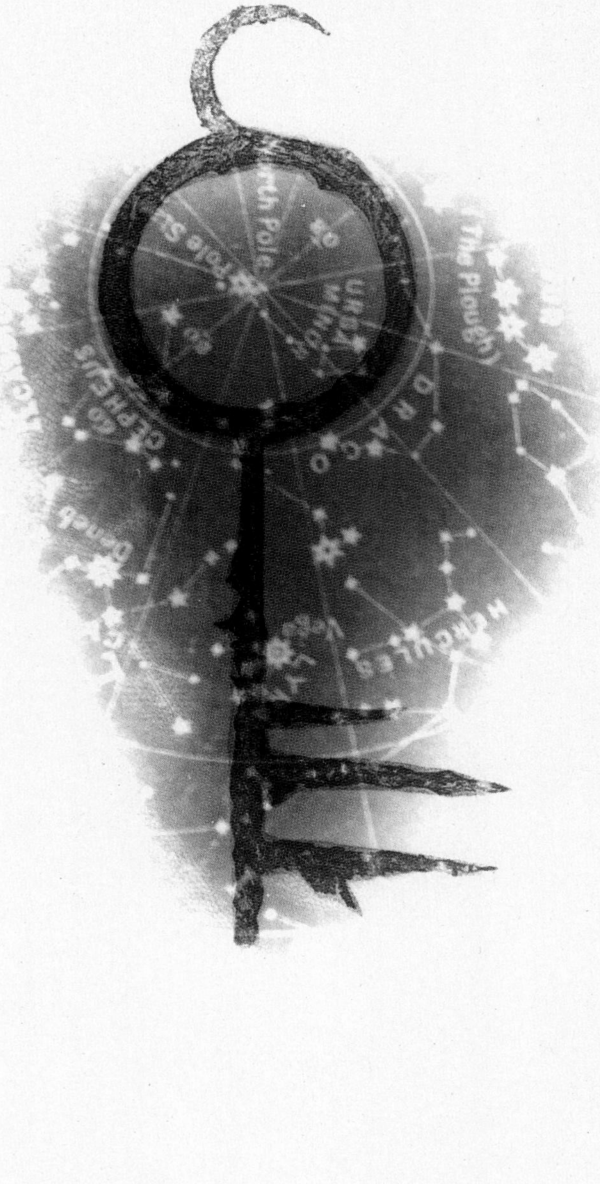
(The Plough)
DRACO
Deneb
Vega

In which the dead return; and Charles Rowland concludes his education.

EPISODE 4

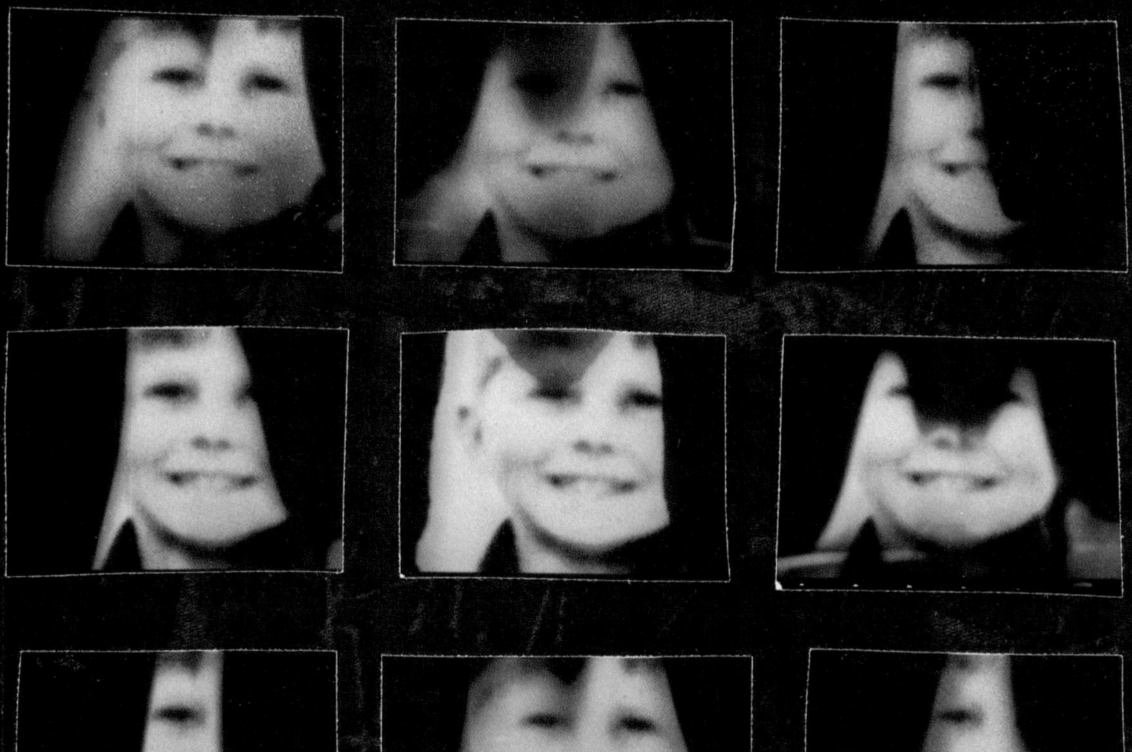

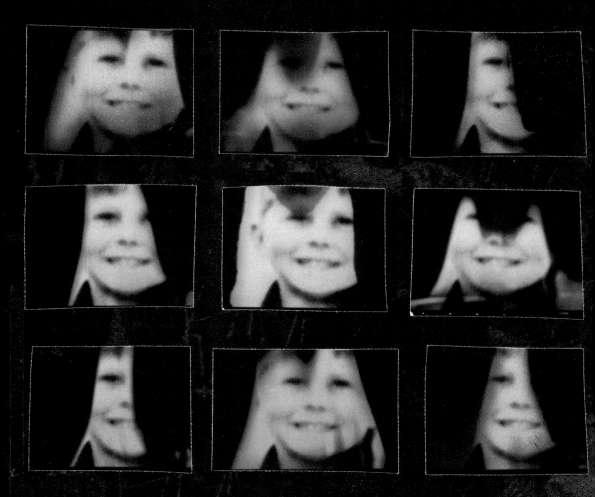

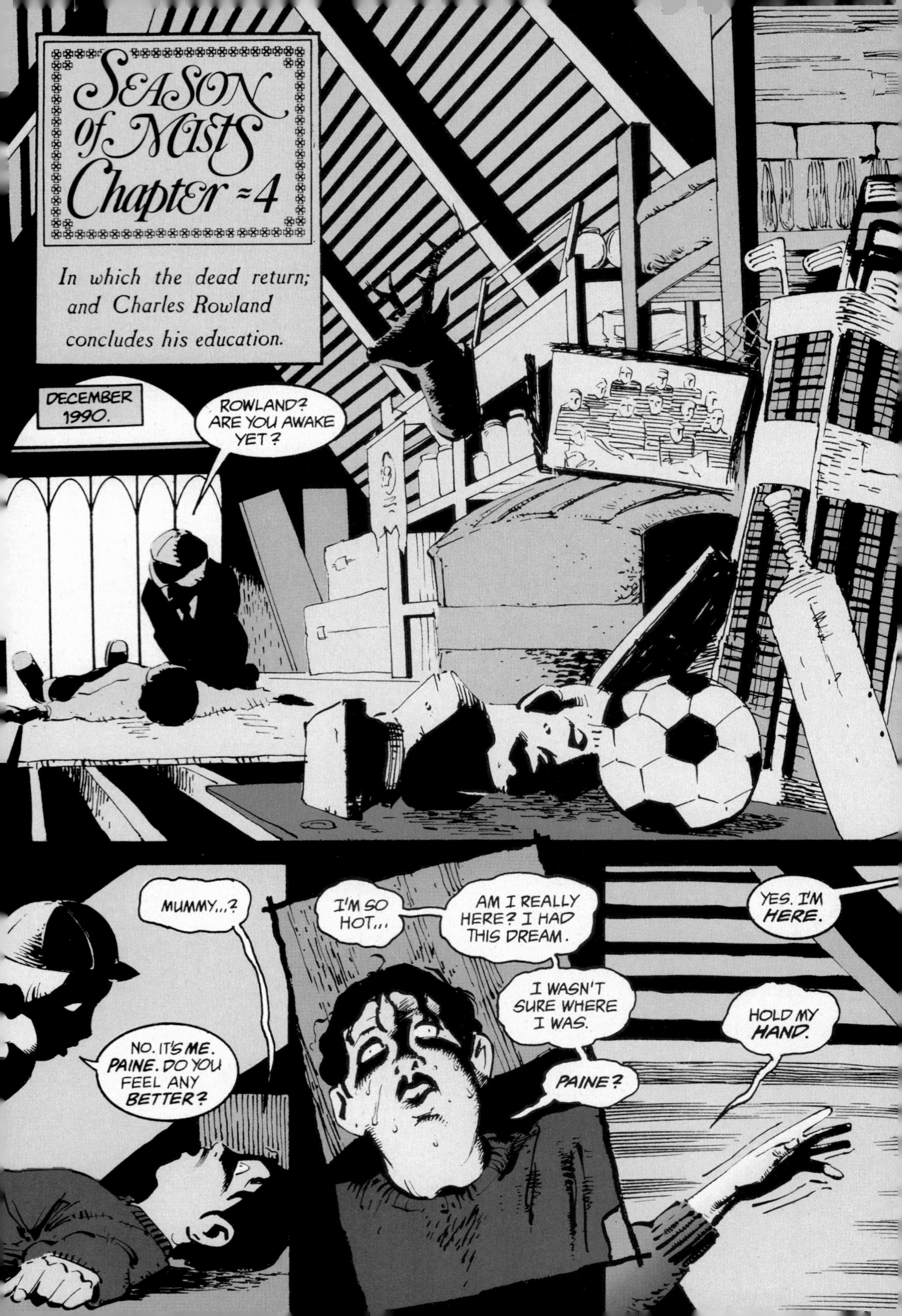

SEASON of MISTS Chapter ≈4
In which the dead return; and Charles Rowland concludes his education.
DECEMBER 1990.
ROWLAND? ARE YOU AWAKE YET?
MUMMY...?
NO. IT'S ME. PAINE. DO YOU FEEL ANY BETTER?
I'M SO HOT...
AM I REALLY HERE? I HAD THIS DREAM.
I WASN'T SURE WHERE I WAS.
PAINE?
YES. I'M HERE.
HOLD MY HAND.

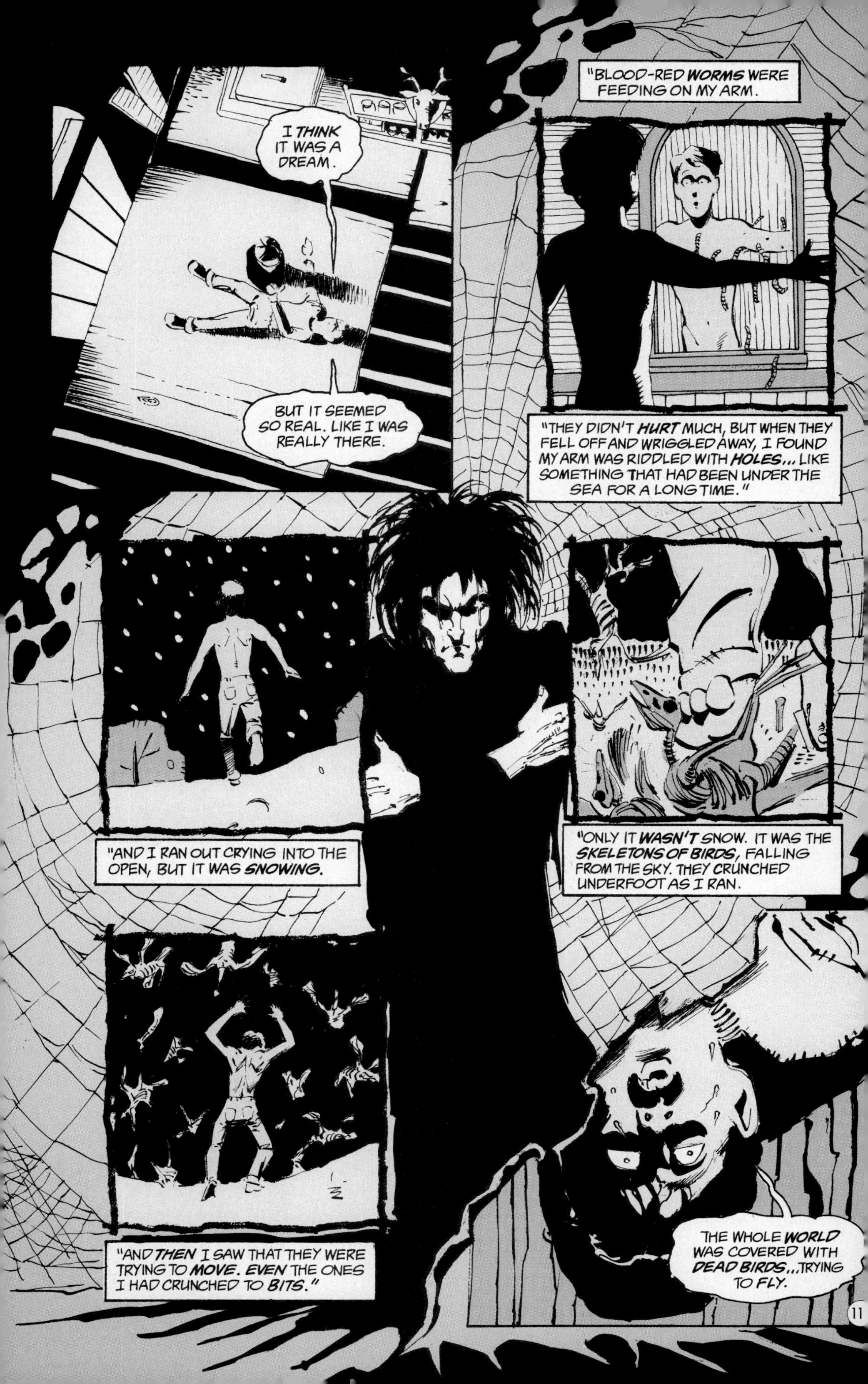

I *THINK* IT WAS A DREAM.
BUT IT SEEMED SO REAL. LIKE I WAS REALLY THERE.
"BLOOD-RED *WORMS* WERE FEEDING ON MY ARM.
"THEY DIDN'T *HURT* MUCH, BUT WHEN THEY FELL OFF AND WRIGGLED AWAY, I FOUND MY ARM WAS RIDDLED WITH *HOLES*... LIKE SOMETHING THAT HAD BEEN UNDER THE SEA FOR A LONG TIME."
"AND I RAN OUT CRYING INTO THE OPEN, BUT IT WAS *SNOWING*.
"ONLY IT *WASN'T* SNOW. IT WAS THE *SKELETONS OF BIRDS*, FALLING FROM THE SKY. THEY CRUNCHED UNDERFOOT AS I RAN.
"AND *THEN* I SAW THAT THEY WERE TRYING TO *MOVE*. *EVEN* THE ONES I HAD CRUNCHED TO *BITS*."
THE WHOLE *WORLD* WAS COVERED WITH *DEAD BIRDS*... TRYING TO *FLY*.

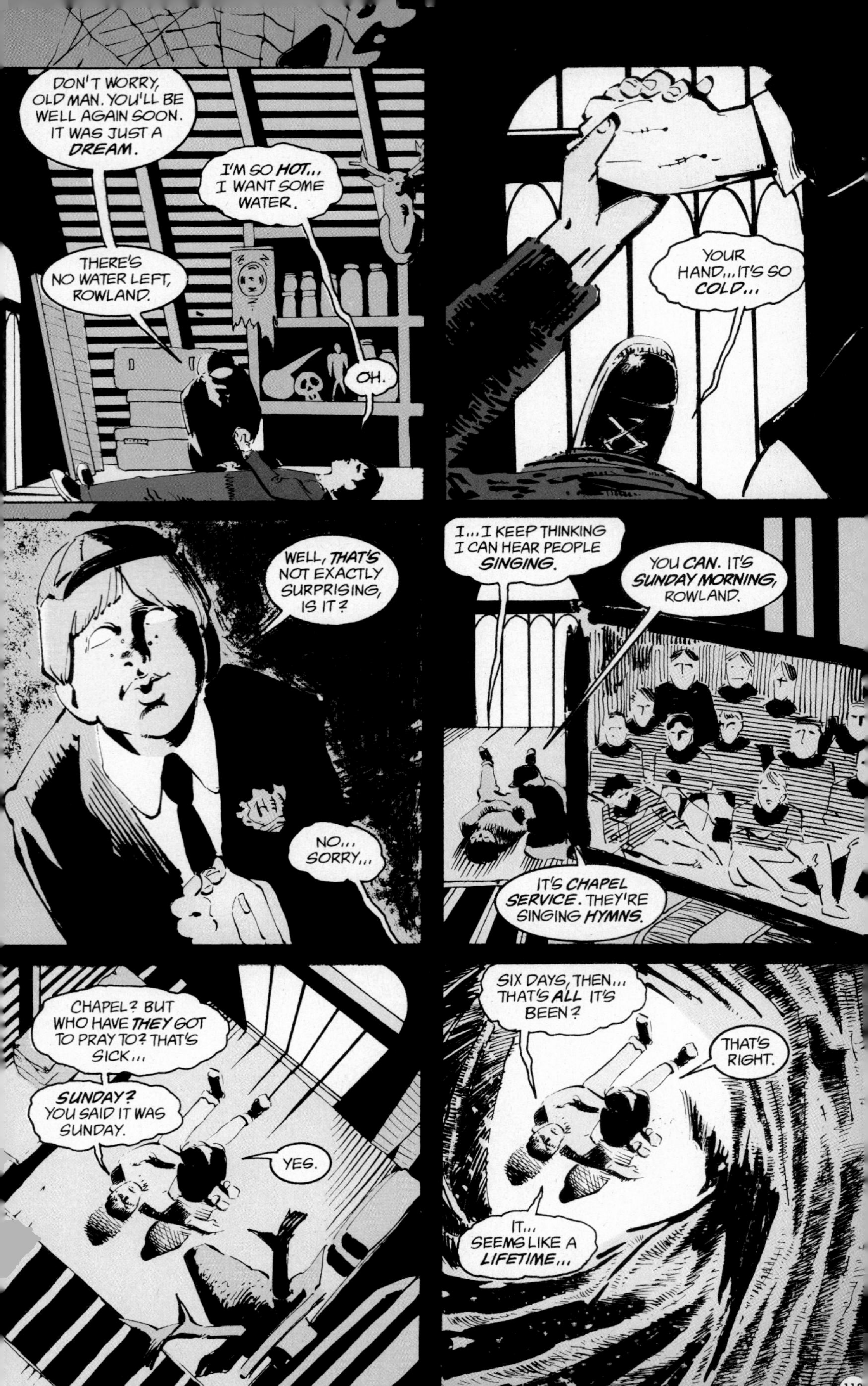
DON'T WORRY, OLD MAN. YOU'LL BE WELL AGAIN SOON. IT WAS JUST A DREAM.
I'M SO HOT... I WANT SOME WATER.
THERE'S NO WATER LEFT, ROWLAND.
OH.
YOUR HAND... IT'S SO COLD...
WELL, THAT'S NOT EXACTLY SURPRISING, IS IT?
NO... SORRY...
I... I KEEP THINKING I CAN HEAR PEOPLE SINGING.
YOU CAN. IT'S SUNDAY MORNING, ROWLAND.
IT'S CHAPEL SERVICE. THEY'RE SINGING HYMNS.
CHAPEL? BUT WHO HAVE THEY GOT TO PRAY TO? THAT'S SICK...
SUNDAY? YOU SAID IT WAS SUNDAY.
YES.
SIX DAYS, THEN... THAT'S ALL IT'S BEEN?
THAT'S RIGHT.
IT... SEEMS LIKE A LIFETIME...

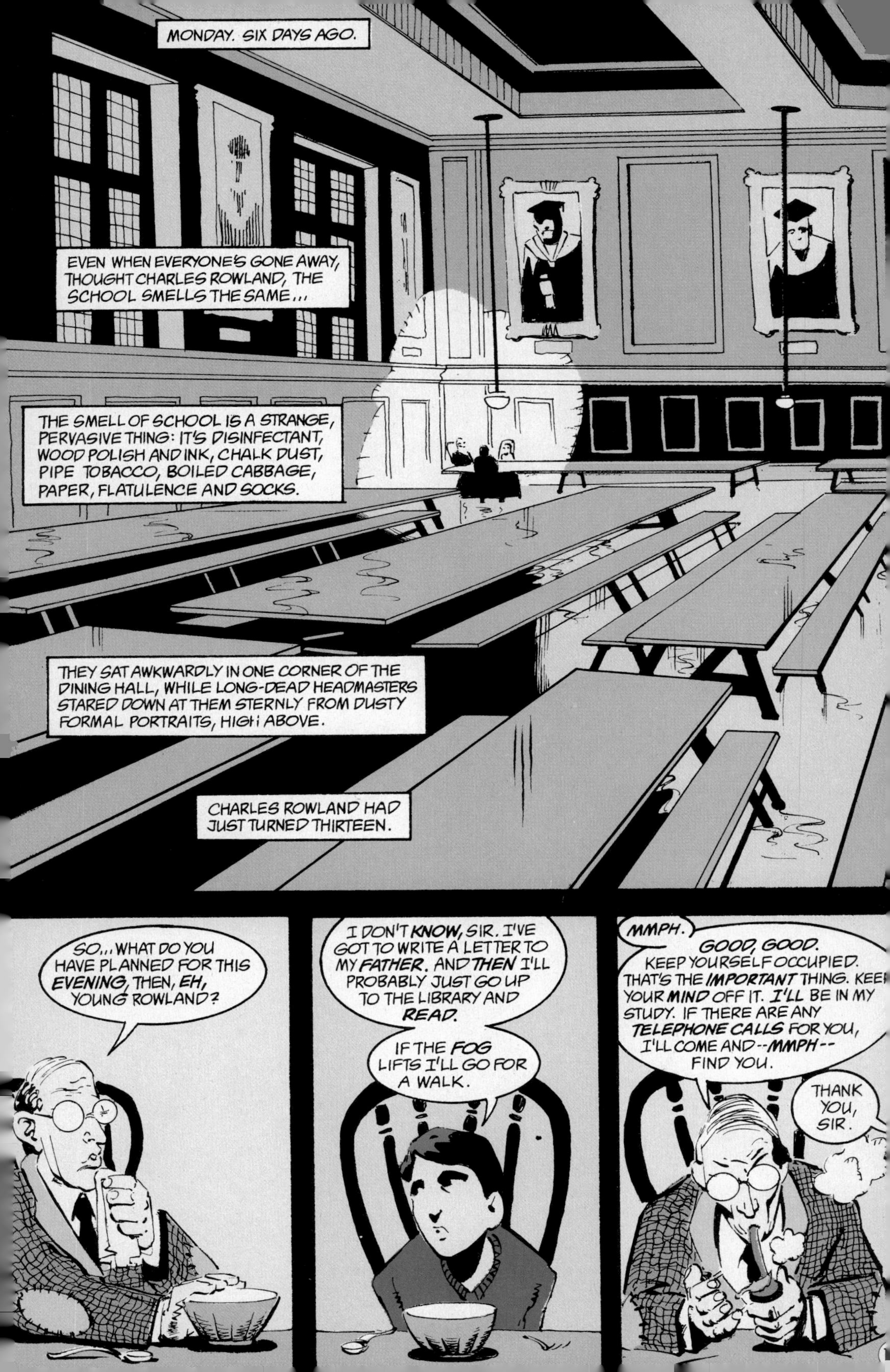

MONDAY. SIX DAYS AGO.
EVEN WHEN EVERYONE'S GONE AWAY, THOUGHT CHARLES ROWLAND, THE SCHOOL SMELLS THE SAME...
THE SMELL OF SCHOOL IS A STRANGE, PERVASIVE THING: IT'S DISINFECTANT, WOOD POLISH AND INK, CHALK DUST, PIPE TOBACCO, BOILED CABBAGE, PAPER, FLATULENCE AND SOCKS.
THEY SAT AWKWARDLY IN ONE CORNER OF THE DINING HALL, WHILE LONG-DEAD HEADMASTERS STARED DOWN AT THEM STERNLY FROM DUSTY FORMAL PORTRAITS, HIGH ABOVE.
CHARLES ROWLAND HAD JUST TURNED THIRTEEN.
SO... WHAT DO YOU HAVE PLANNED FOR THIS EVENING, THEN, EH, YOUNG ROWLAND?
I DON'T KNOW, SIR. I'VE GOT TO WRITE A LETTER TO MY FATHER. AND THEN I'LL PROBABLY JUST GO UP TO THE LIBRARY AND READ.
IF THE FOG LIFTS I'LL GO FOR A WALK.
MMPH.
GOOD, GOOD. KEEP YOURSELF OCCUPIED. THAT'S THE IMPORTANT THING. KEEP YOUR MIND OFF IT. I'LL BE IN MY STUDY. IF THERE ARE ANY TELEPHONE CALLS FOR YOU, I'LL COME AND --MMPH-- FIND YOU.
THANK YOU, SIR.

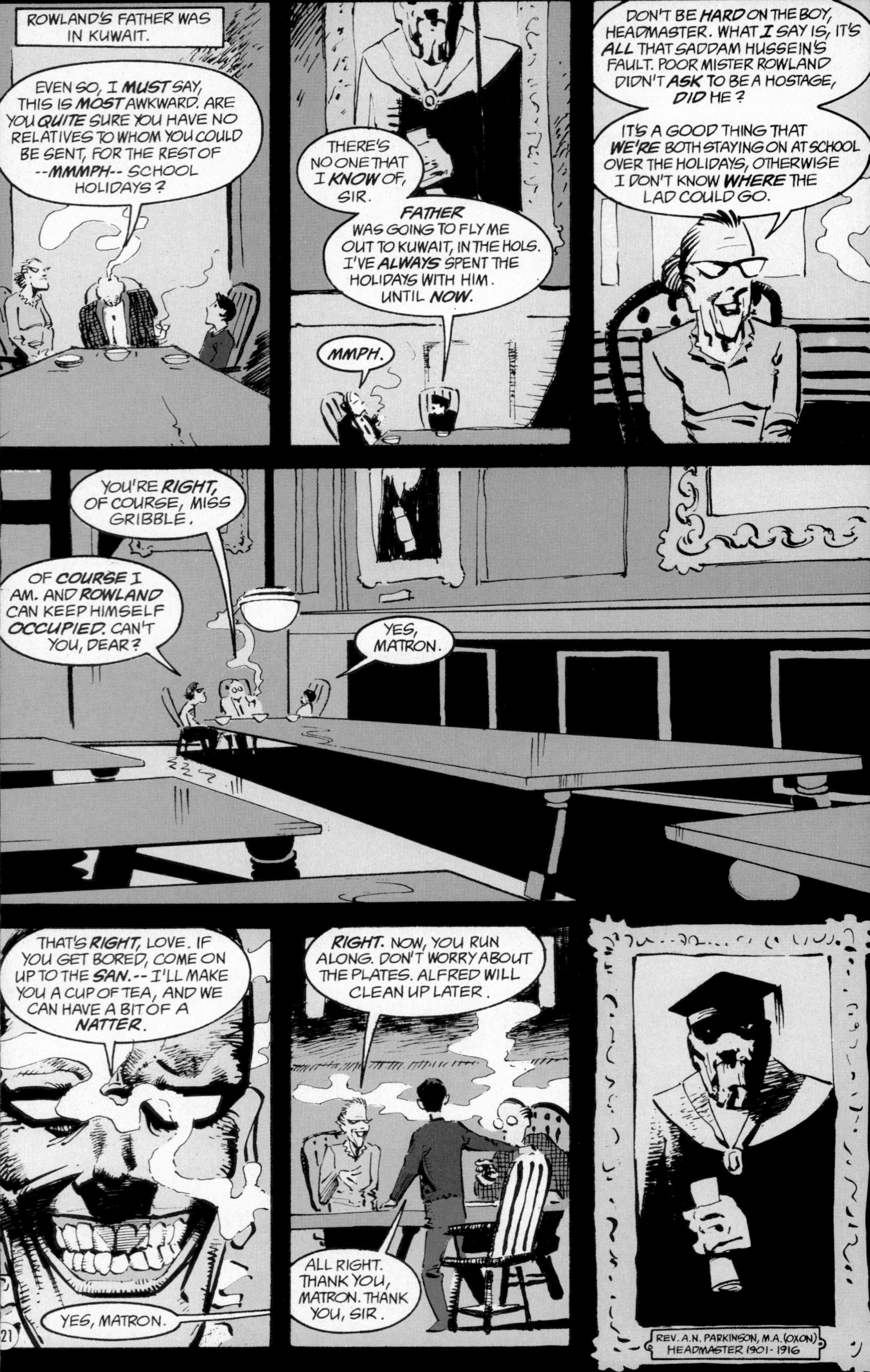
ROWLAND'S FATHER WAS IN KUWAIT.
EVEN SO, I **MUST** SAY, THIS IS **MOST** AWKWARD. ARE YOU **QUITE** SURE YOU HAVE NO RELATIVES TO WHOM YOU COULD BE SENT, FOR THE REST OF --**MMMPH**-- SCHOOL HOLIDAYS?
THERE'S NO ONE THAT I **KNOW** OF, SIR.
FATHER WAS GOING TO FLY ME OUT TO KUWAIT, IN THE HOLS. I'VE **ALWAYS** SPENT THE HOLIDAYS WITH HIM. UNTIL **NOW**.
MMPH.
DON'T BE **HARD** ON THE BOY, HEADMASTER. WHAT **I** SAY IS, IT'S **ALL** THAT SADDAM HUSSEIN'S FAULT. POOR MISTER ROWLAND DIDN'T **ASK** TO BE A HOSTAGE, **DID** HE?
IT'S A GOOD THING THAT **WE'RE** BOTH STAYING ON AT SCHOOL OVER THE HOLIDAYS, OTHERWISE I DON'T KNOW **WHERE** THE LAD COULD GO.
YOU'RE **RIGHT,** OF COURSE, MISS GRIBBLE.
OF **COURSE** I AM. AND **ROWLAND** CAN KEEP HIMSELF **OCCUPIED**. CAN'T YOU, DEAR?
YES, MATRON.
THAT'S **RIGHT,** LOVE. IF YOU GET BORED, COME ON UP TO THE **SAN**.-- I'LL MAKE YOU A CUP OF TEA, AND WE CAN HAVE A BIT OF A **NATTER**.
YES, MATRON.
RIGHT. NOW, YOU RUN ALONG. DON'T WORRY ABOUT THE PLATES. ALFRED WILL CLEAN UP LATER.
ALL RIGHT. THANK YOU, MATRON. THANK YOU, SIR.
REV. A.N. PARKINSON, M.A. (OXON) HEADMASTER 1901-1916

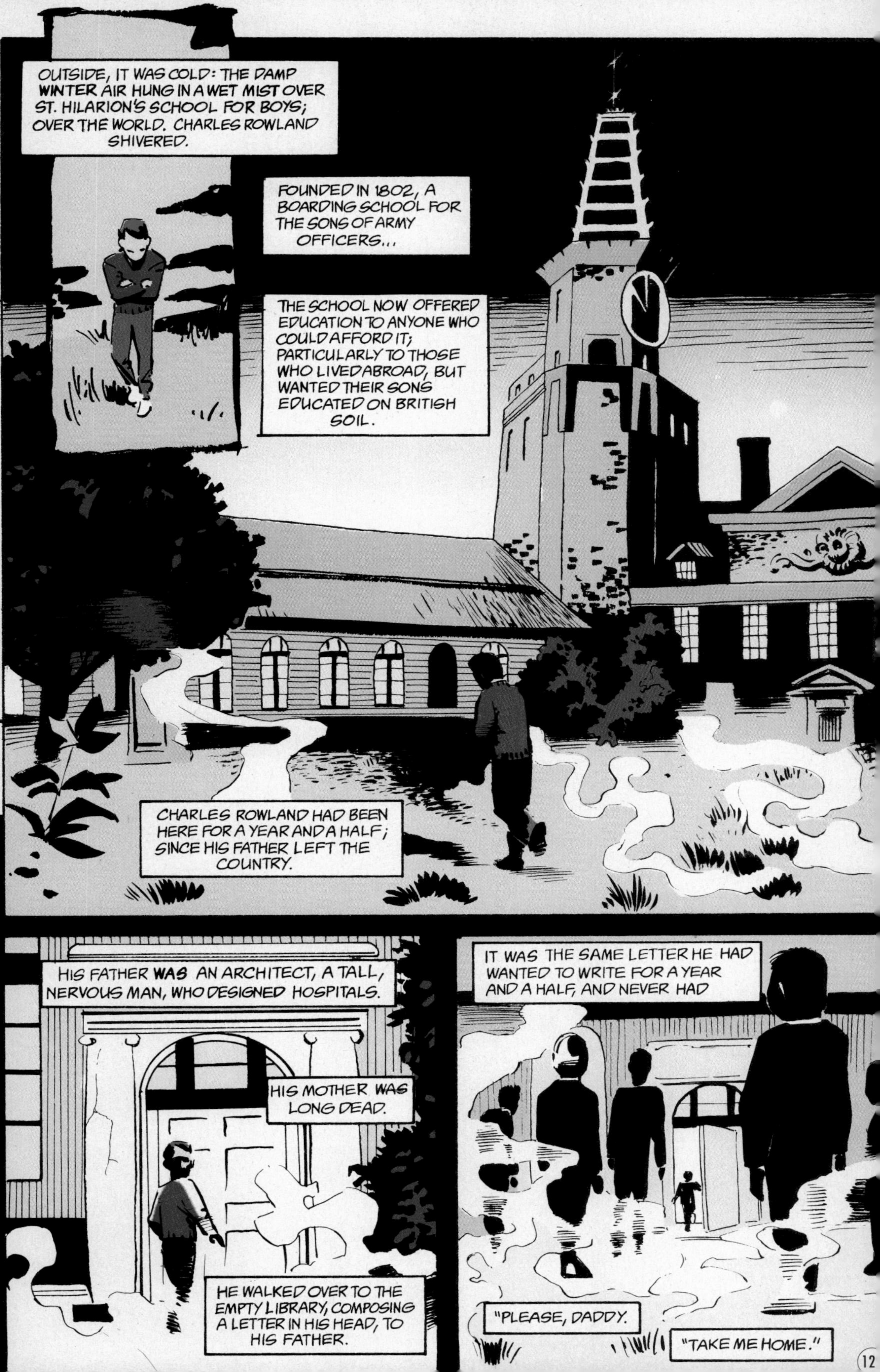
OUTSIDE, IT WAS COLD: THE DAMP **WINTER** AIR HUNG IN A WET MIST OVER ST. HILARION'S SCHOOL FOR BOYS; OVER THE WORLD. CHARLES ROWLAND SHIVERED.
FOUNDED IN 1802, A BOARDING SCHOOL FOR THE SONS OF ARMY OFFICERS...
THE SCHOOL NOW OFFERED EDUCATION TO ANYONE WHO COULD AFFORD IT; PARTICULARLY TO THOSE WHO LIVED ABROAD, BUT WANTED THEIR SONS EDUCATED ON BRITISH SOIL.
CHARLES ROWLAND HAD BEEN HERE FOR A YEAR AND A HALF; SINCE HIS FATHER LEFT THE COUNTRY.
HIS FATHER **WAS** AN ARCHITECT, A TALL, NERVOUS MAN, WHO DESIGNED HOSPITALS.
HIS MOTHER WAS LONG DEAD.
HE WALKED OVER TO THE EMPTY LIBRARY, COMPOSING A LETTER IN HIS HEAD, TO HIS FATHER.
IT WAS THE SAME LETTER HE HAD WANTED TO WRITE FOR A YEAR AND A HALF, AND NEVER HAD
"PLEASE, DADDY.
"TAKE ME HOME."

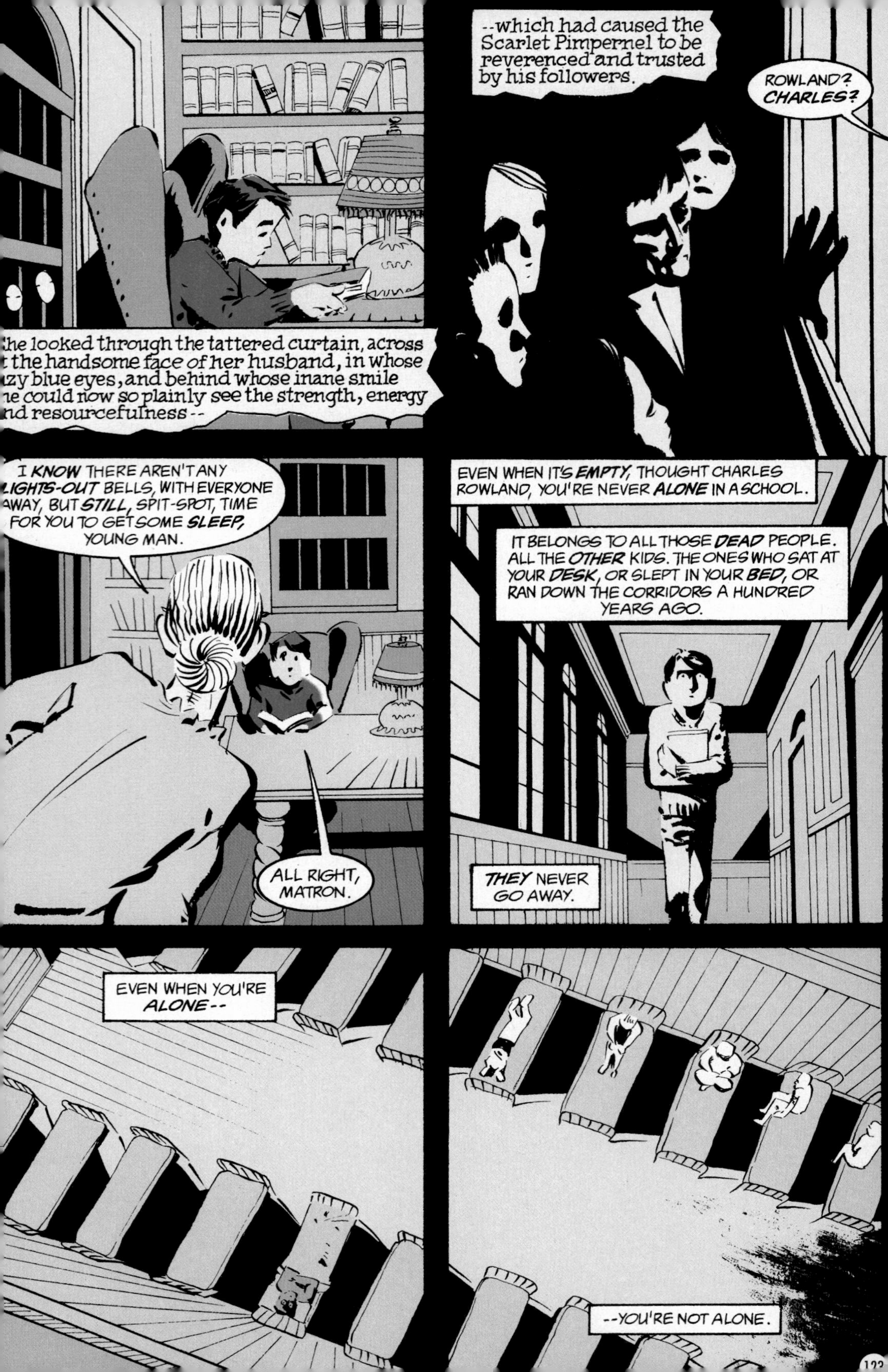

he looked through the tattered curtain, across
t the handsome face of her husband, in whose
zy blue eyes, and behind whose inane smile
he could now so plainly see the strength, energy
nd resourcefulness --
--which had caused the Scarlet Pimpernel to be reverenced and trusted by his followers.
ROWLAND? CHARLES?
I KNOW THERE AREN'T ANY LIGHTS-OUT BELLS, WITH EVERYONE AWAY, BUT STILL, SPIT-SPOT, TIME FOR YOU TO GET SOME SLEEP, YOUNG MAN.
ALL RIGHT, MATRON.
EVEN WHEN IT'S EMPTY, THOUGHT CHARLES ROWLAND, YOU'RE NEVER ALONE IN A SCHOOL.
IT BELONGS TO ALL THOSE DEAD PEOPLE. ALL THE OTHER KIDS. THE ONES WHO SAT AT YOUR DESK, OR SLEPT IN YOUR BED, OR RAN DOWN THE CORRIDORS A HUNDRED YEARS AGO.
THEY NEVER GO AWAY.
EVEN WHEN YOU'RE ALONE--
--YOU'RE NOT ALONE.

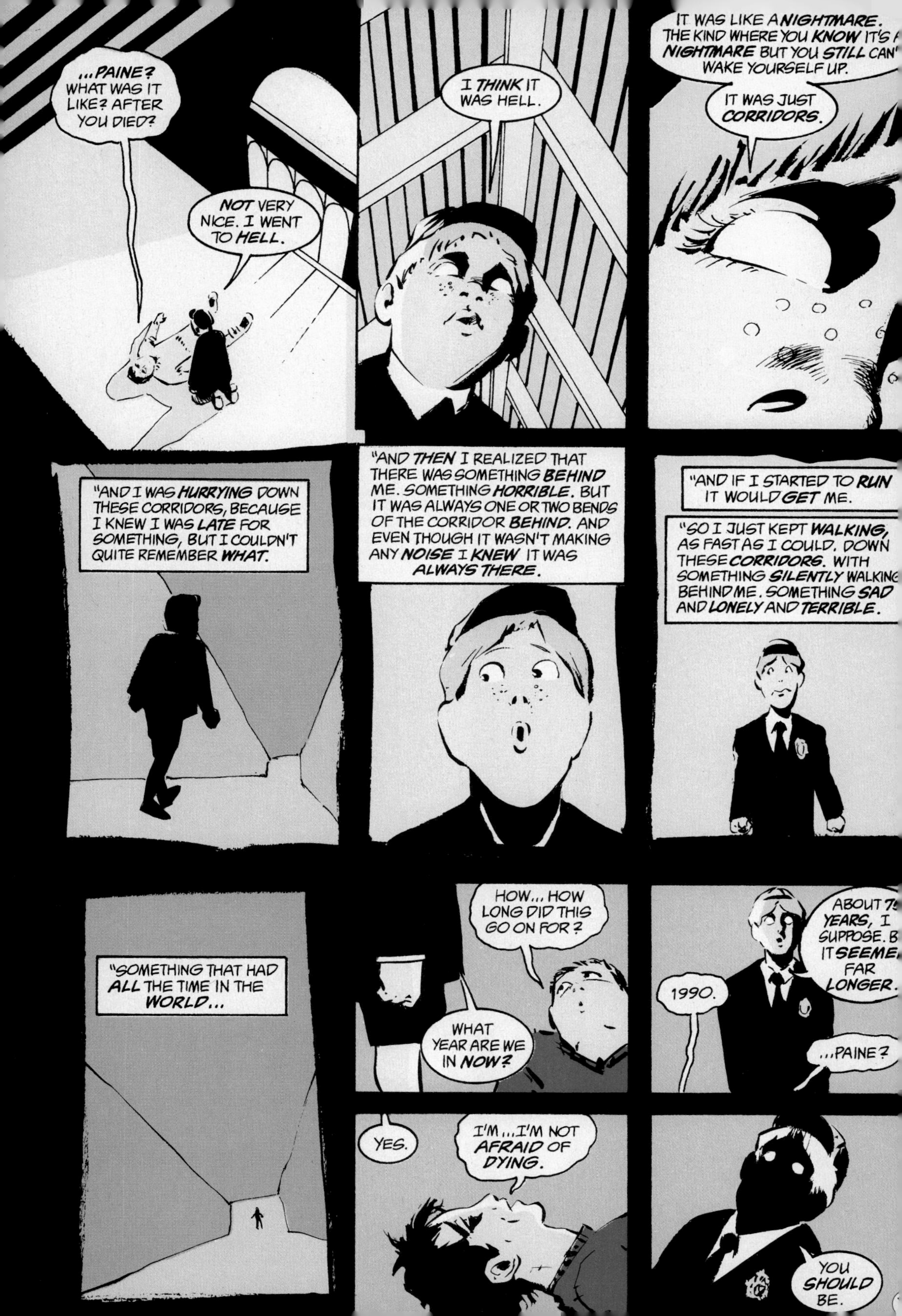
...PAINE? WHAT WAS IT LIKE? AFTER YOU DIED?
NOT VERY NICE. I WENT TO HELL.
I THINK IT WAS HELL.
IT WAS LIKE A NIGHTMARE. THE KIND WHERE YOU KNOW IT'S A NIGHTMARE BUT YOU STILL CAN'T WAKE YOURSELF UP.
IT WAS JUST CORRIDORS.
"AND I WAS HURRYING DOWN THESE CORRIDORS, BECAUSE I KNEW I WAS LATE FOR SOMETHING, BUT I COULDN'T QUITE REMEMBER WHAT.
"AND THEN I REALIZED THAT THERE WAS SOMETHING BEHIND ME. SOMETHING HORRIBLE. BUT IT WAS ALWAYS ONE OR TWO BENDS OF THE CORRIDOR BEHIND. AND EVEN THOUGH IT WASN'T MAKING ANY NOISE I KNEW IT WAS ALWAYS THERE.
"AND IF I STARTED TO RUN IT WOULD GET ME.
"SO I JUST KEPT WALKING, AS FAST AS I COULD, DOWN THESE CORRIDORS. WITH SOMETHING SILENTLY WALKING BEHIND ME. SOMETHING SAD AND LONELY AND TERRIBLE.
"SOMETHING THAT HAD ALL THE TIME IN THE WORLD...
HOW... HOW LONG DID THIS GO ON FOR?
WHAT YEAR ARE WE IN NOW?
1990.
ABOUT 75 YEARS, I SUPPOSE. BUT IT SEEMED FAR LONGER.
...PAINE?
YES.
I'M...I'M NOT AFRAID OF DYING.
YOU SHOULD BE.

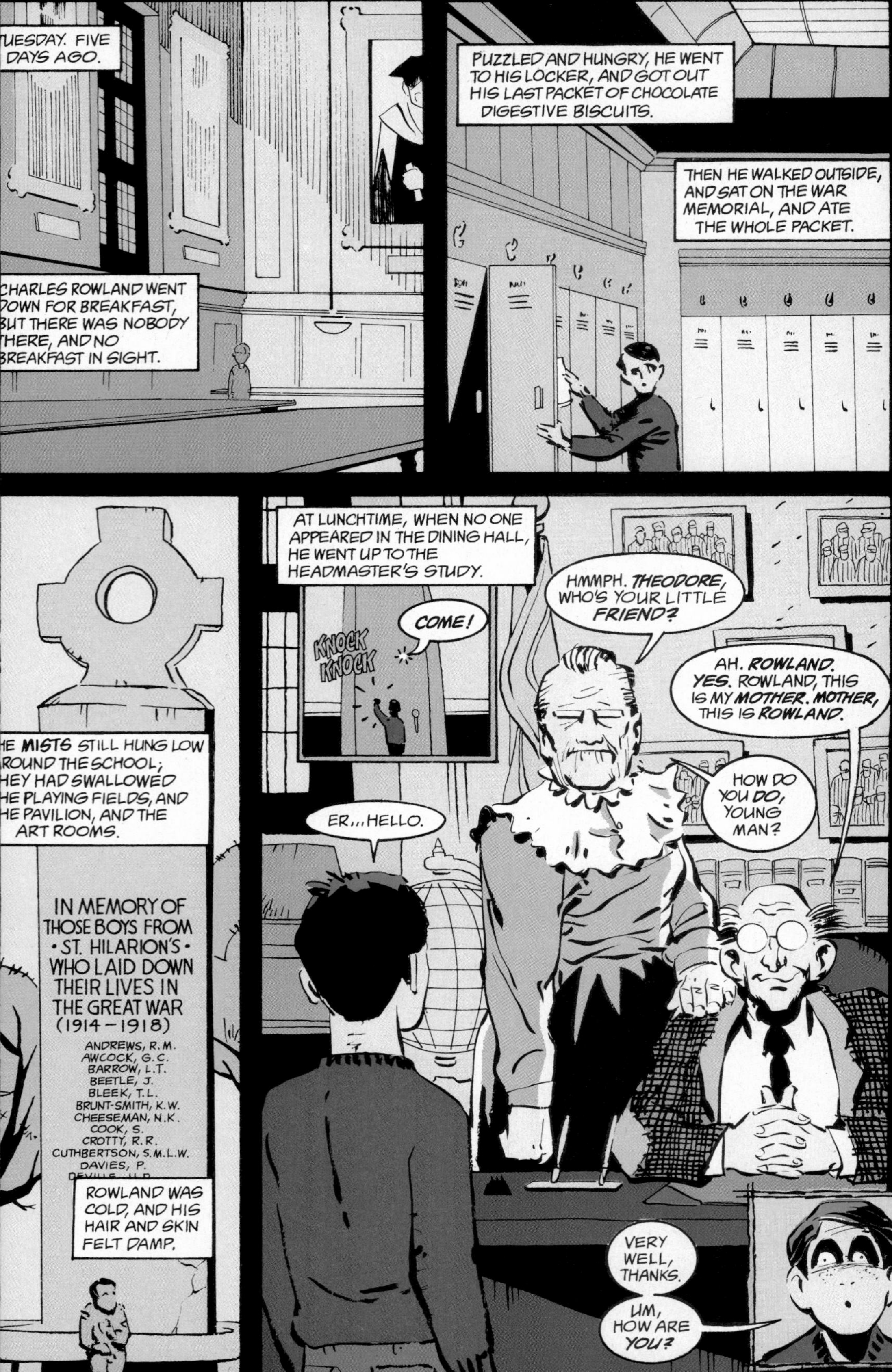

TUESDAY. FIVE DAYS AGO.
CHARLES ROWLAND WENT DOWN FOR BREAKFAST, BUT THERE WAS NOBODY THERE, AND NO BREAKFAST IN SIGHT.
PUZZLED AND HUNGRY, HE WENT TO HIS LOCKER, AND GOT OUT HIS LAST PACKET OF CHOCOLATE DIGESTIVE BISCUITS.
THEN HE WALKED OUTSIDE, AND SAT ON THE WAR MEMORIAL, AND ATE THE WHOLE PACKET.
HE **MISTS** STILL HUNG LOW AROUND THE SCHOOL; HEY HAD SWALLOWED HE PLAYING FIELDS, AND HE PAVILION, AND THE ART ROOMS.
IN MEMORY OF THOSE BOYS FROM • ST. HILARION'S • WHO LAID DOWN THEIR LIVES IN THE GREAT WAR (1914 – 1918)
ANDREWS, R.M.
AWCOCK, G.C.
BARROW, L.T.
BEETLE, J.
BLEEK, T.L.
BRUNT-SMITH, K.W.
CHEESEMAN, N.K.
COOK, S.
CROTTY, R.R.
CUTHBERTSON, S.M.L.W.
DAVIES, P.
ROWLAND WAS COLD, AND HIS HAIR AND SKIN FELT DAMP.
AT LUNCHTIME, WHEN NO ONE APPEARED IN THE DINING HALL, HE WENT UP TO THE HEADMASTER'S STUDY.
KNOCK KNOCK
COME!
HMMPH. ***THEODORE***, WHO'S YOUR LITTLE ***FRIEND?***
AH. ***ROWLAND. YES.*** ROWLAND, THIS IS MY ***MOTHER. MOTHER***, THIS IS ***ROWLAND***.
ER... HELLO.
HOW DO YOU ***DO***, YOUNG MAN?
VERY WELL, THANKS.
UM, HOW ARE ***YOU?***

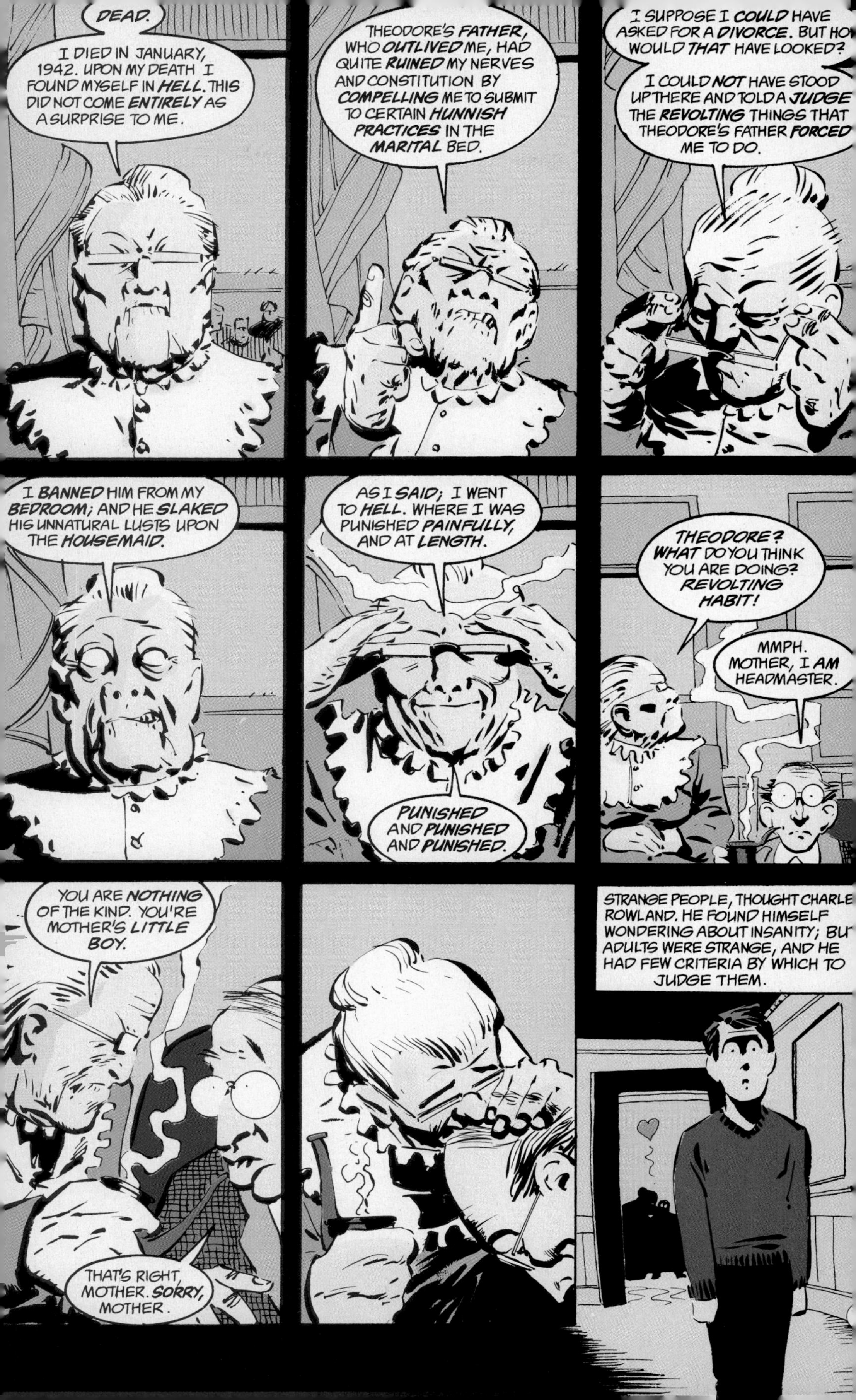
DEAD.
I DIED IN JANUARY, 1942. UPON MY DEATH I FOUND MYSELF IN HELL. THIS DID NOT COME ENTIRELY AS A SURPRISE TO ME.
THEODORE'S FATHER, WHO OUTLIVED ME, HAD QUITE RUINED MY NERVES AND CONSTITUTION BY COMPELLING ME TO SUBMIT TO CERTAIN HUNNISH PRACTICES IN THE MARITAL BED.
I SUPPOSE I COULD HAVE ASKED FOR A DIVORCE. BUT HOW WOULD THAT HAVE LOOKED?
I COULD NOT HAVE STOOD UP THERE AND TOLD A JUDGE THE REVOLTING THINGS THAT THEODORE'S FATHER FORCED ME TO DO.
I BANNED HIM FROM MY BEDROOM; AND HE SLAKED HIS UNNATURAL LUSTS UPON THE HOUSEMAID.
AS I SAID; I WENT TO HELL. WHERE I WAS PUNISHED PAINFULLY, AND AT LENGTH.
PUNISHED AND PUNISHED AND PUNISHED.
THEODORE? WHAT DO YOU THINK YOU ARE DOING? REVOLTING HABIT!
MMPH. MOTHER, I AM HEADMASTER.
YOU ARE NOTHING OF THE KIND. YOU'RE MOTHER'S LITTLE BOY.
THAT'S RIGHT, MOTHER. SORRY, MOTHER.
STRANGE PEOPLE, THOUGHT CHARLES ROWLAND. HE FOUND HIMSELF WONDERING ABOUT INSANITY; BUT ADULTS WERE STRANGE, AND HE HAD FEW CRITERIA BY WHICH TO JUDGE THEM.

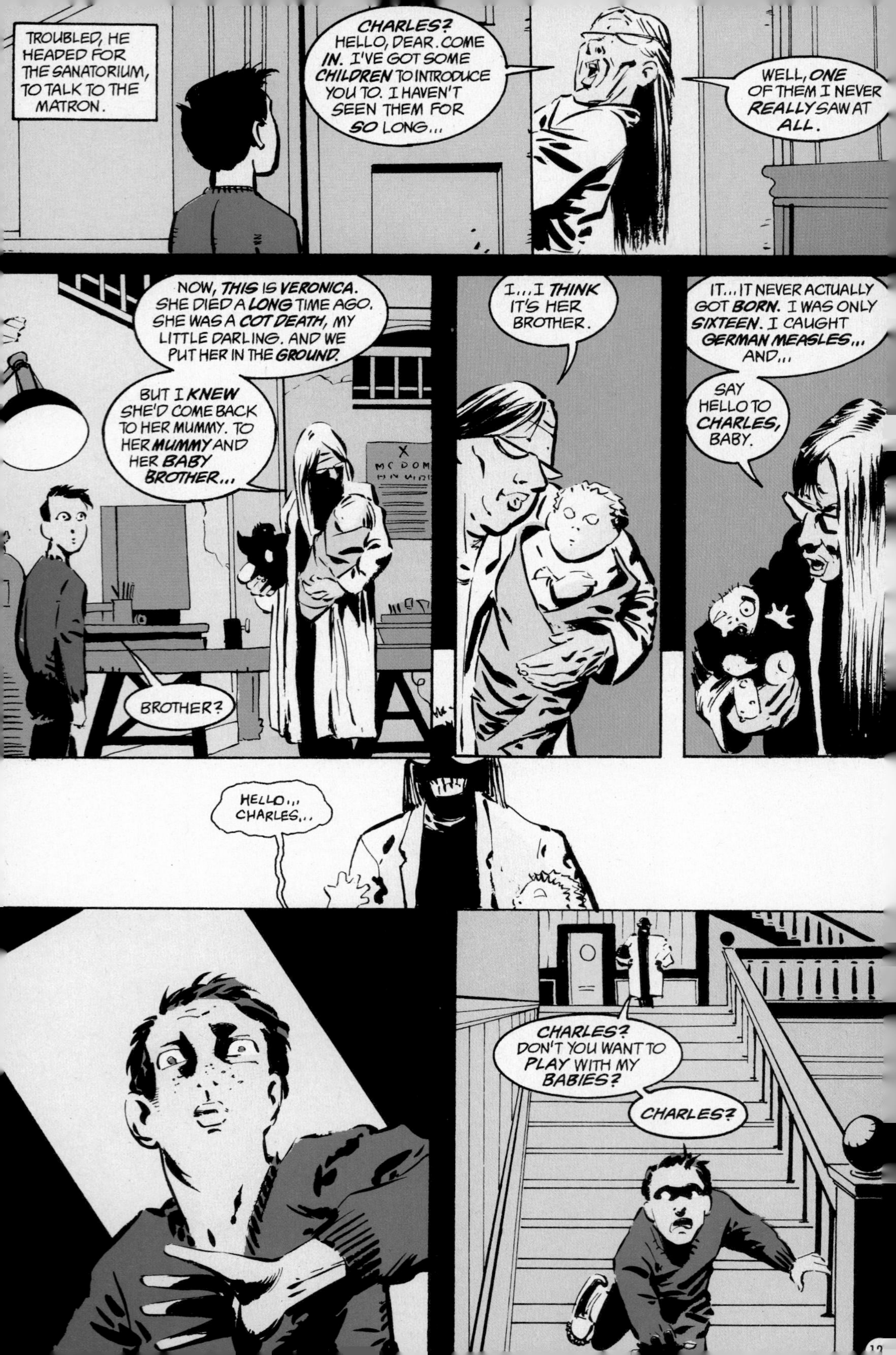
TROUBLED, HE HEADED FOR THE SANATORIUM, TO TALK TO THE MATRON.
CHARLES? HELLO, DEAR. COME IN. I'VE GOT SOME CHILDREN TO INTRODUCE YOU TO. I HAVEN'T SEEN THEM FOR SO LONG...
WELL, ONE OF THEM I NEVER REALLY SAW AT ALL.
NOW, THIS IS VERONICA. SHE DIED A LONG TIME AGO. SHE WAS A COT DEATH, MY LITTLE DARLING. AND WE PUT HER IN THE GROUND.
BUT I KNEW SHE'D COME BACK TO HER MUMMY. TO HER MUMMY AND HER BABY BROTHER...
BROTHER?
I... I THINK IT'S HER BROTHER.
IT... IT NEVER ACTUALLY GOT BORN. I WAS ONLY SIXTEEN. I CAUGHT GERMAN MEASLES... AND...
SAY HELLO TO CHARLES, BABY.
HELLO... CHARLES...
CHARLES? DON'T YOU WANT TO PLAY WITH MY BABIES?
CHARLES?

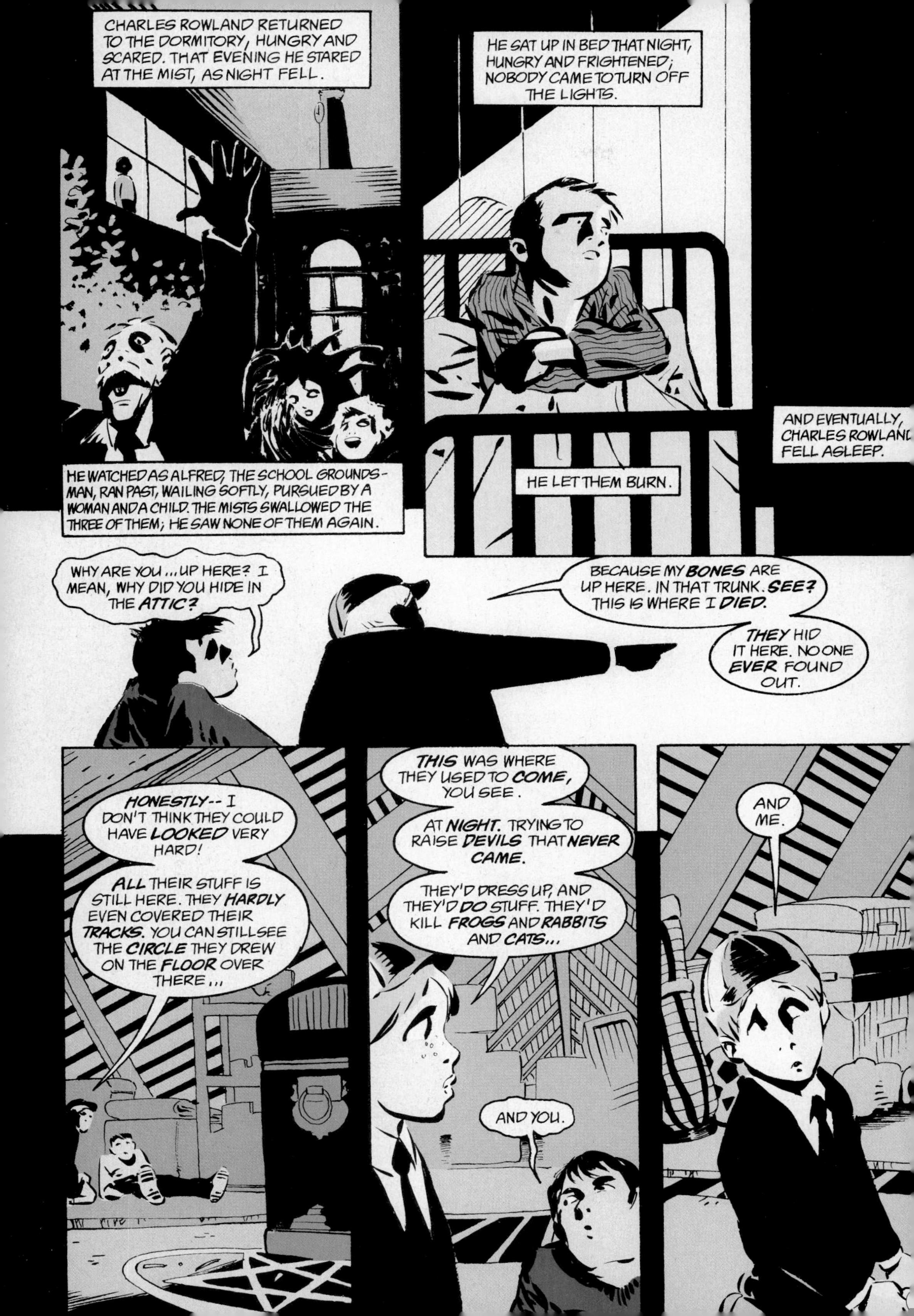
CHARLES ROWLAND RETURNED TO THE DORMITORY, HUNGRY AND SCARED. THAT EVENING HE STARED AT THE MIST, AS NIGHT FELL.
HE WATCHED AS ALFRED, THE SCHOOL GROUNDS-MAN, RAN PAST, WAILING SOFTLY, PURSUED BY A WOMAN AND A CHILD. THE MISTS SWALLOWED THE THREE OF THEM; HE SAW NONE OF THEM AGAIN.
HE SAT UP IN BED THAT NIGHT, HUNGRY AND FRIGHTENED; NOBODY CAME TO TURN OFF THE LIGHTS.
HE LET THEM BURN.
AND EVENTUALLY, CHARLES ROWLAND FELL ASLEEP.
WHY ARE YOU ... UP HERE? I MEAN, WHY DID YOU HIDE IN THE ATTIC?
BECAUSE MY BONES ARE UP HERE. IN THAT TRUNK. SEE? THIS IS WHERE I DIED.
THEY HID IT HERE. NO ONE EVER FOUND OUT.
HONESTLY-- I DON'T THINK THEY COULD HAVE LOOKED VERY HARD!
ALL THEIR STUFF IS STILL HERE. THEY HARDLY EVEN COVERED THEIR TRACKS. YOU CAN STILL SEE THE CIRCLE THEY DREW ON THE FLOOR OVER THERE...
THIS WAS WHERE THEY USED TO COME, YOU SEE.
AT NIGHT. TRYING TO RAISE DEVILS THAT NEVER CAME.
THEY'D DRESS UP, AND THEY'D DO STUFF. THEY'D KILL FROGS AND RABBITS AND CATS...
AND YOU.
AND ME.

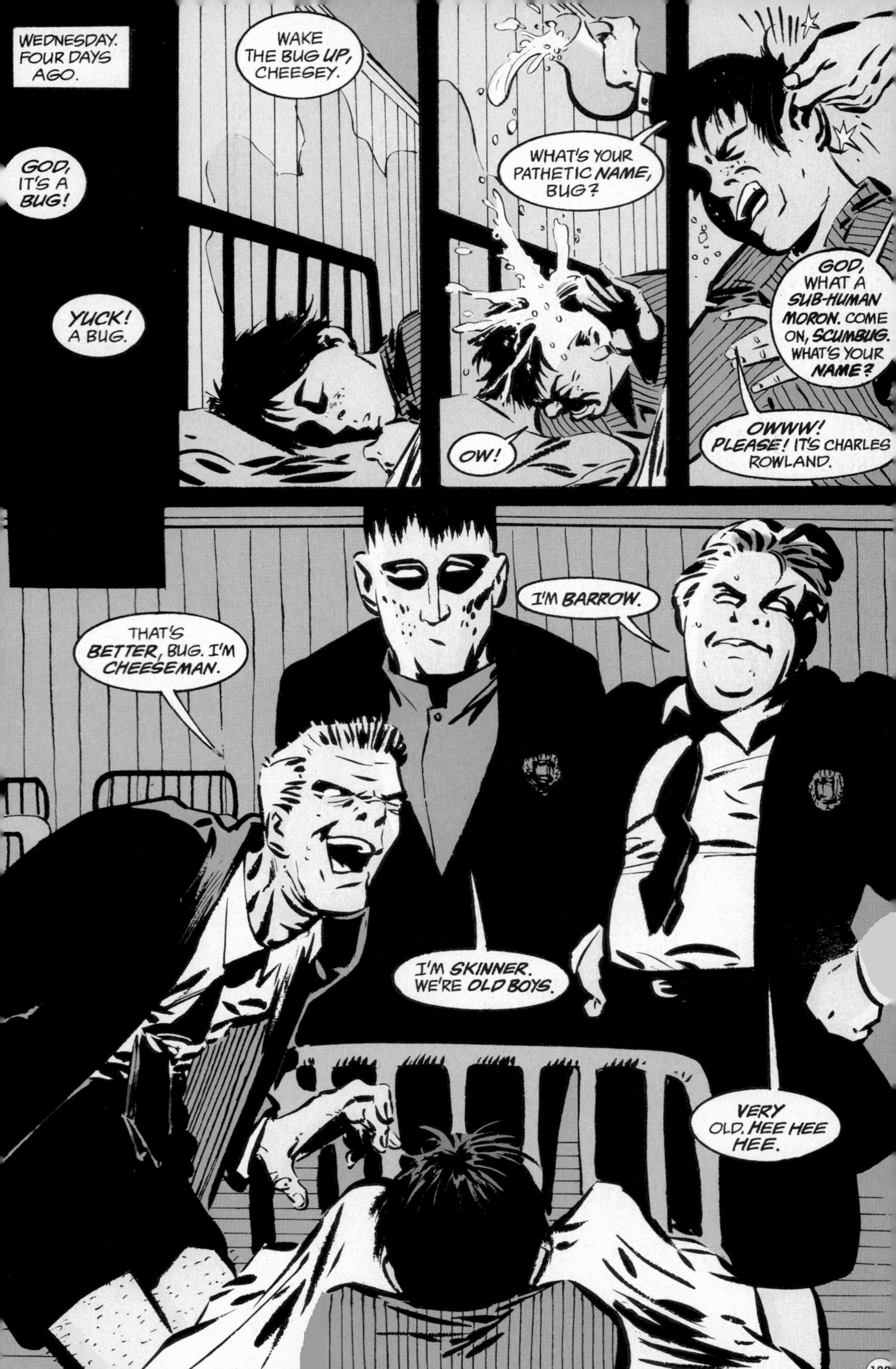
WEDNESDAY. FOUR DAYS AGO.
GOD, IT'S A BUG!
YUCK! A BUG.
WAKE THE BUG UP, CHEESEY.
WHAT'S YOUR PATHETIC NAME, BUG?
OW!
GOD, WHAT A SUB-HUMAN MORON. COME ON, SCUMBUG. WHAT'S YOUR NAME?
OWWW! PLEASE! IT'S CHARLES ROWLAND.
THAT'S BETTER, BUG. I'M CHEESEMAN.
I'M BARROW.
I'M SKINNER. WE'RE OLD BOYS.
VERY OLD. HEE HEE HEE.

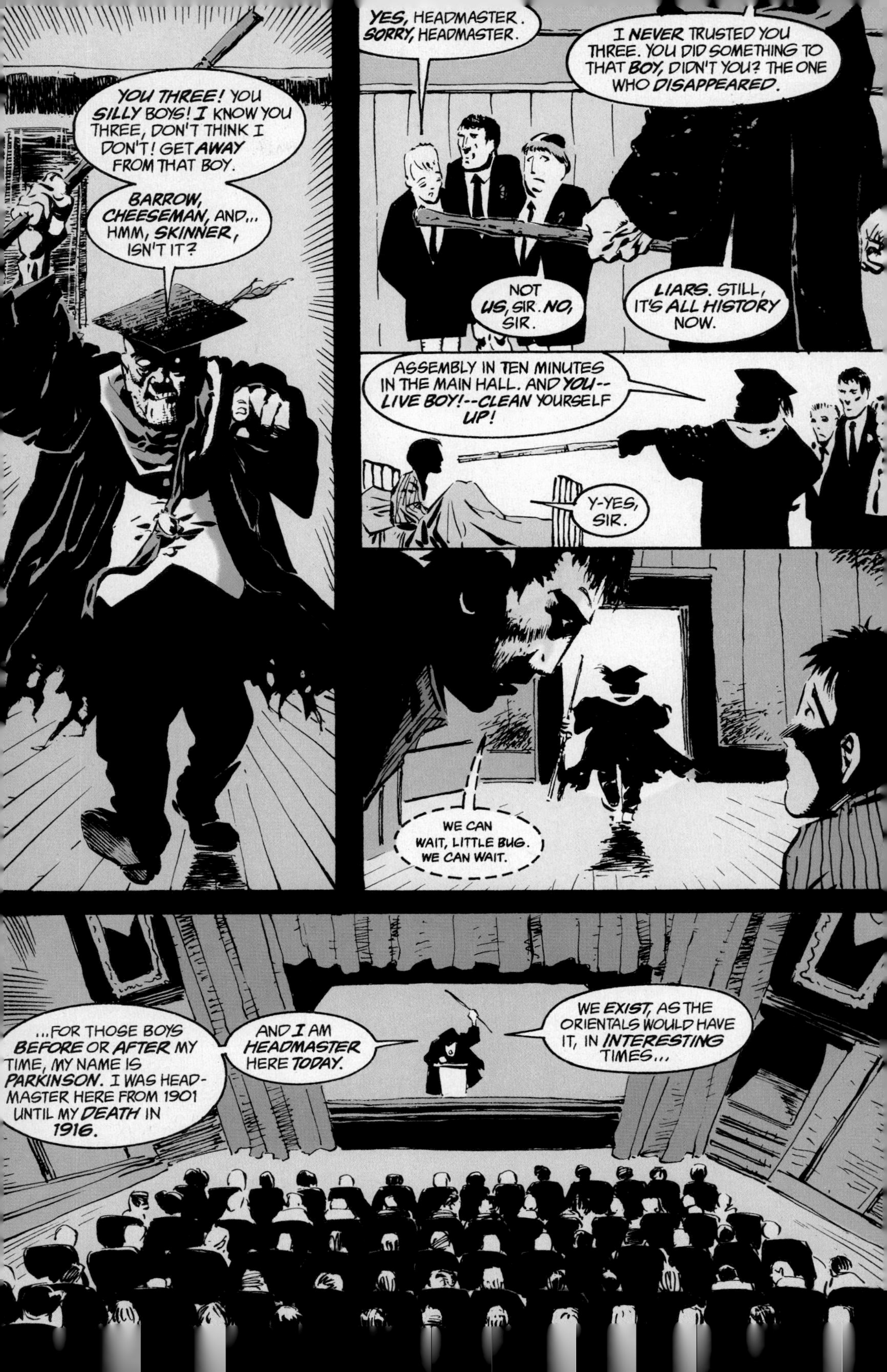
YOU THREE! YOU SILLY BOYS! I KNOW YOU THREE, DON'T THINK I DON'T! GET AWAY FROM THAT BOY.
BARROW, CHEESEMAN, AND... HMM, SKINNER, ISN'T IT?
YES, HEADMASTER. SORRY, HEADMASTER.
I NEVER TRUSTED YOU THREE. YOU DID SOMETHING TO THAT BOY, DIDN'T YOU? THE ONE WHO DISAPPEARED.
NOT US, SIR. NO, SIR.
LIARS. STILL, IT'S ALL HISTORY NOW.
ASSEMBLY IN TEN MINUTES IN THE MAIN HALL. AND YOU--LIVE BOY!--CLEAN YOURSELF UP!
Y-YES, SIR.
WE CAN WAIT, LITTLE BUG. WE CAN WAIT.
...FOR THOSE BOYS BEFORE OR AFTER MY TIME, MY NAME IS PARKINSON. I WAS HEAD-MASTER HERE FROM 1901 UNTIL MY DEATH IN 1916.
AND I AM HEADMASTER HERE TODAY.
WE EXIST, AS THE ORIENTALS WOULD HAVE IT, IN INTERESTING TIMES...

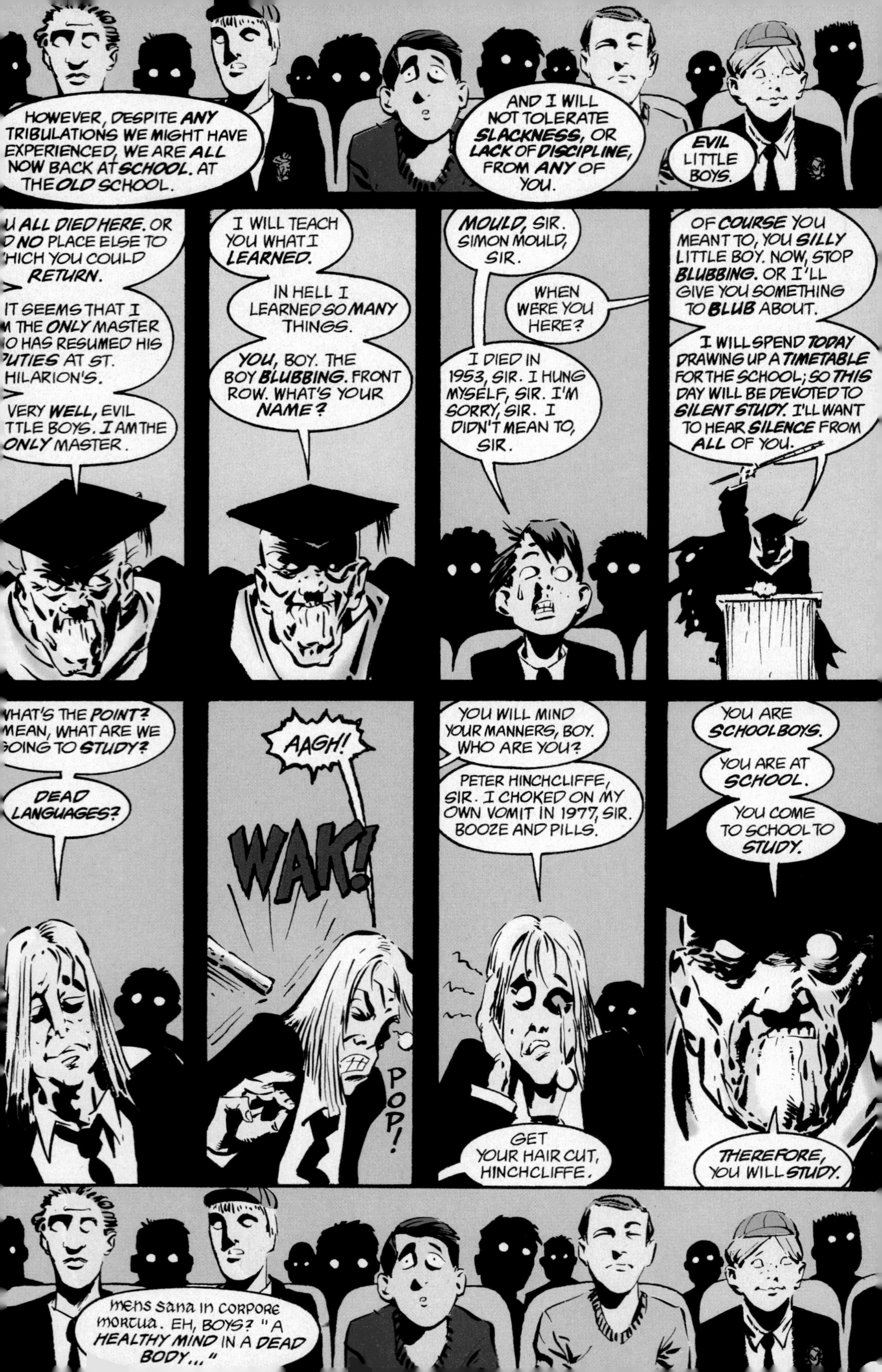
HOWEVER, DESPITE ANY TRIBULATIONS WE MIGHT HAVE EXPERIENCED, WE ARE ALL NOW BACK AT SCHOOL. AT THE OLD SCHOOL.
AND I WILL NOT TOLERATE SLACKNESS, OR LACK OF DISCIPLINE, FROM ANY OF YOU.
EVIL LITTLE BOYS.
U ALL DIED HERE. OR D NO PLACE ELSE TO HICH YOU COULD RETURN.
IT SEEMS THAT I M THE ONLY MASTER O HAS RESUMED HIS UTIES AT ST. HILARION'S.
VERY WELL, EVIL TTLE BOYS. I AM THE ONLY MASTER.
I WILL TEACH YOU WHAT I LEARNED.
IN HELL I LEARNED SO MANY THINGS.
YOU, BOY. THE BOY BLUBBING. FRONT ROW. WHAT'S YOUR NAME?
MOULD, SIR. SIMON MOULD, SIR.
WHEN WERE YOU HERE?
I DIED IN 1953, SIR. I HUNG MYSELF, SIR. I'M SORRY, SIR. I DIDN'T MEAN TO, SIR.
OF COURSE YOU MEANT TO, YOU SILLY LITTLE BOY. NOW, STOP BLUBBING. OR I'LL GIVE YOU SOMETHING TO BLUB ABOUT.
I WILL SPEND TODAY DRAWING UP A TIMETABLE FOR THE SCHOOL; SO THIS DAY WILL BE DEVOTED TO SILENT STUDY. I'LL WANT TO HEAR SILENCE FROM ALL OF YOU.
HAT'S THE POINT? MEAN, WHAT ARE WE GOING TO STUDY?
DEAD LANGUAGES?
AAGH!
WAK!
POP!
YOU WILL MIND YOUR MANNERS, BOY. WHO ARE YOU?
PETER HINCHCLIFFE, SIR. I CHOKED ON MY OWN VOMIT IN 1977, SIR. BOOZE AND PILLS.
GET YOUR HAIR CUT, HINCHCLIFFE.
YOU ARE SCHOOLBOYS.
YOU ARE AT SCHOOL.
YOU COME TO SCHOOL TO STUDY.
THEREFORE, YOU WILL STUDY.
mens sana in corpore mortua. EH, BOYS? "A HEALTHY MIND IN A DEAD BODY..."

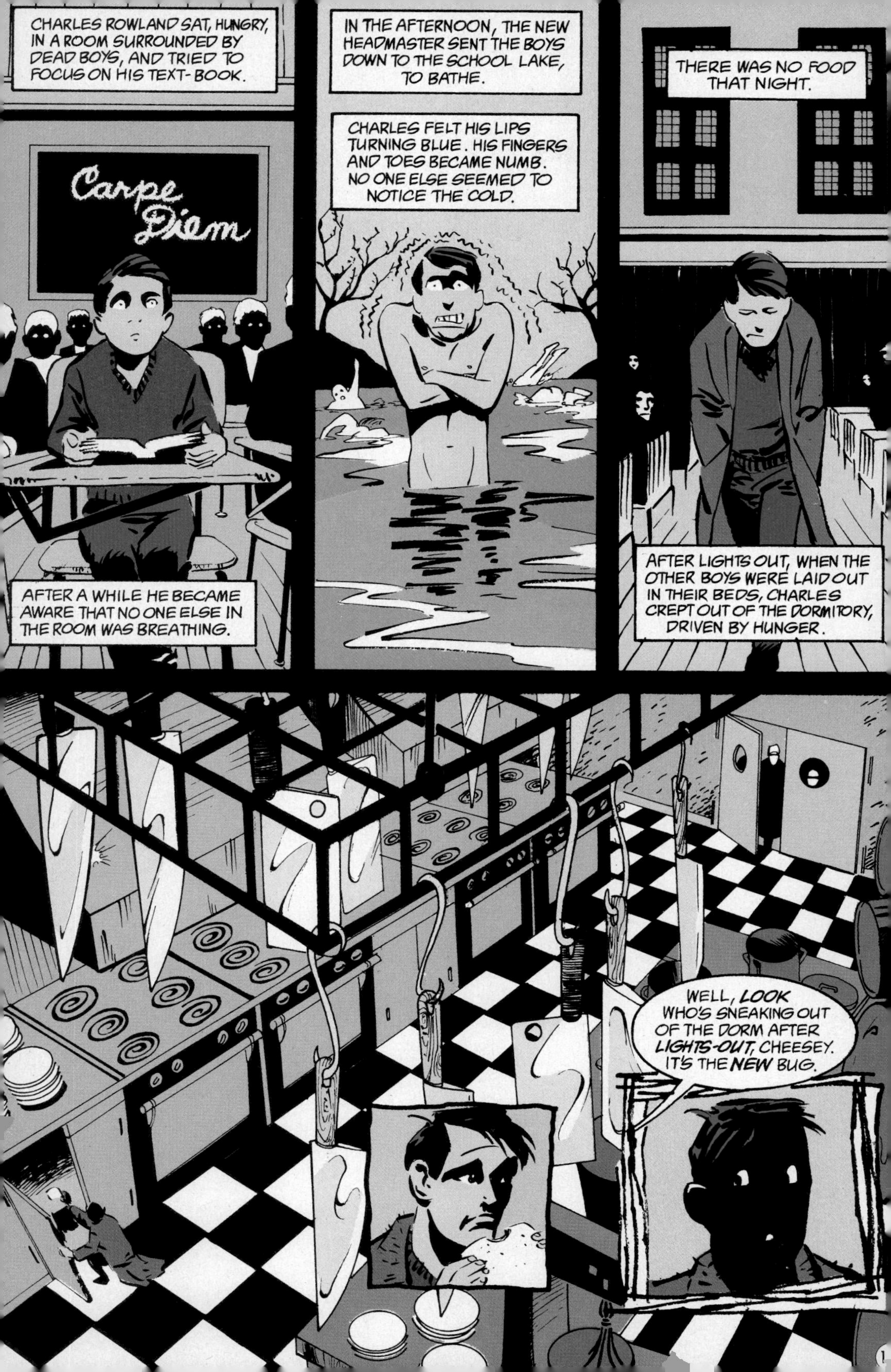
CHARLES ROWLAND SAT, HUNGRY, IN A ROOM SURROUNDED BY DEAD BOYS, AND TRIED TO FOCUS ON HIS TEXT-BOOK.
Carpe Diem
AFTER A WHILE HE BECAME AWARE THAT NO ONE ELSE IN THE ROOM WAS BREATHING.
IN THE AFTERNOON, THE NEW HEADMASTER SENT THE BOYS DOWN TO THE SCHOOL LAKE, TO BATHE.
CHARLES FELT HIS LIPS TURNING BLUE. HIS FINGERS AND TOES BECAME NUMB. NO ONE ELSE SEEMED TO NOTICE THE COLD.
THERE WAS NO FOOD THAT NIGHT.
AFTER LIGHTS OUT, WHEN THE OTHER BOYS WERE LAID OUT IN THEIR BEDS, CHARLES CREPT OUT OF THE DORMITORY, DRIVEN BY HUNGER.
WELL, **LOOK** WHO'S SNEAKING OUT OF THE DORM AFTER ***LIGHTS-OUT***, CHEESEY. IT'S THE ***NEW*** BUG.

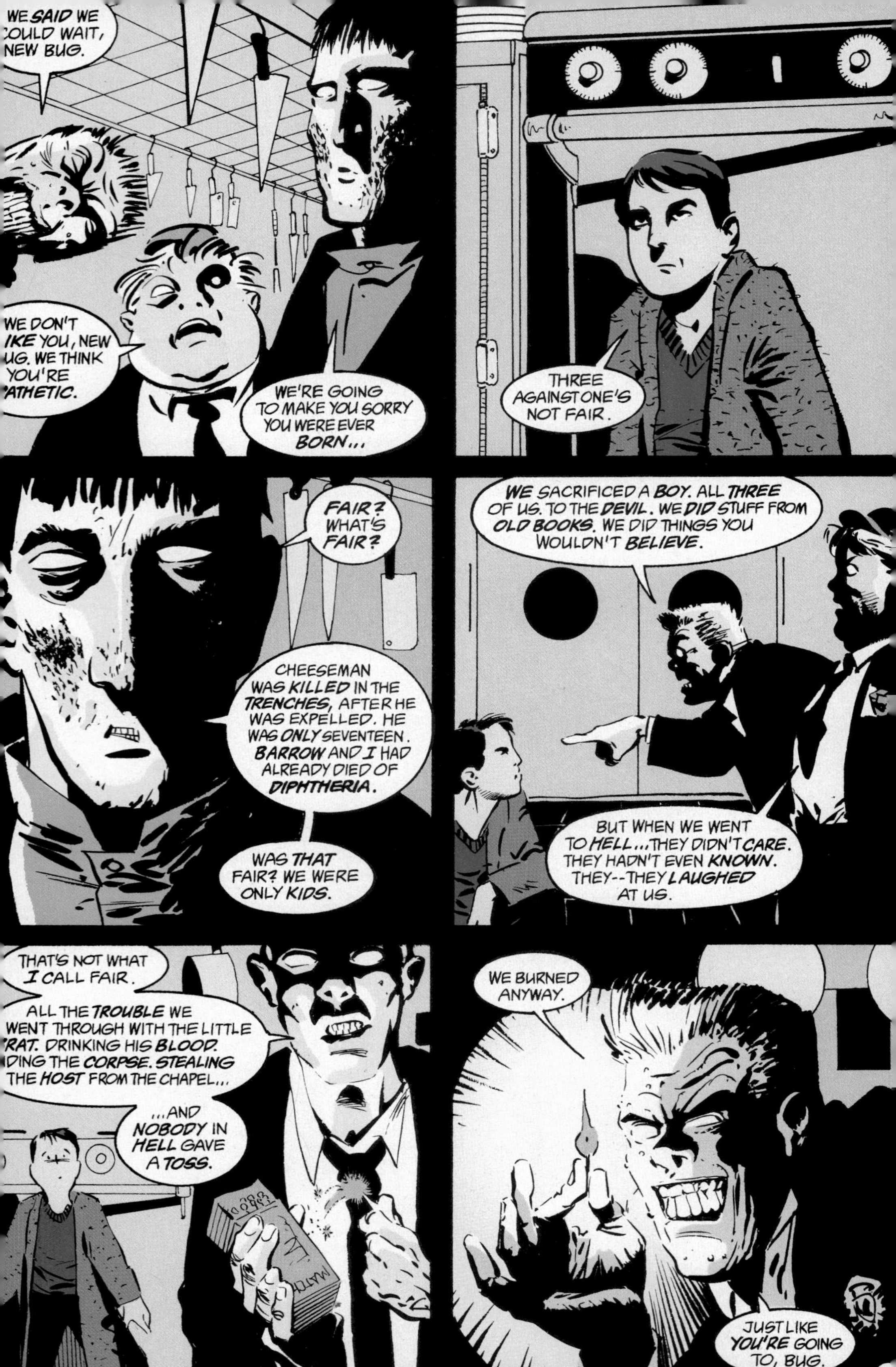

WE SAID WE
:OULD WAIT,
NEW BUG.
WE DON'T
IKE YOU, NEW
UG. WE THINK
YOU'RE
ATHETIC.
WE'RE GOING TO MAKE YOU SORRY YOU WERE EVER BORN...
THREE AGAINST ONE'S NOT FAIR.
FAIR? WHAT'S FAIR?
CHEESEMAN WAS KILLED IN THE TRENCHES, AFTER HE WAS EXPELLED. HE WAS ONLY SEVENTEEN. BARROW AND I HAD ALREADY DIED OF DIPHTHERIA.
WAS THAT FAIR? WE WERE ONLY KIDS.
WE SACRIFICED A BOY. ALL THREE OF US. TO THE DEVIL. WE DID STUFF FROM OLD BOOKS. WE DID THINGS YOU WOULDN'T BELIEVE.
BUT WHEN WE WENT TO HELL...THEY DIDN'T CARE. THEY HADN'T EVEN KNOWN. THEY--THEY LAUGHED AT US.
THAT'S NOT WHAT I CALL FAIR.
ALL THE TROUBLE WE
WENT THROUGH WITH THE LITTLE
RAT. DRINKING HIS BLOOD.
DING THE CORPSE. STEALING
THE HOST FROM THE CHAPEL...
...AND NOBODY IN HELL GAVE A TOSS.
WE BURNED ANYWAY.
JUST LIKE YOU'RE GOING TO, BUG.

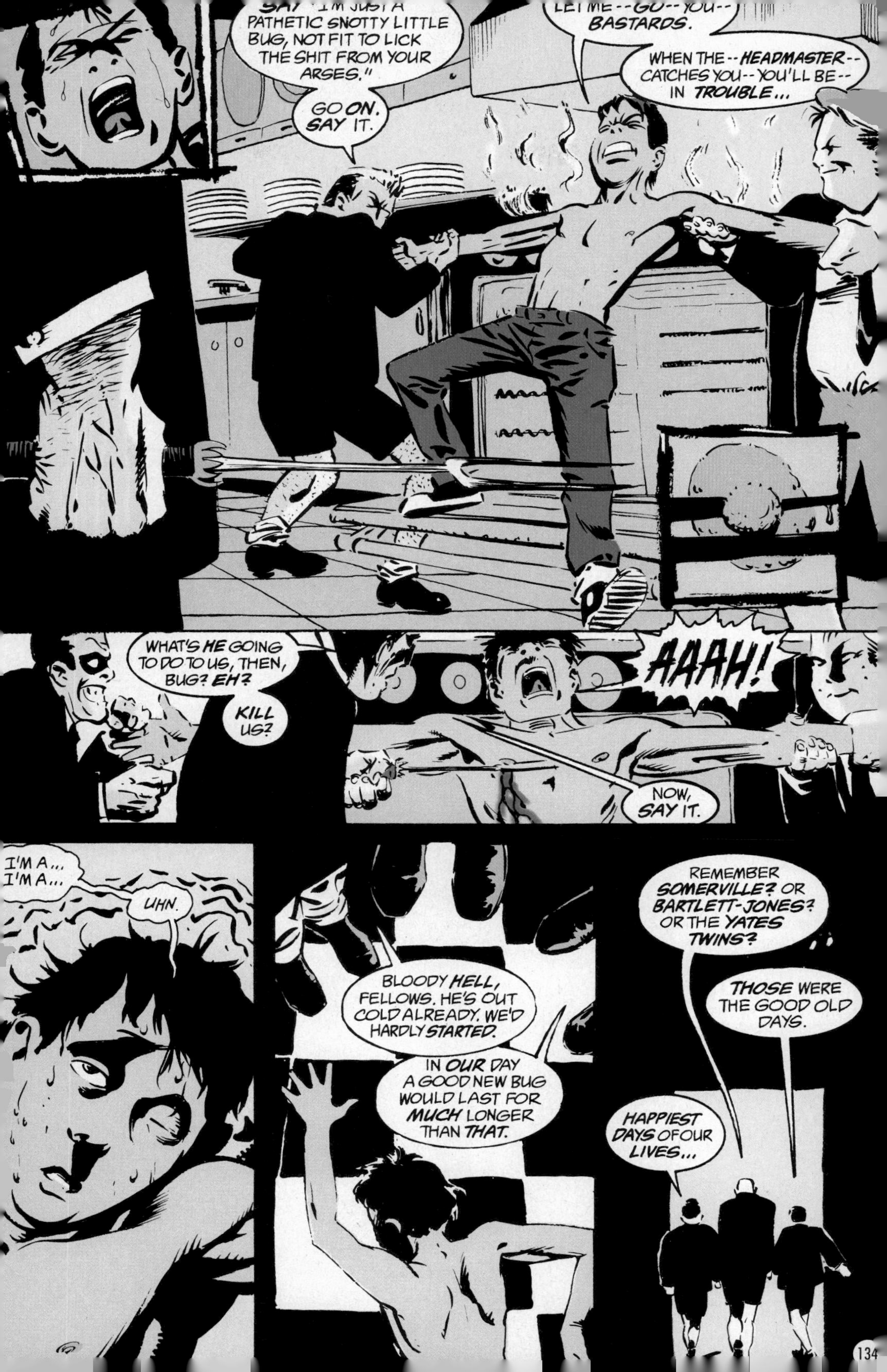
SAY "I'M JUST A PATHETIC SNOTTY LITTLE BUG, NOT FIT TO LICK THE SHIT FROM YOUR ARSES."
GO ON. SAY IT.
LET ME--GO--YOU--BASTARDS.
WHEN THE--HEADMASTER--CATCHES YOU--YOU'LL BE--IN TROUBLE...
WHAT'S HE GOING TO DO TO US, THEN, BUG? EH?
KILL US?
AAAH!
NOW, SAY IT.
I'M A... I'M A...
UHN.
BLOODY HELL, FELLOWS. HE'S OUT COLD ALREADY. WE'D HARDLY STARTED.
IN OUR DAY A GOOD NEW BUG WOULD LAST FOR MUCH LONGER THAN THAT.
REMEMBER SOMERVILLE? OR BARTLETT-JONES? OR THE YATES TWINS?
THOSE WERE THE GOOD OLD DAYS.
HAPPIEST DAYS OF OUR LIVES...

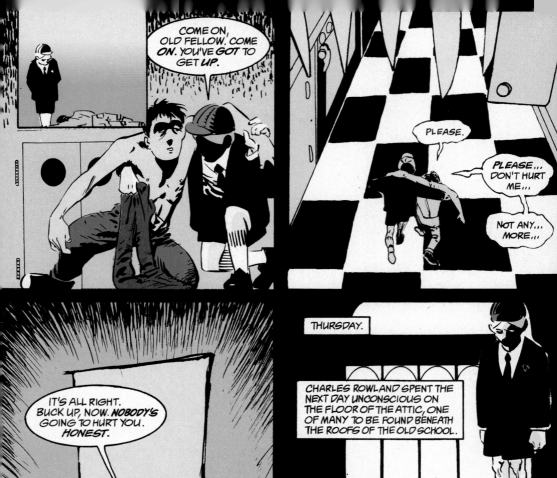

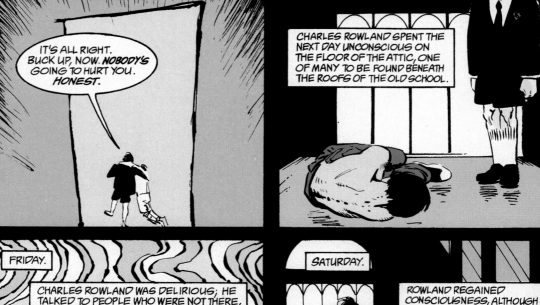

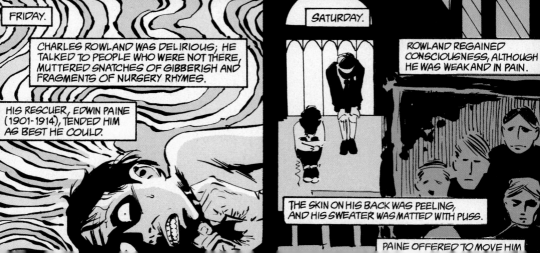

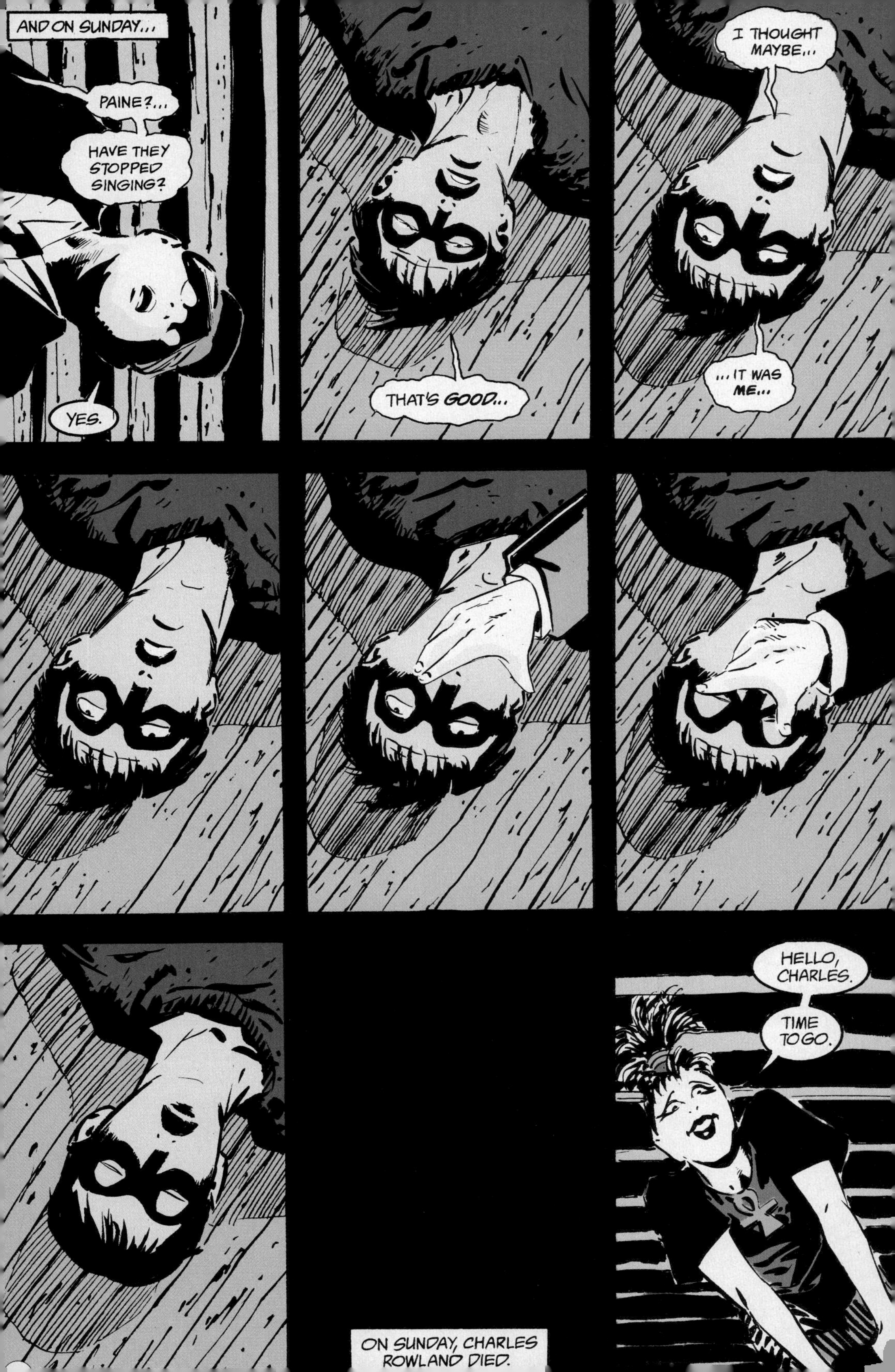
AND ON SUNDAY...
PAINE?...
HAVE THEY STOPPED SINGING?
YES.
THAT'S GOOD...
I THOUGHT MAYBE...
...IT WAS ME...
HELLO, CHARLES.
TIME TO GO.
ON SUNDAY, CHARLES ROWLAND DIED.

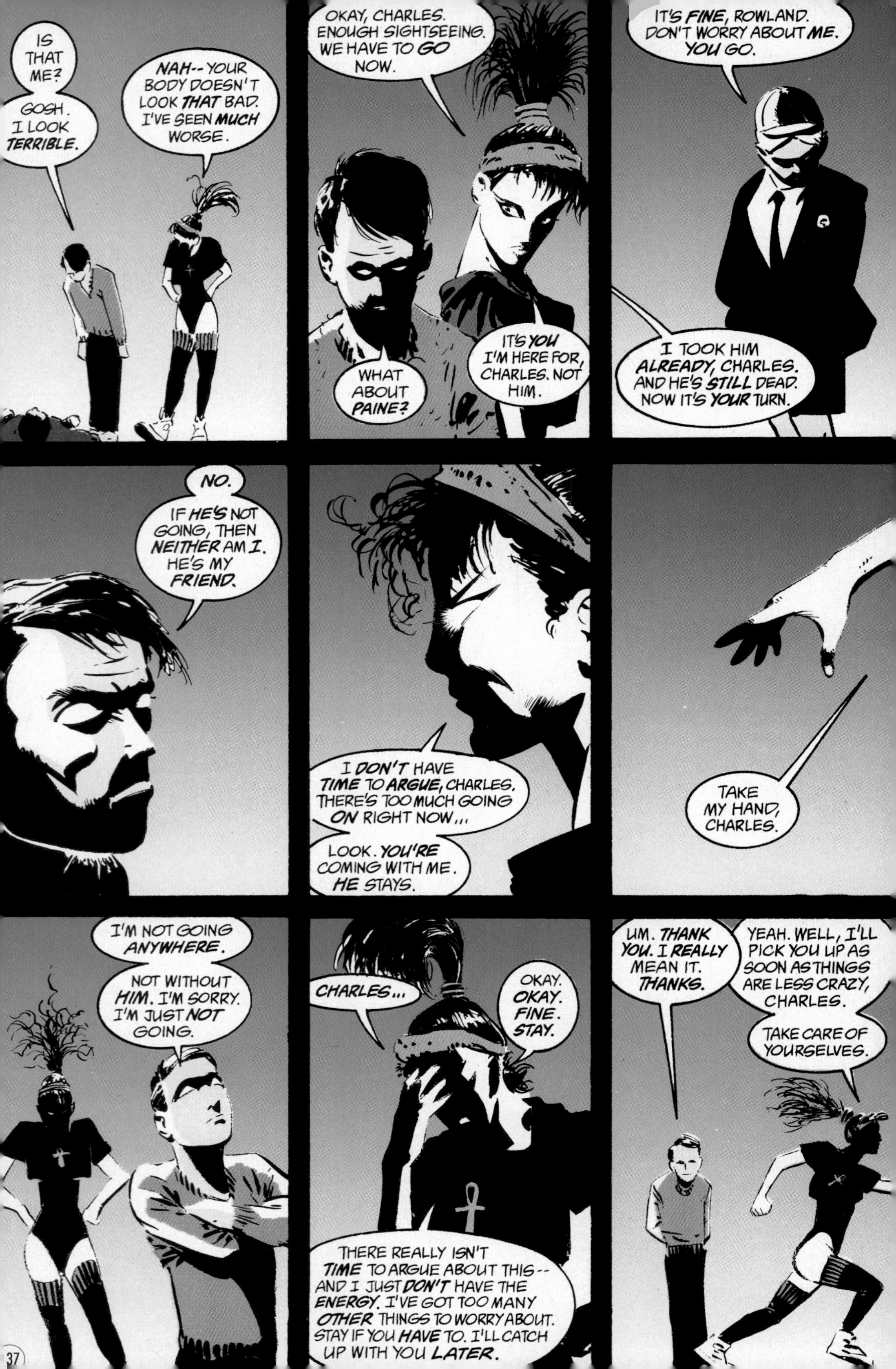
IS THAT ME?
GOSH. I LOOK TERRIBLE.
NAH-- YOUR BODY DOESN'T LOOK THAT BAD. I'VE SEEN MUCH WORSE.
OKAY, CHARLES. ENOUGH SIGHTSEEING. WE HAVE TO GO NOW.
WHAT ABOUT PAINE?
IT'S YOU I'M HERE FOR, CHARLES. NOT HIM.
IT'S FINE, ROWLAND. DON'T WORRY ABOUT ME. YOU GO.
I TOOK HIM ALREADY, CHARLES. AND HE'S STILL DEAD. NOW IT'S YOUR TURN.
NO.
IF HE'S NOT GOING, THEN NEITHER AM I. HE'S MY FRIEND.
I DON'T HAVE TIME TO ARGUE, CHARLES. THERE'S TOO MUCH GOING ON RIGHT NOW...
LOOK. YOU'RE COMING WITH ME. HE STAYS.
TAKE MY HAND, CHARLES.
I'M NOT GOING ANYWHERE.
NOT WITHOUT HIM. I'M SORRY. I'M JUST NOT GOING.
CHARLES...
OKAY. OKAY. FINE. STAY.
THERE REALLY ISN'T TIME TO ARGUE ABOUT THIS-- AND I JUST DON'T HAVE THE ENERGY. I'VE GOT TOO MANY OTHER THINGS TO WORRY ABOUT. STAY IF YOU HAVE TO. I'LL CATCH UP WITH YOU LATER.
UM. THANK YOU. I REALLY MEAN IT. THANKS.
YEAH. WELL, I'LL PICK YOU UP AS SOON AS THINGS ARE LESS CRAZY, CHARLES.
TAKE CARE OF YOURSELVES.

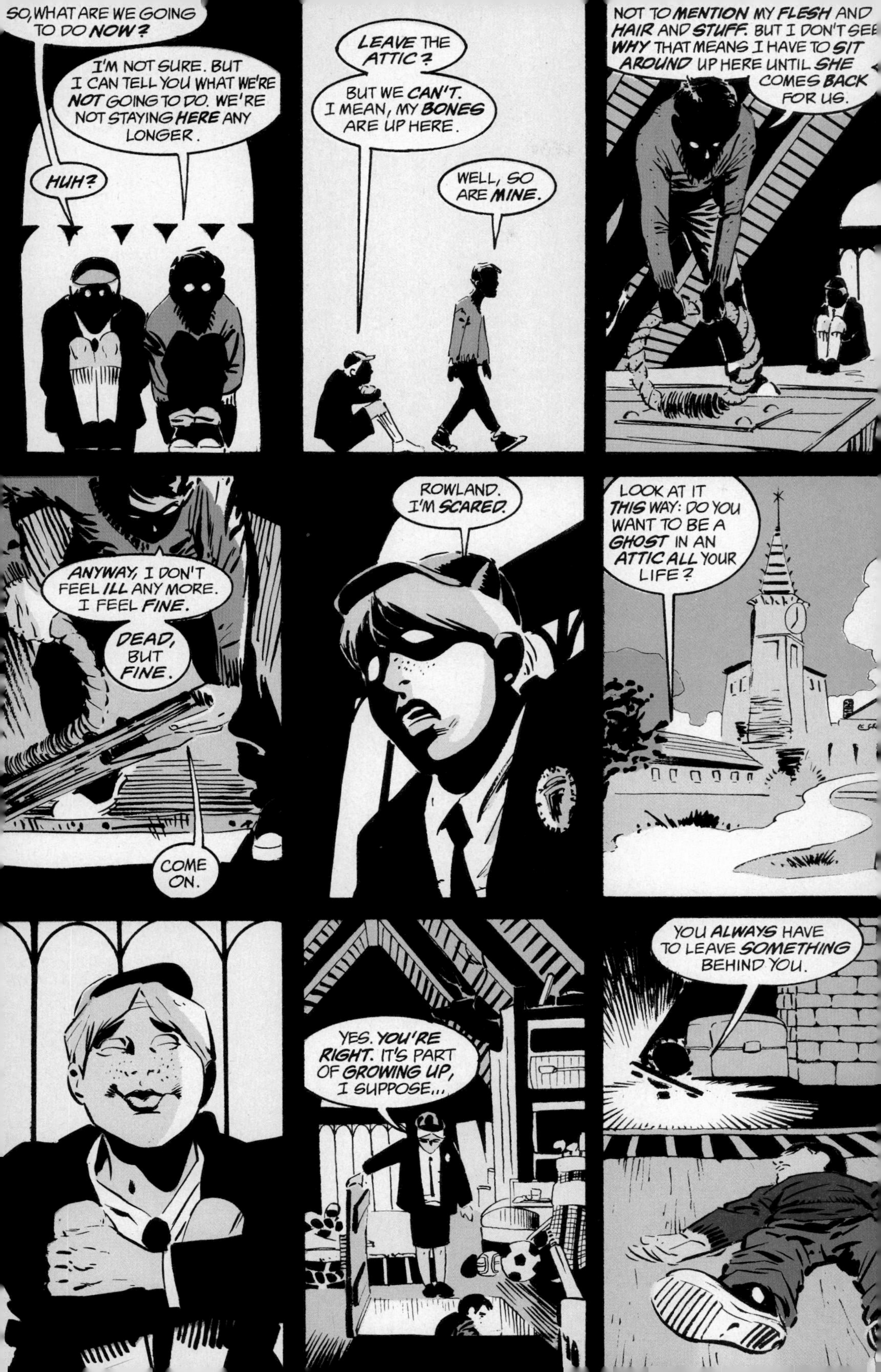
SO, WHAT ARE WE GOING TO DO NOW?
I'M NOT SURE. BUT I CAN TELL YOU WHAT WE'RE NOT GOING TO DO. WE'RE NOT STAYING HERE ANY LONGER.
HUH?
LEAVE THE ATTIC?
BUT WE CAN'T. I MEAN, MY BONES ARE UP HERE.
WELL, SO ARE MINE.
NOT TO MENTION MY FLESH AND HAIR AND STUFF. BUT I DON'T SEE WHY THAT MEANS I HAVE TO SIT AROUND UP HERE UNTIL SHE COMES BACK FOR US.
ANYWAY, I DON'T FEEL ILL ANY MORE. I FEEL FINE.
DEAD, BUT FINE.
COME ON.
ROWLAND. I'M SCARED.
LOOK AT IT THIS WAY: DO YOU WANT TO BE A GHOST IN AN ATTIC ALL YOUR LIFE?
YES. YOU'RE RIGHT. IT'S PART OF GROWING UP, I SUPPOSE...
YOU ALWAYS HAVE TO LEAVE SOMETHING BEHIND YOU.

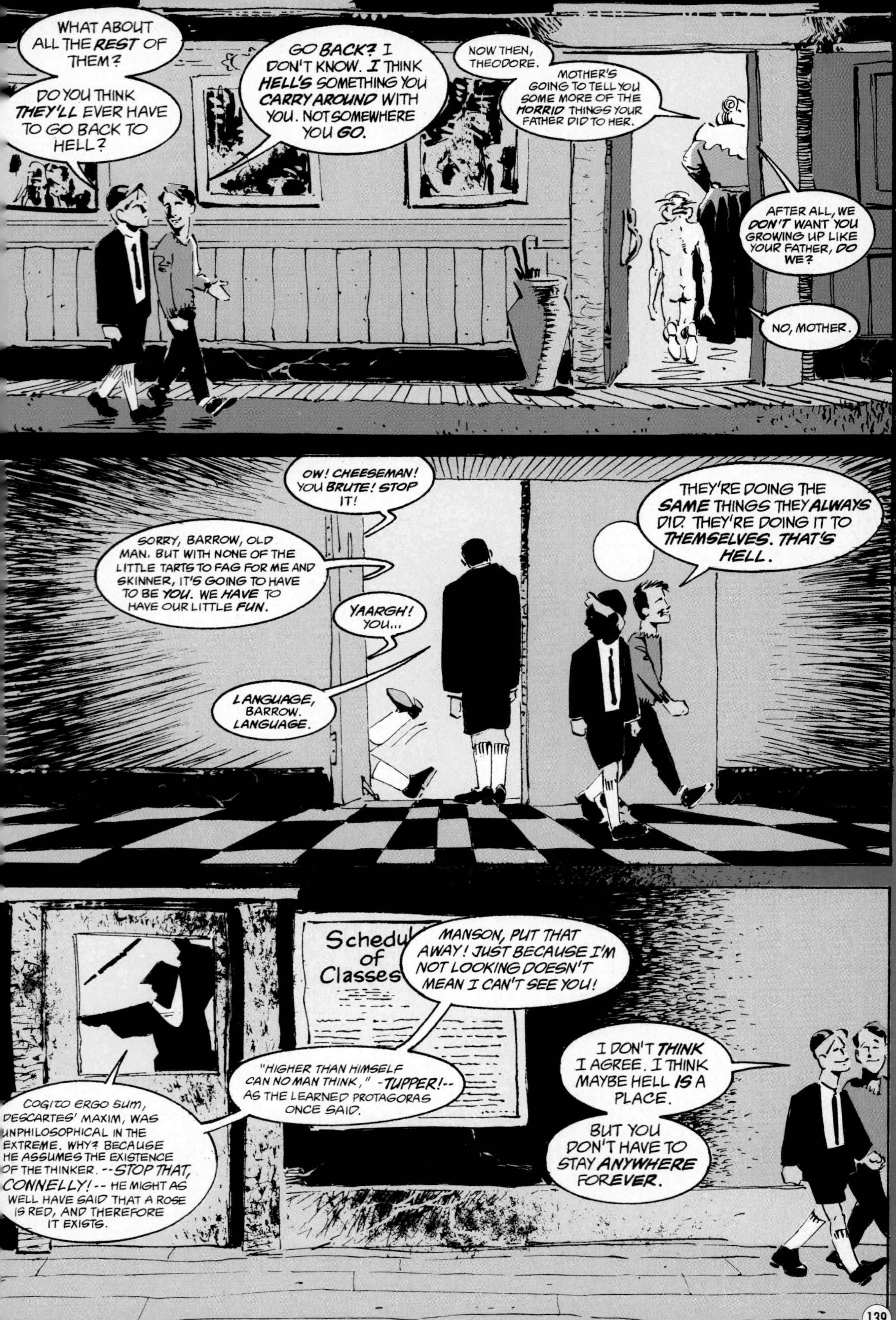
WHAT ABOUT ALL THE REST OF THEM?
DO YOU THINK THEY'LL EVER HAVE TO GO BACK TO HELL?
GO BACK? I DON'T KNOW. I THINK HELL'S SOMETHING YOU CARRY AROUND WITH YOU. NOT SOMEWHERE YOU GO.
NOW THEN, THEODORE.
MOTHER'S GOING TO TELL YOU SOME MORE OF THE HORRID THINGS YOUR FATHER DID TO HER.
AFTER ALL, WE DON'T WANT YOU GROWING UP LIKE YOUR FATHER, DO WE?
NO, MOTHER.
SORRY, BARROW, OLD MAN. BUT WITH NONE OF THE LITTLE TARTS TO FAG FOR ME AND SKINNER, IT'S GOING TO HAVE TO BE YOU. WE HAVE TO HAVE OUR LITTLE FUN.
OW! CHEESEMAN! YOU BRUTE! STOP IT!
YAARGH! YOU...
LANGUAGE, BARROW. LANGUAGE.
THEY'RE DOING THE SAME THINGS THEY ALWAYS DID. THEY'RE DOING IT TO THEMSELVES. THAT'S HELL.
COGITO ERGO SUM, DESCARTES' MAXIM, WAS UNPHILOSOPHICAL IN THE EXTREME. WHY? BECAUSE HE ASSUMES THE EXISTENCE OF THE THINKER. --STOP THAT, CONNELLY!-- HE MIGHT AS WELL HAVE SAID THAT A ROSE IS RED, AND THEREFORE IT EXISTS.
Schedul... of Classes
"HIGHER THAN HIMSELF CAN NO MAN THINK," -TUPPER!-- AS THE LEARNED PROTAGORAS ONCE SAID.
MANSON, PUT THAT AWAY! JUST BECAUSE I'M NOT LOOKING DOESN'T MEAN I CAN'T SEE YOU!
I DON'T THINK I AGREE. I THINK MAYBE HELL IS A PLACE.
BUT YOU DON'T HAVE TO STAY ANYWHERE FOREVER.

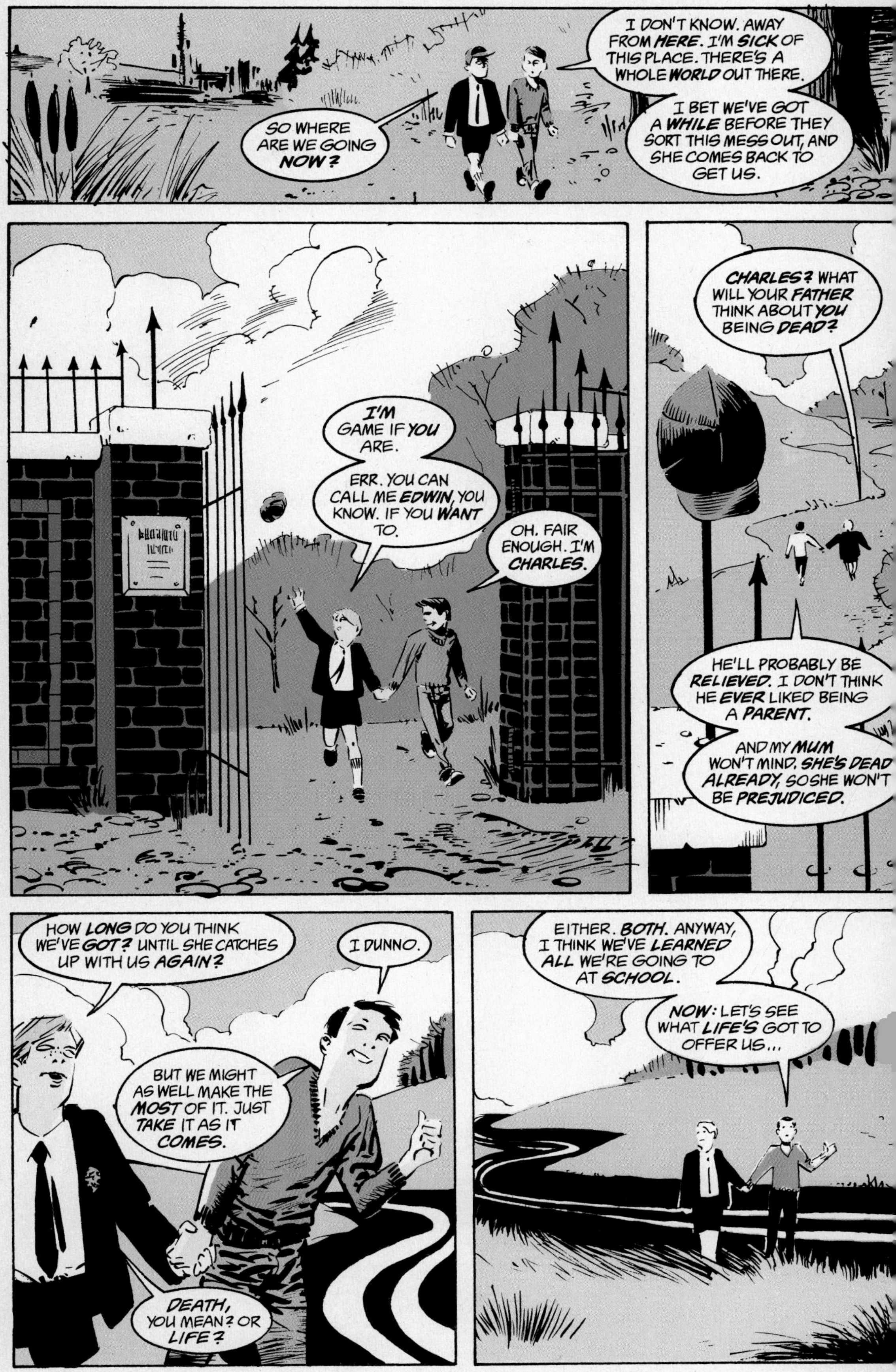
SO WHERE ARE WE GOING NOW?
I DON'T KNOW. AWAY FROM HERE. I'M SICK OF THIS PLACE. THERE'S A WHOLE WORLD OUT THERE.
I BET WE'VE GOT A WHILE BEFORE THEY SORT THIS MESS OUT, AND SHE COMES BACK TO GET US.
I'M GAME IF YOU ARE.
ERR. YOU CAN CALL ME EDWIN, YOU KNOW. IF YOU WANT TO.
OH. FAIR ENOUGH. I'M CHARLES.
CHARLES? WHAT WILL YOUR FATHER THINK ABOUT YOU BEING DEAD?
HE'LL PROBABLY BE RELIEVED. I DON'T THINK HE EVER LIKED BEING A PARENT.
AND MY MUM WON'T MIND. SHE'S DEAD ALREADY, SO SHE WON'T BE PREJUDICED.
HOW LONG DO YOU THINK WE'VE GOT? UNTIL SHE CATCHES UP WITH US AGAIN?
I DUNNO.
BUT WE MIGHT AS WELL MAKE THE MOST OF IT. JUST TAKE IT AS IT COMES.
DEATH, YOU MEAN? OR LIFE?
EITHER. BOTH. ANYWAY, I THINK WE'VE LEARNED ALL WE'RE GOING TO AT SCHOOL.
NOW: LET'S SEE WHAT LIFE'S GOT TO OFFER US...

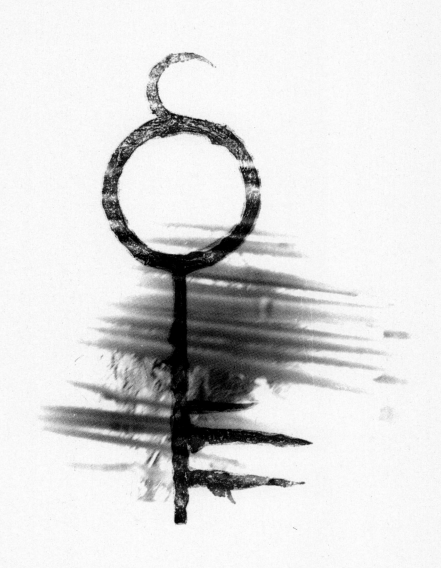

In which a banquet is held, and of what comes after; concerning diplomacy and bedrooms, blackmail and threats; and an unusual recipe for sausages.

EPISODE 5

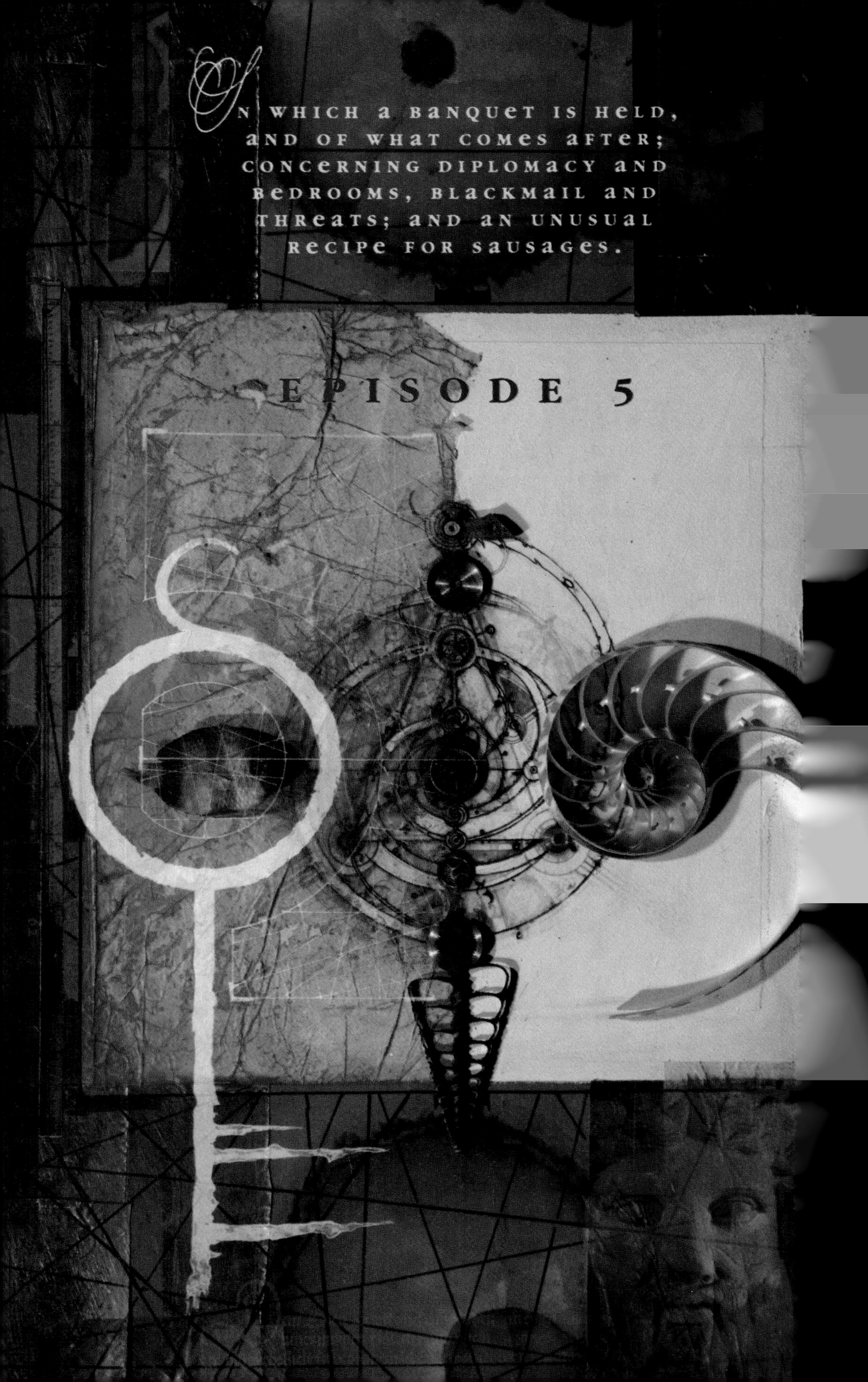

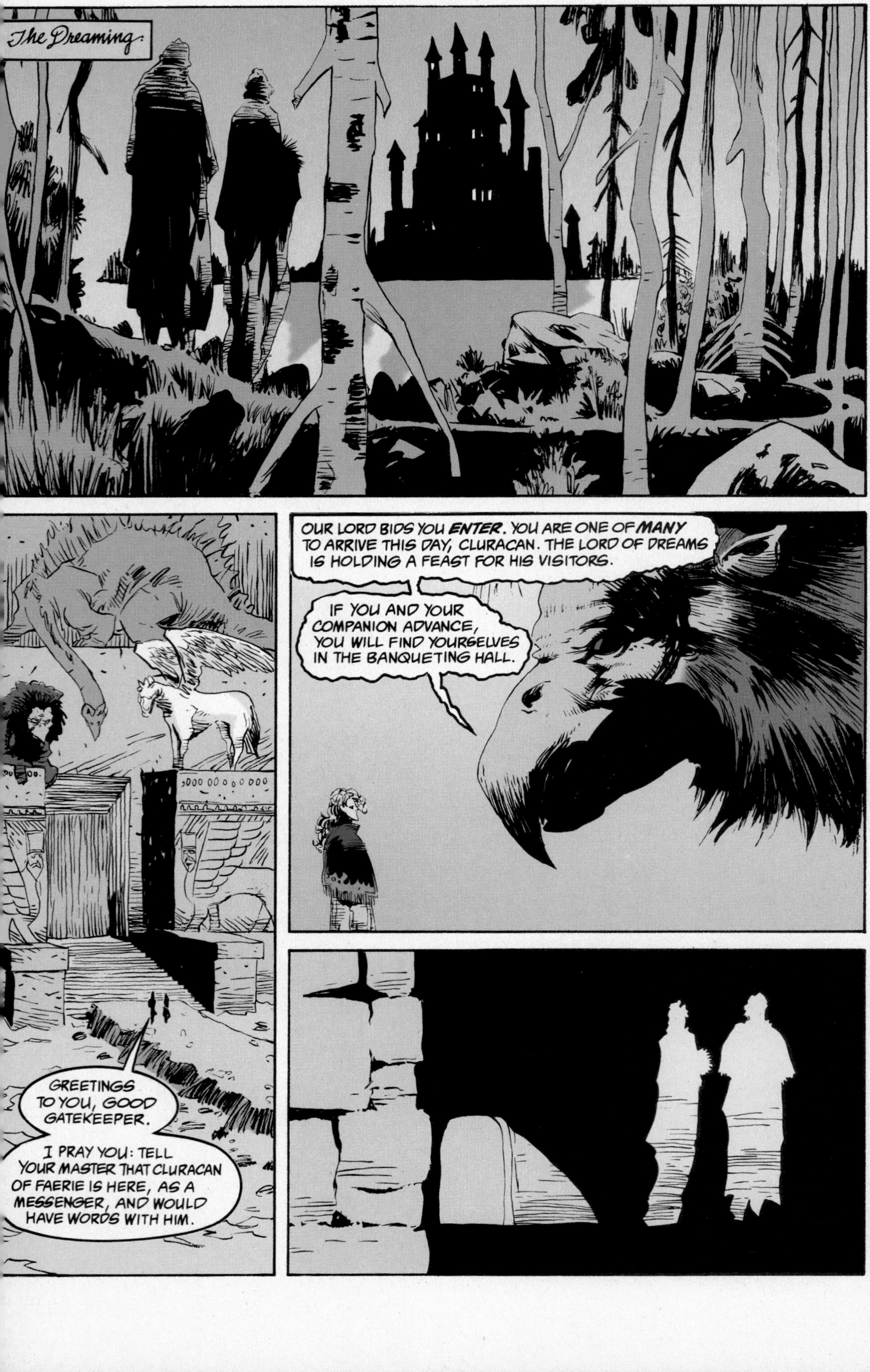
The Dreaming:
GREETINGS TO YOU, GOOD GATEKEEPER.
I PRAY YOU: TELL YOUR MASTER THAT CLURACAN OF FAERIE IS HERE, AS A MESSENGER, AND WOULD HAVE WORDS WITH HIM.
OUR LORD BIDS YOU ENTER. YOU ARE ONE OF MANY TO ARRIVE THIS DAY, CLURACAN. THE LORD OF DREAMS IS HOLDING A FEAST FOR HIS VISITORS.
IF YOU AND YOUR COMPANION ADVANCE, YOU WILL FIND YOURSELVES IN THE BANQUETING HALL.

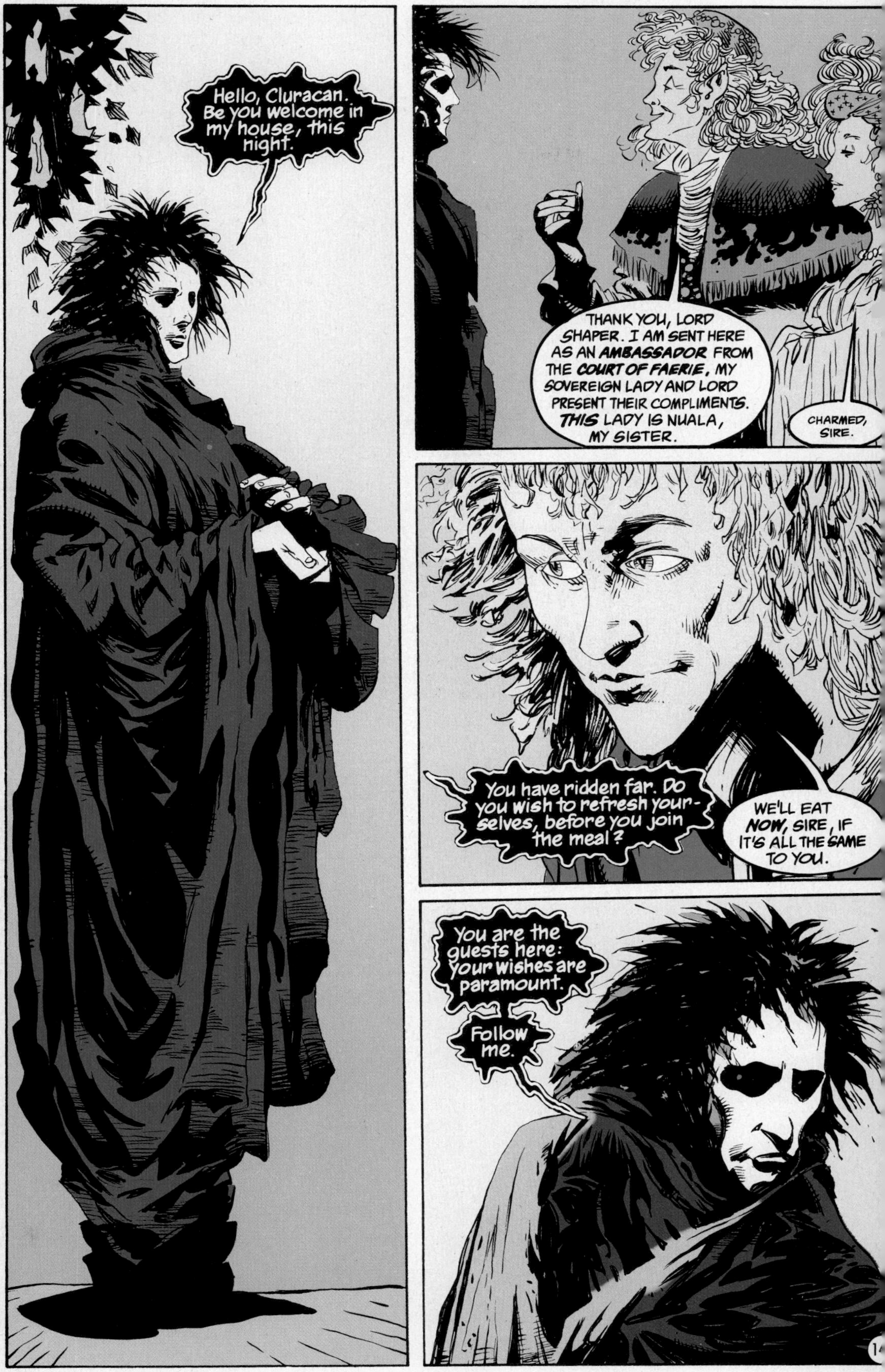

Hello, Cluracan. Be you welcome in my house, this night.
THANK YOU, LORD SHAPER. I AM SENT HERE AS AN **AMBASSADOR** FROM THE **COURT OF FAERIE**, MY SOVEREIGN LADY AND LORD PRESENT THEIR COMPLIMENTS. **THIS** LADY IS NUALA, MY SISTER.
CHARMED, SIRE.
You have ridden far. Do you wish to refresh yourselves, before you join the meal?
WE'LL EAT **NOW**, SIRE, IF IT'S ALL THE SAME TO YOU.
You are the guests here: your wishes are paramount.
Follow me.

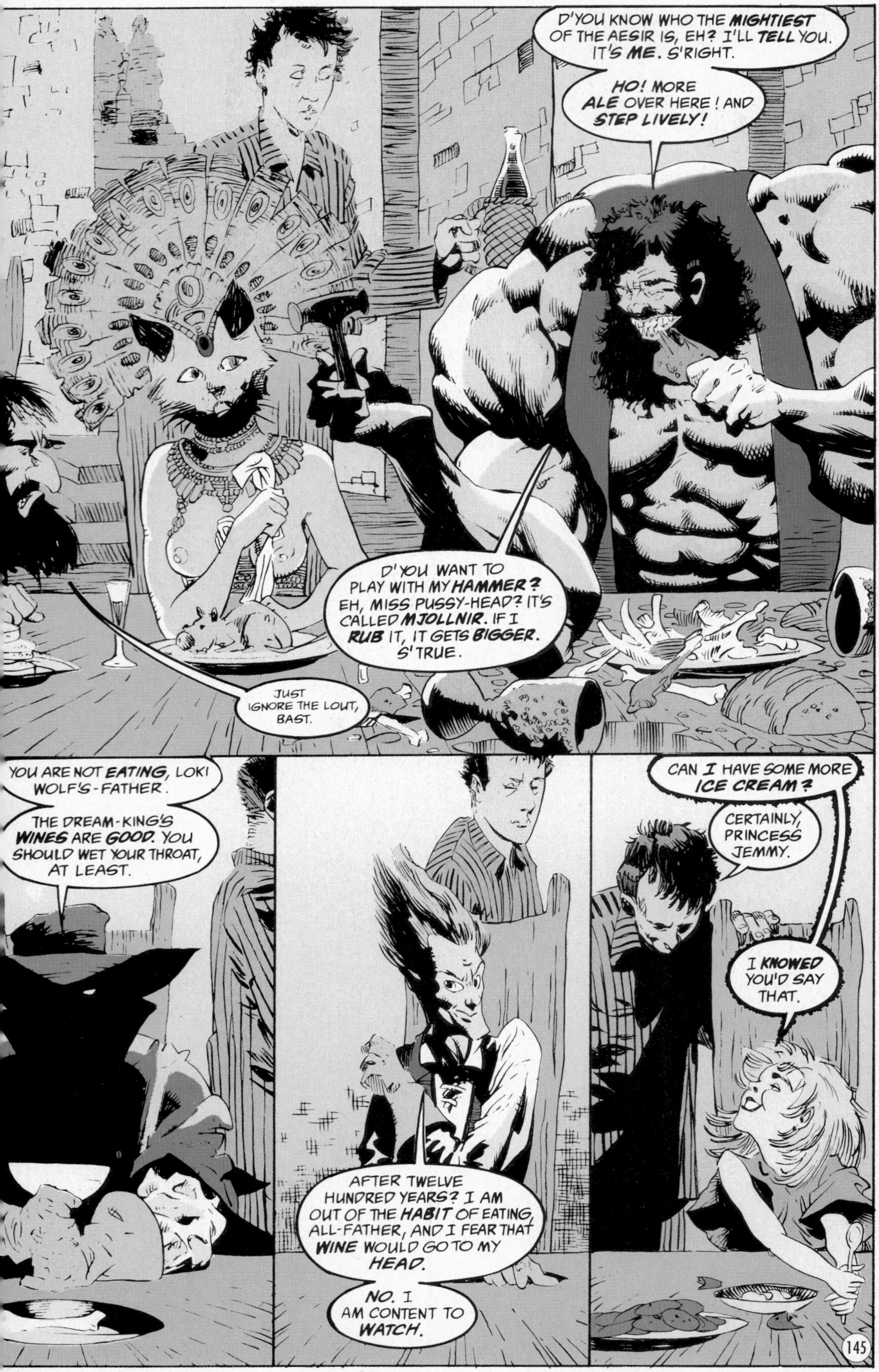
D'YOU KNOW WHO THE MIGHTIEST OF THE AESIR IS, EH? I'LL TELL YOU. IT'S ME. S'RIGHT.
HO! MORE ALE OVER HERE! AND STEP LIVELY!
D'YOU WANT TO PLAY WITH MY HAMMER? EH, MISS PUSSY-HEAD? IT'S CALLED MJOLLNIR. IF I RUB IT, IT GETS BIGGER. S'TRUE.
JUST IGNORE THE LOUT, BAST.
YOU ARE NOT EATING, LOKI WOLF'S-FATHER.
THE DREAM-KING'S WINES ARE GOOD. YOU SHOULD WET YOUR THROAT, AT LEAST.
AFTER TWELVE HUNDRED YEARS? I AM OUT OF THE HABIT OF EATING, ALL-FATHER, AND I FEAR THAT WINE WOULD GO TO MY HEAD.
NO. I AM CONTENT TO WATCH.
CAN I HAVE SOME MORE ICE CREAM?
CERTAINLY, PRINCESS JEMMY.
I KNOWED YOU'D SAY THAT.

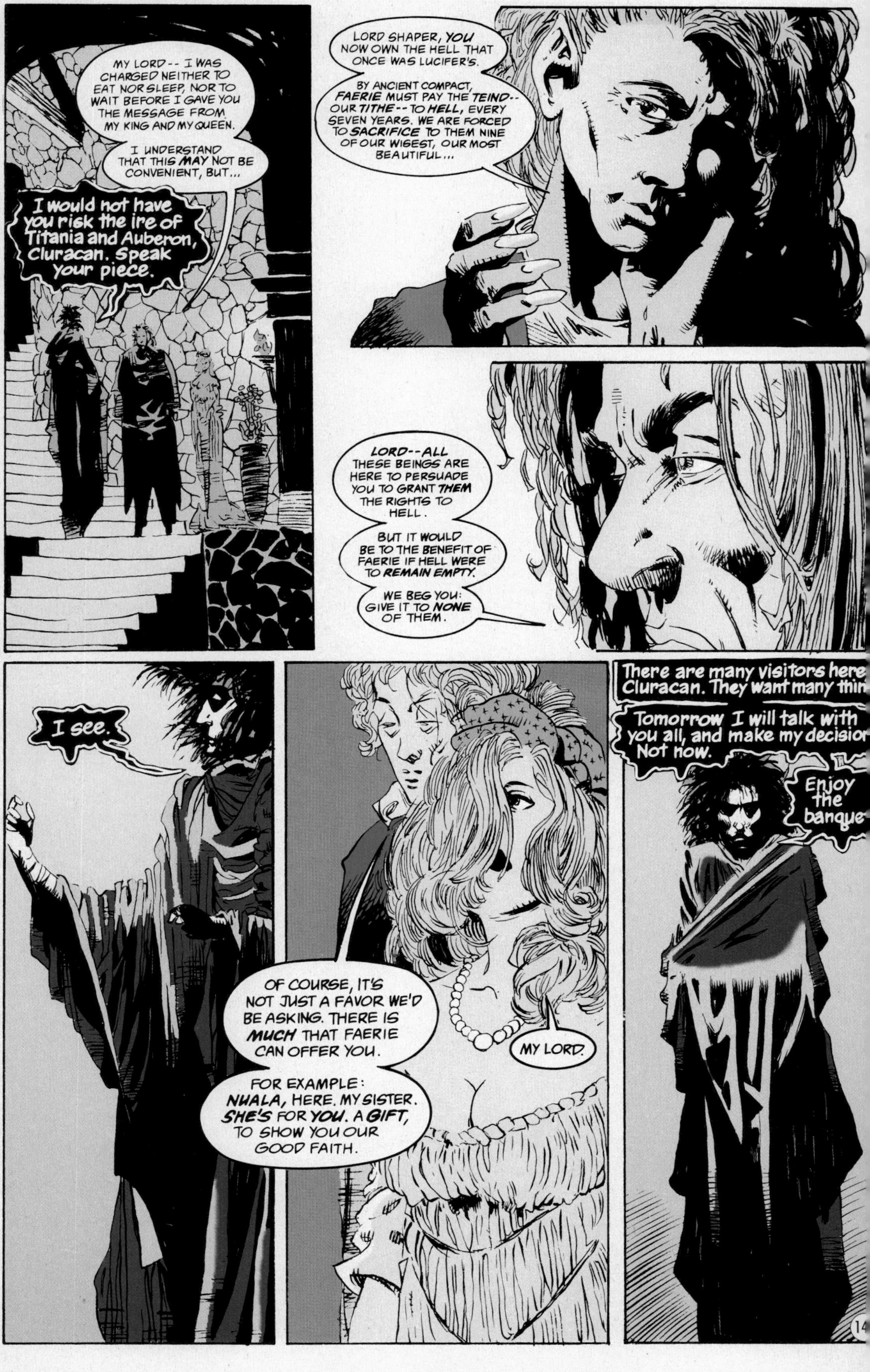

MY LORD -- I WAS CHARGED NEITHER TO EAT NOR SLEEP, NOR TO WAIT BEFORE I GAVE YOU THE MESSAGE FROM MY KING AND MY QUEEN.
I UNDERSTAND THAT THIS MAY NOT BE CONVENIENT, BUT...
I would not have you risk the ire of Titania and Auberon, Cluracan. Speak your piece.
LORD SHAPER, YOU NOW OWN THE HELL THAT ONCE WAS LUCIFER'S.
BY ANCIENT COMPACT, FAERIE MUST PAY THE TEIND-- OUR TITHE -- TO HELL, EVERY SEVEN YEARS. WE ARE FORCED TO SACRIFICE TO THEM NINE OF OUR WISEST, OUR MOST BEAUTIFUL...
LORD--ALL THESE BEINGS ARE HERE TO PERSUADE YOU TO GRANT THEM THE RIGHTS TO HELL.
BUT IT WOULD BE TO THE BENEFIT OF FAERIE IF HELL WERE TO REMAIN EMPTY.
WE BEG YOU: GIVE IT TO NONE OF THEM.
I see.
OF COURSE, IT'S NOT JUST A FAVOR WE'D BE ASKING. THERE IS MUCH THAT FAERIE CAN OFFER YOU.
FOR EXAMPLE: NUALA, HERE. MY SISTER. SHE'S FOR YOU. A GIFT, TO SHOW YOU OUR GOOD FAITH.
MY LORD.
There are many visitors here Cluracan. They want many thin
Tomorrow I will talk with you all, and make my decisio Not now.
Enjoy the banque

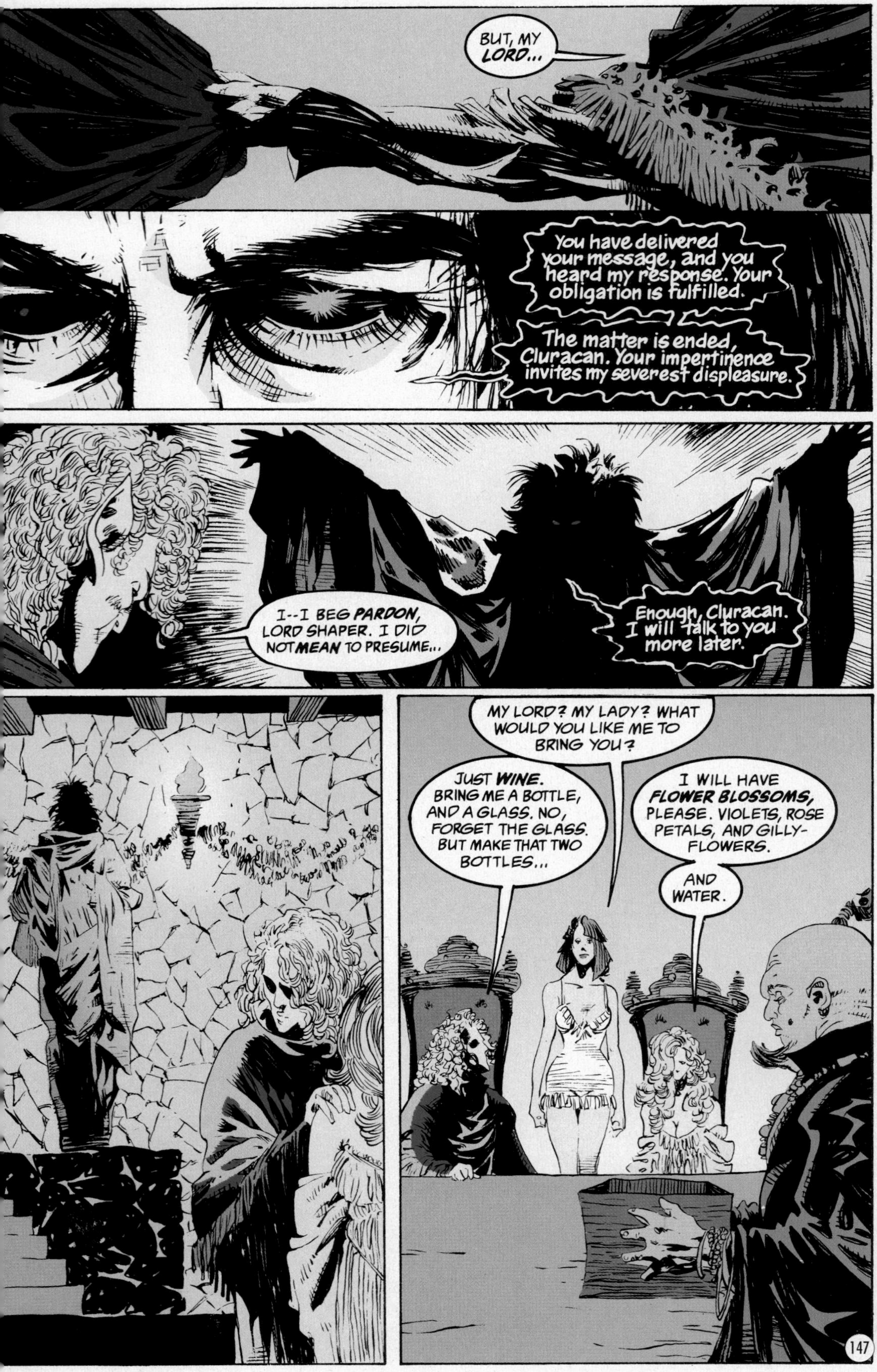
BUT, MY LORD...
You have delivered your message, and you heard my response. Your obligation is fulfilled.
The matter is ended, Cluracan. Your impertinence invites my severest displeasure.
I--I BEG PARDON, LORD SHAPER. I DID NOT MEAN TO PRESUME...
Enough, Cluracan. I will talk to you more later.
MY LORD? MY LADY? WHAT WOULD YOU LIKE ME TO BRING YOU?
JUST WINE. BRING ME A BOTTLE, AND A GLASS. NO, FORGET THE GLASS. BUT MAKE THAT TWO BOTTLES...
I WILL HAVE FLOWER BLOSSOMS, PLEASE. VIOLETS, ROSE PETALS, AND GILLY-FLOWERS.
AND WATER.

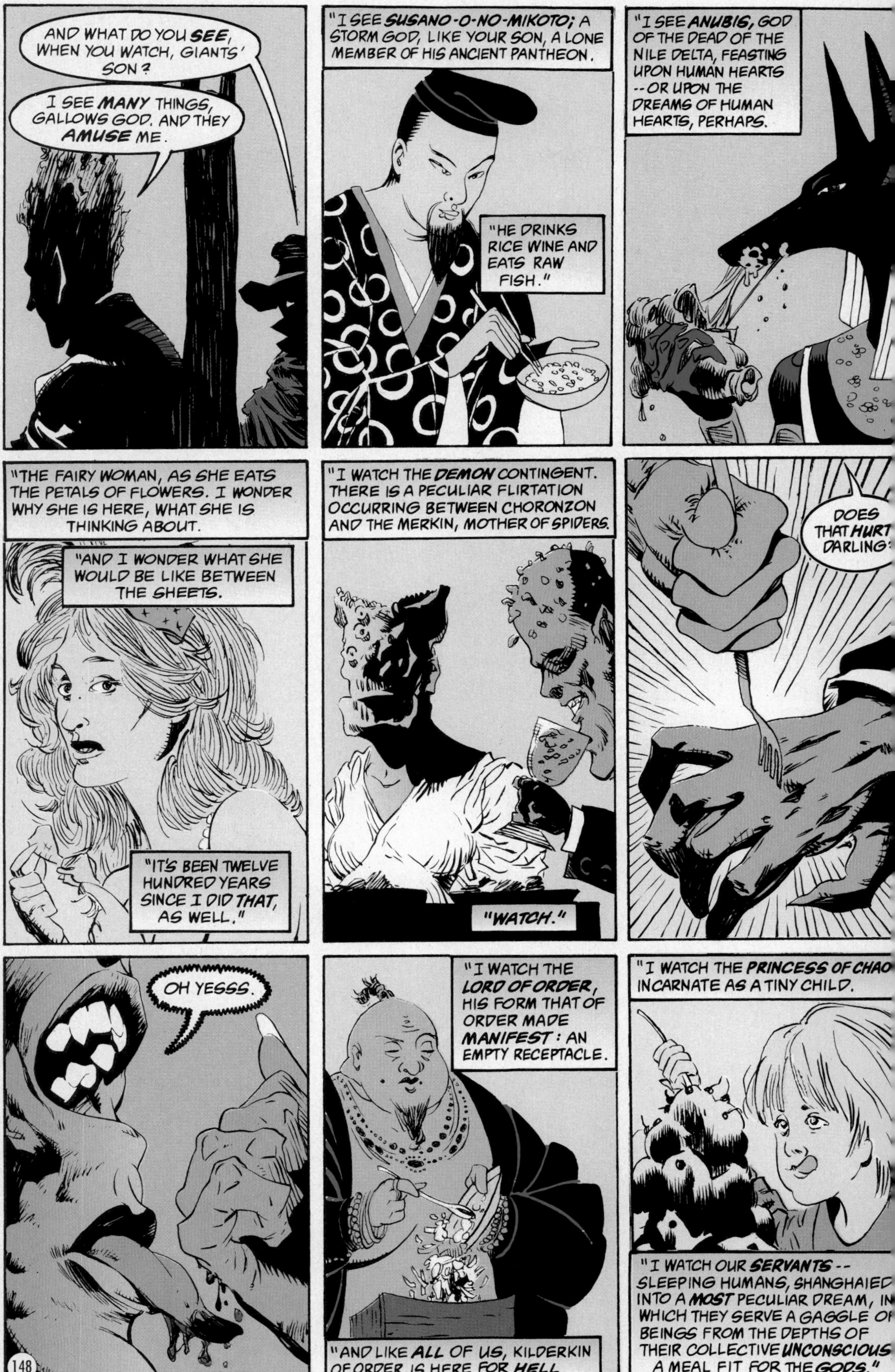
AND WHAT DO YOU SEE, WHEN YOU WATCH, GIANTS' SON?
I SEE MANY THINGS, GALLOWS GOD. AND THEY AMUSE ME.
"I SEE SUSANO-O-NO-MIKOTO; A STORM GOD, LIKE YOUR SON, A LONE MEMBER OF HIS ANCIENT PANTHEON.
"HE DRINKS RICE WINE AND EATS RAW FISH."
"I SEE ANUBIS, GOD OF THE DEAD OF THE NILE DELTA, FEASTING UPON HUMAN HEARTS --OR UPON THE DREAMS OF HUMAN HEARTS, PERHAPS.
"THE FAIRY WOMAN, AS SHE EATS THE PETALS OF FLOWERS. I WONDER WHY SHE IS HERE, WHAT SHE IS THINKING ABOUT.
"AND I WONDER WHAT SHE WOULD BE LIKE BETWEEN THE SHEETS.
"IT'S BEEN TWELVE HUNDRED YEARS SINCE I DID THAT, AS WELL."
"I WATCH THE DEMON CONTINGENT. THERE IS A PECULIAR FLIRTATION OCCURRING BETWEEN CHORONZON AND THE MERKIN, MOTHER OF SPIDERS.
"WATCH."
DOES THAT HURT DARLING
OH YESSS.
"I WATCH THE LORD OF ORDER, HIS FORM THAT OF ORDER MADE MANIFEST: AN EMPTY RECEPTACLE.
"AND LIKE ALL OF US, KILDERKIN OF ORDER IS HERE FOR HELL.
"I WATCH THE PRINCESS OF CHAO INCARNATE AS A TINY CHILD.
"I WATCH OUR SERVANTS -- SLEEPING HUMANS, SHANGHAIED INTO A MOST PECULIAR DREAM, IN WHICH THEY SERVE A GAGGLE OF BEINGS FROM THE DEPTHS OF THEIR COLLECTIVE UNCONSCIOUS A MEAL FIT FOR THE GODS."

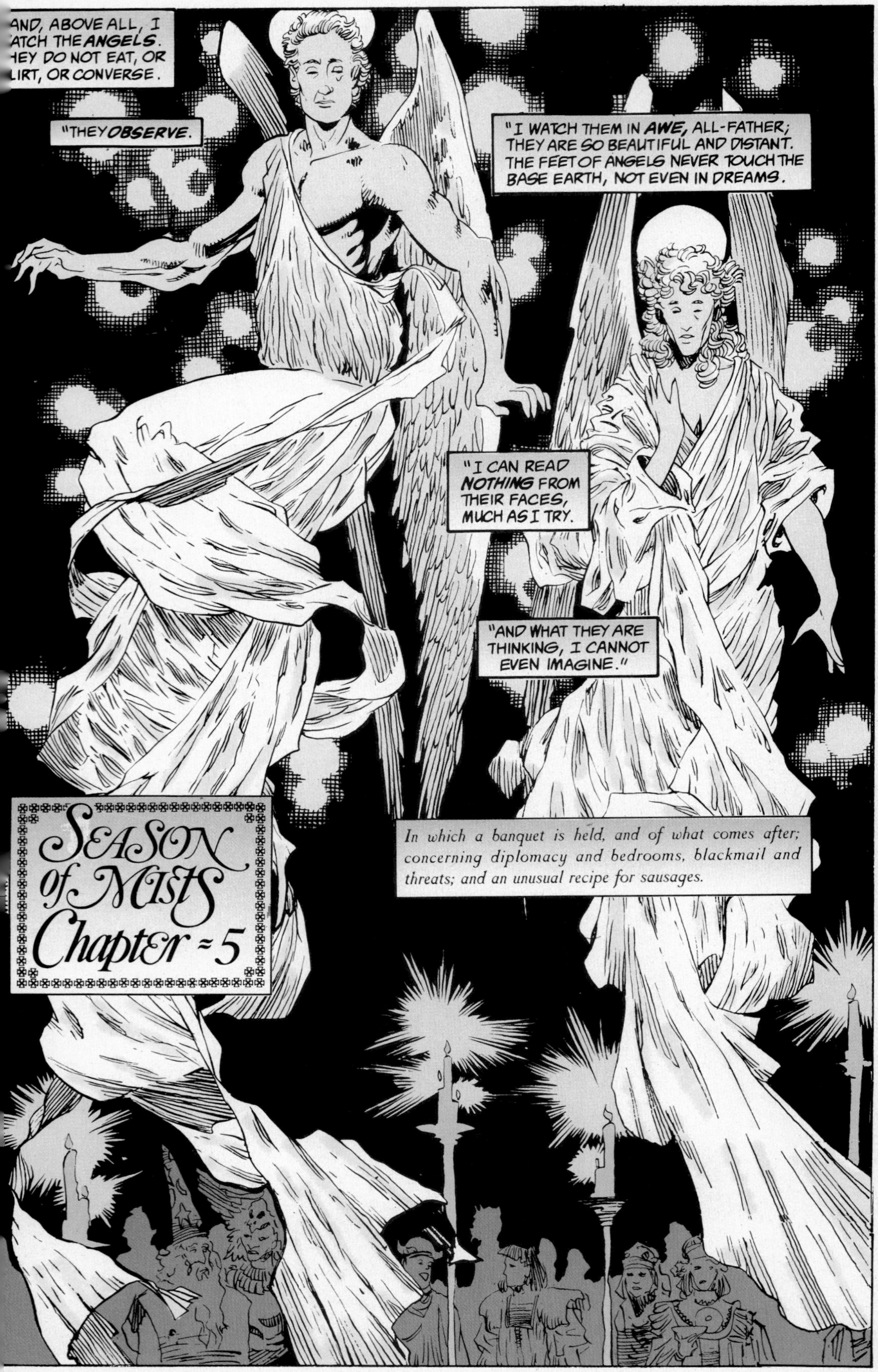
AND, ABOVE ALL, I WATCH THE ANGELS. THEY DO NOT EAT, OR FLIRT, OR CONVERSE.
"THEY OBSERVE.
"I WATCH THEM IN AWE, ALL-FATHER; THEY ARE SO BEAUTIFUL AND DISTANT. THE FEET OF ANGELS NEVER TOUCH THE BASE EARTH, NOT EVEN IN DREAMS.
"I CAN READ NOTHING FROM THEIR FACES, MUCH AS I TRY.
"AND WHAT THEY ARE THINKING, I CANNOT EVEN IMAGINE."
SEASON of MISTS Chapter 5
In which a banquet is held, and of what comes after; concerning diplomacy and bedrooms, blackmail and threats; and an unusual recipe for sausages.

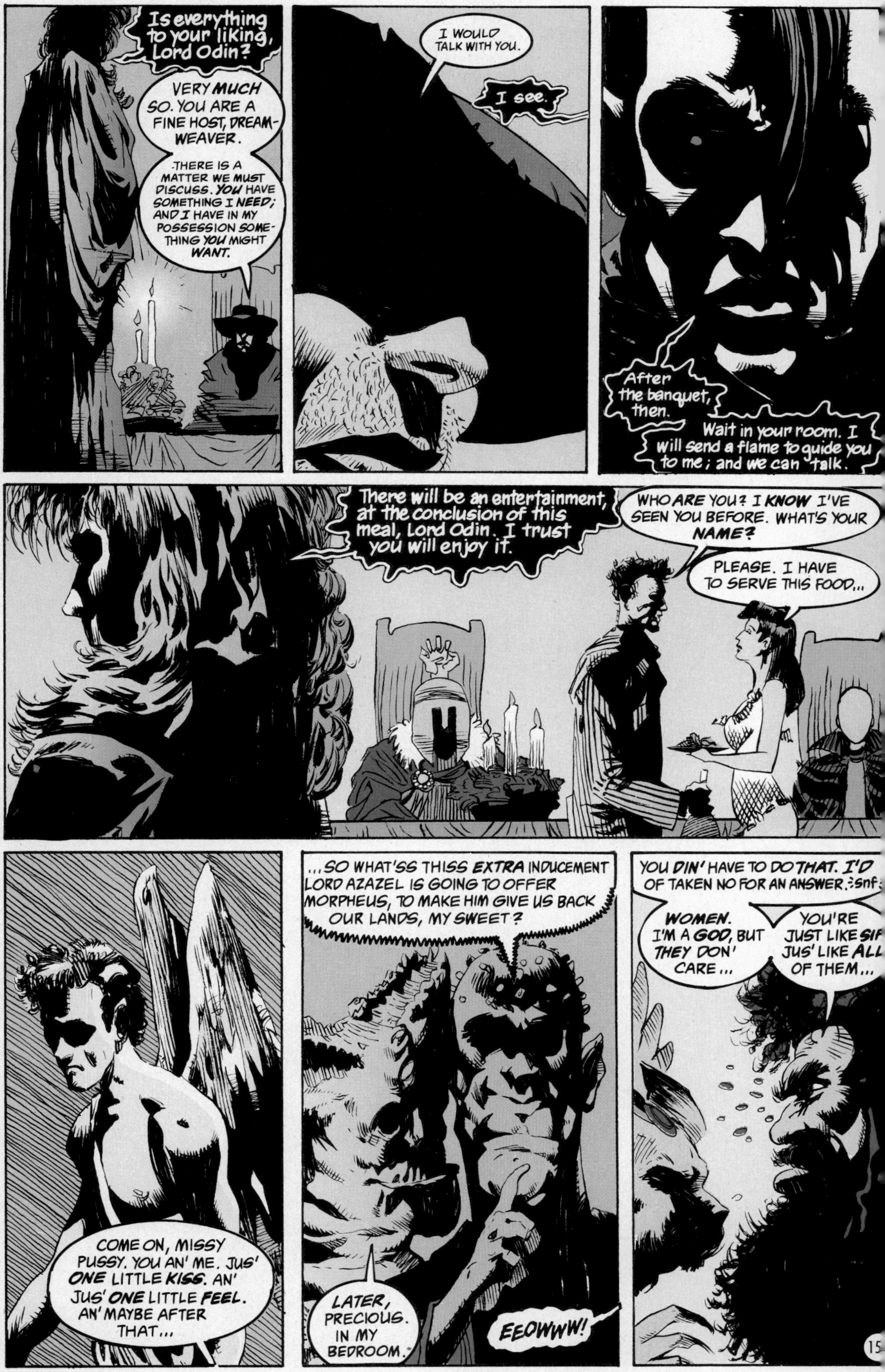
Is everything to your liking, Lord Odin?
VERY MUCH SO. YOU ARE A FINE HOST, DREAM-WEAVER.
THERE IS A MATTER WE MUST DISCUSS. YOU HAVE SOMETHING I NEED; AND I HAVE IN MY POSSESSION SOMETHING YOU MIGHT WANT.
I WOULD TALK WITH YOU.
I see.
After the banquet, then.
Wait in your room. I will send a flame to guide you to me; and we can talk.
There will be an entertainment, at the conclusion of this meal, Lord Odin. I trust you will enjoy it.
WHO ARE YOU? I KNOW I'VE SEEN YOU BEFORE. WHAT'S YOUR NAME?
PLEASE. I HAVE TO SERVE THIS FOOD...
COME ON, MISSY PUSSY. YOU AN' ME. JUS' ONE LITTLE KISS. AN' JUS' ONE LITTLE FEEL. AN' MAYBE AFTER THAT...
...SO WHAT'SS THISS EXTRA INDUCEMENT LORD AZAZEL IS GOING TO OFFER MORPHEUS, TO MAKE HIM GIVE US BACK OUR LANDS, MY SWEET?
LATER, PRECIOUS. IN MY BEDROOM.
EEOWWW!
YOU DIN' HAVE TO DO THAT. I'D OF TAKEN NO FOR AN ANSWER. snf
WOMEN. I'M A GOD, BUT THEY DON' CARE...
YOU'RE JUST LIKE SIF JUS' LIKE ALL OF THEM...

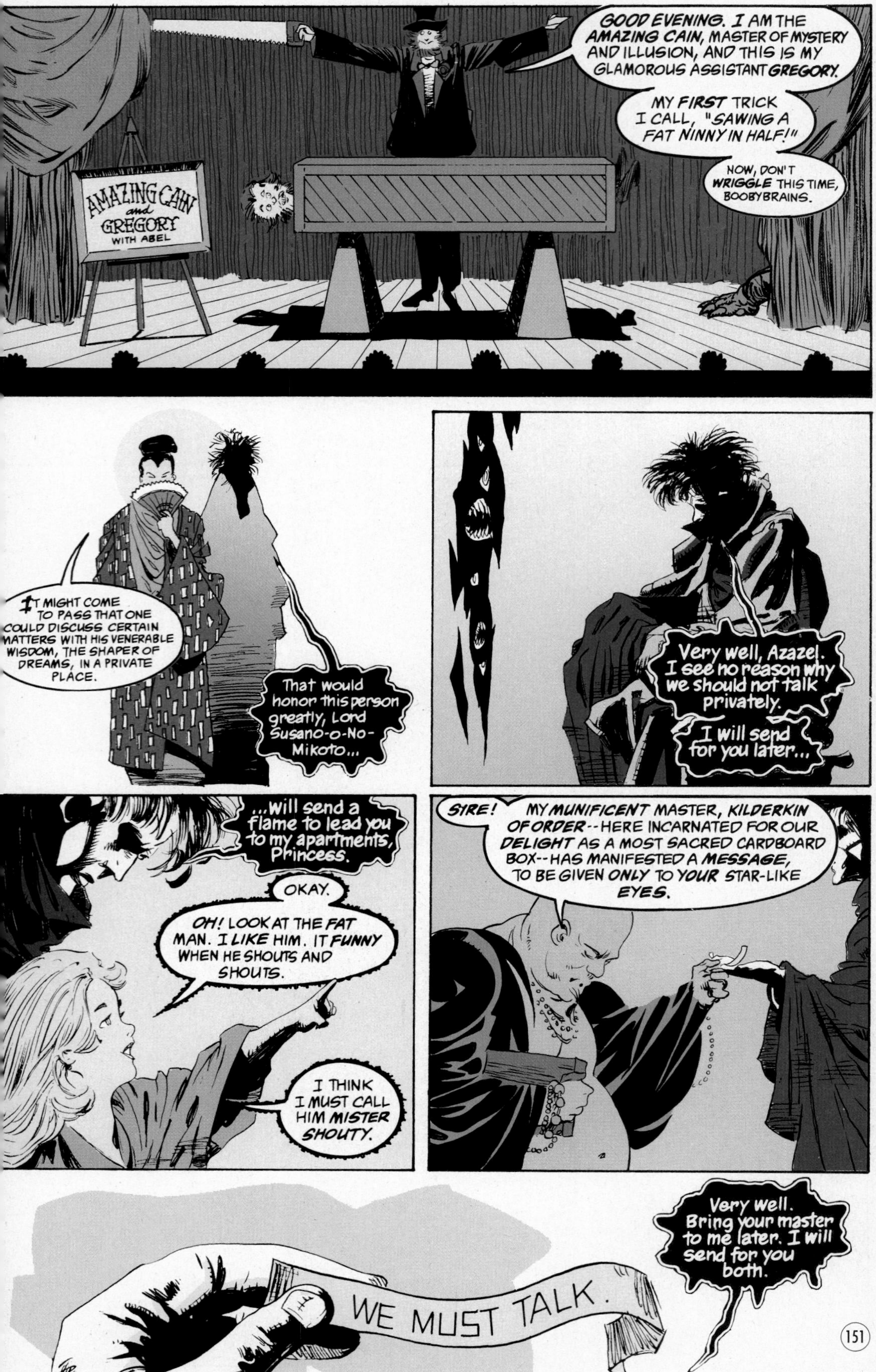
GOOD EVENING. I AM THE AMAZING CAIN, MASTER OF MYSTERY AND ILLUSION, AND THIS IS MY GLAMOROUS ASSISTANT GREGORY.
MY FIRST TRICK I CALL, "SAWING A FAT NINNY IN HALF!"
NOW, DON'T WRIGGLE THIS TIME, BOOBYBRAINS.
AMAZING CAIN and GREGORY WITH ABEL
IT MIGHT COME TO PASS THAT ONE COULD DISCUSS CERTAIN MATTERS WITH HIS VENERABLE WISDOM, THE SHAPER OF DREAMS, IN A PRIVATE PLACE.
That would honor this person greatly, Lord Susano-o-No-Mikoto...
Very well, Azazel. I see no reason why we should not talk privately.
I will send for you later...
...will send a flame to lead you to my apartments, Princess.
OKAY.
OH! LOOK AT THE FAT MAN. I LIKE HIM. IT FUNNY WHEN HE SHOUTS AND SHOUTS.
I THINK I MUST CALL HIM MISTER SHOUTY.
SIRE!
MY MUNIFICENT MASTER, KILDERKIN OF ORDER--HERE INCARNATED FOR OUR DELIGHT AS A MOST SACRED CARDBOARD BOX--HAS MANIFESTED A MESSAGE, TO BE GIVEN ONLY TO YOUR STAR-LIKE EYES.
WE MUST TALK.
Very well. Bring your master to me later. I will send for you both.

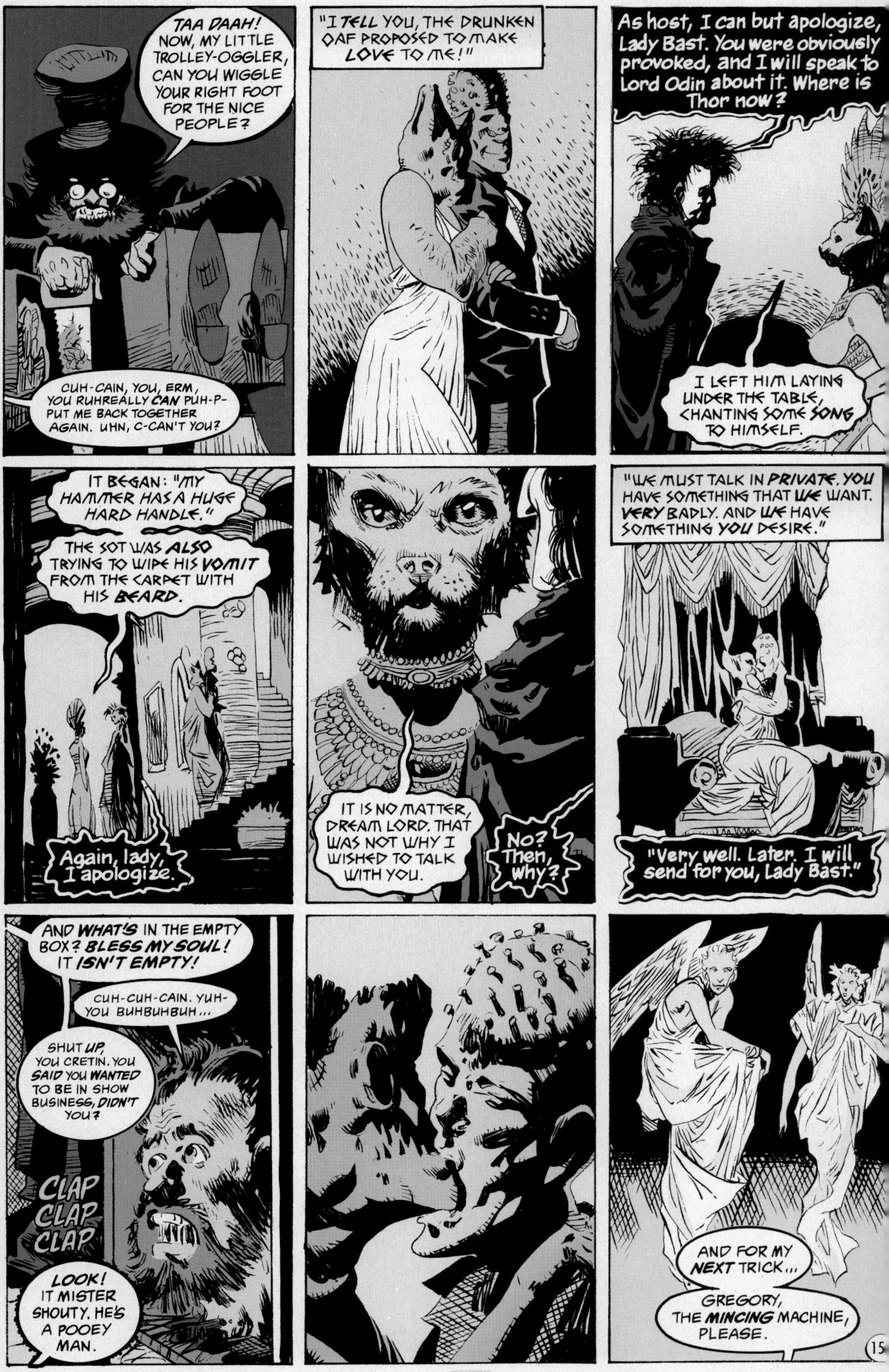
TAA DAAH! NOW, MY LITTLE TROLLEY-OGGLER, CAN YOU WIGGLE YOUR RIGHT FOOT FOR THE NICE PEOPLE?
CUH-CAIN, YOU, ERM, YOU RUHREALLY CAN PUH-P-PUT ME BACK TOGETHER AGAIN. UHN, C-CAN'T YOU?
"I TELL YOU, THE DRUNKEN OAF PROPOSED TO MAKE LOVE TO ME!"
As host, I can but apologize, Lady Bast. You were obviously provoked, and I will speak to Lord Odin about it. Where is Thor now?
I LEFT HIM LAYING UNDER THE TABLE, CHANTING SOME SONG TO HIMSELF.
IT BEGAN: "MY HAMMER HAS A HUGE HARD HANDLE."
THE SOT WAS ALSO TRYING TO WIPE HIS VOMIT FROM THE CARPET WITH HIS BEARD.
Again, lady, I apologize.
IT IS NO MATTER, DREAM LORD. THAT WAS NOT WHY I WISHED TO TALK WITH YOU.
No? Then, why?
"WE MUST TALK IN PRIVATE. YOU HAVE SOMETHING THAT WE WANT. VERY BADLY. AND WE HAVE SOMETHING YOU DESIRE."
"Very well. Later. I will send for you, Lady Bast."
AND WHAT'S IN THE EMPTY BOX? BLESS MY SOUL! IT ISN'T EMPTY!
CUH-CUH-CAIN. YUH-YOU BUHBUHBUH...
SHUT UP, YOU CRETIN. YOU SAID YOU WANTED TO BE IN SHOW BUSINESS, DIDN'T YOU?
CLAP CLAP CLAP
LOOK! IT MISTER SHOUTY. HE'S A POOEY MAN.
AND FOR MY NEXT TRICK...
GREGORY, THE MINCING MACHINE, PLEASE.

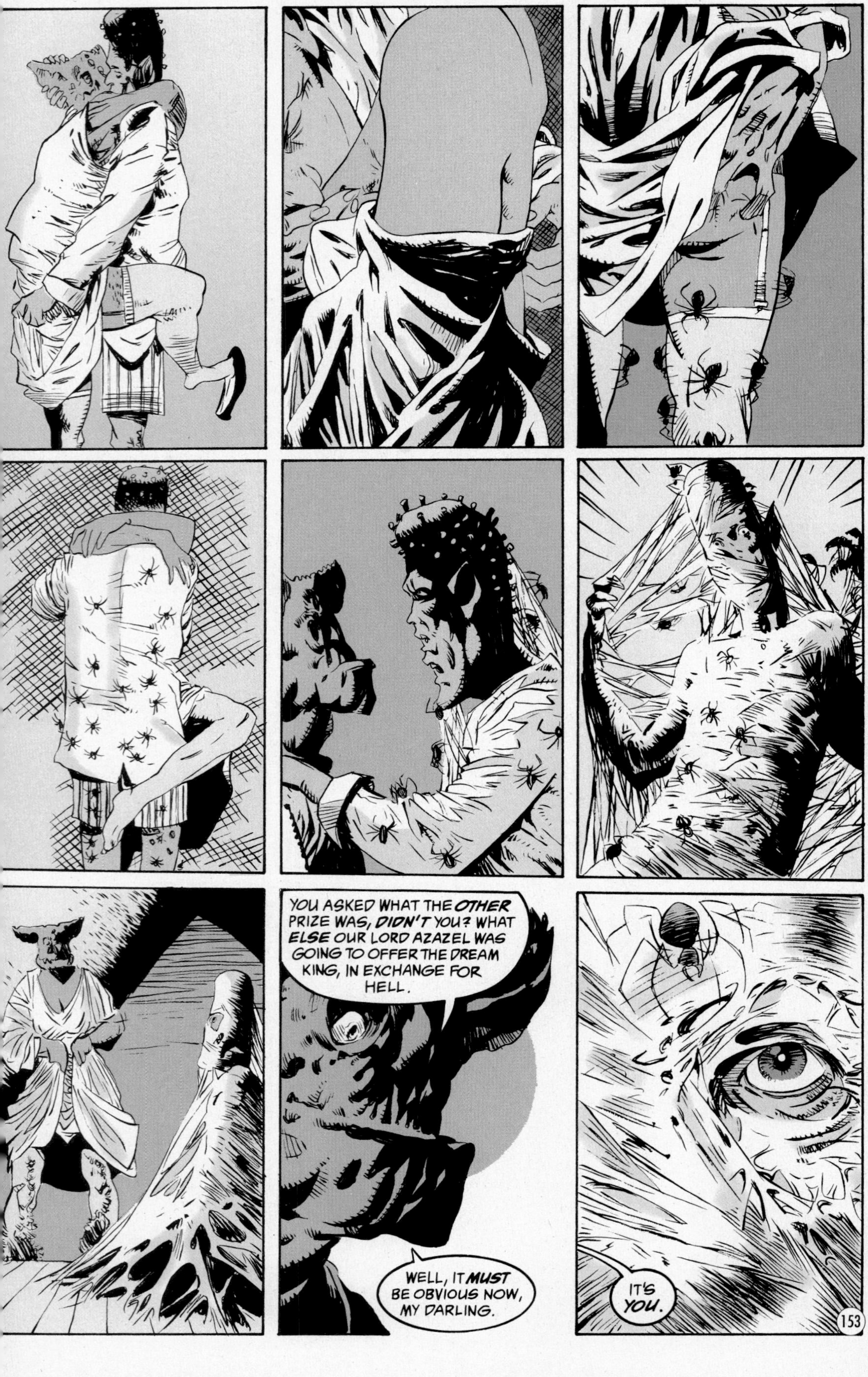
YOU ASKED WHAT THE OTHER PRIZE WAS, DIDN'T YOU? WHAT ELSE OUR LORD AZAZEL WAS GOING TO OFFER THE DREAM KING, IN EXCHANGE FOR HELL.
WELL, IT MUST BE OBVIOUS NOW, MY DARLING.
IT'S YOU.

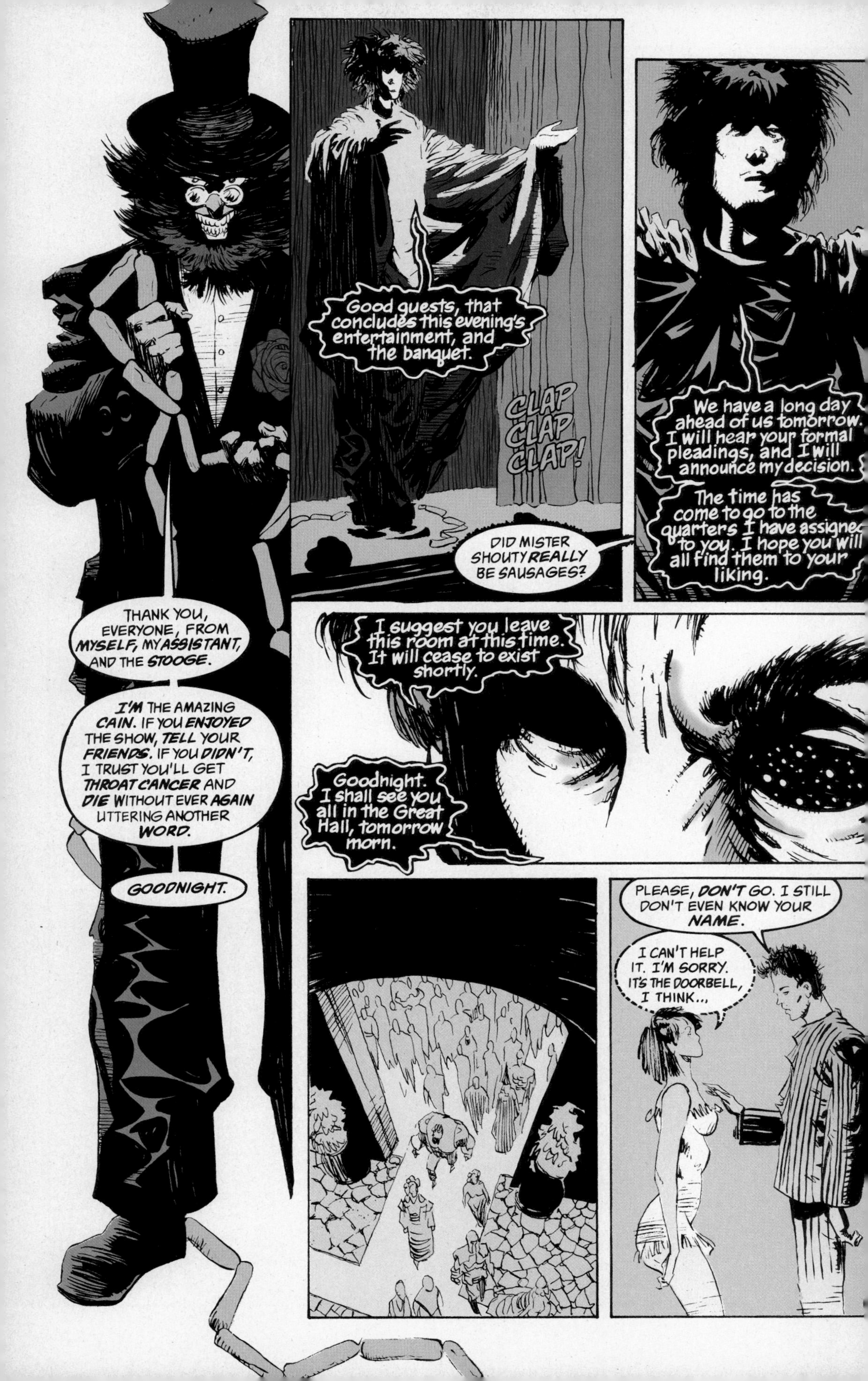

THANK YOU, EVERYONE, FROM MYSELF, MY ASSISTANT, AND THE STOOGE.
I'M THE AMAZING CAIN. IF YOU ENJOYED THE SHOW, TELL YOUR FRIENDS. IF YOU DIDN'T, I TRUST YOU'LL GET THROAT CANCER AND DIE WITHOUT EVER AGAIN UTTERING ANOTHER WORD.
GOODNIGHT.
Good guests, that concludes this evening's entertainment, and the banquet.
CLAP CLAP CLAP!
DID MISTER SHOUTY REALLY BE SAUSAGES?
We have a long day ahead of us tomorrow. I will hear your formal pleadings, and I will announce my decision.
The time has come to go to the quarters I have assigned to you. I hope you will all find them to your liking.
I suggest you leave this room at this time. It will cease to exist shortly.
Goodnight. I shall see you all in the Great Hall, tomorrow morn.
PLEASE, DON'T GO. I STILL DON'T EVEN KNOW YOUR NAME.
I CAN'T HELP IT. I'M SORRY. IT'S THE DOORBELL, I THINK...

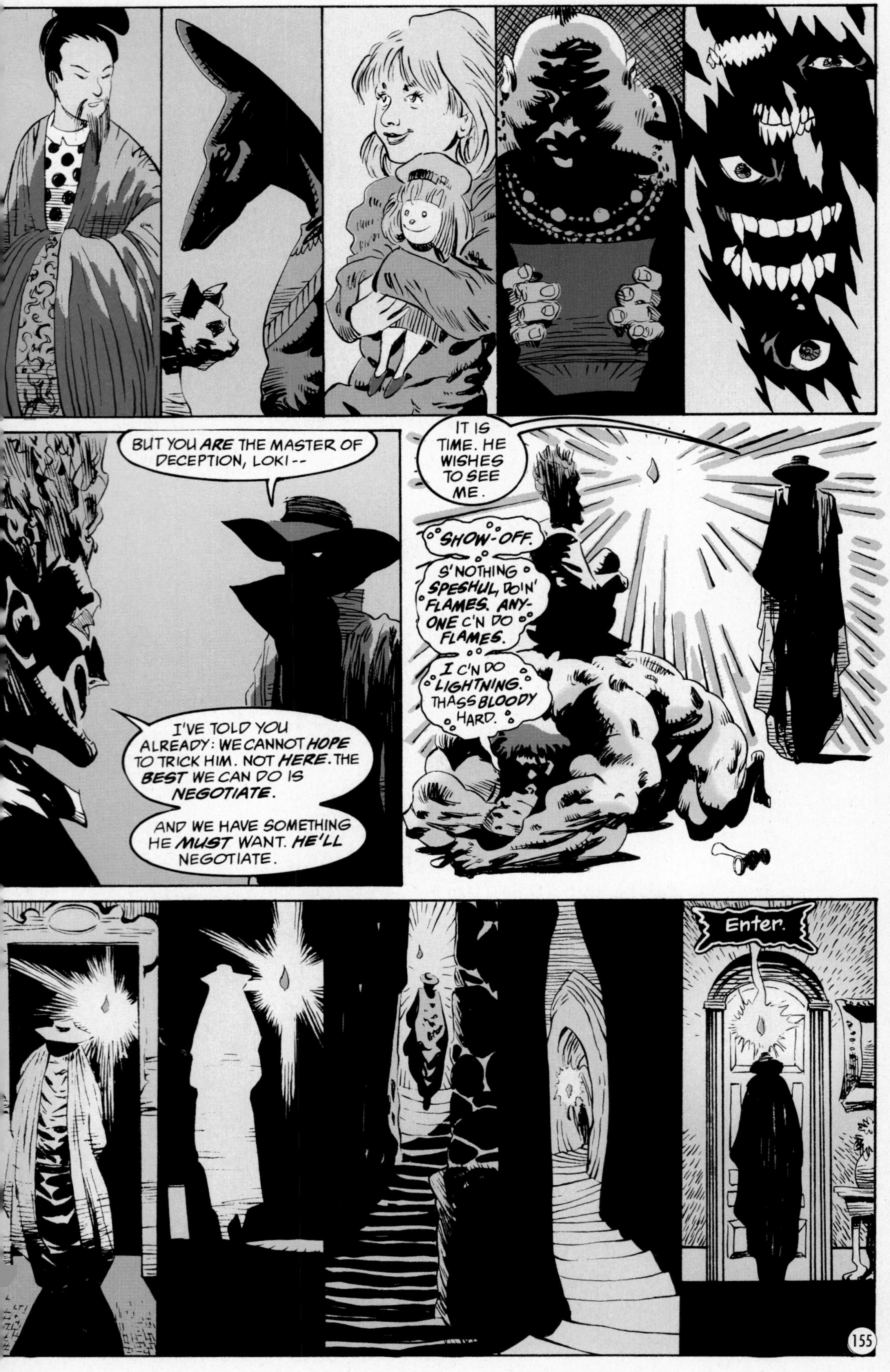
BUT YOU *ARE* THE MASTER OF DECEPTION, LOKI--
I'VE TOLD YOU ALREADY: WE CANNOT *HOPE* TO TRICK HIM. NOT *HERE*. THE *BEST* WE CAN DO IS *NEGOTIATE*.
AND WE HAVE SOMETHING HE *MUST* WANT. *HE'LL* NEGOTIATE.
IT IS TIME. HE WISHES TO SEE ME.
SHOW-OFF.
S'NOTHING *SPESHUL,* DOIN' *FLAMES. ANY-ONE* C'N DO *FLAMES.*
I C'N DO *LIGHTNING.* THASS *BLOODY* HARD.
Enter.

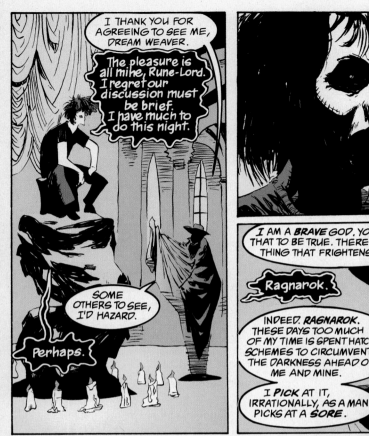

I THANK YOU FOR AGREEING TO SEE ME, DREAM WEAVER.

The pleasure is all mine, Rune-Lord. I regret our discussion must be brief. I have much to do this night.

SOME OTHERS TO SEE, I'D HAZARD.

Perhaps.

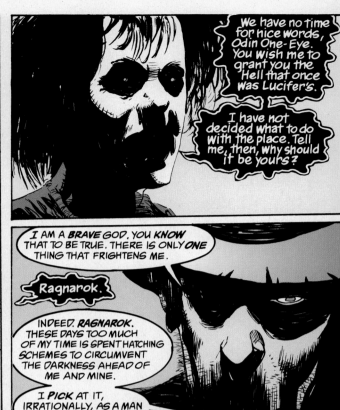

We have no time for nice words, Odin One-Eye. You wish me to grant you the Hell that once was Lucifer's.

I have not decided what to do with the place. Tell me, then, why should it be yours?

I AM A *BRAVE* GOD. YOU *KNOW* THAT TO BE TRUE. THERE IS ONLY *ONE* THING THAT FRIGHTENS ME.

Ragnarok.

INDEED. *RAGNAROK.* THESE DAYS TOO MUCH OF MY TIME IS SPENT HATCHING SCHEMES TO CIRCUMVENT THE DARKNESS AHEAD OF ME AND MINE.

I *PICK* AT IT, IRRATIONALLY, AS A MAN PICKS AT A *SORE.*

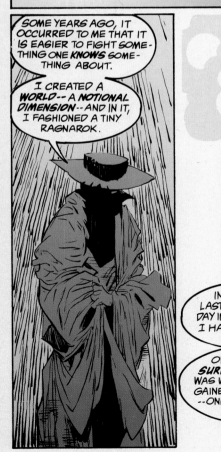

SOME YEARS AGO, IT OCCURRED TO ME THAT IT IS EASIER TO FIGHT SOMETHING ONE *KNOWS* SOMETHING ABOUT.

I CREATED A *WORLD* -- A *NOTIONAL DIMENSION* -- AND IN IT, I FASHIONED A TINY *RAGNAROK.*

IN MY WORLD, THE LAST BATTLE IS FOUGHT, DAY IN, DAY OUT, FOR *EVER.* I HAVE LEARNED *MUCH* FROM IT.

ONE THING THAT *SURPRISED* ME, THOUGH, WAS WHEN MY LITTLE WORLD GAINED *FURTHER* WARRIORS --ONES I HAD NOT CREATED.

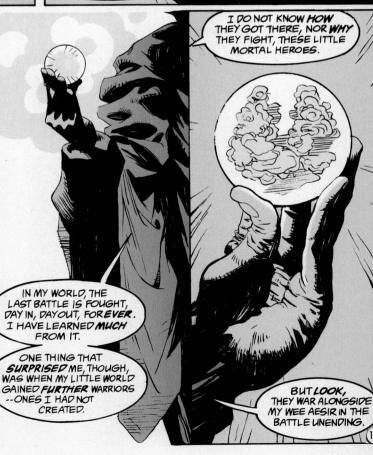

I DO NOT KNOW *HOW* THEY GOT THERE, NOR *WHY* THEY FIGHT, THESE LITTLE MORTAL HEROES.

BUT *LOOK,* THEY WAR ALONGSIDE MY WEE AESIR IN THE BATTLE UNENDING.

19

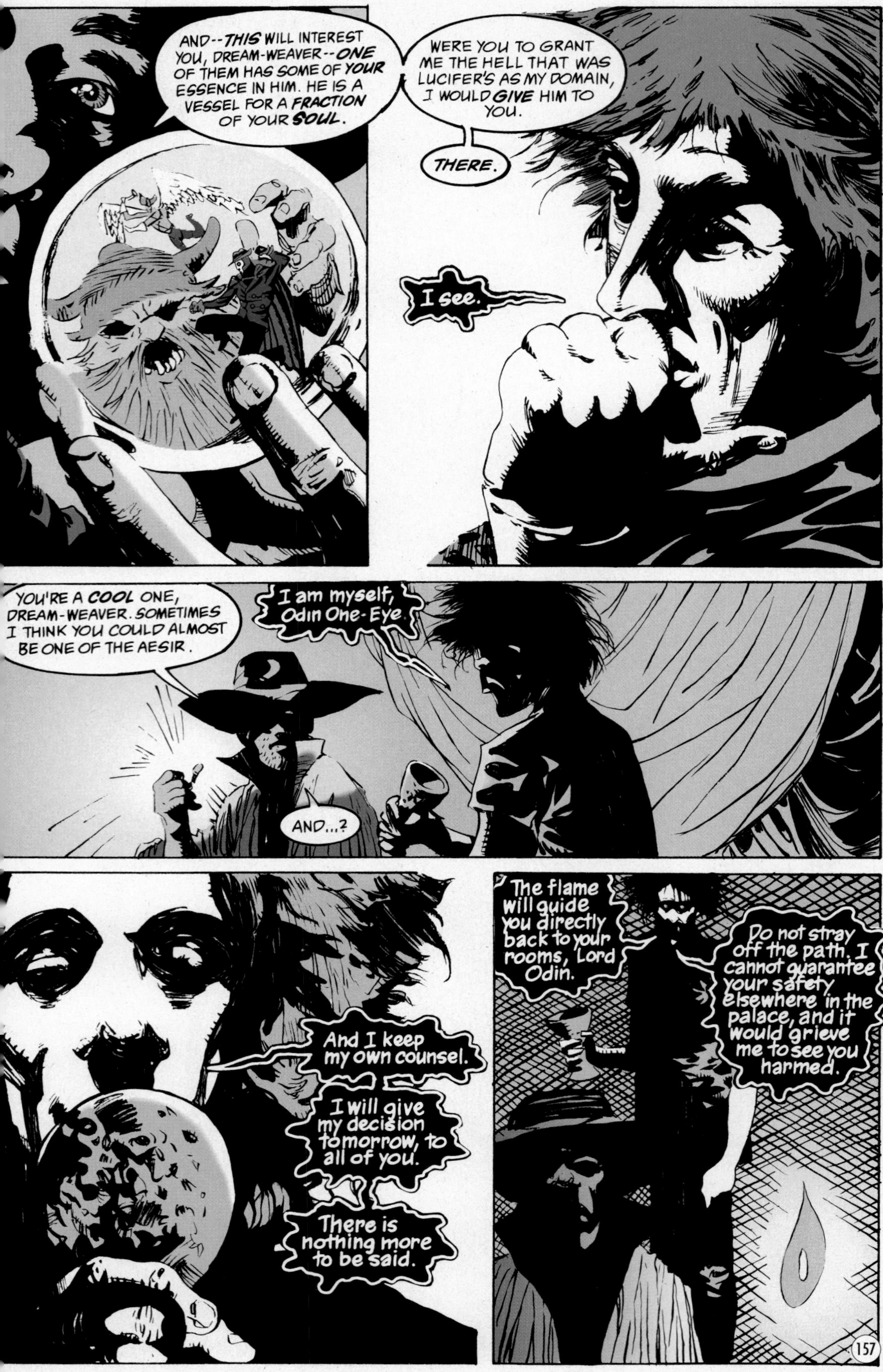
AND--THIS WILL INTEREST YOU, DREAM-WEAVER--ONE OF THEM HAS SOME OF YOUR ESSENCE IN HIM. HE IS A VESSEL FOR A FRACTION OF YOUR SOUL.
WERE YOU TO GRANT ME THE HELL THAT WAS LUCIFER'S AS MY DOMAIN, I WOULD GIVE HIM TO YOU.
THERE.
I see.
YOU'RE A COOL ONE, DREAM-WEAVER. SOMETIMES I THINK YOU COULD ALMOST BE ONE OF THE AESIR.
I am myself, Odin One-Eye.
AND...?
And I keep my own counsel.
I will give my decision tomorrow, to all of you.
There is nothing more to be said.
The flame will guide you directly back to your rooms, Lord Odin.
Do not stray off the path. I cannot guarantee your safety elsewhere in the palace, and it would grieve me to see you harmed.

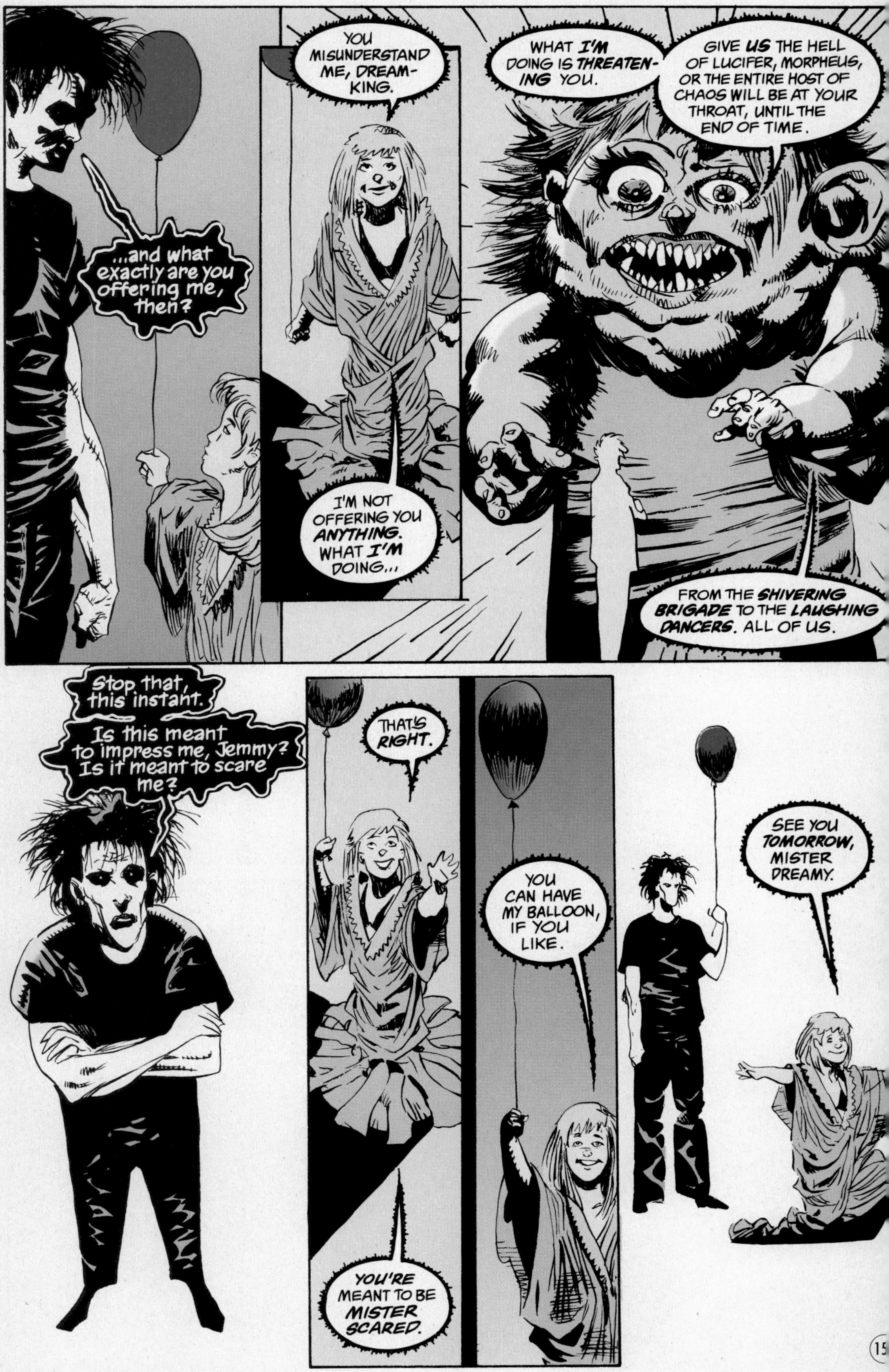
...and what exactly are you offering me, then?
YOU MISUNDERSTAND ME, DREAM-KING.
I'M NOT OFFERING YOU ANYTHING. WHAT I'M DOING...
WHAT I'M DOING IS THREATENING YOU.
GIVE US THE HELL OF LUCIFER, MORPHEUS, OR THE ENTIRE HOST OF CHAOS WILL BE AT YOUR THROAT, UNTIL THE END OF TIME.
FROM THE SHIVERING BRIGADE TO THE LAUGHING DANCERS. ALL OF US.
Stop that, this instant.
Is this meant to impress me, Jemmy? Is it meant to scare me?
THAT'S RIGHT.
YOU'RE MEANT TO BE MISTER SCARED.
YOU CAN HAVE MY BALLOON, IF YOU LIKE.
SEE YOU TOMORROW, MISTER DREAMY.

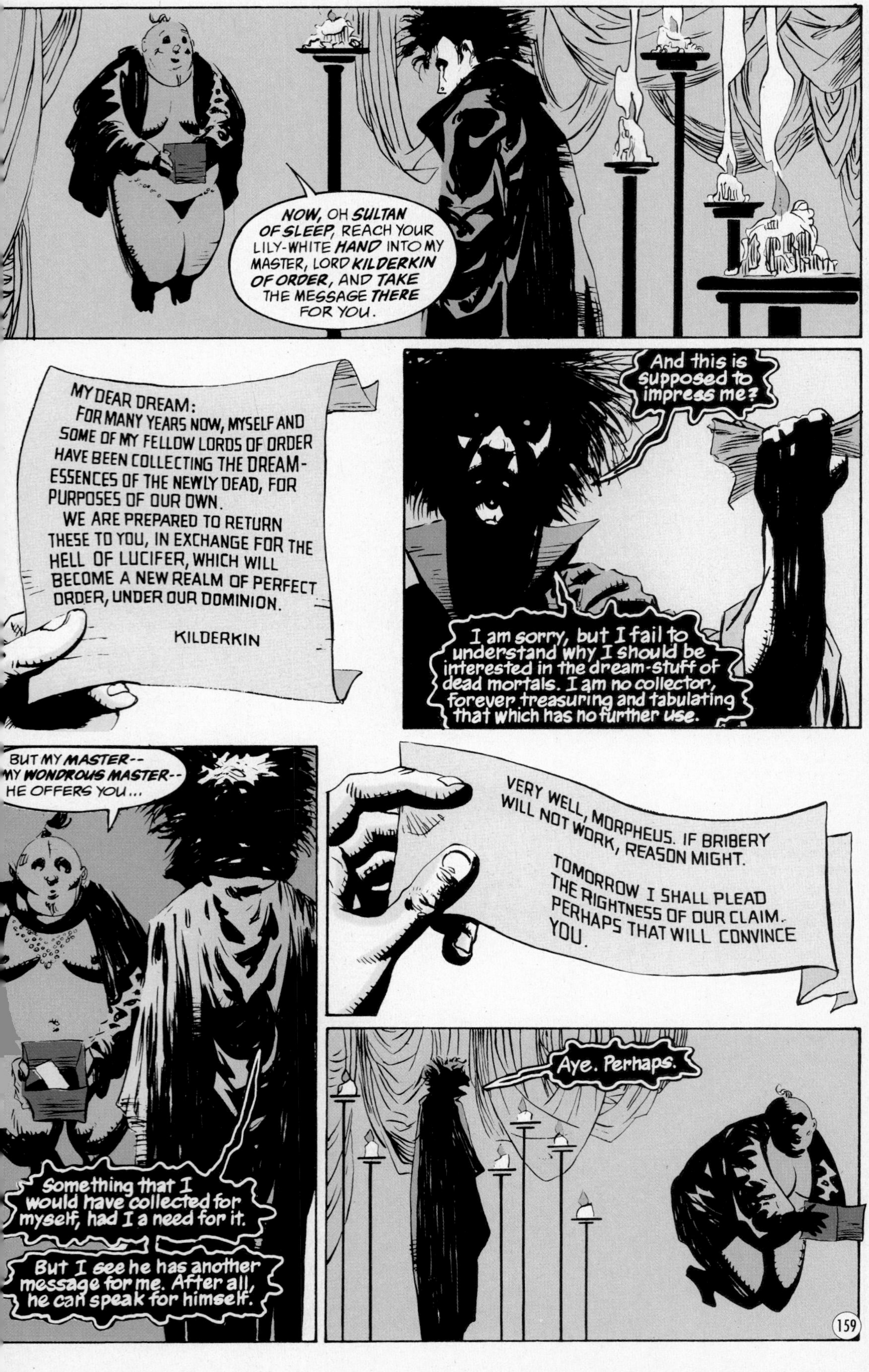
NOW, OH SULTAN OF SLEEP, REACH YOUR LILY-WHITE HAND INTO MY MASTER, LORD KILDERKIN OF ORDER, AND TAKE THE MESSAGE THERE FOR YOU.
MY DEAR DREAM: FOR MANY YEARS NOW, MYSELF AND SOME OF MY FELLOW LORDS OF ORDER HAVE BEEN COLLECTING THE DREAM-ESSENCES OF THE NEWLY DEAD, FOR PURPOSES OF OUR OWN. WE ARE PREPARED TO RETURN THESE TO YOU, IN EXCHANGE FOR THE HELL OF LUCIFER, WHICH WILL BECOME A NEW REALM OF PERFECT ORDER, UNDER OUR DOMINION. KILDERKIN
And this is supposed to impress me?
I am sorry, but I fail to understand why I should be interested in the dream-stuff of dead mortals. I am no collector, forever treasuring and tabulating that which has no further use.
BUT MY MASTER-- MY WONDROUS MASTER-- HE OFFERS YOU...
Something that I would have collected for myself, had I a need for it.
But I see he has another message for me. After all, he can speak for himself.
VERY WELL, MORPHEUS. IF BRIBERY WILL NOT WORK, REASON MIGHT. TOMORROW I SHALL PLEAD THE RIGHTNESS OF OUR CLAIM. PERHAPS THAT WILL CONVINCE YOU.
Aye. Perhaps.

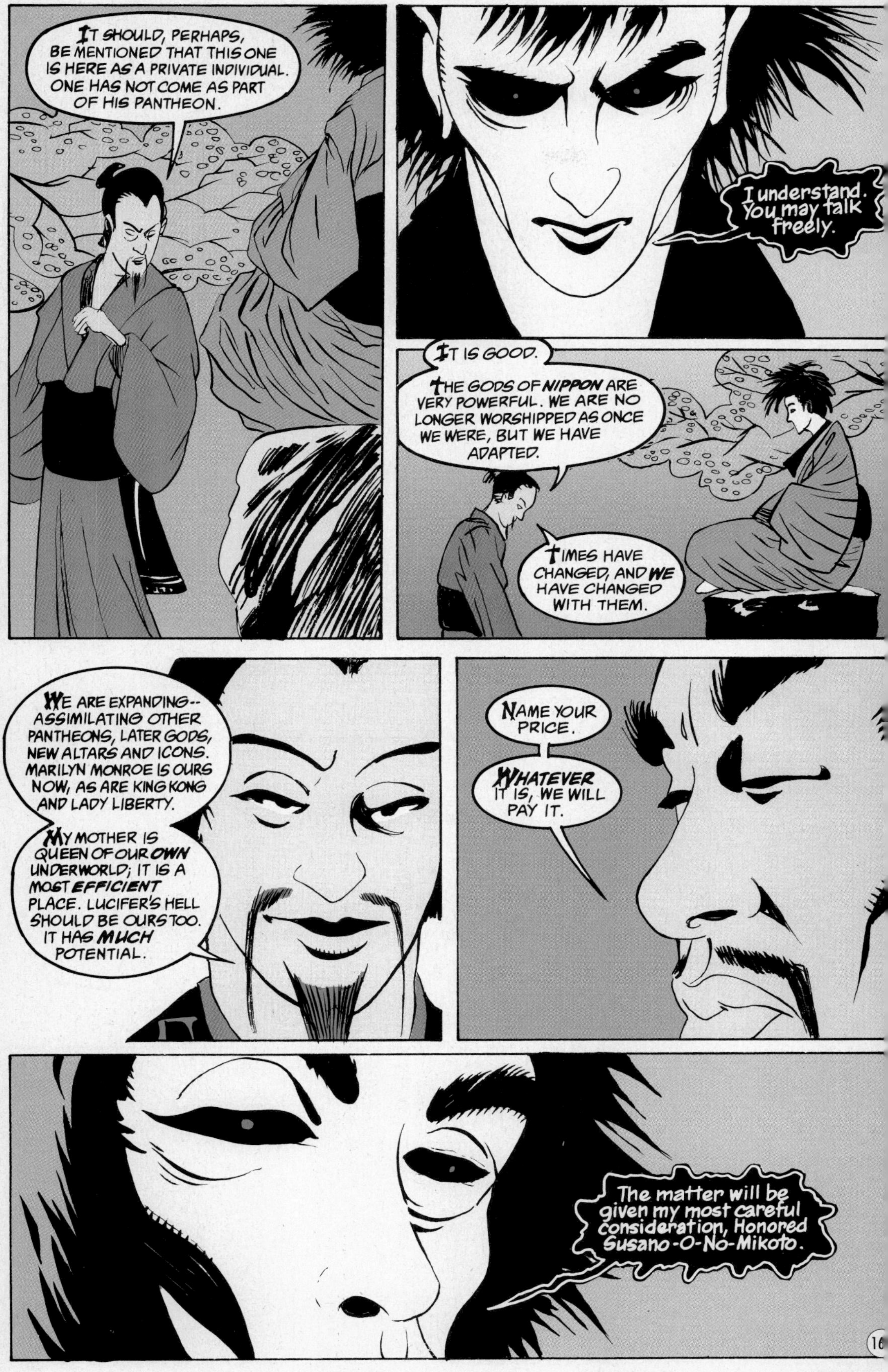
IT SHOULD, PERHAPS, BE MENTIONED THAT THIS ONE IS HERE AS A PRIVATE INDIVIDUAL. ONE HAS NOT COME AS PART OF HIS PANTHEON.
I understand. You may talk freely.
IT IS GOOD.
THE GODS OF NIPPON ARE VERY POWERFUL. WE ARE NO LONGER WORSHIPPED AS ONCE WE WERE, BUT WE HAVE ADAPTED.
TIMES HAVE CHANGED, AND WE HAVE CHANGED WITH THEM.
WE ARE EXPANDING-- ASSIMILATING OTHER PANTHEONS, LATER GODS, NEW ALTARS AND ICONS. MARILYN MONROE IS OURS NOW, AS ARE KING KONG AND LADY LIBERTY.
MY MOTHER IS QUEEN OF OUR OWN UNDERWORLD; IT IS A MOST EFFICIENT PLACE. LUCIFER'S HELL SHOULD BE OURS TOO. IT HAS MUCH POTENTIAL.
NAME YOUR PRICE.
WHATEVER IT IS, WE WILL PAY IT.
The matter will be given my most careful consideration, Honored Susano-O-No-Mikoto.

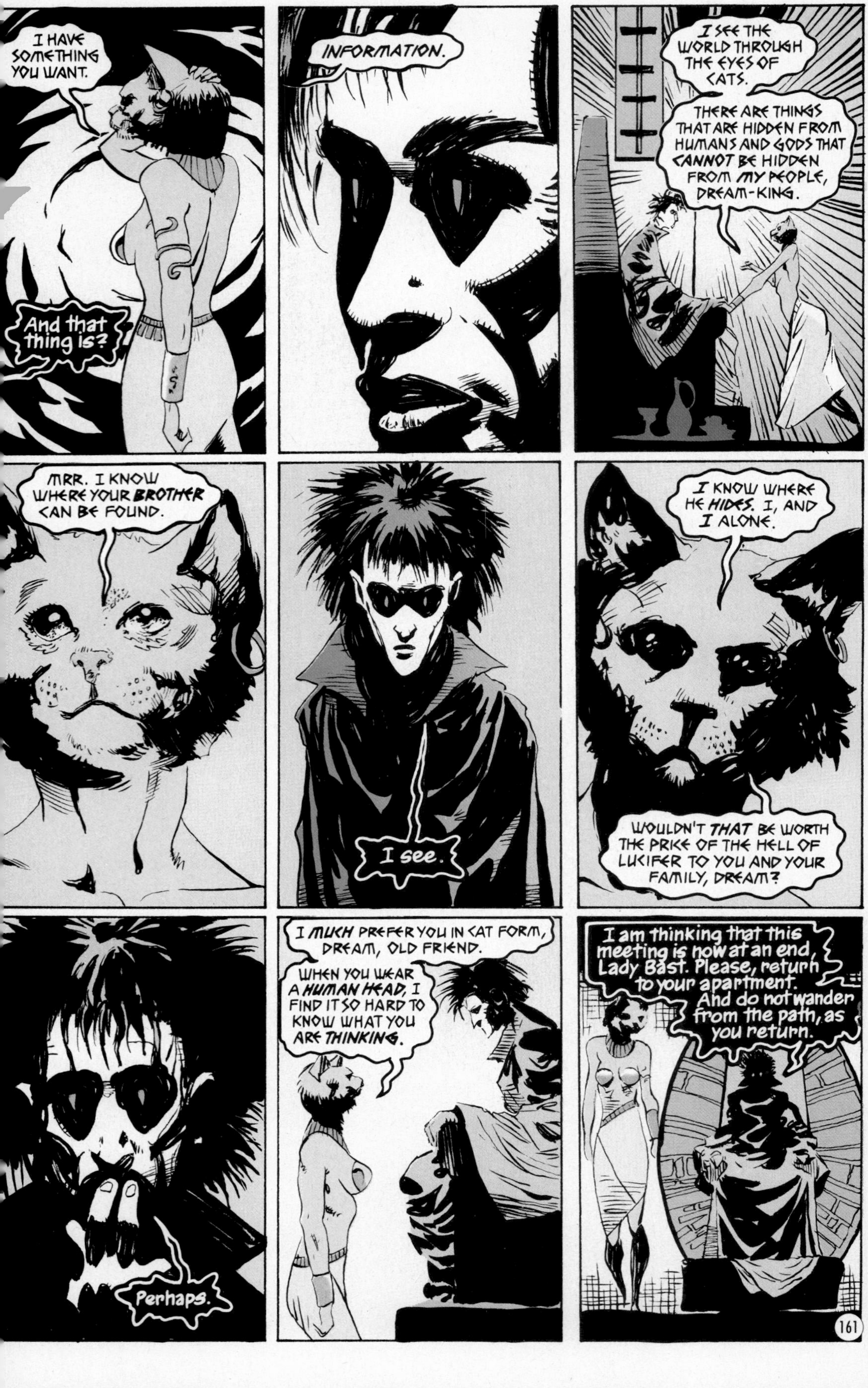
I HAVE SOMETHING YOU WANT.
And that thing is?
INFORMATION.
I SEE THE WORLD THROUGH THE EYES OF CATS.
THERE ARE THINGS THAT ARE HIDDEN FROM HUMANS AND GODS THAT CANNOT BE HIDDEN FROM MY PEOPLE, DREAM-KING.
MRR. I KNOW WHERE YOUR BROTHER CAN BE FOUND.
I see.
I KNOW WHERE HE HIDES. I, AND I ALONE.
WOULDN'T THAT BE WORTH THE PRICE OF THE HELL OF LUCIFER TO YOU AND YOUR FAMILY, DREAM?
Perhaps.
I MUCH PREFER YOU IN CAT FORM, DREAM, OLD FRIEND.
WHEN YOU WEAR A HUMAN HEAD, I FIND IT SO HARD TO KNOW WHAT YOU ARE THINKING.
I am thinking that this meeting is now at an end, Lady Bast. Please, return to your apartment. And do not wander from the path, as you return.

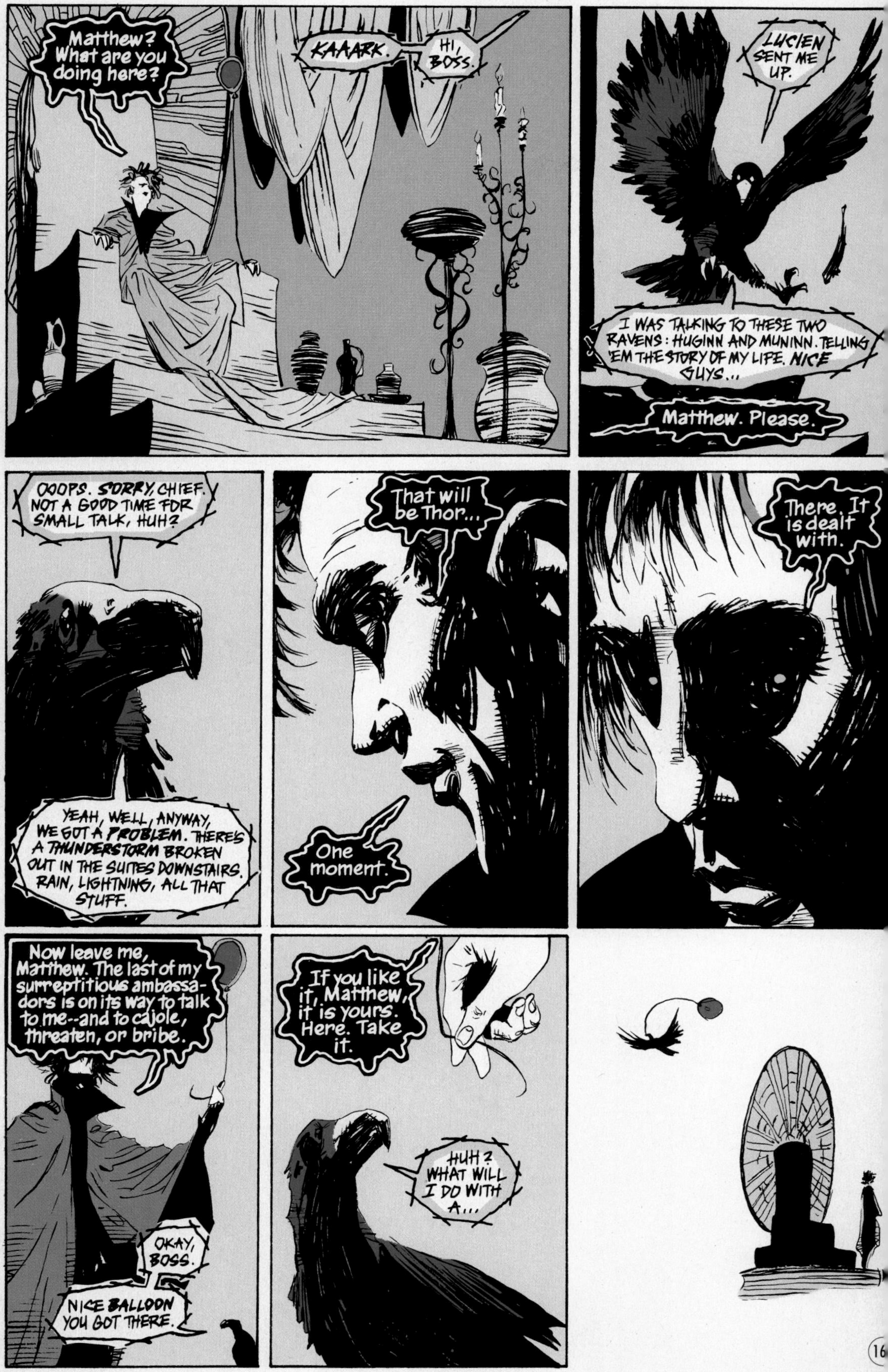
Matthew? What are you doing here?
KAAARK.
HI, BOSS.
LUCIEN SENT ME UP.
I WAS TALKING TO THESE TWO RAVENS: HUGINN AND MUNINN. TELLING 'EM THE STORY OF MY LIFE. NICE GUYS...
Matthew. Please.
OOPS. SORRY, CHIEF. NOT A GOOD TIME FOR SMALL TALK, HUH?
YEAH, WELL, ANYWAY, WE GOT A PROBLEM. THERE'S A THUNDERSTORM BROKEN OUT IN THE SUITES DOWNSTAIRS. RAIN, LIGHTNING, ALL THAT STUFF.
That will be Thor...
One moment.
There. It is dealt with.
Now leave me, Matthew. The last of my surreptitious ambassadors is on its way to talk to me--and to cajole, threaten, or bribe.
OKAY, BOSS.
NICE BALLOON YOU GOT THERE.
If you like it, Matthew, it is yours. Here. Take it.
HUH? WHAT WILL I DO WITH A...

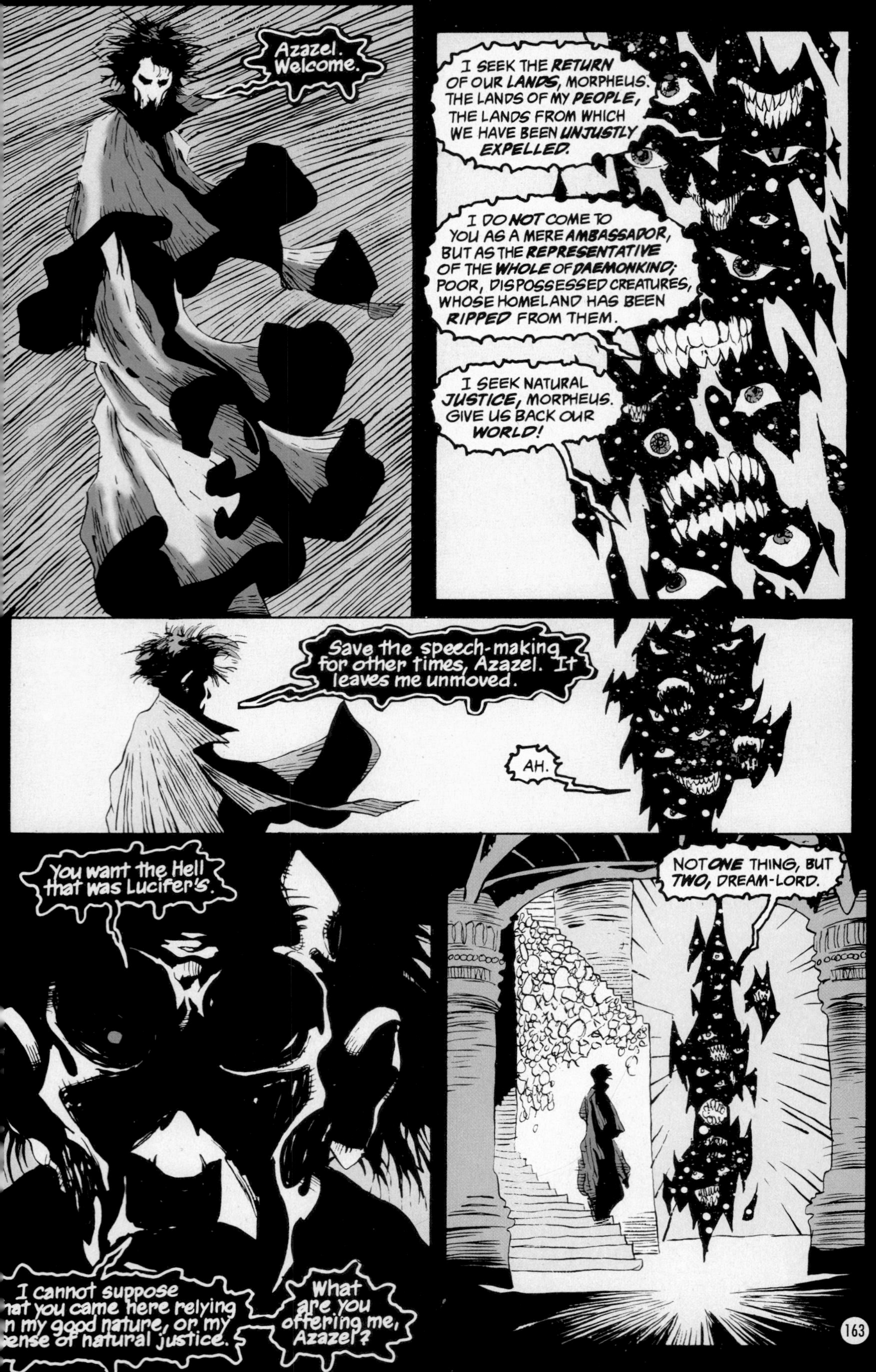
Azazel. Welcome.
I SEEK THE RETURN OF OUR LANDS, MORPHEUS. THE LANDS OF MY PEOPLE, THE LANDS FROM WHICH WE HAVE BEEN UNJUSTLY EXPELLED.
I DO NOT COME TO YOU AS A MERE AMBASSADOR, BUT AS THE REPRESENTATIVE OF THE WHOLE OF DAEMONKIND; POOR, DISPOSSESSED CREATURES, WHOSE HOMELAND HAS BEEN RIPPED FROM THEM.
I SEEK NATURAL JUSTICE, MORPHEUS. GIVE US BACK OUR WORLD!
Save the speech-making for other times, Azazel. It leaves me unmoved.
AH.
You want the Hell that was Lucifer's.
I cannot suppose hat you came here relying n my good nature, or my ense of natural justice.
What are you offering me, Azazel?
NOT ONE THING, BUT TWO, DREAM-LORD.

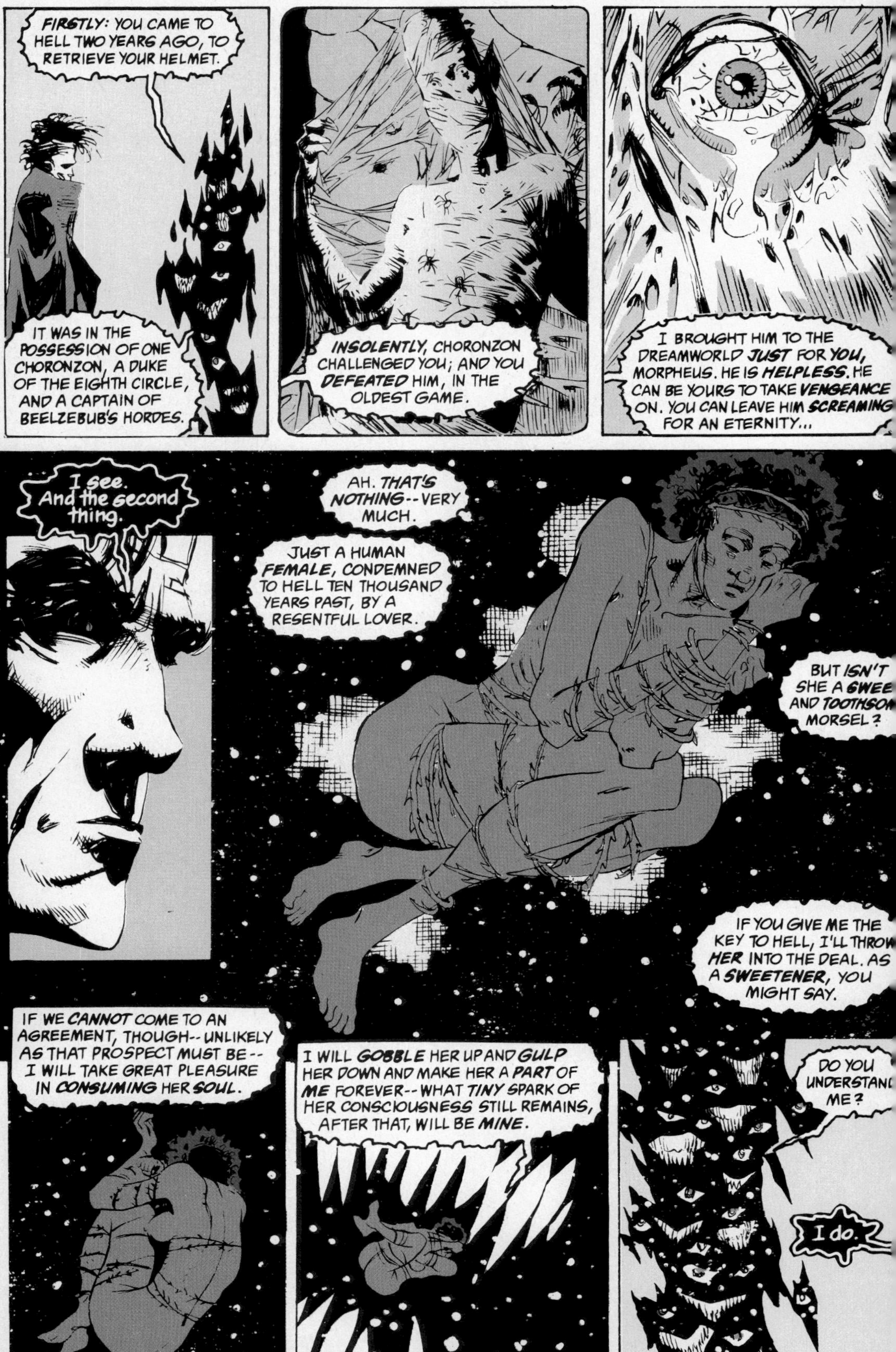
FIRSTLY: YOU CAME TO HELL TWO YEARS AGO, TO RETRIEVE YOUR HELMET.
IT WAS IN THE POSSESSION OF ONE CHORONZON, A DUKE OF THE EIGHTH CIRCLE, AND A CAPTAIN OF BEELZEBUB'S HORDES.
INSOLENTLY, CHORONZON CHALLENGED YOU; AND YOU DEFEATED HIM, IN THE OLDEST GAME.
I BROUGHT HIM TO THE DREAMWORLD JUST FOR YOU, MORPHEUS. HE IS HELPLESS. HE CAN BE YOURS TO TAKE VENGEANCE ON. YOU CAN LEAVE HIM SCREAMING FOR AN ETERNITY...
I see. And the second thing.
AH. THAT'S NOTHING--VERY MUCH.
JUST A HUMAN FEMALE, CONDEMNED TO HELL TEN THOUSAND YEARS PAST, BY A RESENTFUL LOVER.
BUT ISN'T SHE A SWEE AND TOOTHSO MORSEL?
IF YOU GIVE ME THE KEY TO HELL, I'LL THROW HER INTO THE DEAL. AS A SWEETENER, YOU MIGHT SAY.
IF WE CANNOT COME TO AN AGREEMENT, THOUGH-- UNLIKELY AS THAT PROSPECT MUST BE -- I WILL TAKE GREAT PLEASURE IN CONSUMING HER SOUL.
I WILL GOBBLE HER UP AND GULP HER DOWN AND MAKE HER A PART OF ME FOREVER--WHAT TINY SPARK OF HER CONSCIOUSNESS STILL REMAINS, AFTER THAT, WILL BE MINE.
DO YOU UNDERSTAN ME?
I do.

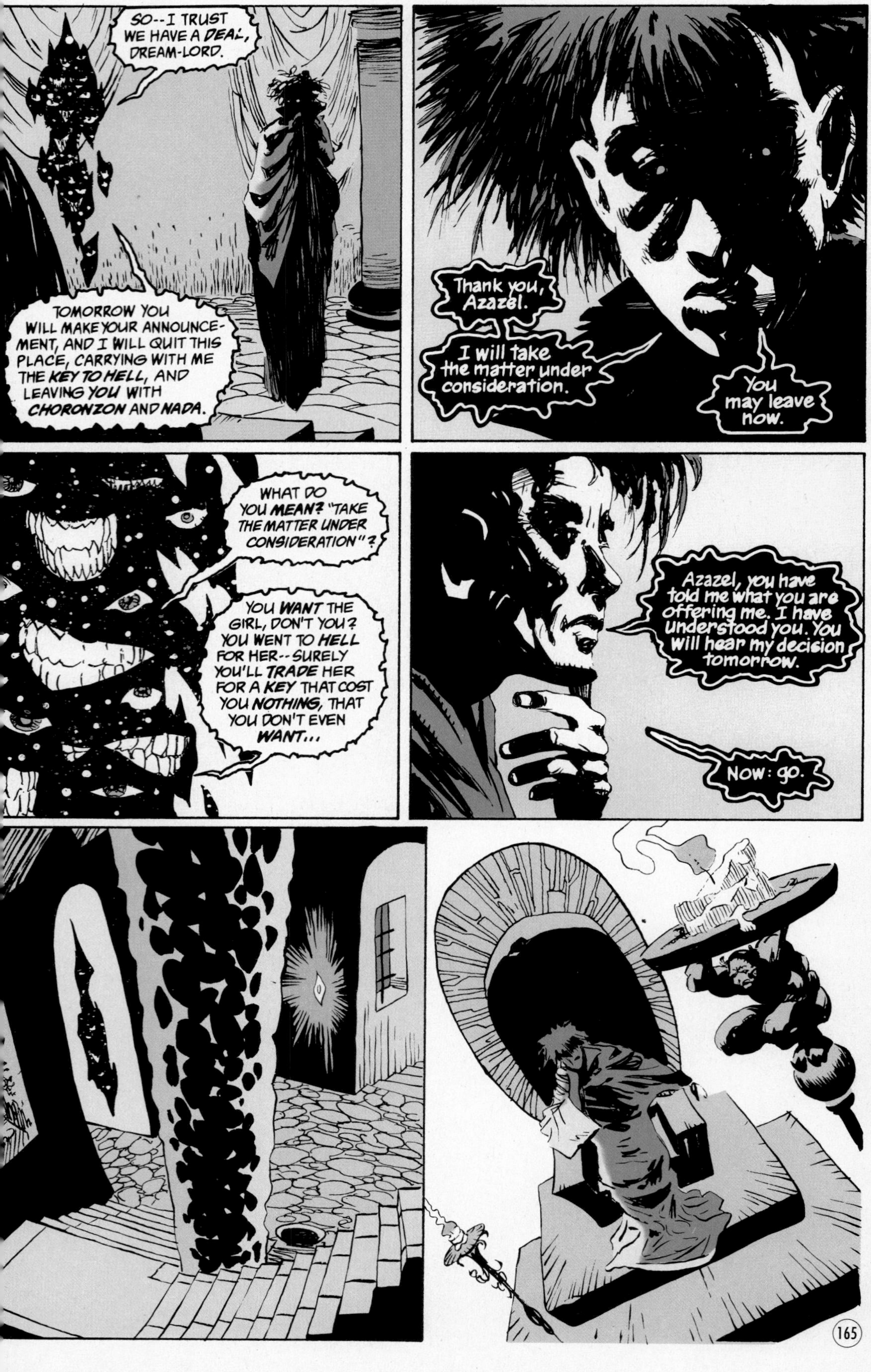
SO--I TRUST WE HAVE A DEAL, DREAM-LORD.
TOMORROW YOU WILL MAKE YOUR ANNOUNCE-MENT, AND I WILL QUIT THIS PLACE, CARRYING WITH ME THE KEY TO HELL, AND LEAVING YOU WITH CHORONZON AND NADA.
Thank you, Azazel.
I will take the matter under consideration.
You may leave now.
WHAT DO YOU MEAN? "TAKE THE MATTER UNDER CONSIDERATION"?
YOU WANT THE GIRL, DON'T YOU? YOU WENT TO HELL FOR HER--SURELY YOU'LL TRADE HER FOR A KEY THAT COST YOU NOTHING, THAT YOU DON'T EVEN WANT...
Azazel, you have told me what you are offering me. I have understood you. You will hear my decision tomorrow.
Now: go.

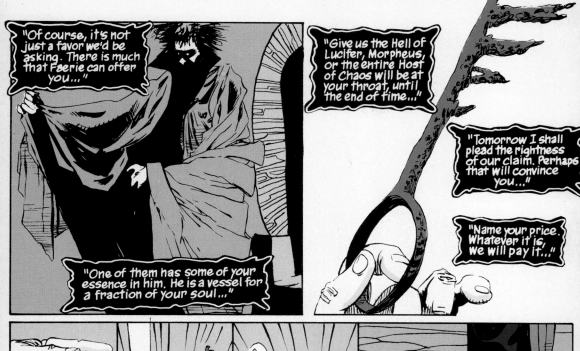

"Of course, it's not just a favor we'd be asking. There is much that Faerie can offer you..."

"One of them has some of your essence in him. He is a vessel for a fraction of your soul..."

"Give us the Hell of Lucifer, Morpheus, or the entire Host of Chaos will be at your throat, until the end of time..."

"Tomorrow I shall plead the rightness of our claim. Perhaps that will convince you..."

"Name your price. Whatever it is, we will pay it..."

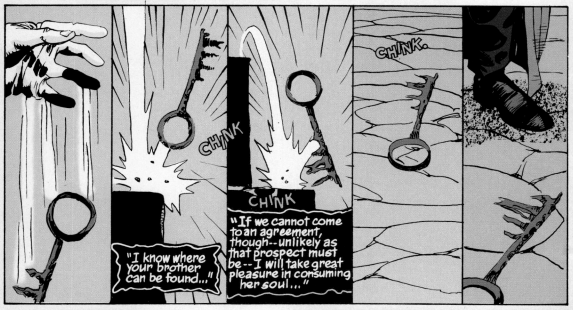

CHINK

CHINK

CHINK.

"I know where your brother can be found..."

"If we cannot come to an agreement, though--unlikely as that prospect must be--I will take great pleasure in consuming her soul..."

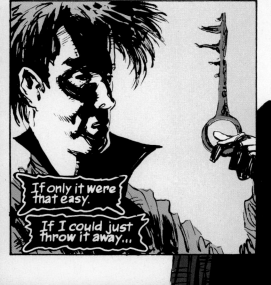

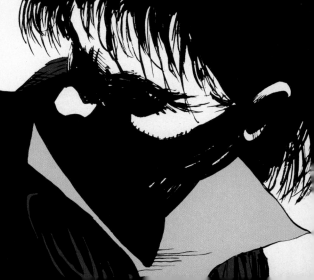

If only it were that easy.

If I could just throw it away...

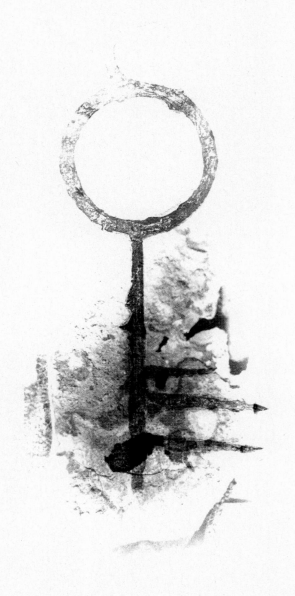

IN WHICH THE VEXING QUESTION OF THE SOVEREIGNTY OF HELL IS FINALLY SETTLED, TO THE SATISFACTION OF SOME; THE FINER POINTS OF HOSPITALITY; AND IN WHICH IT IS DEMONSTRATED THAT WHILE SOME MAY FALL, OTHERS ARE PUSHED.

EPISODE 6

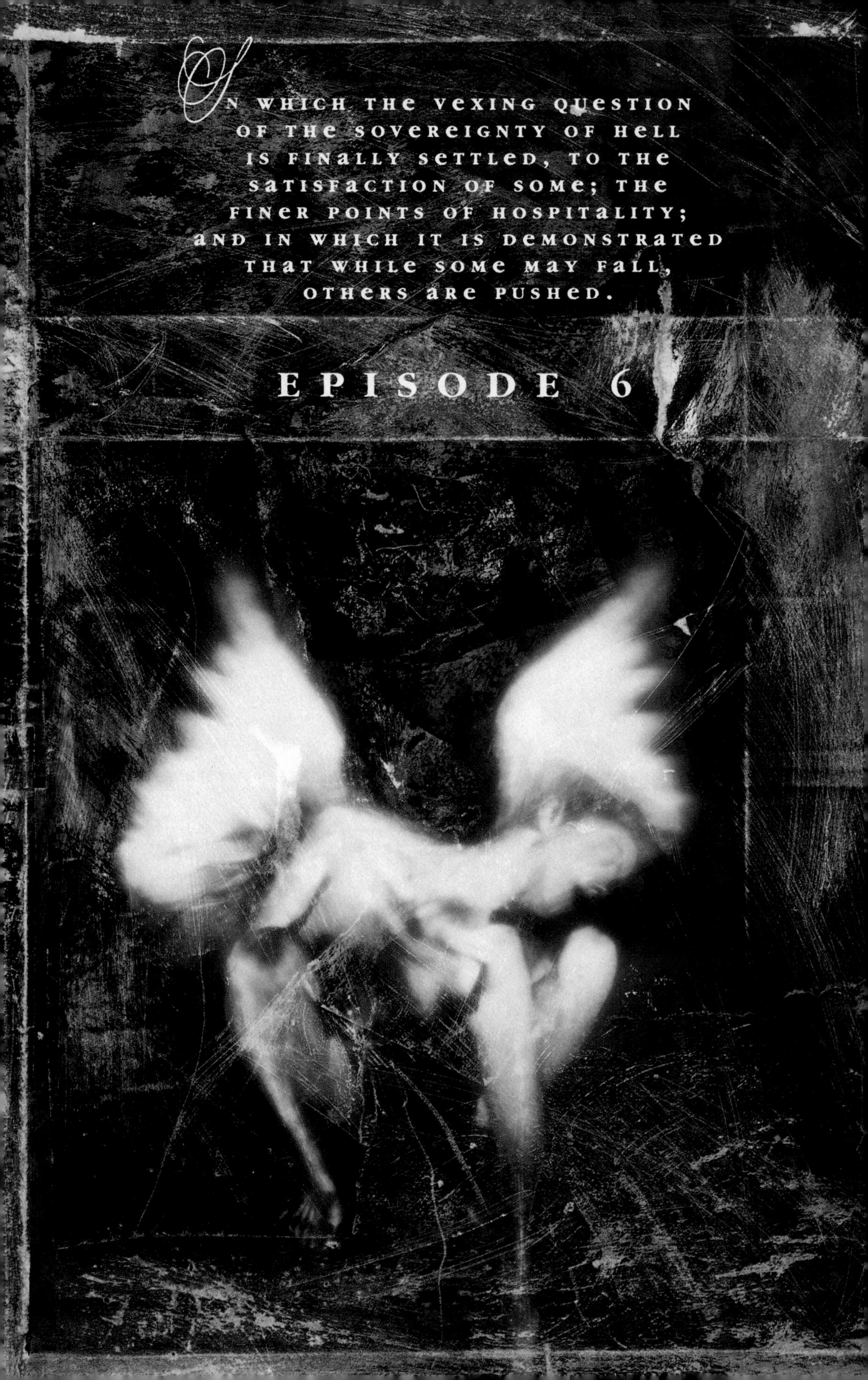

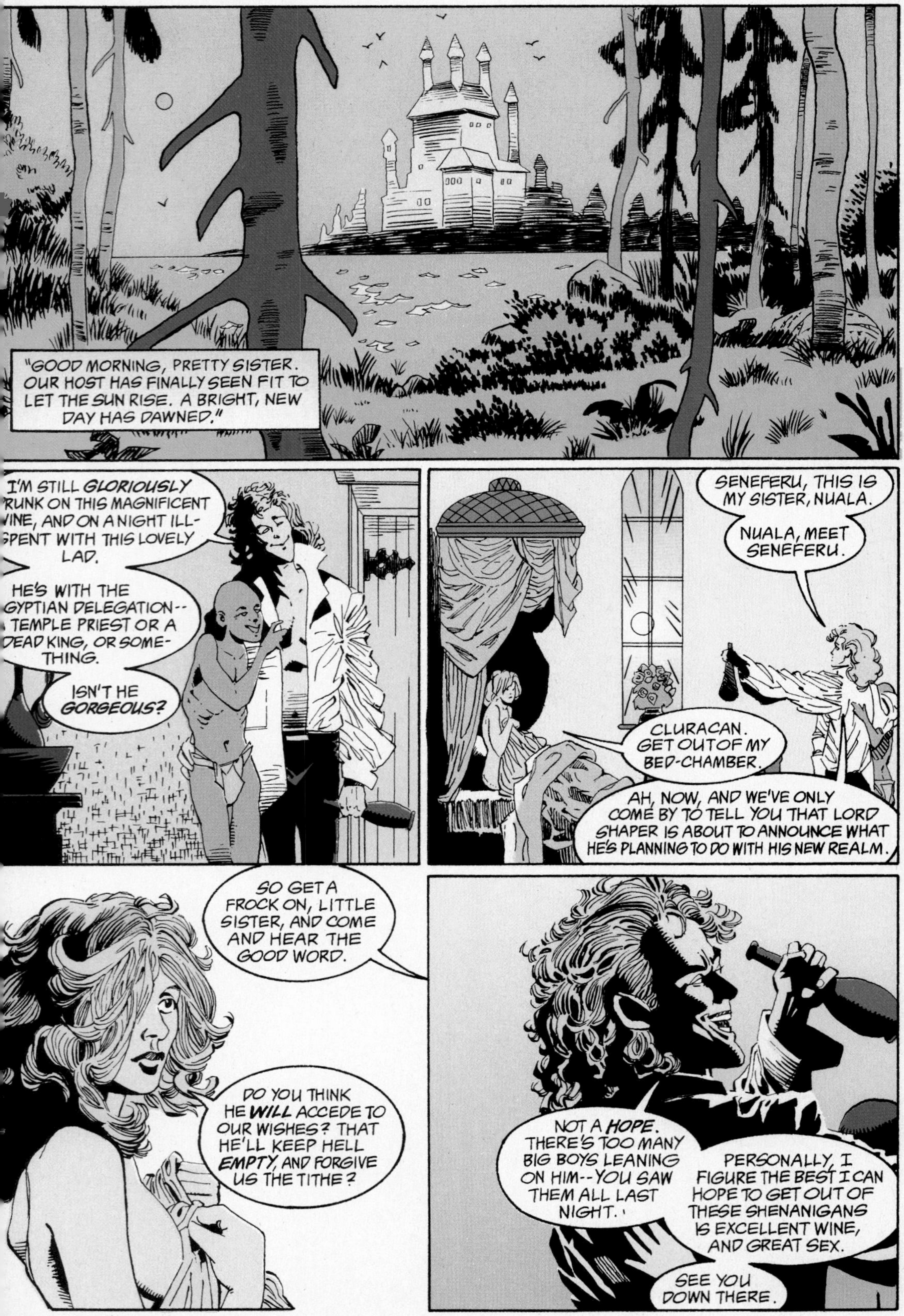
"GOOD MORNING, PRETTY SISTER. OUR HOST HAS FINALLY SEEN FIT TO LET THE SUN RISE. A BRIGHT, NEW DAY HAS DAWNED."
I'M STILL GLORIOUSLY RUNK ON THIS MAGNIFICENT INE, AND ON A NIGHT ILL-SPENT WITH THIS LOVELY LAD.
HE'S WITH THE GYPTIAN DELEGATION-- TEMPLE PRIEST OR A DEAD KING, OR SOMETHING.
ISN'T HE GORGEOUS?
SENEFERU, THIS IS MY SISTER, NUALA.
NUALA, MEET SENEFERU.
CLURACAN. GET OUT OF MY BED-CHAMBER.
AH, NOW, AND WE'VE ONLY COME BY TO TELL YOU THAT LORD SHAPER IS ABOUT TO ANNOUNCE WHAT HE'S PLANNING TO DO WITH HIS NEW REALM.
SO GET A FROCK ON, LITTLE SISTER, AND COME AND HEAR THE GOOD WORD.
DO YOU THINK HE WILL ACCEDE TO OUR WISHES? THAT HE'LL KEEP HELL EMPTY, AND FORGIVE US THE TITHE?
NOT A HOPE. THERE'S TOO MANY BIG BOYS LEANING ON HIM--YOU SAW THEM ALL LAST NIGHT.
PERSONALLY, I FIGURE THE BEST I CAN HOPE TO GET OUT OF THESE SHENANIGANS IS EXCELLENT WINE, AND GREAT SEX.
SEE YOU DOWN THERE.

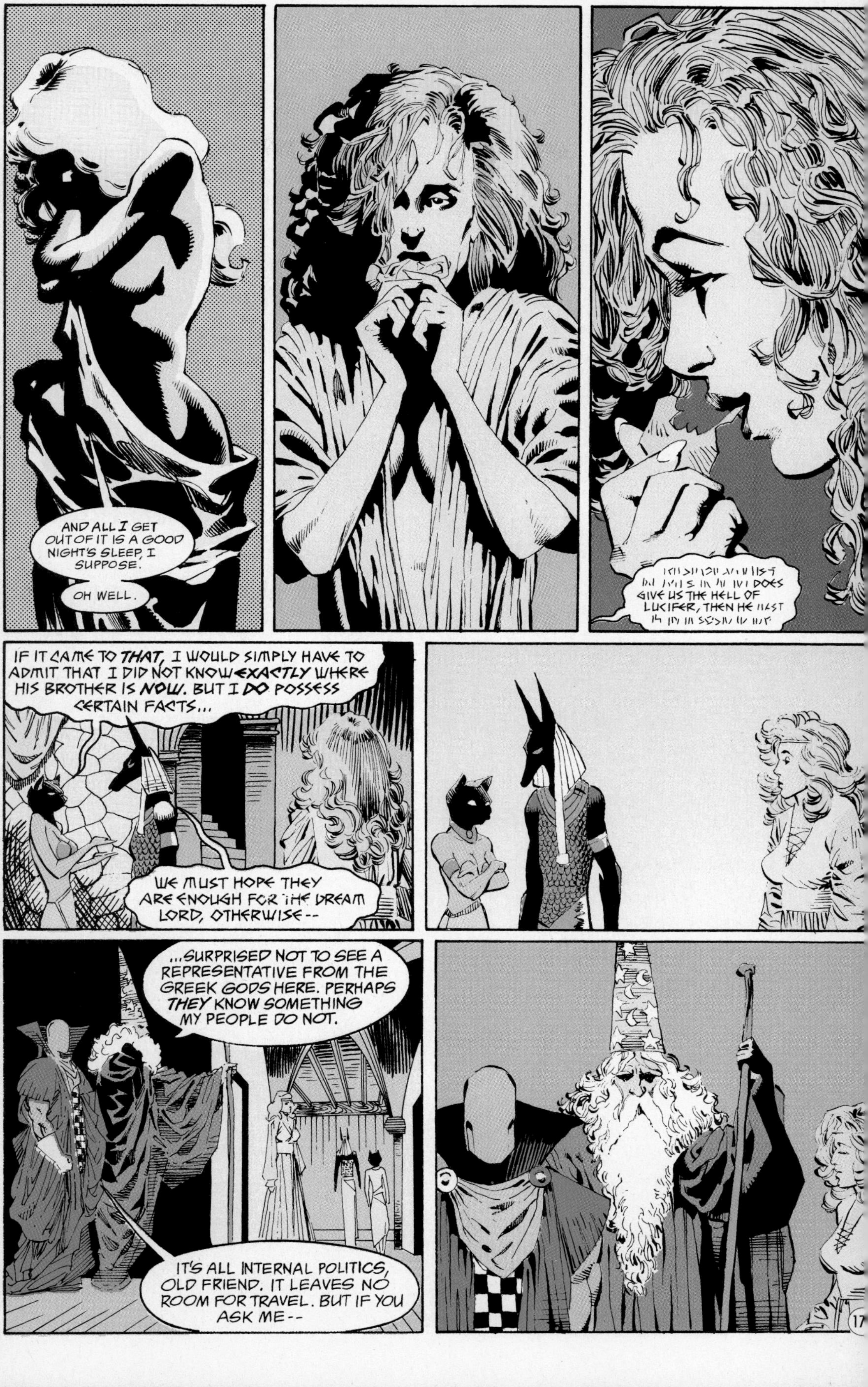
AND ALL I GET OUT OF IT IS A GOOD NIGHT'S SLEEP, I SUPPOSE.
OH WELL.
DOES GIVE US THE HELL OF LUCIFER, THEN HE
IF IT CAME TO THAT, I WOULD SIMPLY HAVE TO ADMIT THAT I DID NOT KNOW EXACTLY WHERE HIS BROTHER IS NOW. BUT I DO POSSESS CERTAIN FACTS...
WE MUST HOPE THEY ARE ENOUGH FOR THE DREAM LORD, OTHERWISE--
...SURPRISED NOT TO SEE A REPRESENTATIVE FROM THE GREEK GODS HERE. PERHAPS THEY KNOW SOMETHING MY PEOPLE DO NOT.
IT'S ALL INTERNAL POLITICS, OLD FRIEND. IT LEAVES NO ROOM FOR TRAVEL. BUT IF YOU ASK ME--

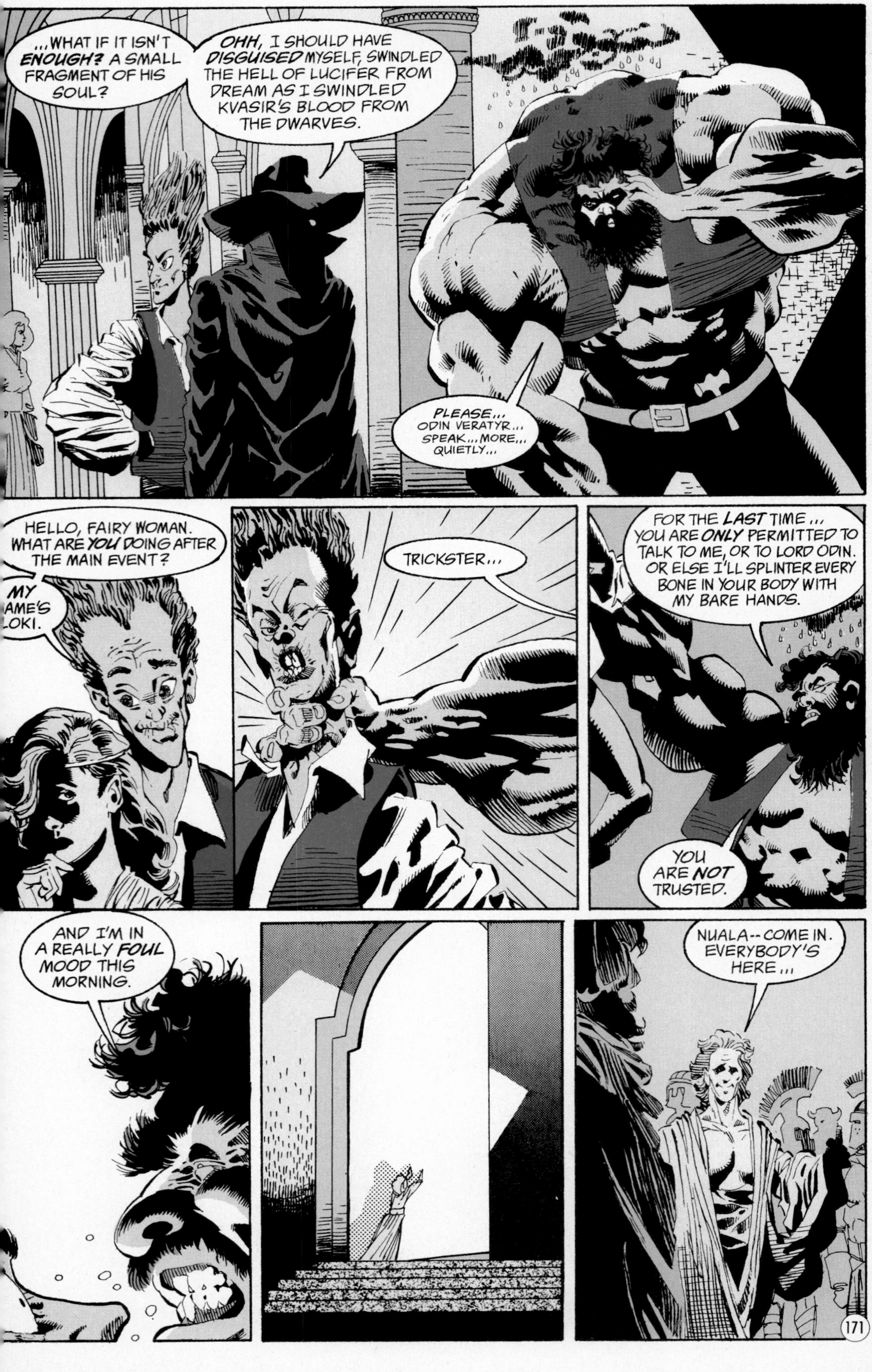

...WHAT IF IT ISN'T ENOUGH? A SMALL FRAGMENT OF HIS SOUL?
OHH, I SHOULD HAVE DISGUISED MYSELF, SWINDLED THE HELL OF LUCIFER FROM DREAM AS I SWINDLED KVASIR'S BLOOD FROM THE DWARVES.
PLEASE... ODIN VERATYR... SPEAK... MORE... QUIETLY...
HELLO, FAIRY WOMAN. WHAT ARE YOU DOING AFTER THE MAIN EVENT?
MY AME'S LOKI.
TRICKSTER...
FOR THE LAST TIME... YOU ARE ONLY PERMITTED TO TALK TO ME, OR TO LORD ODIN. OR ELSE I'LL SPLINTER EVERY BONE IN YOUR BODY WITH MY BARE HANDS.
YOU ARE NOT TRUSTED.
AND I'M IN A REALLY FOUL MOOD THIS MORNING.
NUALA--COME IN. EVERYBODY'S HERE...

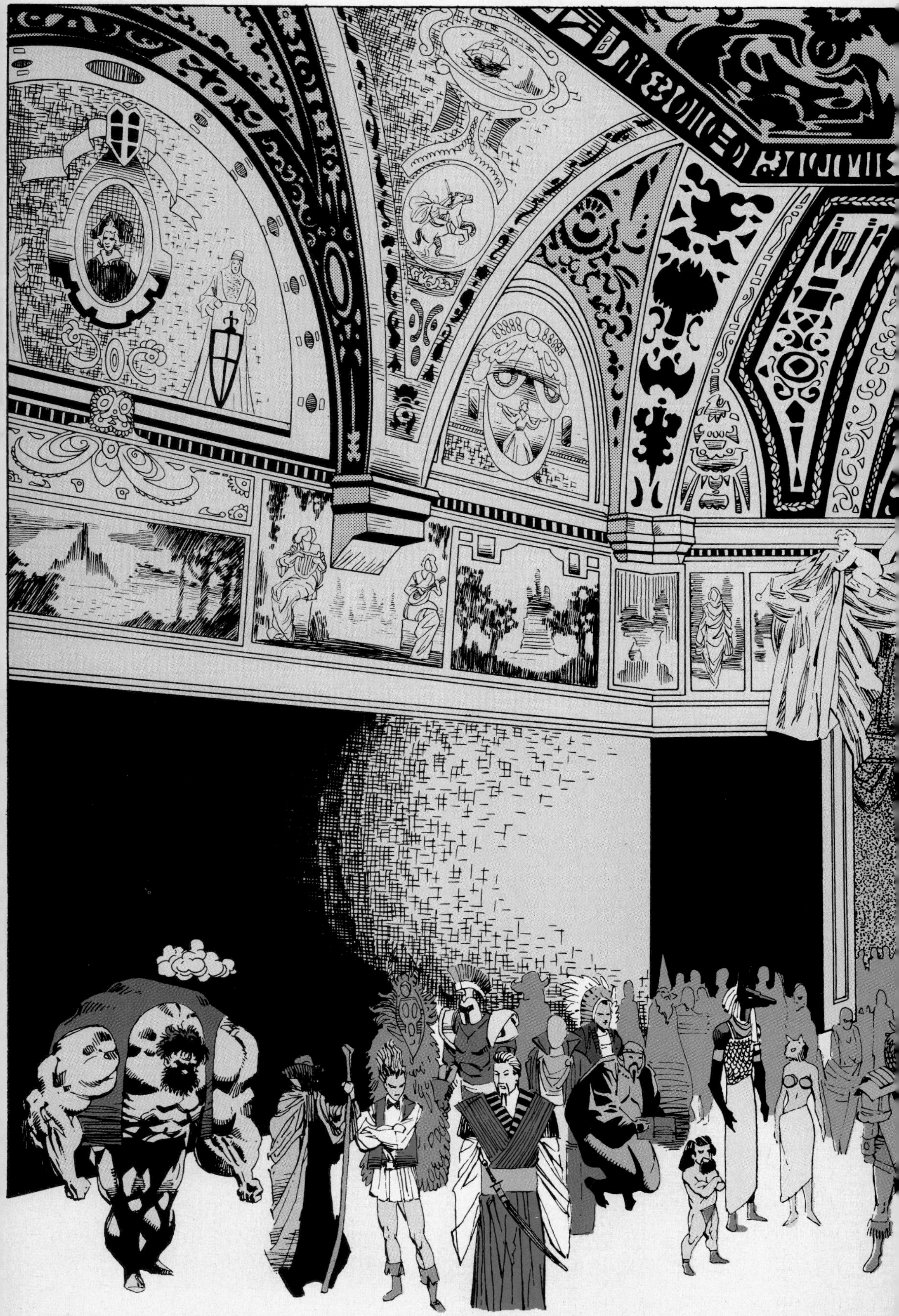

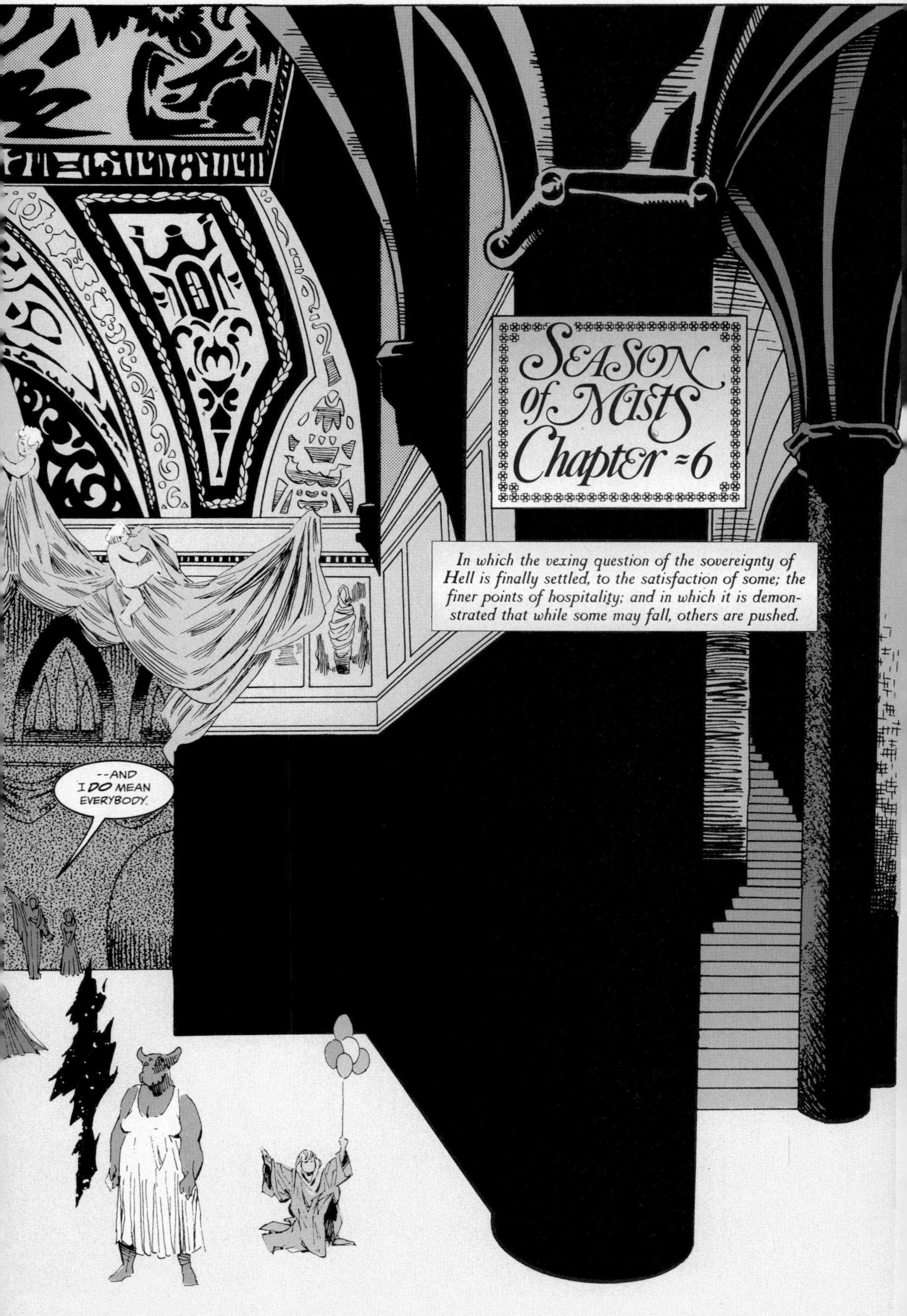
SEASON of MISTS Chapter ≈6
In which the vexing question of the sovereignty of Hell is finally settled, to the satisfaction of some; the finer points of hospitality; and in which it is demonstrated that while some may fall, others are pushed.
--AND I DO MEAN EVERYBODY.

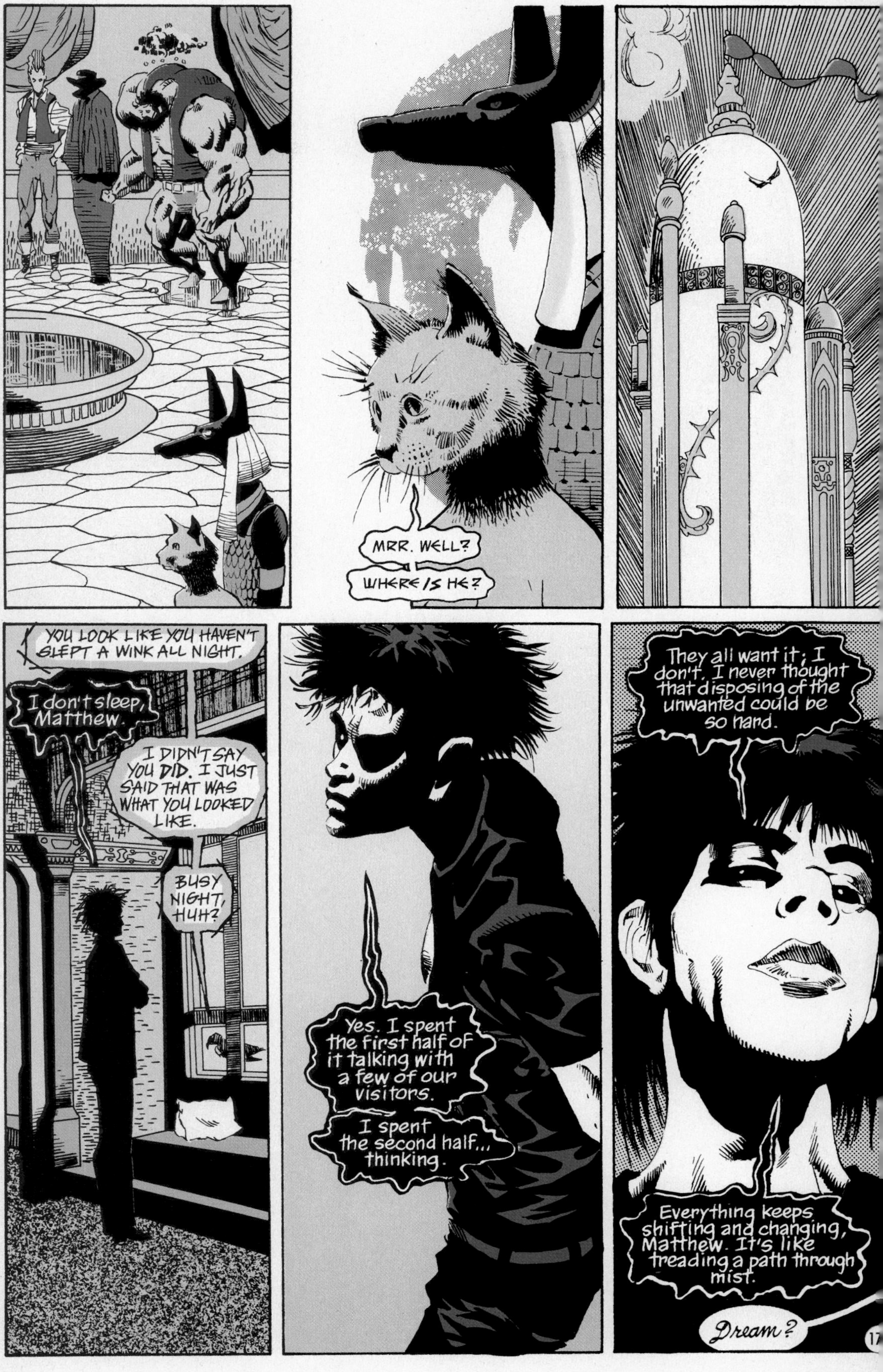
MRR. WELL?
WHERE IS HE?
YOU LOOK LIKE YOU HAVEN'T SLEPT A WINK ALL NIGHT.
I don't sleep, Matthew.
I DIDN'T SAY YOU DID. I JUST SAID THAT WAS WHAT YOU LOOKED LIKE.
BUSY NIGHT, HUH?
Yes. I spent the first half of it talking with a few of our visitors.
I spent the second half... thinking.
They all want it; I don't. I never thought that disposing of the unwanted could be so hard.
Everything keeps shifting and changing, Matthew. It's like treading a path through mist.
Dream?

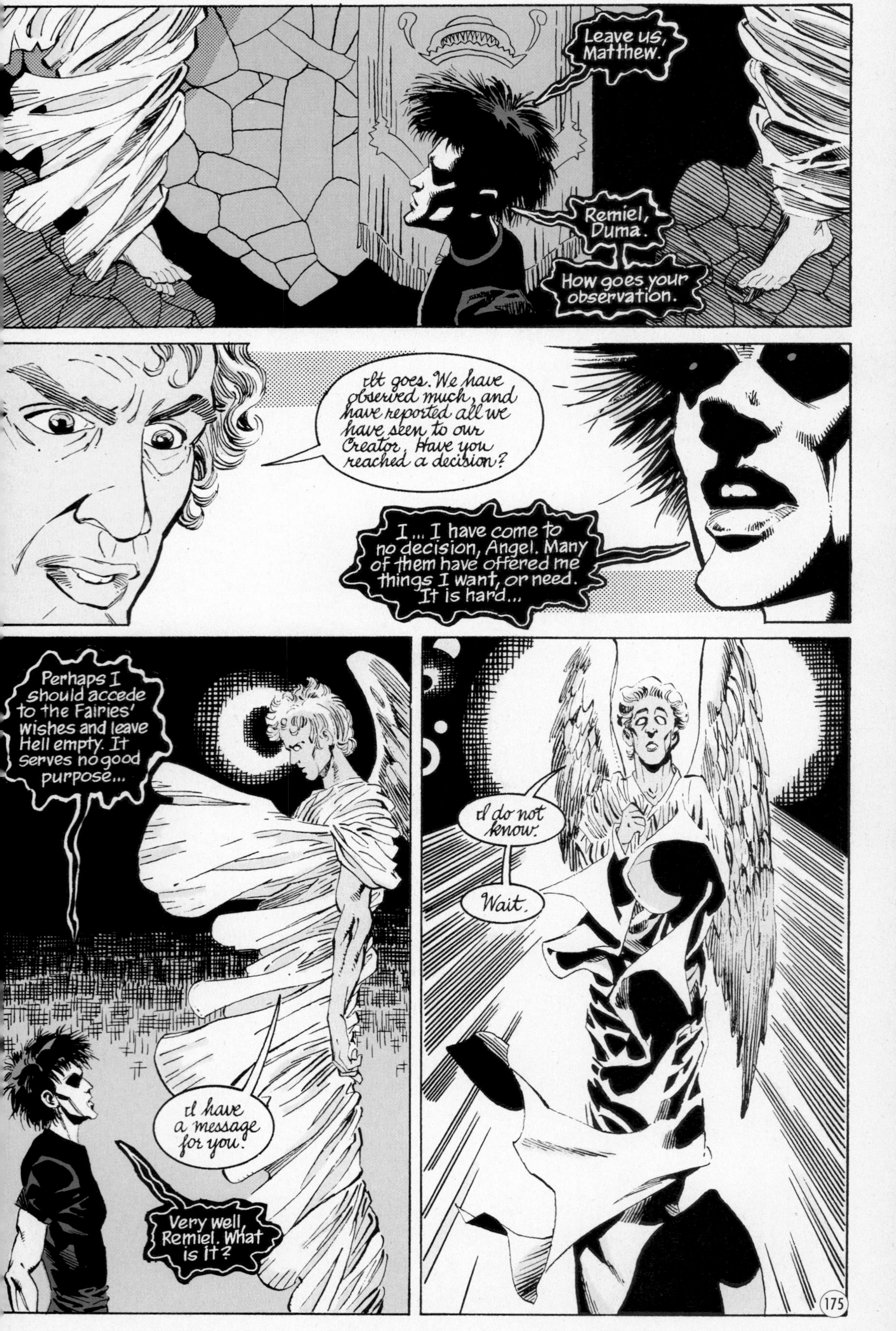
Leave us, Matthew.
Remiel, Duma.
How goes your observation.
It goes. We have observed much, and have reported all we have seen to our Creator. Have you reached a decision?
I... I have come to no decision, Angel. Many of them have offered me things I want, or need. It is hard...
Perhaps I should accede to the Fairies' wishes and leave Hell empty. It serves no good purpose...
I have a message for you.
Very well, Remiel. What is it?
I do not know.
Wait.

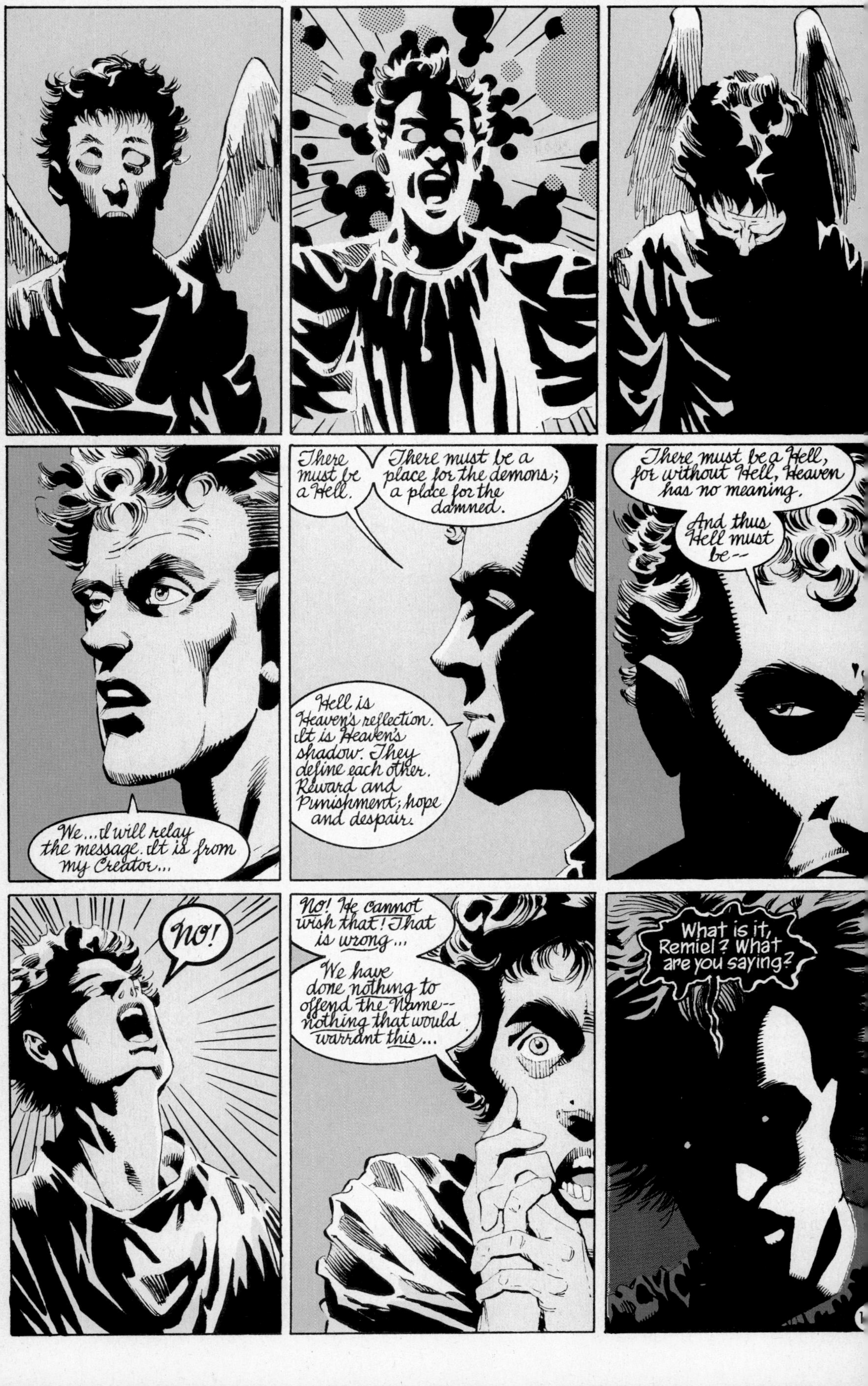
There must be a Hell.
There must be a place for the demons; a place for the damned.
Hell is Heaven's reflection. It is Heaven's shadow. They define each other. Reward and Punishment; hope and despair.
There must be a Hell, for without Hell, Heaven has no meaning.
And thus Hell must be--
We...I will relay the message. It is from my Creator...
NO!
No! He cannot wish that! That is wrong...
We have done nothing to offend the Name--nothing that would warrant this...
What is it, Remiel? What are you saying?

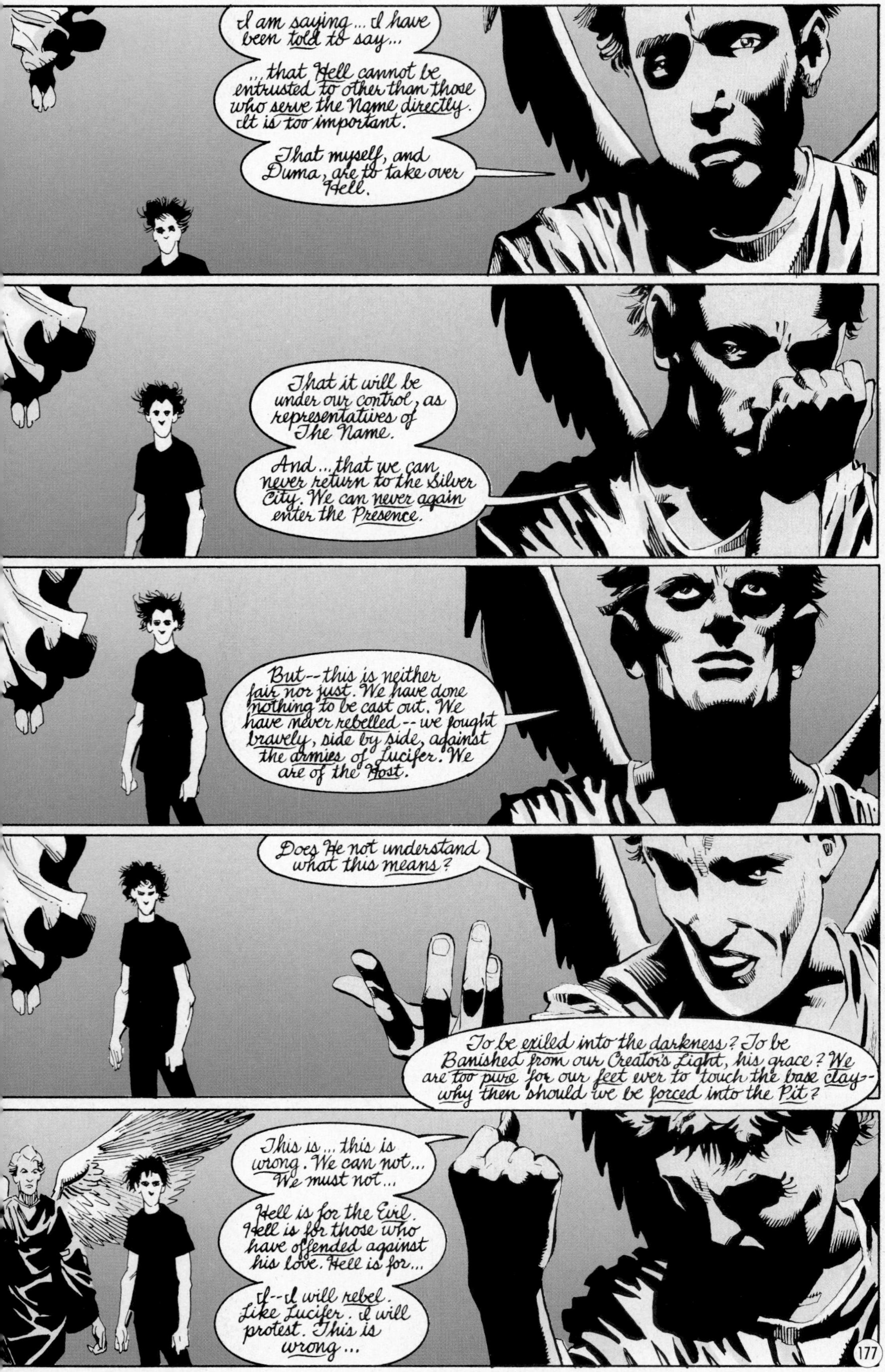
I am saying... I have been told to say...
...that Hell cannot be entrusted to other than those who serve the Name directly. It is too important.
That myself, and Duma, are to take over Hell.
That it will be under our control, as representatives of The Name.
And... that we can never return to the Silver City. We can never again enter the Presence.
But--this is neither fair nor just. We have done nothing to be cast out. We have never rebelled--we fought bravely, side by side, against the armies of Lucifer. We are of the Host.
Does He not understand what this means?
To be exiled into the darkness? To be Banished from our Creator's Light, his grace? We are too pure for our feet ever to touch the base clay-- why then should we be forced into the Pit?
This is... this is wrong. We can not... We must not...
Hell is for the Evil. Hell is for those who have offended against his love. Hell is for...
I--I will rebel. Like Lucifer. I will protest. This is wrong...

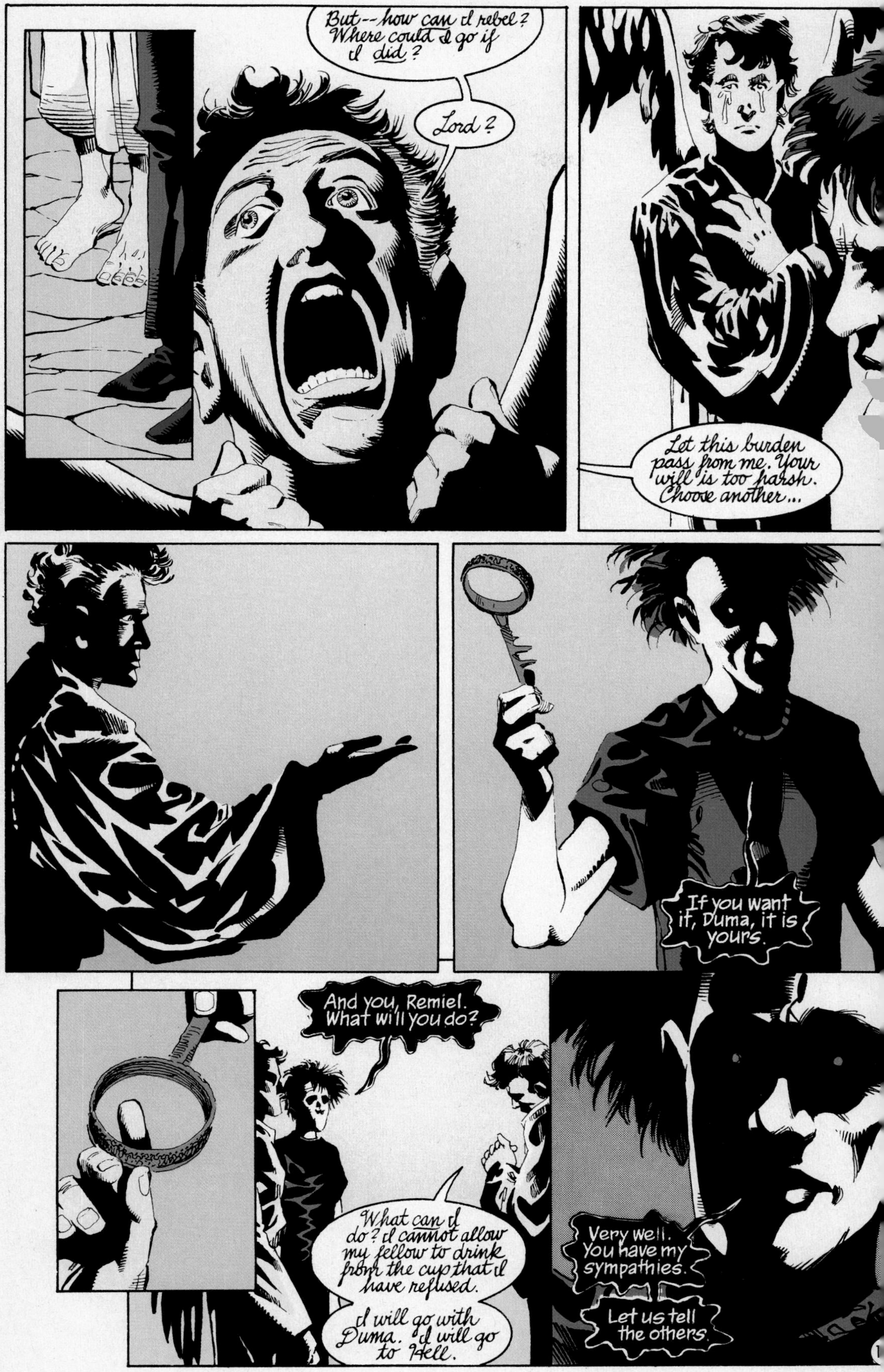
But--how can I rebel? Where could I go if I did?
Lord?
Let this burden pass from me. Your will is too harsh. Choose another...
If you want it, Duma, it is yours.
And you, Remiel. What will you do?
What can I do? I cannot allow my fellow to drink from the cup that I have refused.
I will go with Duma. I will go to Hell.
Very well. You have my sympathies.
Let us tell the others.

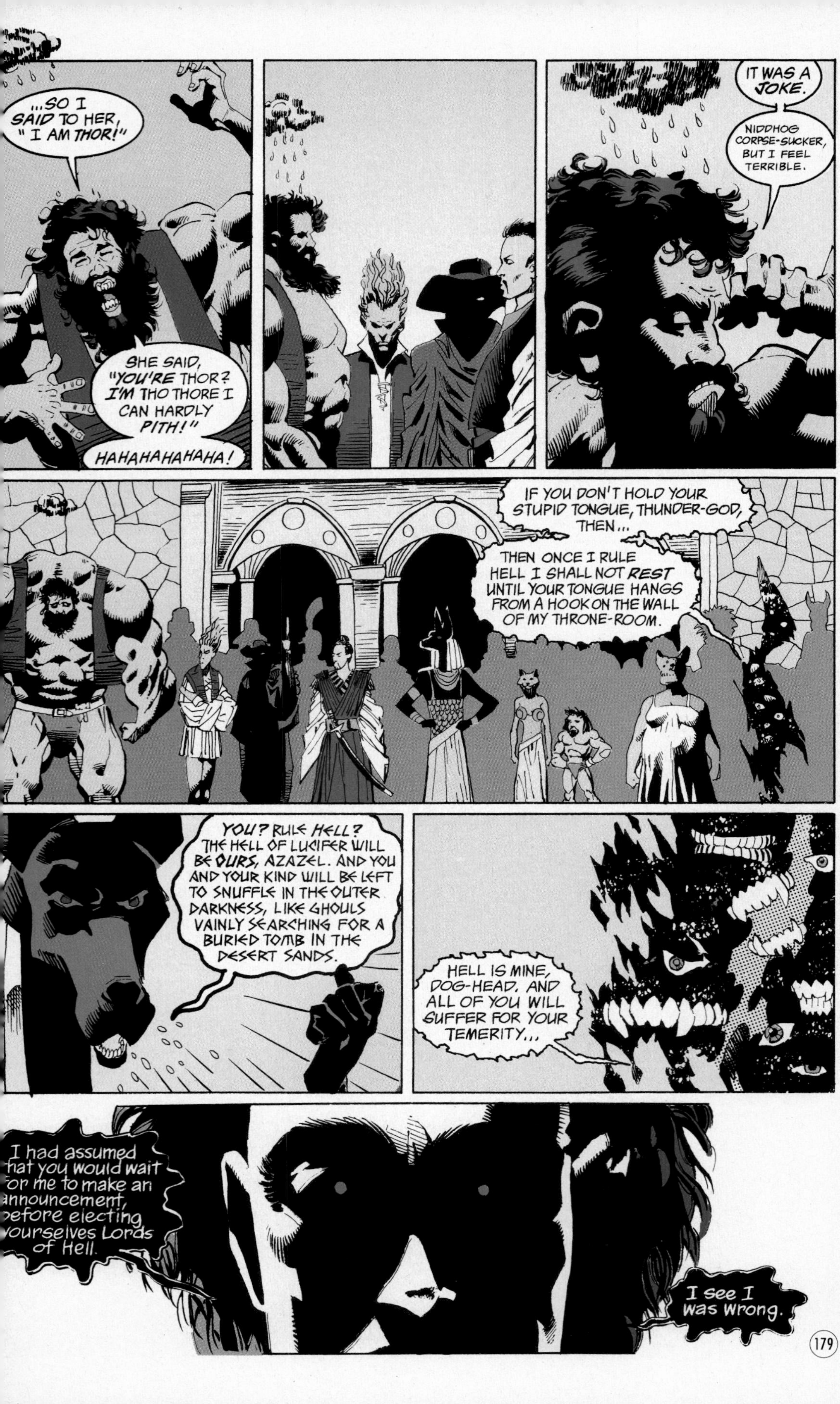
...SO I SAID TO HER, "I AM THOR!"
SHE SAID, "YOU'RE THOR? I'M THO THORE I CAN HARDLY PITH!"
HAHAHAHAHAHA!
IT WAS A JOKE.
NIDDHOG CORPSE-SUCKER, BUT I FEEL TERRIBLE.
IF YOU DON'T HOLD YOUR STUPID TONGUE, THUNDER-GOD, THEN...
THEN ONCE I RULE HELL I SHALL NOT REST UNTIL YOUR TONGUE HANGS FROM A HOOK ON THE WALL OF MY THRONE-ROOM.
YOU? RULE HELL? THE HELL OF LUCIFER WILL BE OURS, AZAZEL. AND YOU AND YOUR KIND WILL BE LEFT TO SNUFFLE IN THE OUTER DARKNESS, LIKE GHOULS VAINLY SEARCHING FOR A BURIED TOMB IN THE DESERT SANDS.
HELL IS MINE, DOG-HEAD. AND ALL OF YOU WILL SUFFER FOR YOUR TEMERITY...
I had assumed that you would wait for me to make an announcement, before electing yourselves Lords of Hell.
I see I was wrong.

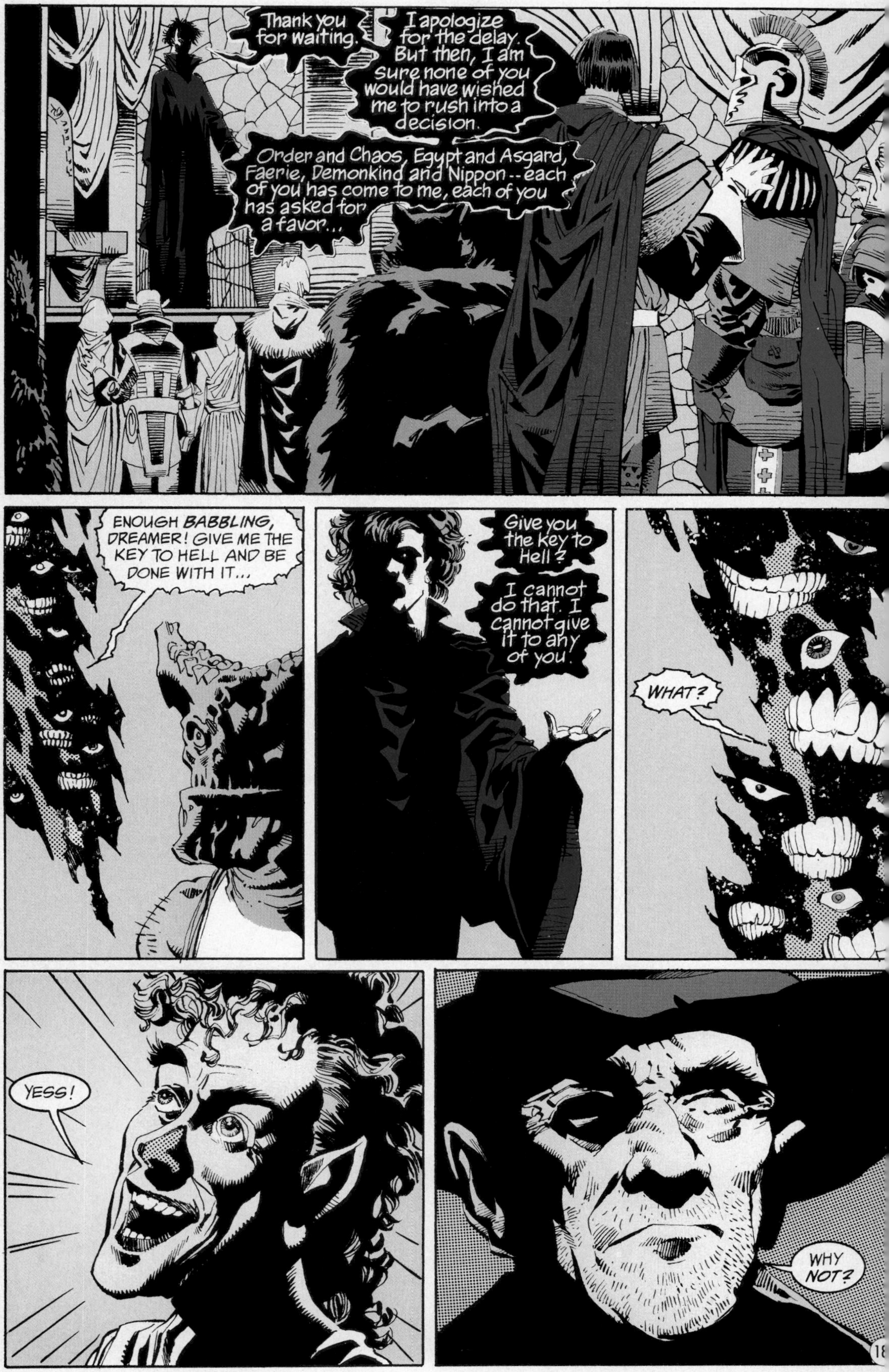
Thank you for waiting.
I apologize for the delay. But then, I am sure none of you would have wished me to rush into a decision.
Order and Chaos, Egypt and Asgard, Faerie, Demonkind and Nippon -- each of you has come to me, each of you has asked for a favor...
ENOUGH BABBLING, DREAMER! GIVE ME THE KEY TO HELL AND BE DONE WITH IT...
Give you the key to Hell?
I cannot do that. I cannot give it to any of you.
WHAT?
YESS!
WHY NOT?

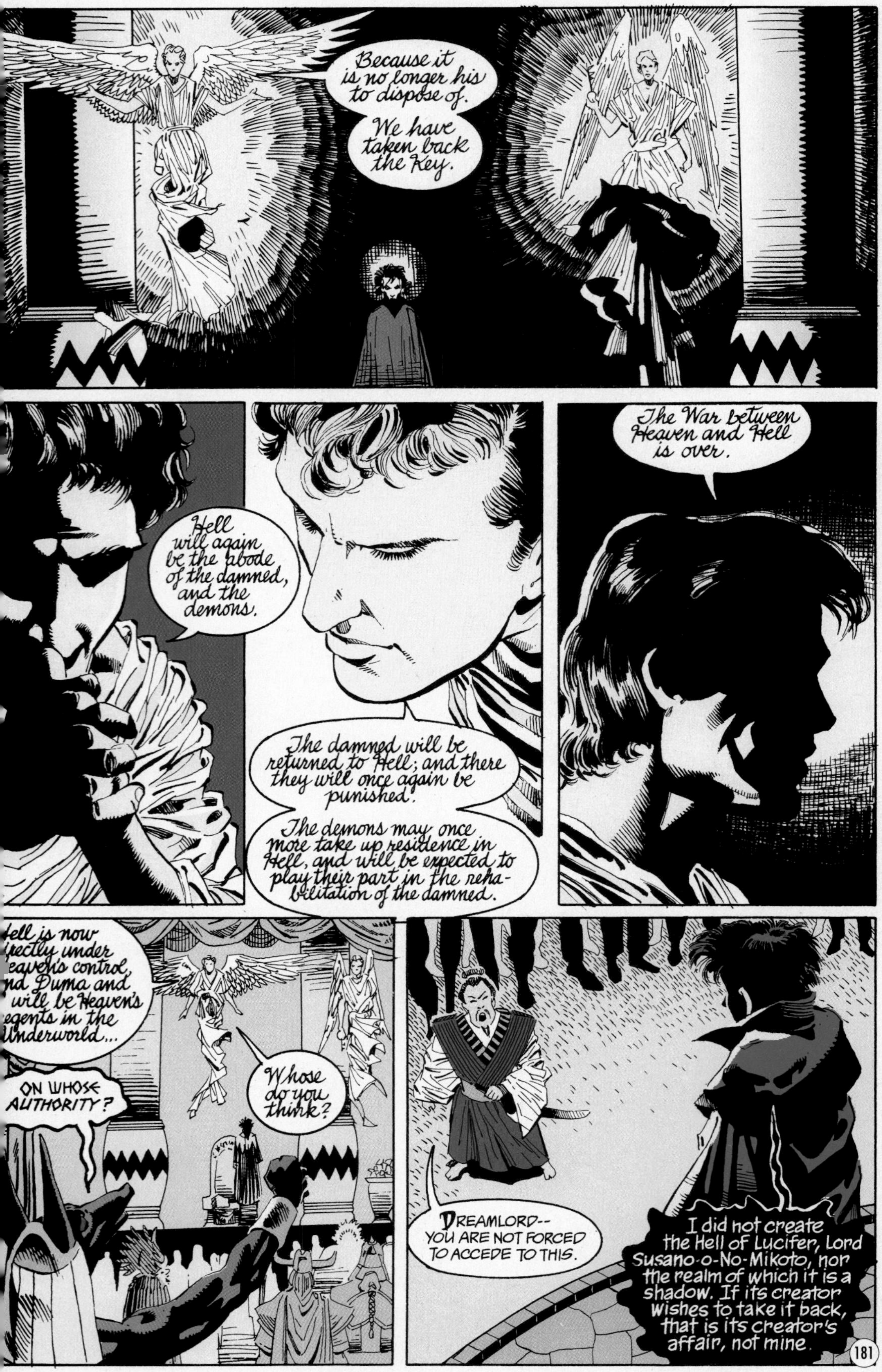
Because it is no longer his to dispose of.
We have taken back the Key.
Hell will again be the abode of the damned, and the demons.
The damned will be returned to Hell; and there they will once again be punished.
The demons may once more take up residence in Hell, and will be expected to play their part in the rehabilitation of the damned.
The War between Heaven and Hell is over.
Hell is now ectly under eaven's control, nd Duma and will be Heaven's egents in the nderworld...
ON WHOSE AUTHORITY?
Whose do you think?
DREAMLORD-- YOU ARE NOT FORCED TO ACCEDE TO THIS.
I did not create the Hell of Lucifer, Lord Susano-o-No-Mikoto, nor the realm of which it is a shadow. If its creator wishes to take it back, that is its creator's affair, not mine.

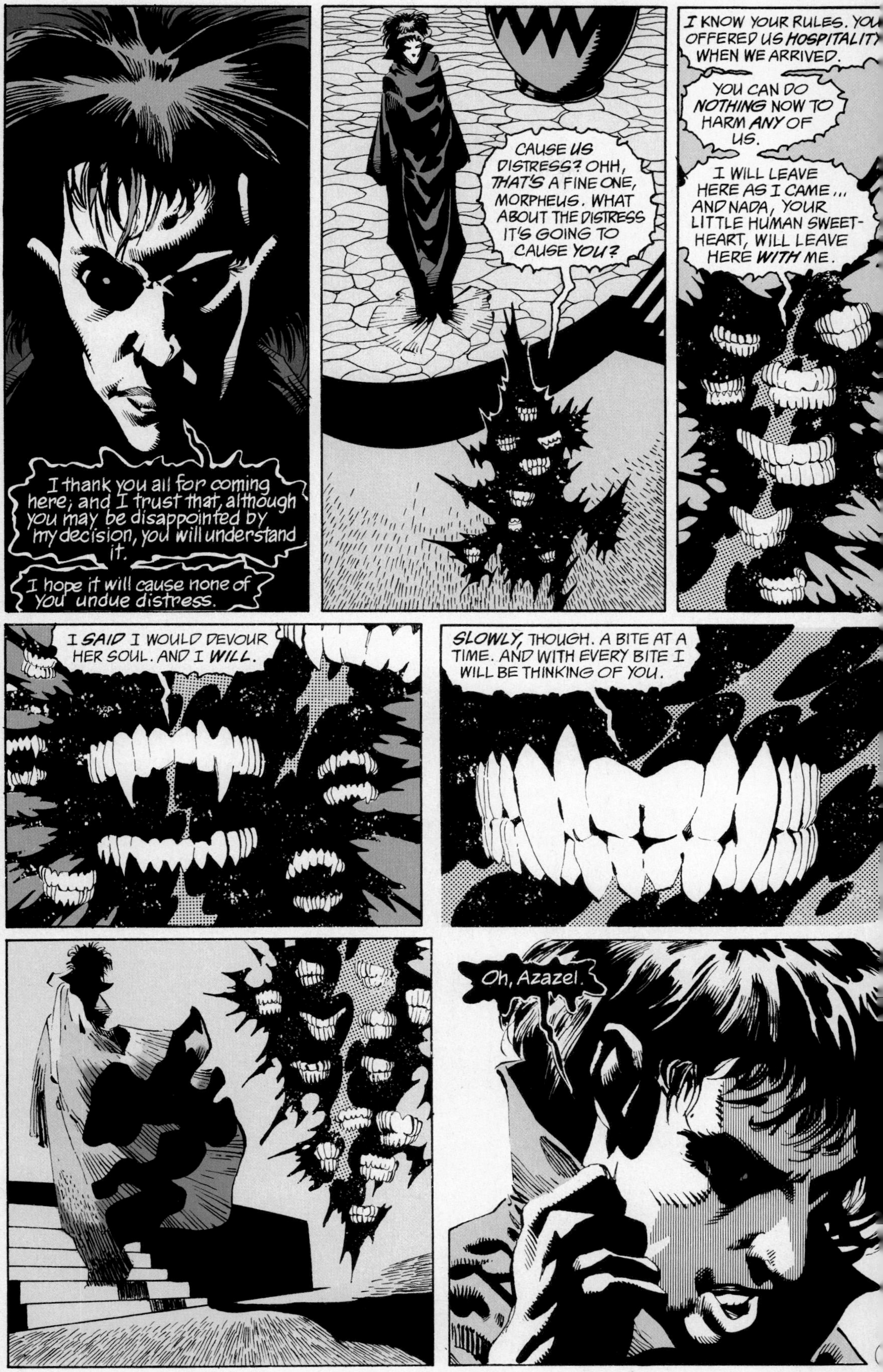

I thank you all for coming here; and I trust that, although you may be disappointed by my decision, you will understand it.
I hope it will cause none of you undue distress.
CAUSE US DISTRESS? OHH, THAT'S A FINE ONE, MORPHEUS. WHAT ABOUT THE DISTRESS IT'S GOING TO CAUSE YOU?
I KNOW YOUR RULES. YOU OFFERED US HOSPITALITY WHEN WE ARRIVED.
YOU CAN DO NOTHING NOW TO HARM ANY OF US.
I WILL LEAVE HERE AS I CAME... AND NADA, YOUR LITTLE HUMAN SWEET-HEART, WILL LEAVE HERE WITH ME.
I SAID I WOULD DEVOUR HER SOUL. AND I WILL.
SLOWLY, THOUGH. A BITE AT A TIME. AND WITH EVERY BITE I WILL BE THINKING OF YOU.
Oh, Azazel.

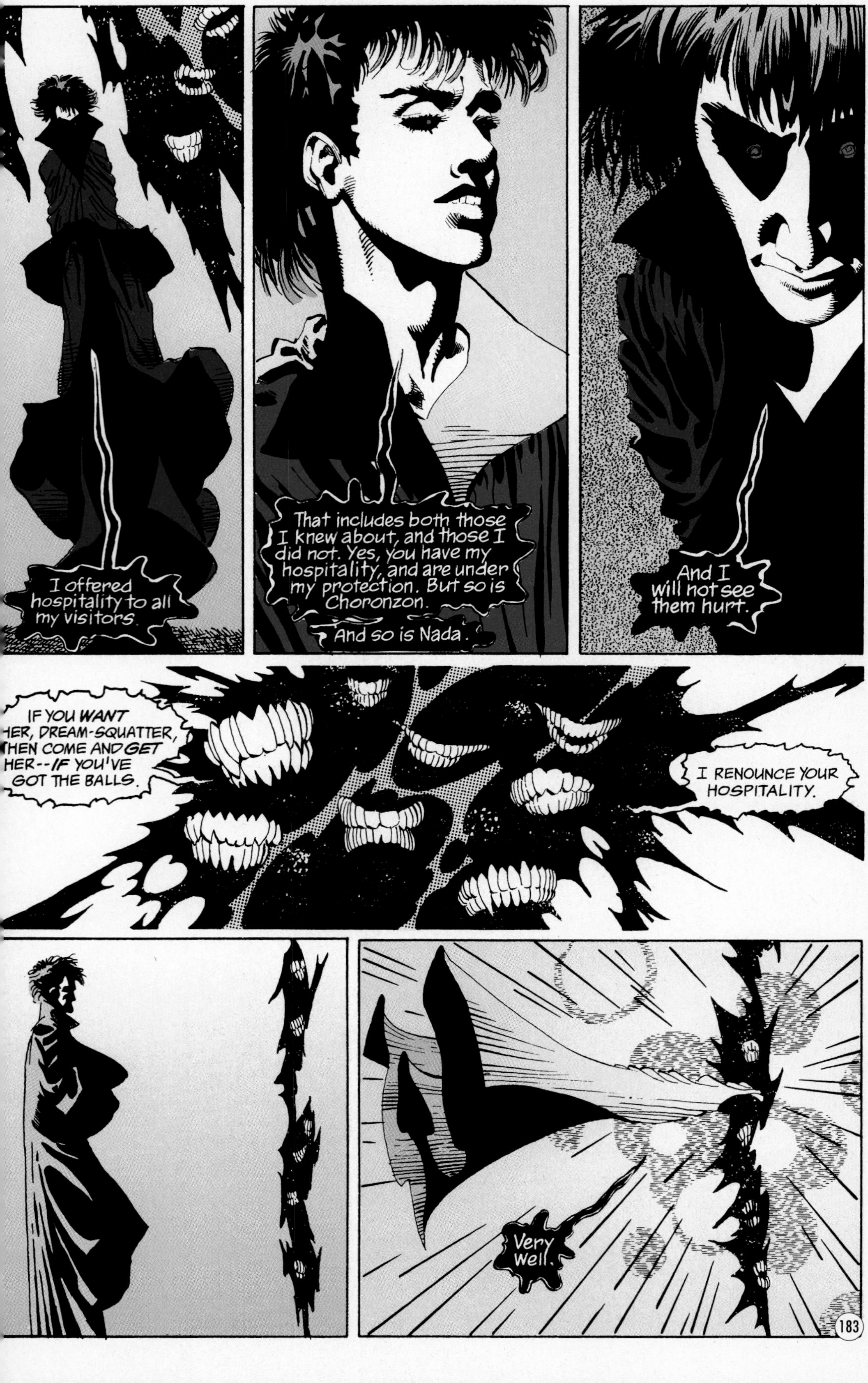
I offered hospitality to all my visitors.
That includes both those I knew about, and those I did not. Yes, you have my hospitality, and are under my protection. But so is Choronzon.
And so is Nada.
And I will not see them hurt.
IF YOU *WANT* HER, DREAM-SQUATTER, THEN COME AND *GET* HER--*IF* YOU'VE GOT THE BALLS.
I RENOUNCE YOUR HOSPITALITY.
Very Well.

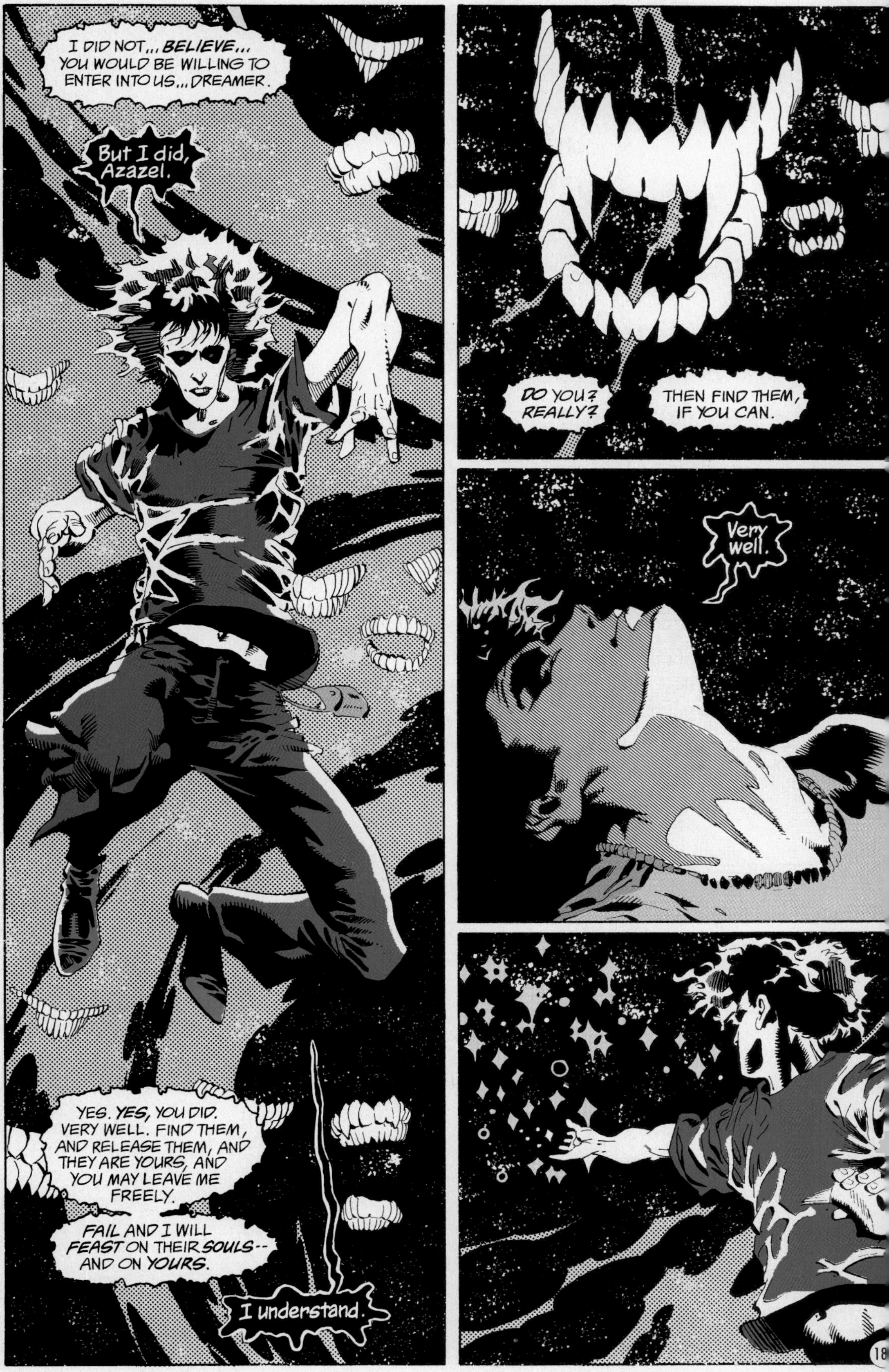

I DID NOT... BELIEVE... YOU WOULD BE WILLING TO ENTER INTO US... DREAMER.
But I did, Azazel.
YES. YES, YOU DID. VERY WELL. FIND THEM, AND RELEASE THEM, AND THEY ARE YOURS, AND YOU MAY LEAVE ME FREELY.
FAIL AND I WILL FEAST ON THEIR SOULS-- AND ON YOURS.
I understand.
DO YOU? REALLY?
THEN FIND THEM, IF YOU CAN.
Very well.

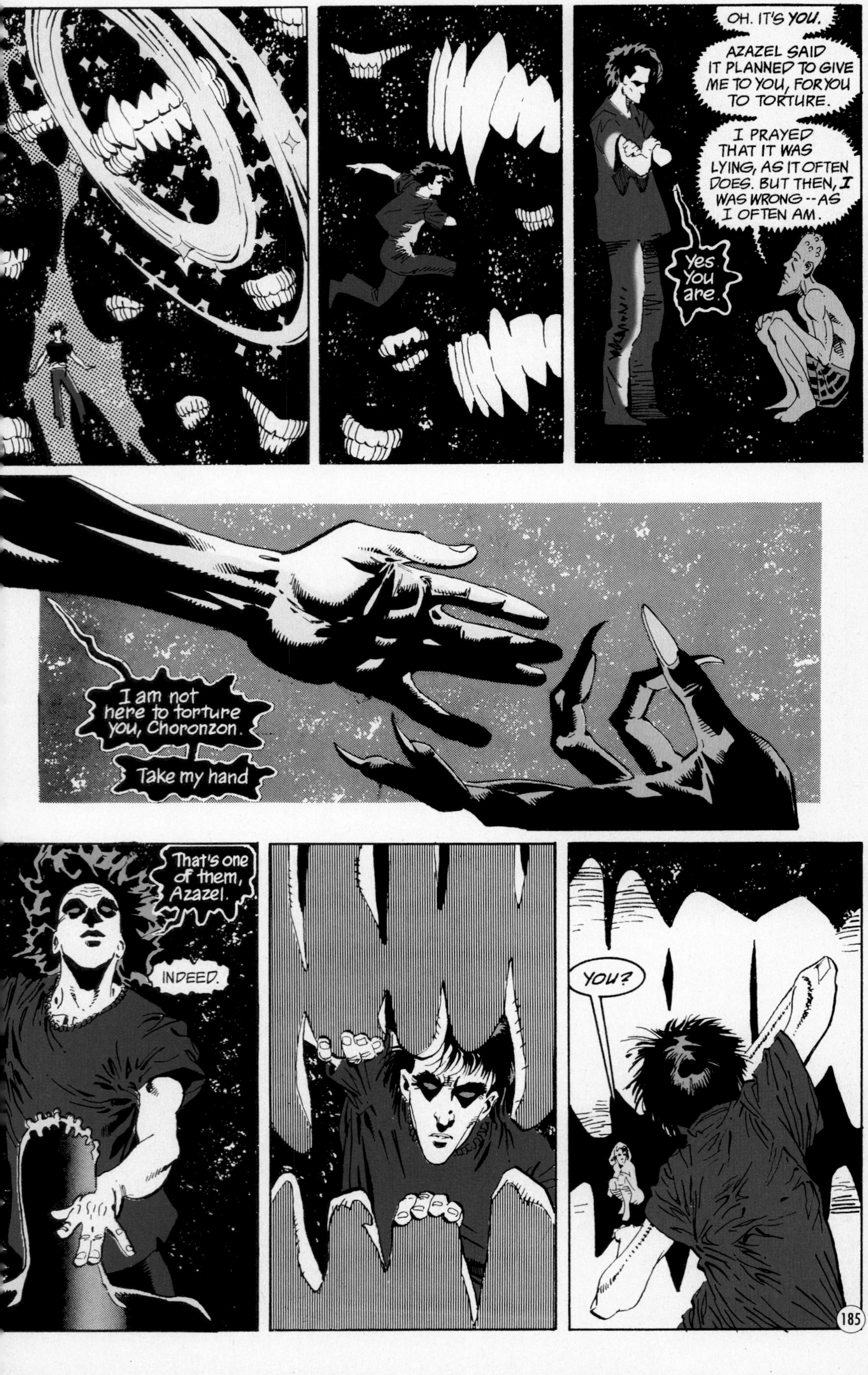
OH. IT'S YOU.
AZAZEL SAID IT PLANNED TO GIVE ME TO YOU, FOR YOU TO TORTURE.
I PRAYED THAT IT WAS LYING, AS IT OFTEN DOES. BUT THEN, I WAS WRONG -- AS I OFTEN AM.
Yes. You are.
I am not here to torture you, Choronzon.
Take my hand
That's one of them, Azazel.
INDEED.
YOU?

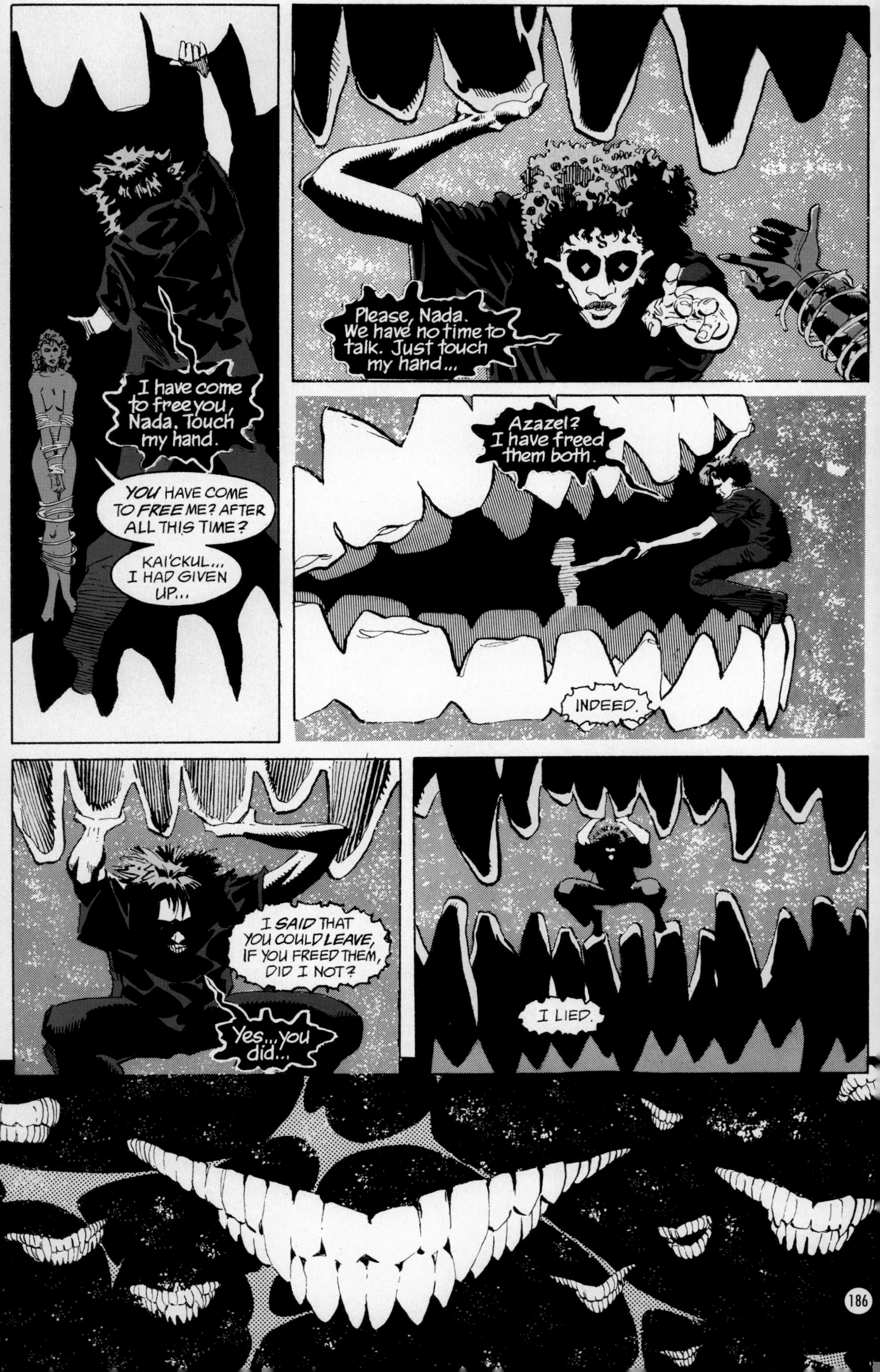
I have come to free you, Nada. Touch my hand.
YOU HAVE COME TO FREE ME? AFTER ALL THIS TIME?
KAI'CKUL... I HAD GIVEN UP...
Please, Nada. We have no time to talk. Just touch my hand...
Azazel? I have freed them both.
INDEED.
I SAID THAT YOU COULD LEAVE, IF YOU FREED THEM, DID I NOT?
Yes... you did...
I LIED.

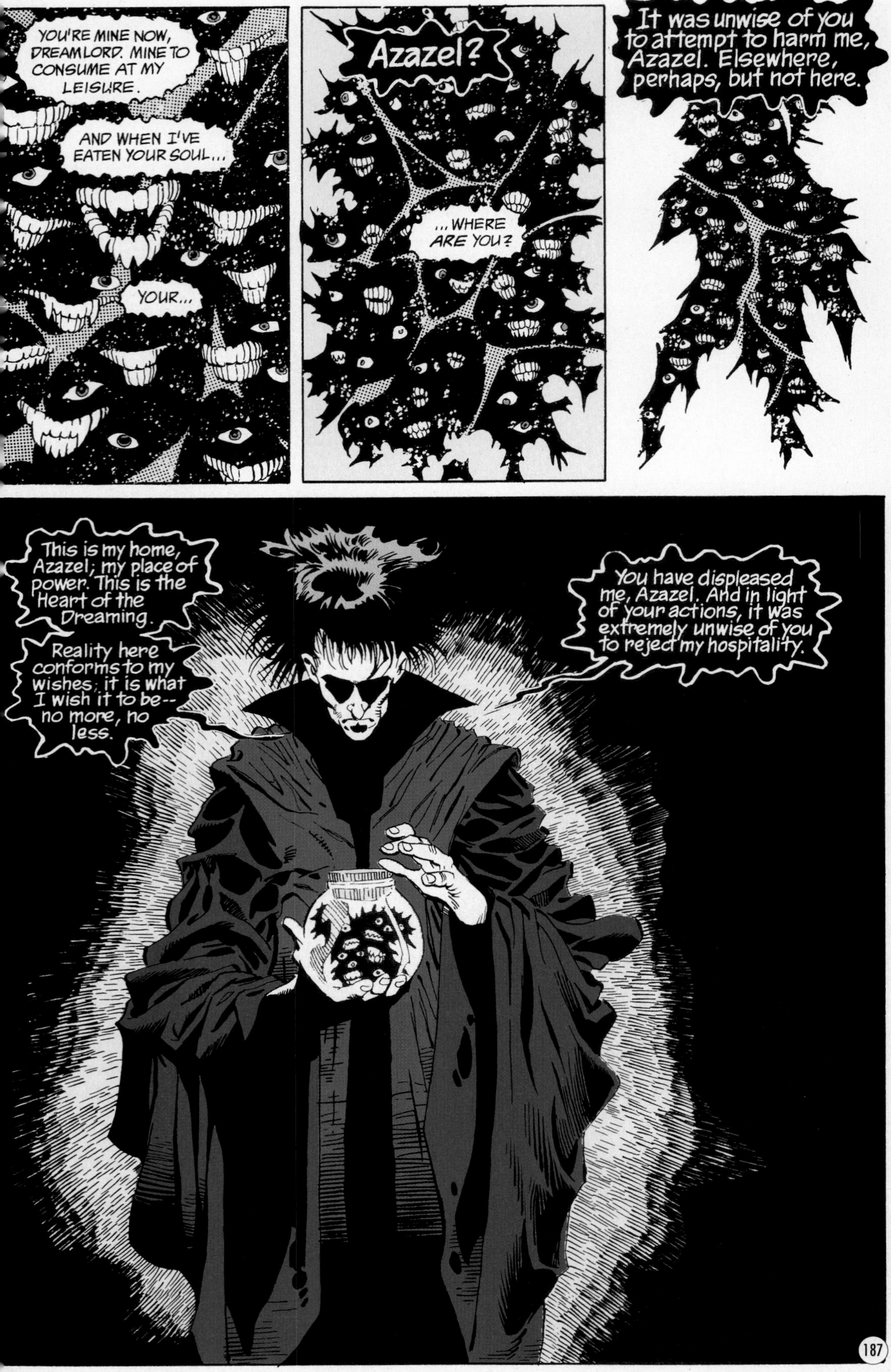
YOU'RE MINE NOW, DREAMLORD. MINE TO CONSUME AT MY LEISURE.
AND WHEN I'VE EATEN YOUR SOUL...
YOUR...
Azazel?
...WHERE ARE YOU?
It was unwise of you to attempt to harm me, Azazel. Elsewhere, perhaps, but not here.
This is my home, Azazel; my place of power. This is the Heart of the Dreaming.
Reality here conforms to my wishes; it is what I wish it to be--no more, no less.
You have displeased me, Azazel. And in light of your actions, it was extremely unwise of you to reject my hospitality.

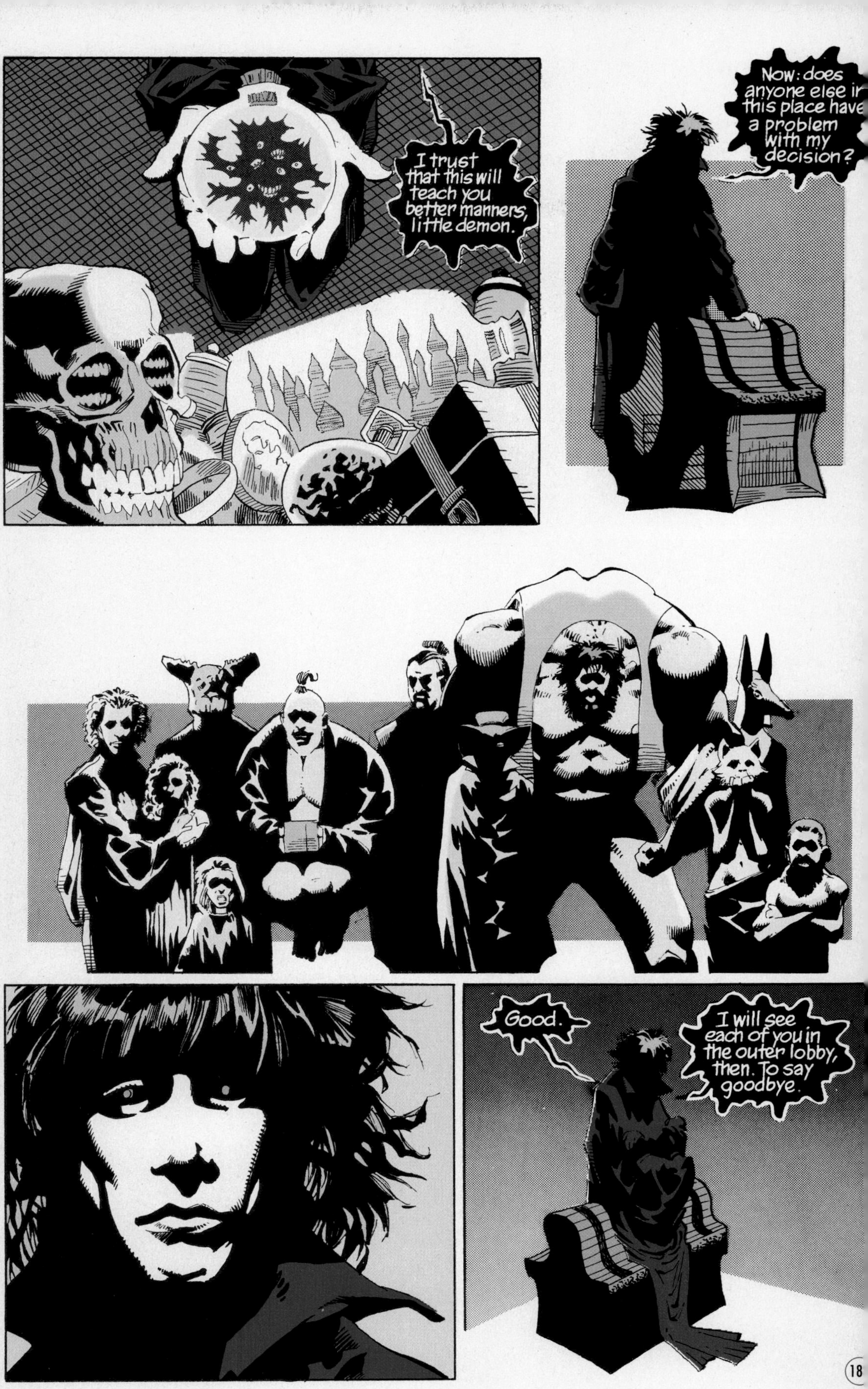
I trust that this will teach you better manners, little demon.
Now: does anyone else in this place have a problem with my decision?
Good.
I will see each of you in the outer lobby, then. To say goodbye.

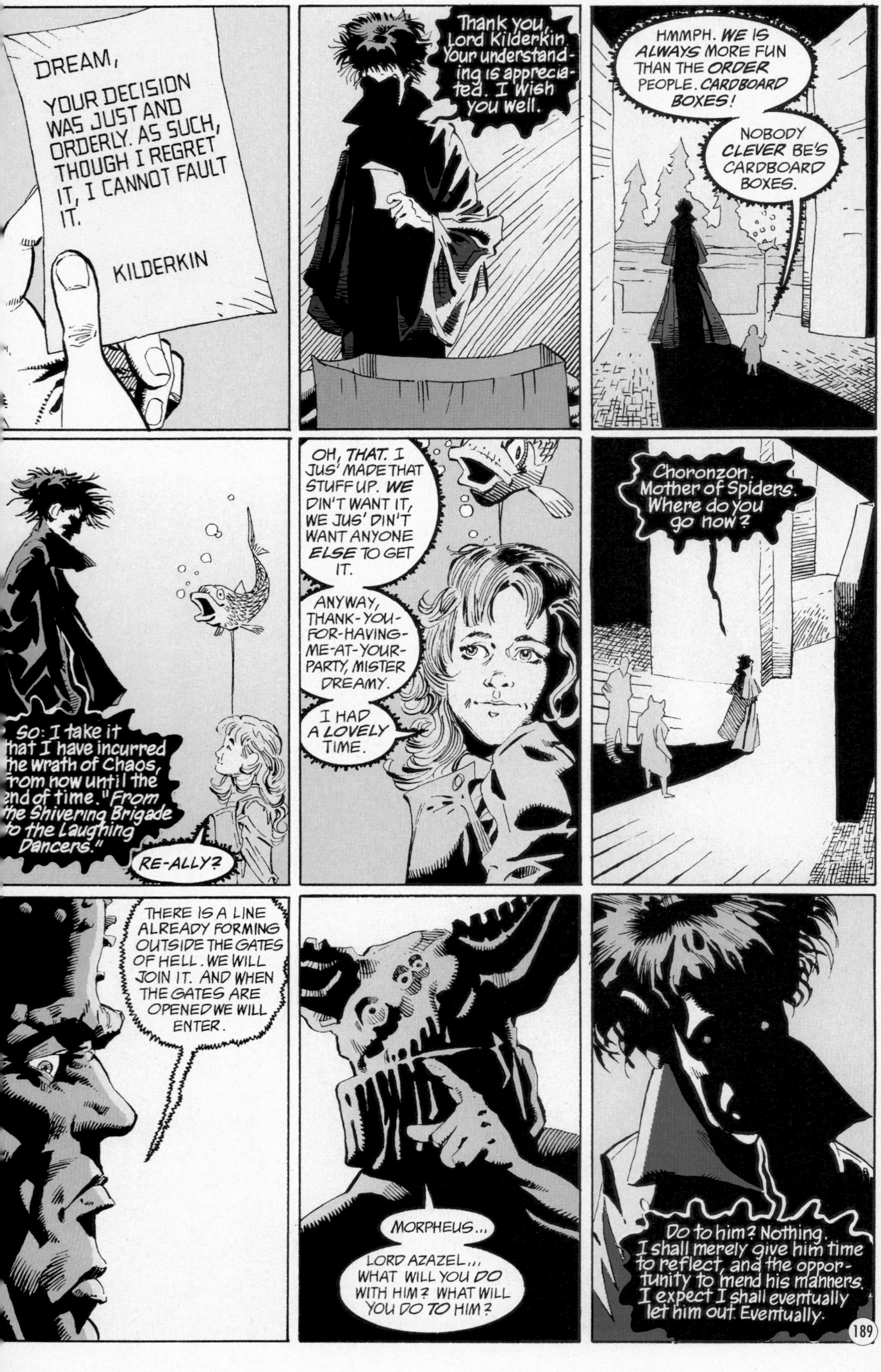
DREAM,
YOUR DECISION WAS JUST AND ORDERLY. AS SUCH, THOUGH I REGRET IT, I CANNOT FAULT IT.
KILDERKIN
Thank you, Lord Kilderkin. Your understanding is appreciated. I wish you well.
HMMPH. WE IS ALWAYS MORE FUN THAN THE ORDER PEOPLE. CARDBOARD BOXES!
NOBODY CLEVER BE'S CARDBOARD BOXES.
So: I take it that I have incurred the wrath of Chaos, from now until the end of time. "From the Shivering Brigade to the Laughing Dancers."
RE-ALLY?
OH, THAT. I JUS' MADE THAT STUFF UP. WE DIN'T WANT IT, WE JUS' DIN'T WANT ANYONE ELSE TO GET IT.
ANYWAY, THANK-YOU-FOR-HAVING-ME-AT-YOUR-PARTY, MISTER DREAMY.
I HAD A LOVELY TIME.
Choronzon. Mother of Spiders. Where do you go now?
THERE IS A LINE ALREADY FORMING OUTSIDE THE GATES OF HELL. WE WILL JOIN IT. AND WHEN THE GATES ARE OPENED WE WILL ENTER.
MORPHEUS...
LORD AZAZEL... WHAT WILL YOU DO WITH HIM? WHAT WILL YOU DO TO HIM?
Do to him? Nothing. I shall merely give him time to reflect, and the opportunity to mend his manners. I expect I shall eventually let him out. Eventually.

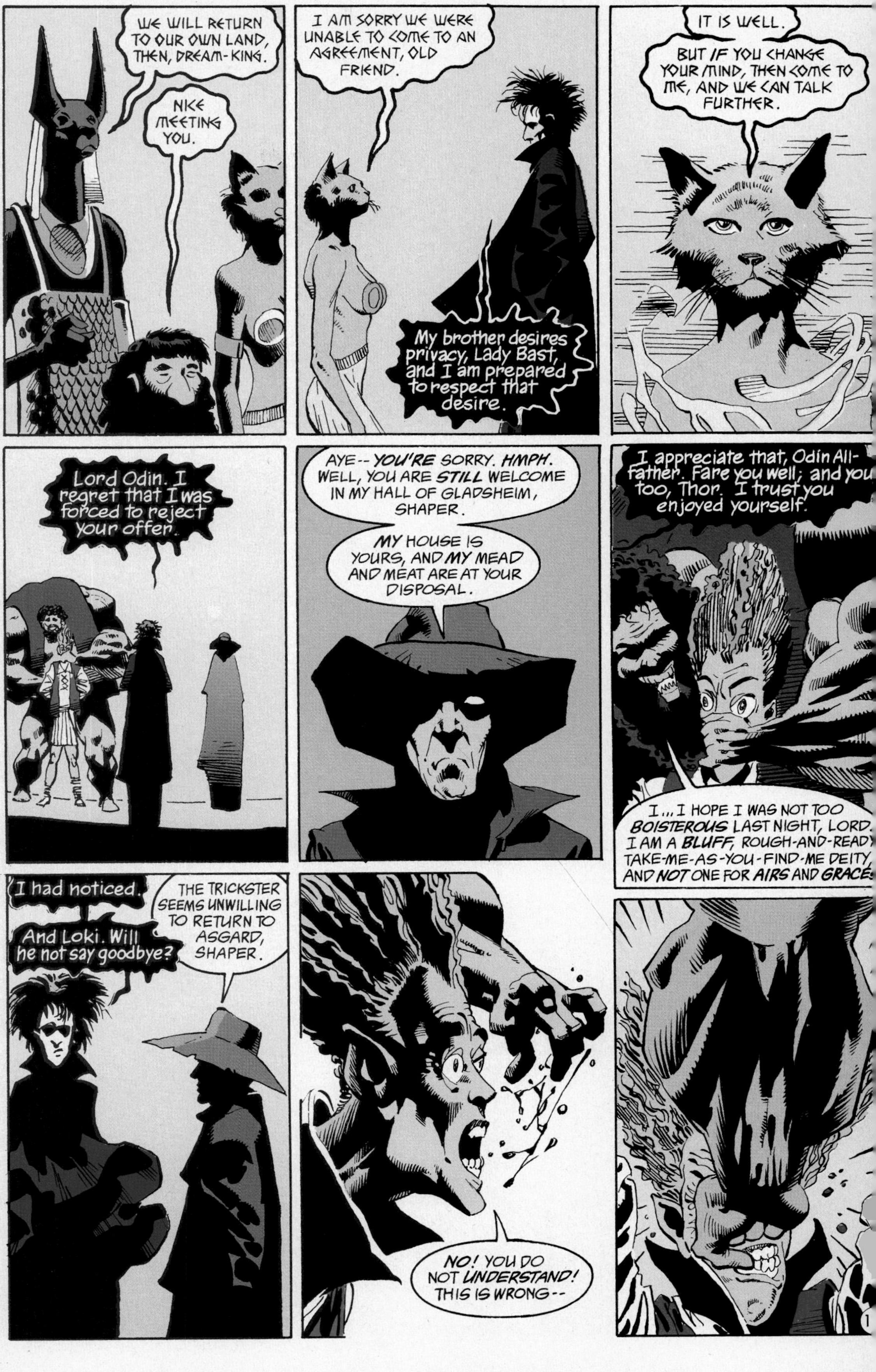
WE WILL RETURN TO OUR OWN LAND, THEN, DREAM-KING.
NICE MEETING YOU.
I AM SORRY WE WERE UNABLE TO COME TO AN AGREEMENT, OLD FRIEND.
My brother desires privacy, Lady Bast, and I am prepared to respect that desire.
IT IS WELL.
BUT *IF* YOU CHANGE YOUR MIND, THEN COME TO ME, AND WE CAN TALK FURTHER.
Lord Odin. I regret that I was forced to reject your offer.
AYE-- ***YOU'RE*** SORRY. ***HMPH.*** WELL, YOU ARE ***STILL*** WELCOME IN MY HALL OF GLADSHEIM, SHAPER.
MY HOUSE IS YOURS, AND ***MY*** MEAD AND MEAT ARE AT YOUR DISPOSAL.
I appreciate that, Odin All-father. Fare you well; and you too, Thor. I trust you enjoyed yourself.
I... I HOPE I WAS NOT TOO ***BOISTEROUS*** LAST NIGHT, LORD. I AM A ***BLUFF***, ROUGH-AND-READY TAKE-ME-AS-YOU-FIND-ME DEITY, AND ***NOT*** ONE FOR ***AIRS*** AND ***GRACE***.
I had noticed.
THE TRICKSTER SEEMS UNWILLING TO RETURN TO ASGARD, SHAPER.
And Loki. Will he not say goodbye?
NO! YOU DO NOT ***UNDERSTAND!*** THIS IS WRONG--

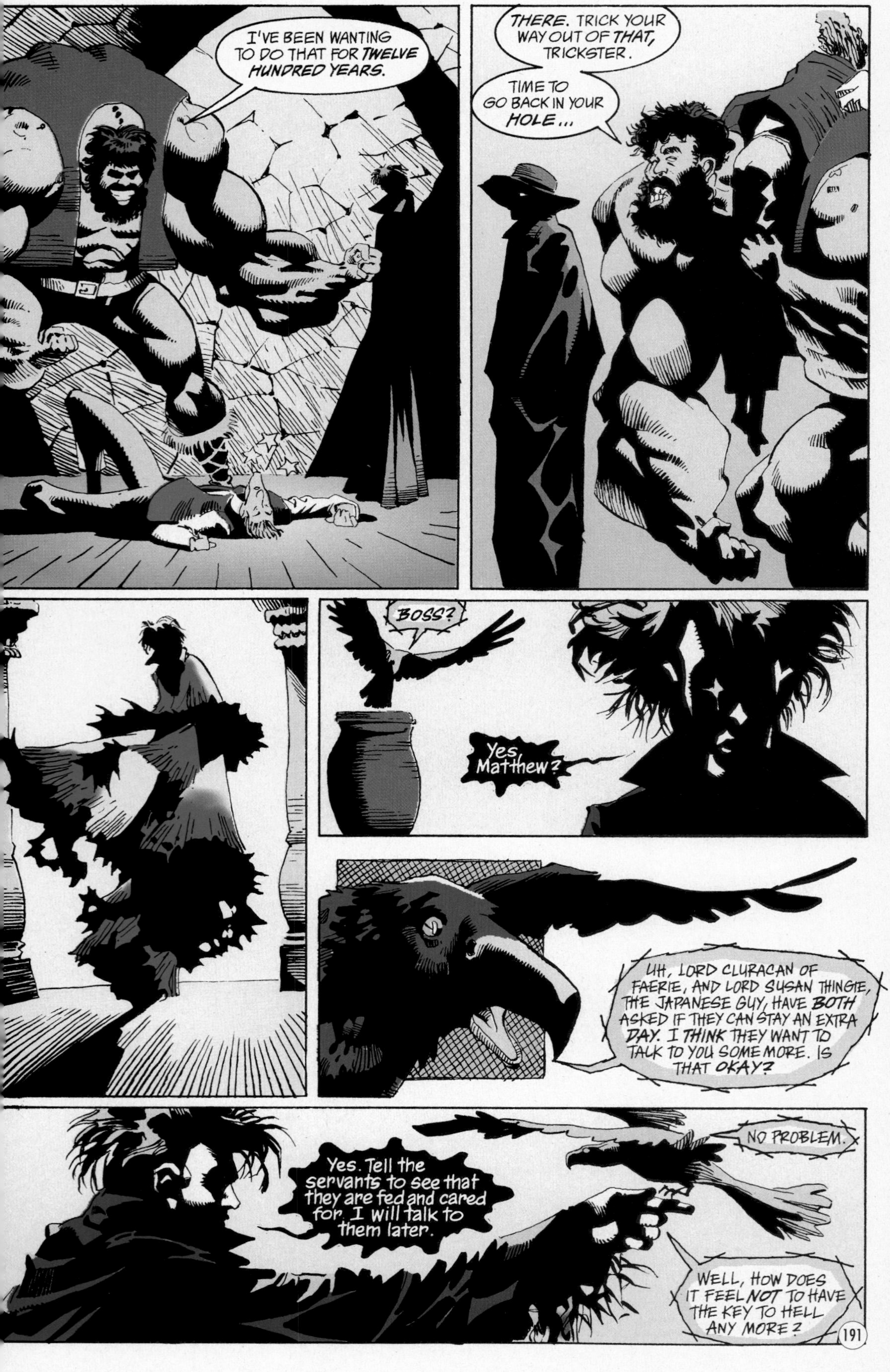
I'VE BEEN WANTING TO DO THAT FOR TWELVE HUNDRED YEARS.
THERE. TRICK YOUR WAY OUT OF THAT, TRICKSTER.
TIME TO GO BACK IN YOUR HOLE...
BOSS?
Yes, Matthew?
UH, LORD CLURACAN OF FAERIE, AND LORD SUSAN THINGIE, THE JAPANESE GUY, HAVE BOTH ASKED IF THEY CAN STAY AN EXTRA DAY. I THINK THEY WANT TO TALK TO YOU SOME MORE. IS THAT OKAY?
Yes. Tell the servants to see that they are fed and cared for. I will talk to them later.
NO PROBLEM.
WELL, HOW DOES IT FEEL NOT TO HAVE THE KEY TO HELL ANY MORE?

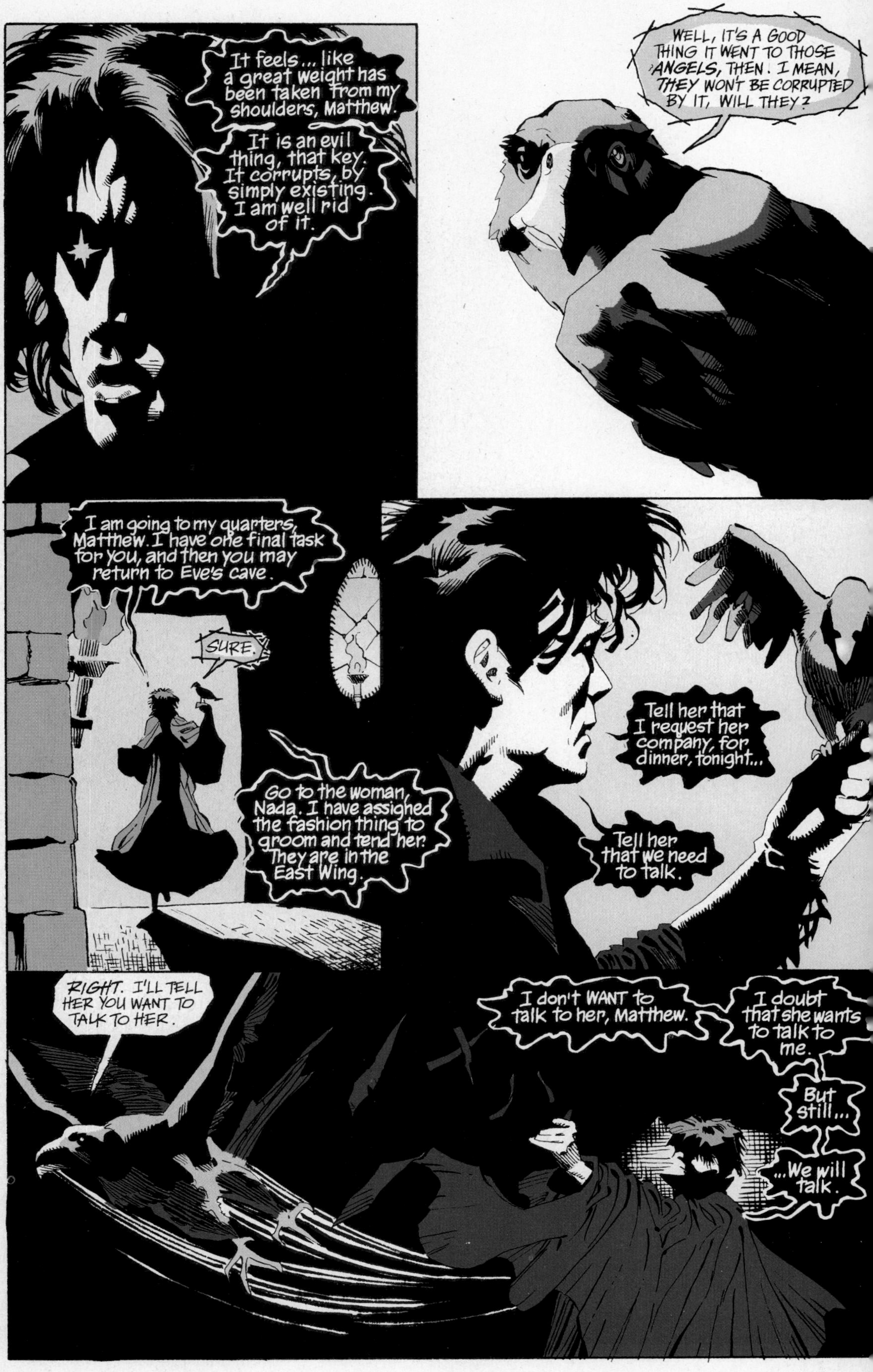
It feels... like a great weight has been taken from my shoulders, Matthew.
It is an evil thing, that key. It corrupts, by simply existing. I am well rid of it.
WELL, IT'S A GOOD THING IT WENT TO THOSE ANGELS, THEN. I MEAN, THEY WON'T BE CORRUPTED BY IT, WILL THEY?
I am going to my quarters, Matthew. I have one final task for you, and then you may return to Eve's cave.
SURE.
Go to the woman, Nada. I have assigned the fashion thing to groom and tend her. They are in the East Wing.
Tell her that I request her company, for dinner, tonight...
Tell her that we need to talk.
RIGHT. I'LL TELL HER YOU WANT TO TALK TO HER.
I don't WANT to talk to her, Matthew.
I doubt that she wants to talk to me.
But still...
...We will talk.

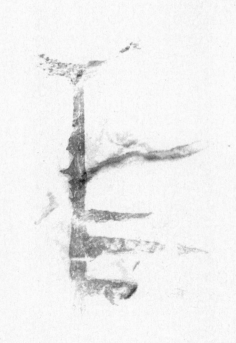

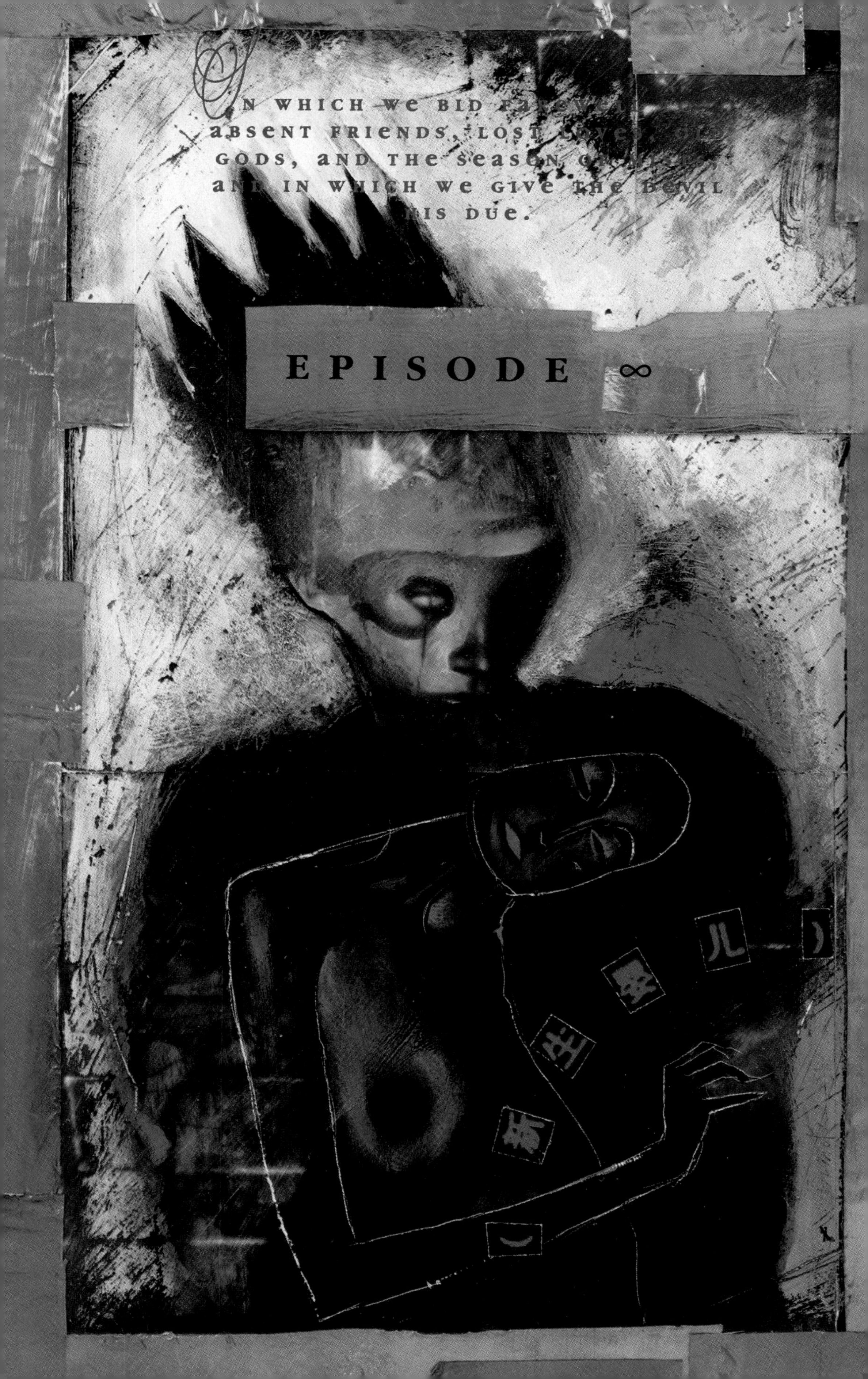
IN WHICH WE BID FAREWELL TO
ABSENT FRIENDS, LOST LOVERS, OLD
GODS, AND THE SEASON OF MISTS;
AND IN WHICH WE GIVE THE DEVIL
HIS DUE.
EPISODE ∞

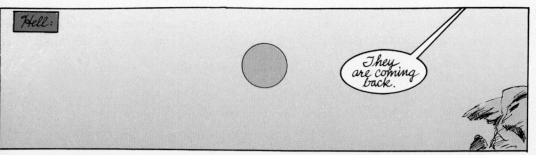

Hell:

They are coming back.

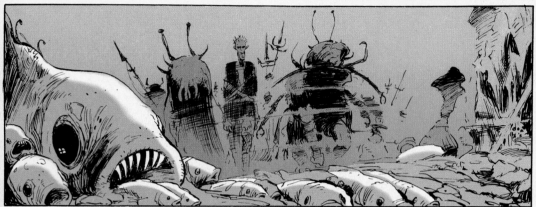

Don't you want to look at them? They are your responsibility too, Duma. No?

It's too late to look away.

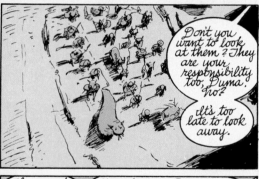

There must be millions of them.

It is strange, Duma: you would think they would be pleased to be back. This is their home, after all. But no.

Each of them walks as if they carry the weight of a thousand worlds on their shoulders. But happy or sad, it matters not...

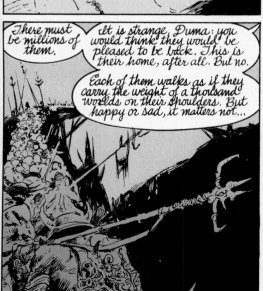

They're coming back.

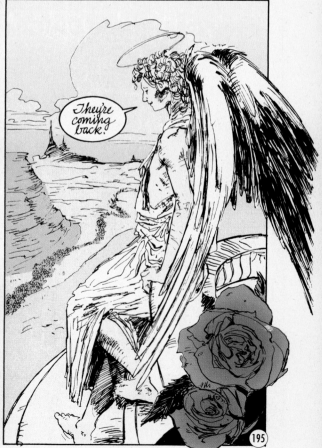

195

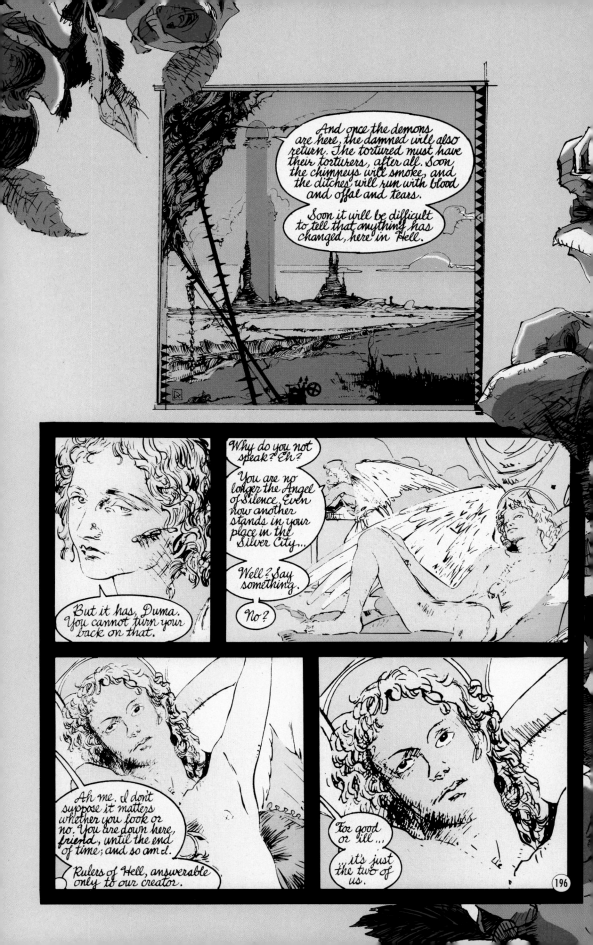

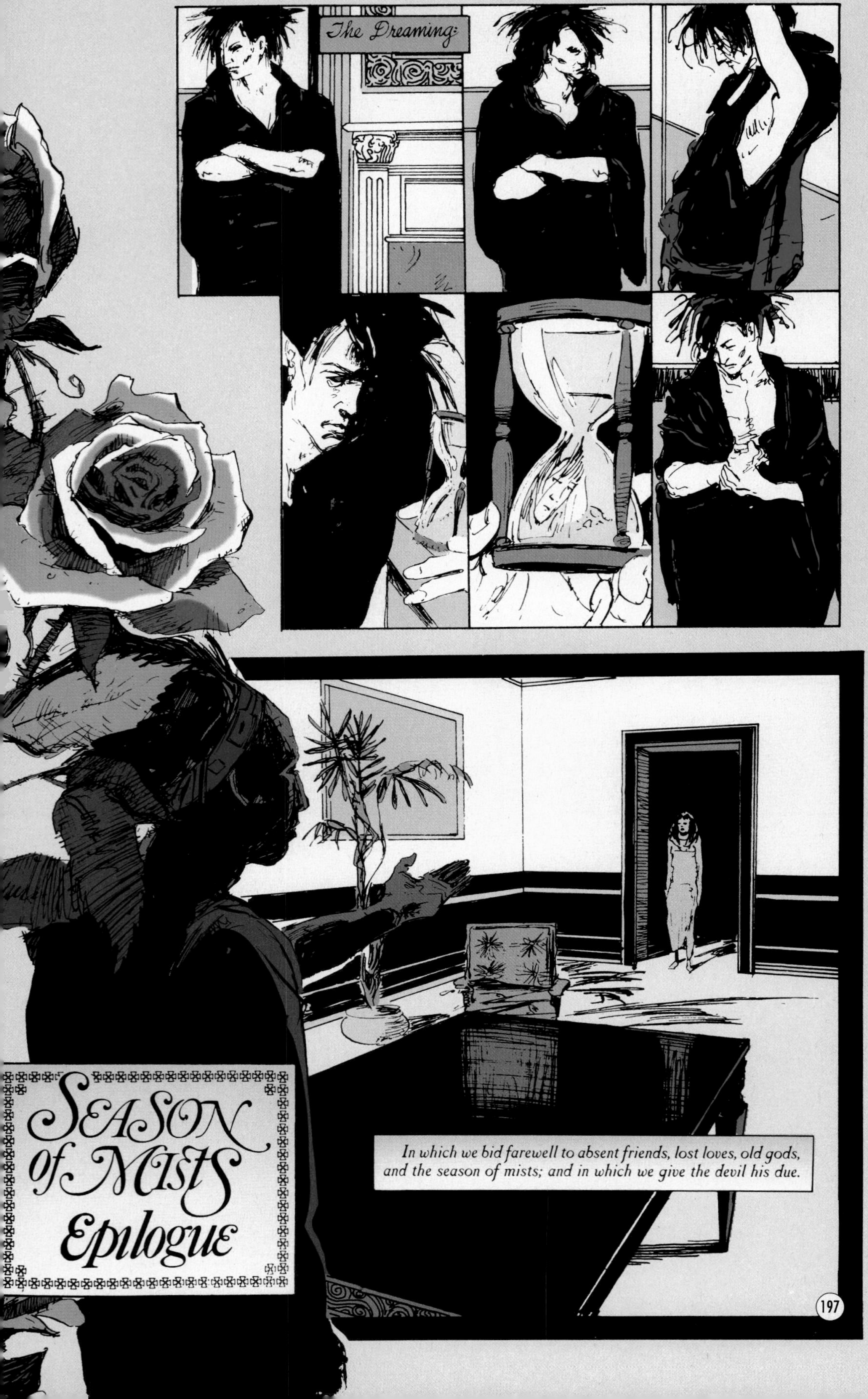
The Dreaming:
SEASON of MISTS
Epilogue
In which we bid farewell to absent friends, lost loves, old gods, and the season of mists; and in which we give the devil his due.

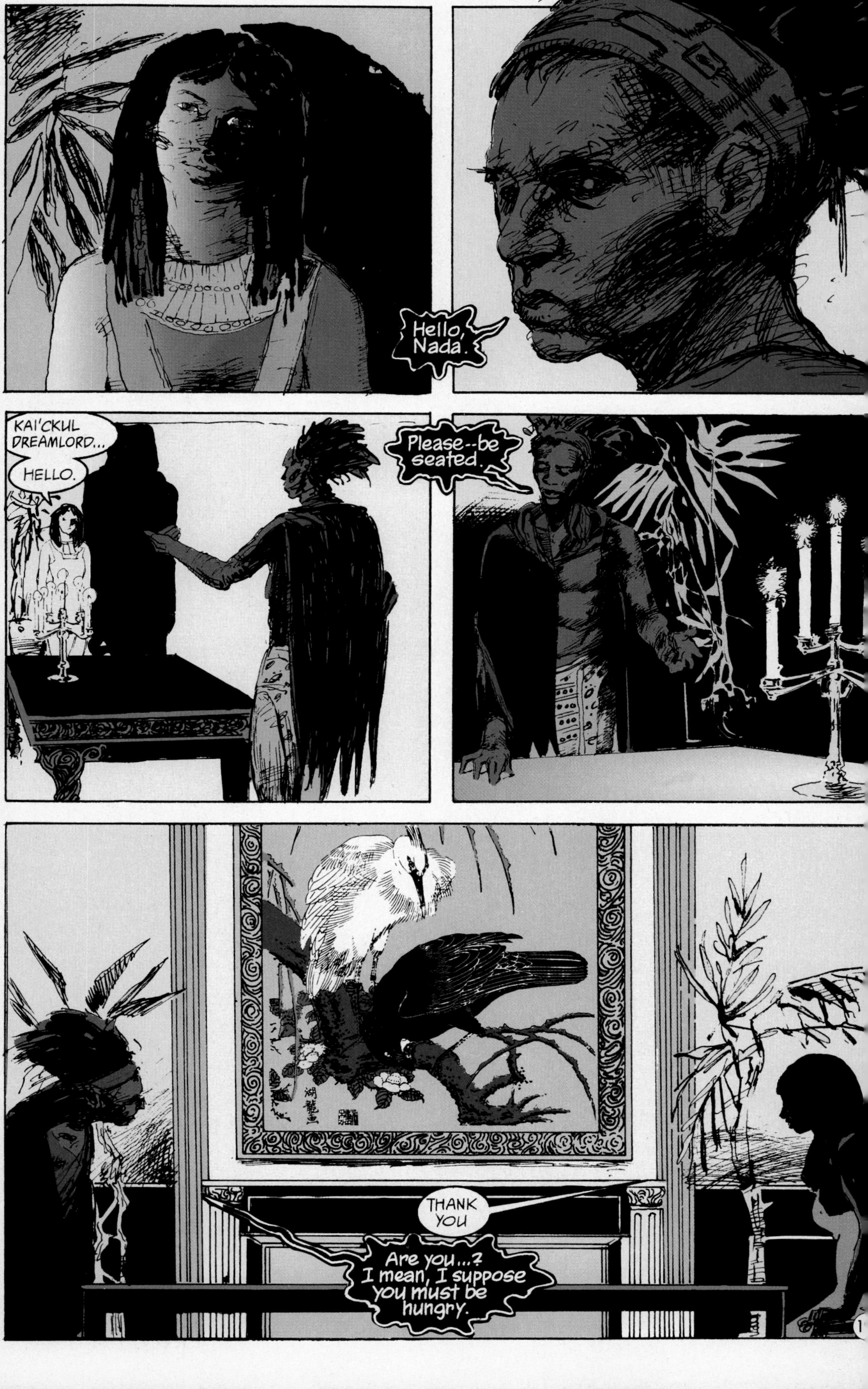
Hello, Nada.
KAI'CKUL DREAMLORD...
HELLO.
Please--be seated.
THANK YOU
Are you...? I mean, I suppose you must be hungry.

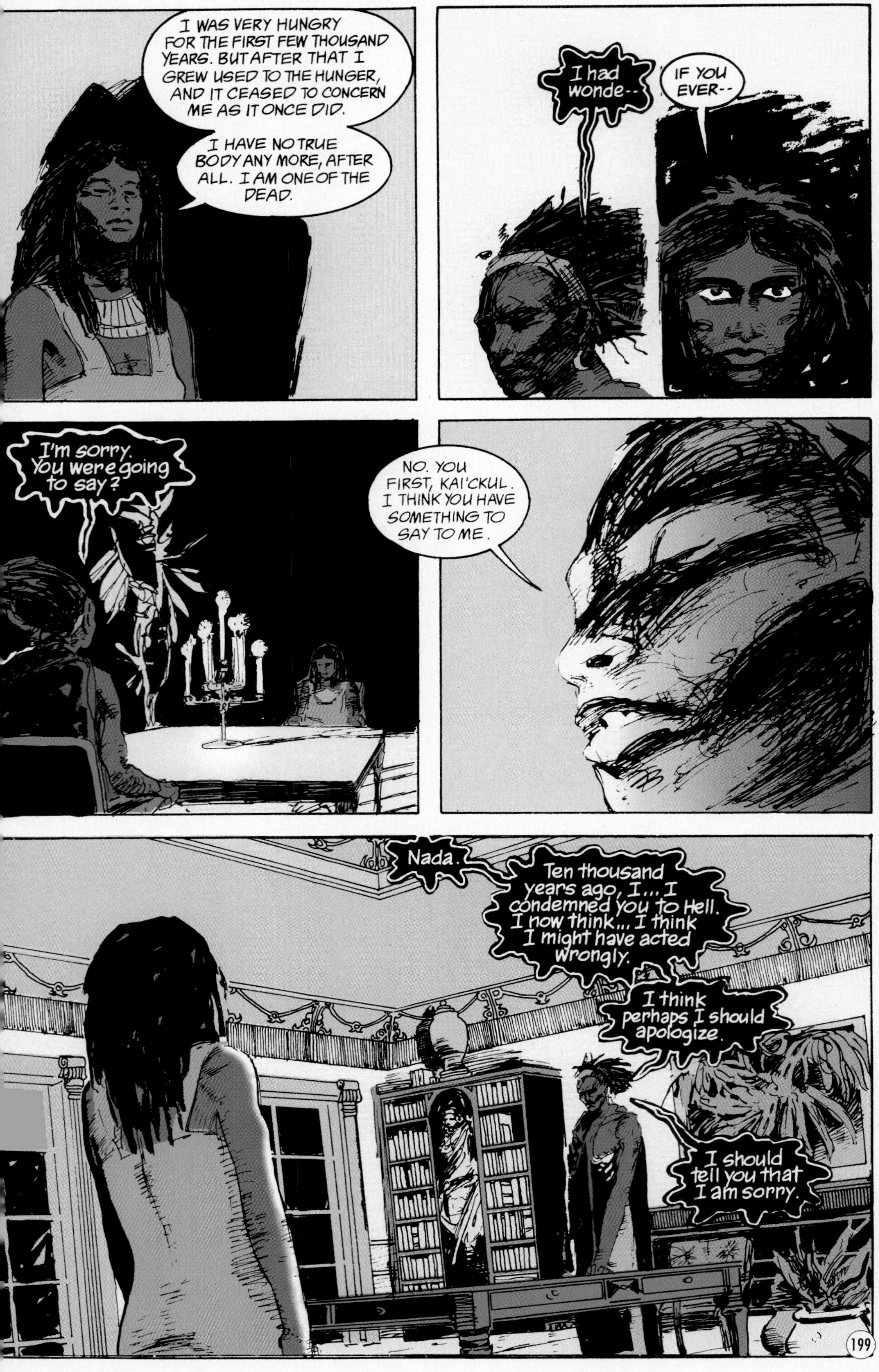
I WAS VERY HUNGRY FOR THE FIRST FEW THOUSAND YEARS. BUT AFTER THAT I GREW USED TO THE HUNGER, AND IT CEASED TO CONCERN ME AS IT ONCE DID.
I HAVE NO TRUE BODY ANY MORE, AFTER ALL. I AM ONE OF THE DEAD.
I had wonde--
IF YOU EVER--
I'm sorry. You were going to say?
NO. YOU FIRST, KAI'CKUL. I THINK YOU HAVE SOMETHING TO SAY TO ME.
Nada.
Ten thousand years ago, I... I condemned you to Hell. I now think... I think I might have acted wrongly.
I think perhaps I should apologize.
I should tell you that I am sorry.

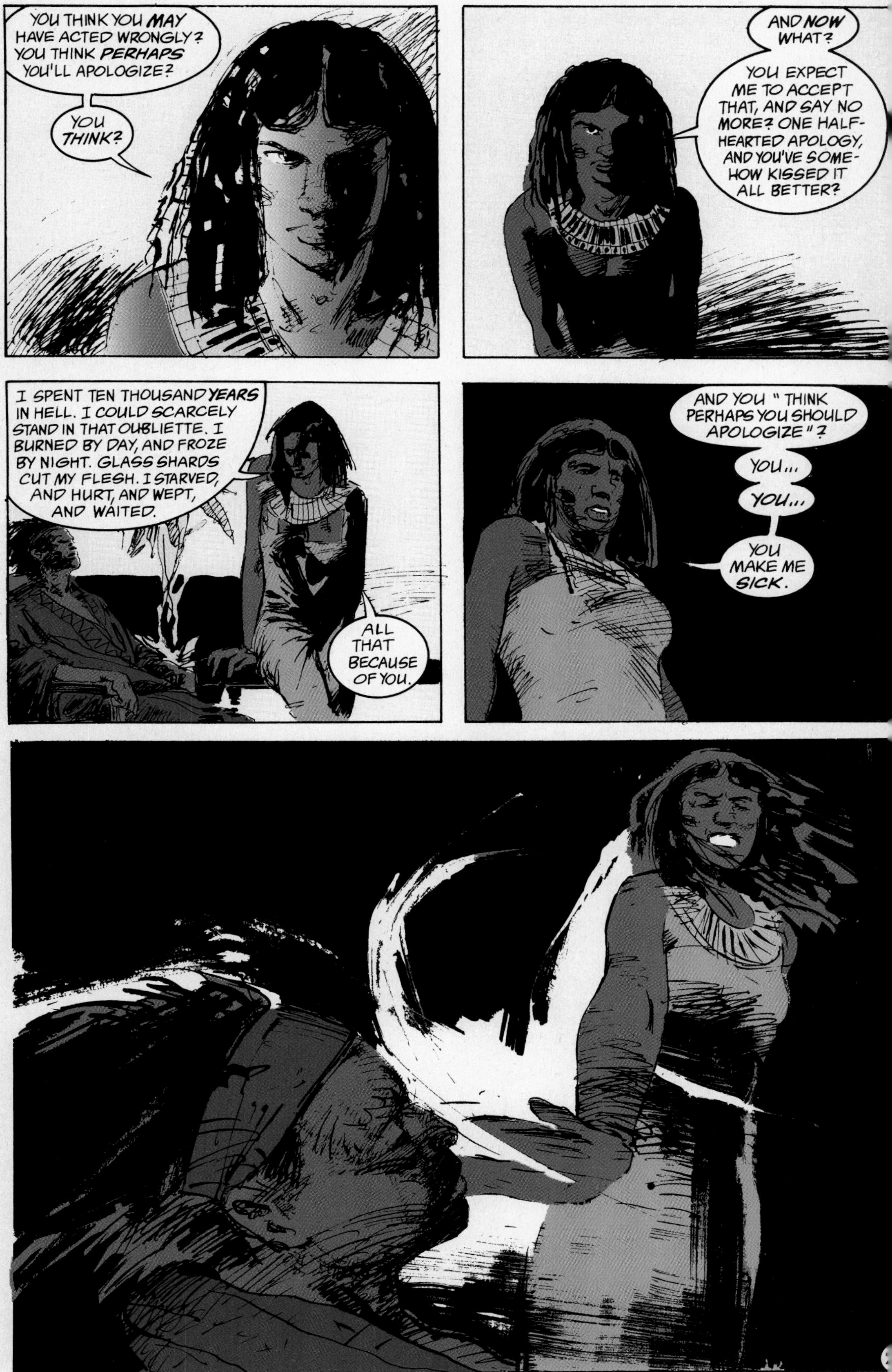
YOU THINK YOU MAY HAVE ACTED WRONGLY? YOU THINK PERHAPS YOU'LL APOLOGIZE?
YOU THINK?
AND NOW WHAT?
YOU EXPECT ME TO ACCEPT THAT, AND SAY NO MORE? ONE HALF-HEARTED APOLOGY, AND YOU'VE SOMEHOW KISSED IT ALL BETTER?
I SPENT TEN THOUSAND YEARS IN HELL. I COULD SCARCELY STAND IN THAT OUBLIETTE. I BURNED BY DAY, AND FROZE BY NIGHT. GLASS SHARDS CUT MY FLESH. I STARVED, AND HURT, AND WEPT, AND WAITED.
ALL THAT BECAUSE OF YOU.
AND YOU "THINK PERHAPS YOU SHOULD APOLOGIZE"?
YOU...
YOU...
YOU MAKE ME SICK.

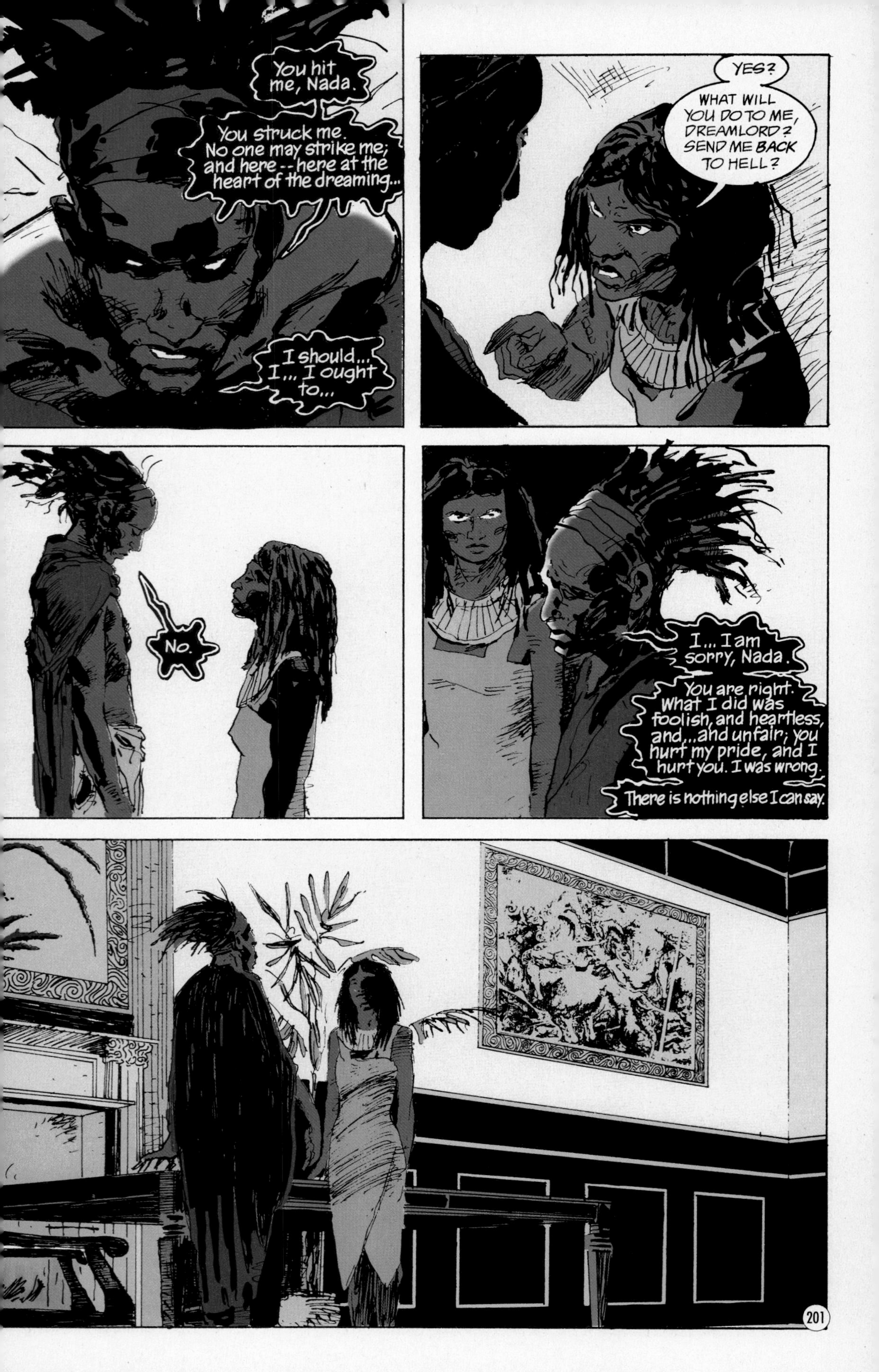

You hit me, Nada.
You struck me. No one may strike me; and here -- here at the heart of the dreaming...
I should... I... I ought to...
YES?
WHAT WILL YOU DO TO ME, DREAMLORD? SEND ME BACK TO HELL?
No.
I... I am sorry, Nada.
You are right. What I did was foolish, and heartless, and... and unfair; you hurt my pride, and I hurt you. I was wrong.
There is nothing else I can say.

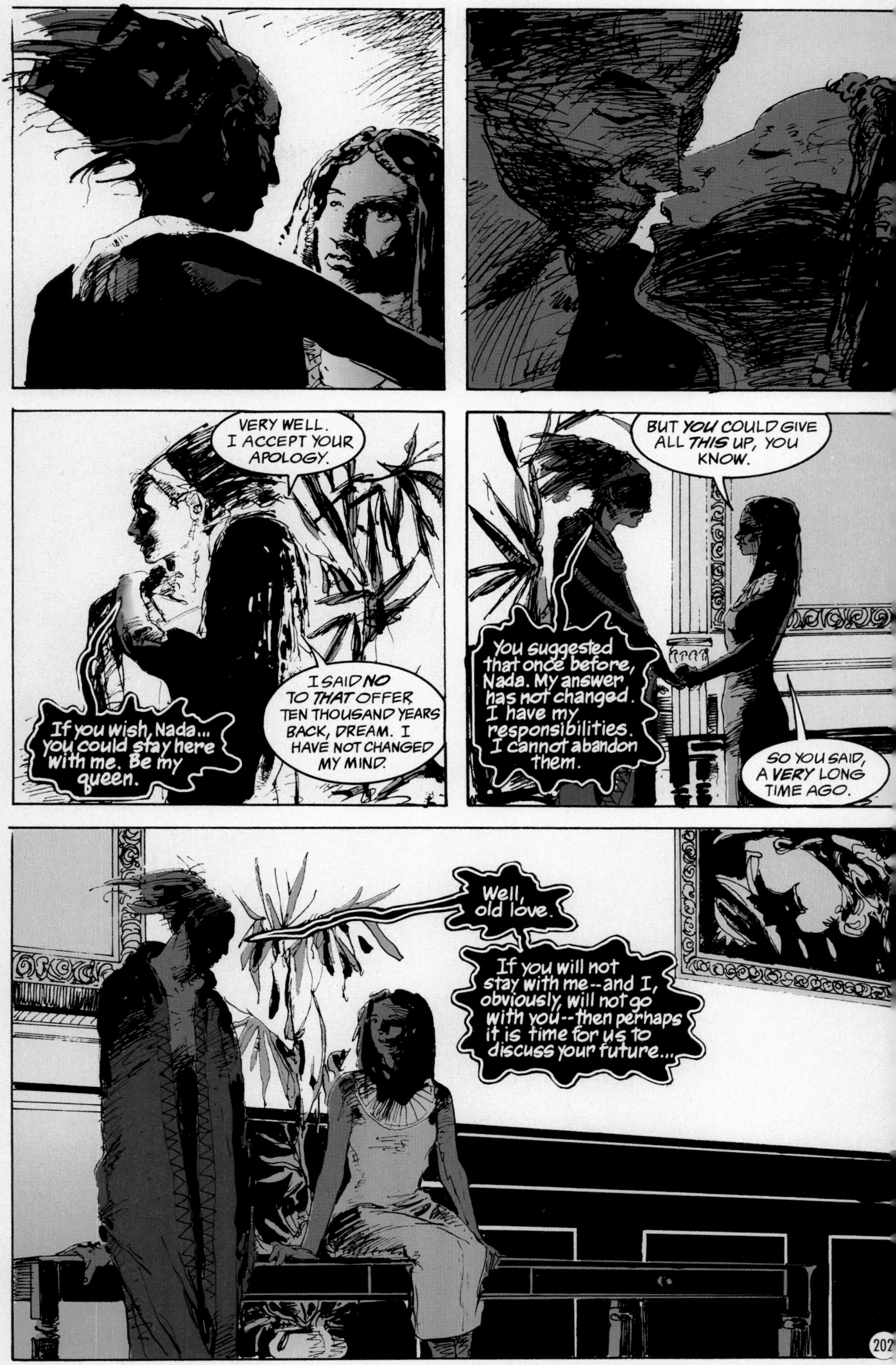
VERY WELL. I ACCEPT YOUR APOLOGY.
If you wish, Nada... you could stay here with me. Be my queen.
I SAID NO TO THAT OFFER TEN THOUSAND YEARS BACK, DREAM. I HAVE NOT CHANGED MY MIND.
BUT YOU COULD GIVE ALL THIS UP, YOU KNOW.
You suggested that once before, Nada. My answer has not changed. I have my responsibilities. I cannot abandon them.
SO YOU SAID, A VERY LONG TIME AGO.
Well, old love.
If you will not stay with me--and I, obviously, will not go with you--then perhaps it is time for us to discuss your future...

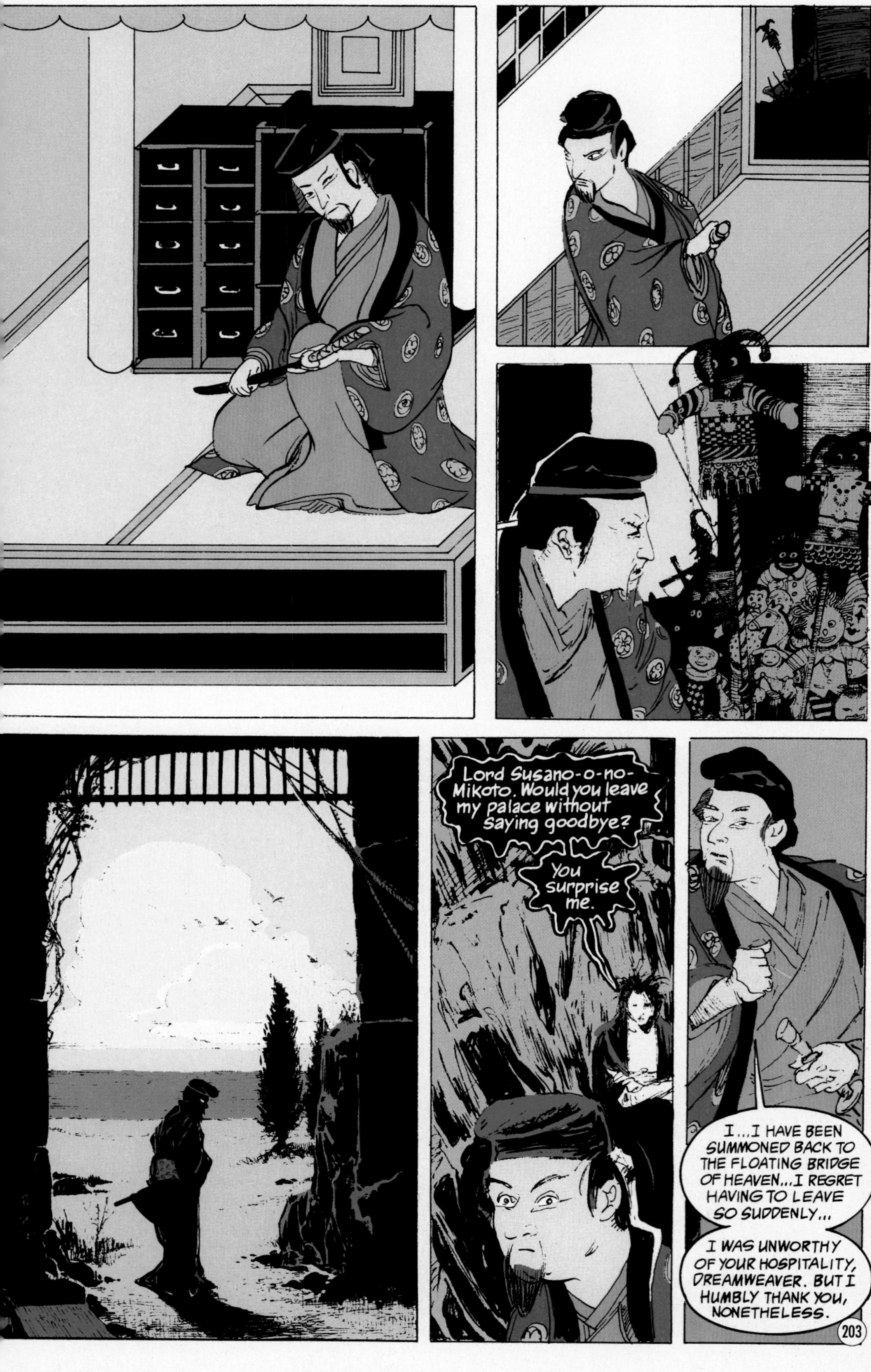
Lord Susano-o-no-Mikoto. Would you leave my palace without saying goodbye?
You surprise me.
I...I HAVE BEEN SUMMONED BACK TO THE FLOATING BRIDGE OF HEAVEN...I REGRET HAVING TO LEAVE SO SUDDENLY...
I WAS UNWORTHY OF YOUR HOSPITALITY, DREAMWEAVER. BUT I HUMBLY THANK YOU, NONETHELESS.

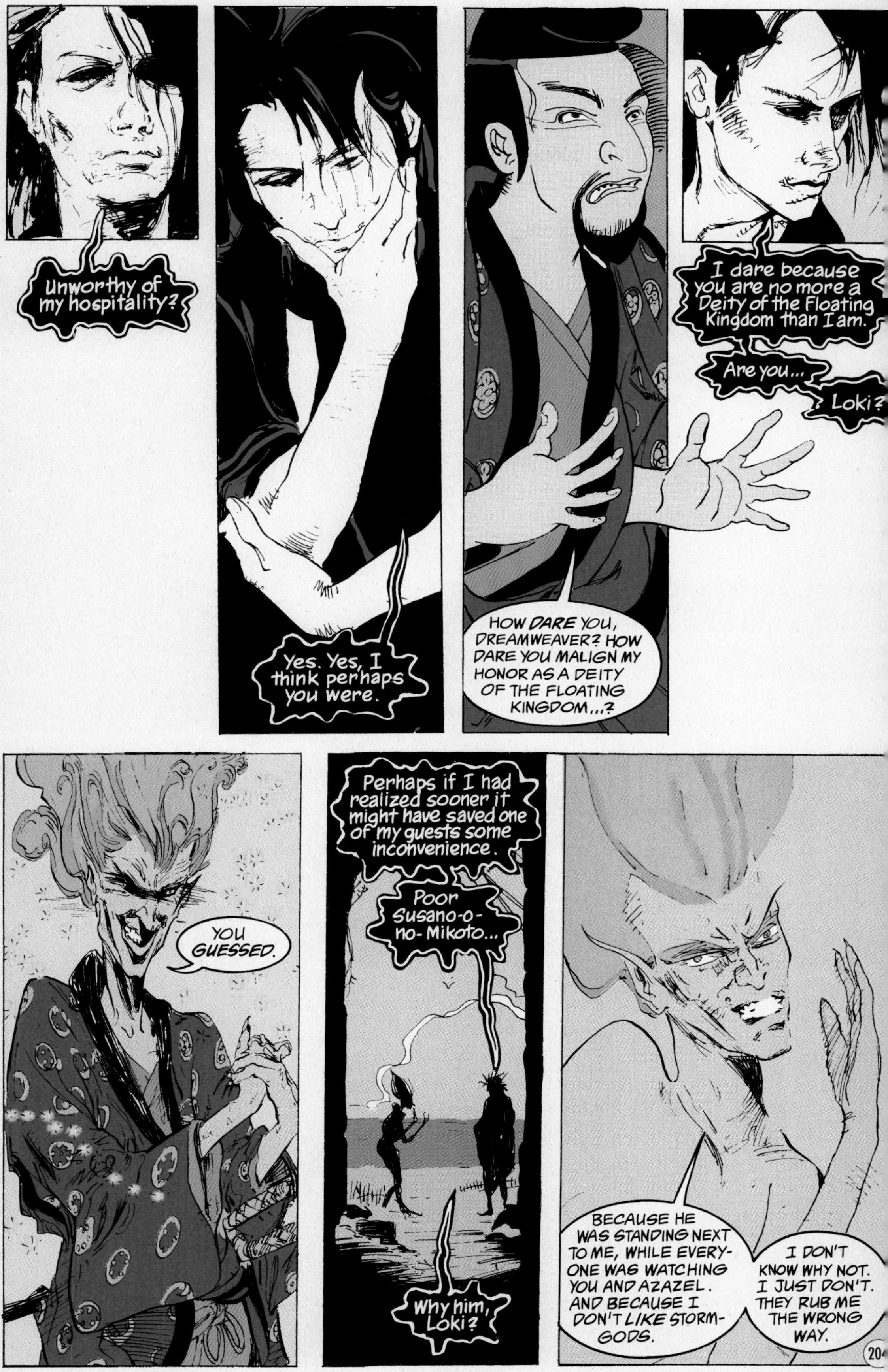
Unworthy of my hospitality?
Yes. Yes, I think perhaps you were.
HOW DARE YOU, DREAMWEAVER? HOW DARE YOU MALIGN MY HONOR AS A DEITY OF THE FLOATING KINGDOM...?
I dare because you are no more a Deity of the Floating Kingdom than I am.
Are you...
Loki?
YOU GUESSED.
Perhaps if I had realized sooner it might have saved one of my guests some inconvenience.
Poor Susano-o-no-Mikoto...
Why him, Loki?
BECAUSE HE WAS STANDING NEXT TO ME, WHILE EVERY-ONE WAS WATCHING YOU AND AZAZEL. AND BECAUSE I DON'T LIKE STORM-GODS.
I DON'T KNOW WHY NOT. I JUST DON'T. THEY RUB ME THE WRONG WAY.

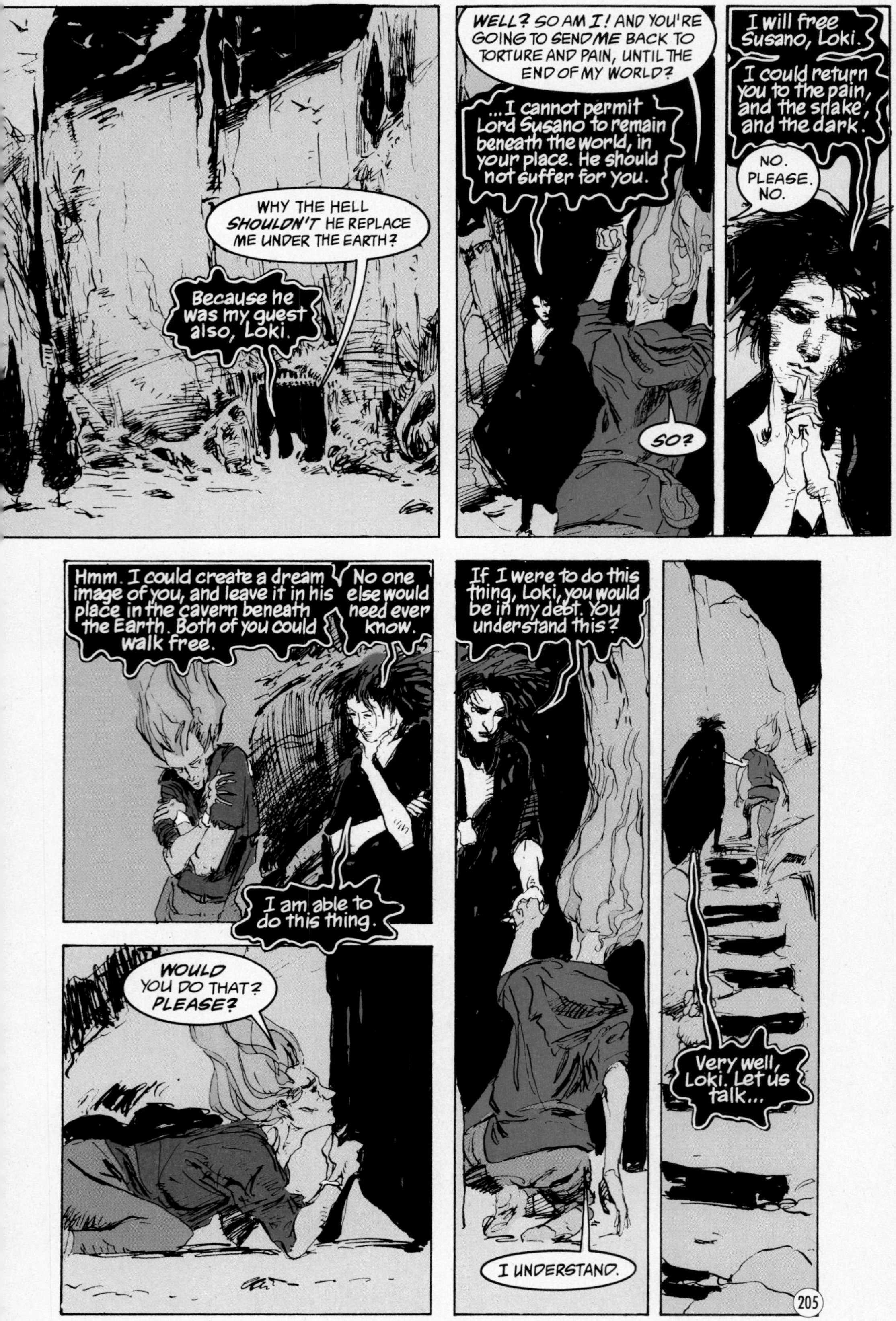
WHY THE HELL SHOULDN'T HE REPLACE ME UNDER THE EARTH?
Because he was my guest also, Loki.
WELL? SO AM I! AND YOU'RE GOING TO SEND ME BACK TO TORTURE AND PAIN, UNTIL THE END OF MY WORLD?
...I cannot permit Lord Susano to remain beneath the world, in your place. He should not suffer for you.
SO?
I will free Susano, Loki.
I could return you to the pain, and the snake, and the dark.
NO. PLEASE. NO.
Hmm. I could create a dream image of you, and leave it in his place in the cavern beneath the Earth. Both of you could walk free.
No one else would need ever know.
I am able to do this thing.
WOULD YOU DO THAT? PLEASE?
If I were to do this thing, Loki, you would be in my debt. You understand this?
I UNDERSTAND.
Very well, Loki. Let us talk...

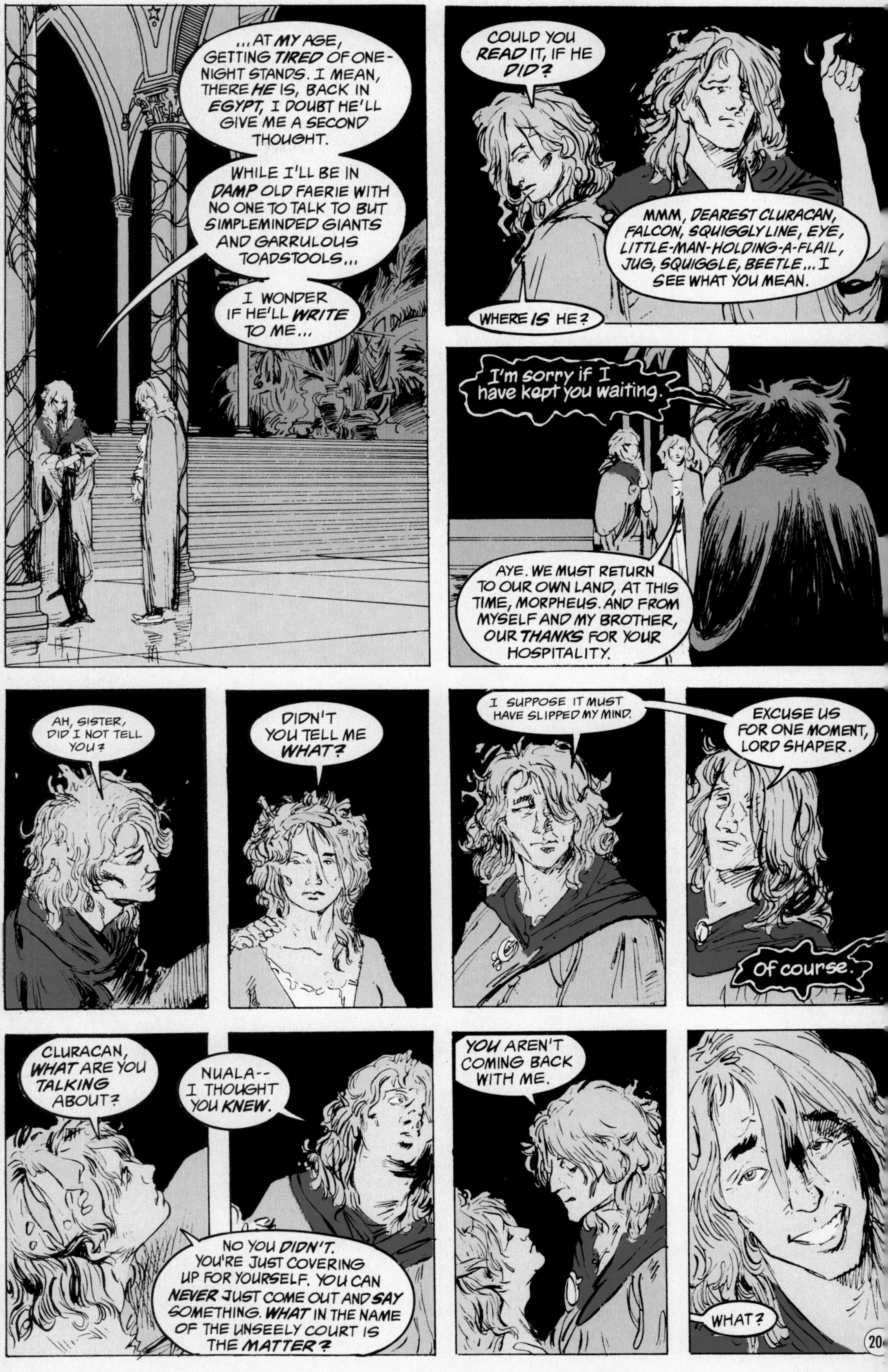
...AT MY AGE, GETTING TIRED OF ONE-NIGHT STANDS. I MEAN, THERE HE IS, BACK IN EGYPT, I DOUBT HE'LL GIVE ME A SECOND THOUGHT.
WHILE I'LL BE IN DAMP OLD FAERIE WITH NO ONE TO TALK TO BUT SIMPLEMINDED GIANTS AND GARRULOUS TOADSTOOLS...
I WONDER IF HE'LL WRITE TO ME...
COULD YOU READ IT, IF HE DID?
MMM, DEAREST CLURACAN, FALCON, SQUIGGLY LINE, EYE, LITTLE-MAN-HOLDING-A-FLAIL, JUG, SQUIGGLE, BEETLE... I SEE WHAT YOU MEAN.
WHERE IS HE?
I'm sorry if I have kept you waiting.
AYE. WE MUST RETURN TO OUR OWN LAND, AT THIS TIME, MORPHEUS. AND FROM MYSELF AND MY BROTHER, OUR THANKS FOR YOUR HOSPITALITY.
AH, SISTER, DID I NOT TELL YOU?
DIDN'T YOU TELL ME WHAT?
I SUPPOSE IT MUST HAVE SLIPPED MY MIND.
EXCUSE US FOR ONE MOMENT, LORD SHAPER.
Of course.
CLURACAN, WHAT ARE YOU TALKING ABOUT?
NUALA-- I THOUGHT YOU KNEW.
NO YOU DIDN'T. YOU'RE JUST COVERING UP FOR YOURSELF. YOU CAN NEVER JUST COME OUT AND SAY SOMETHING. WHAT IN THE NAME OF THE UNSEELY COURT IS THE MATTER?
YOU AREN'T COMING BACK WITH ME.
WHAT?

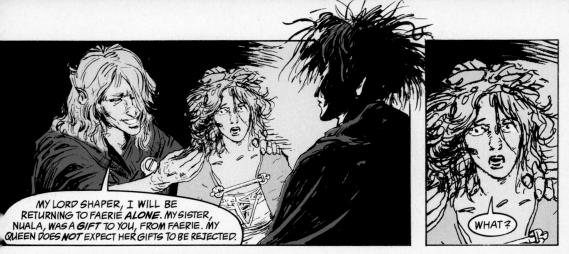

MY LORD SHAPER, I WILL BE RETURNING TO FAERIE *ALONE*. MY SISTER, NUALA, WAS A *GIFT* TO YOU, FROM FAERIE. MY QUEEN DOES *NOT* EXPECT HER GIFTS TO BE REJECTED.

WHAT?

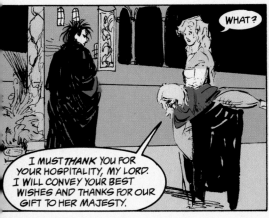

WHAT?

I MUST *THANK* YOU FOR YOUR HOSPITALITY, MY LORD. I WILL CONVEY YOUR BEST WISHES AND THANKS FOR OUR GIFT TO HER MAJESTY.

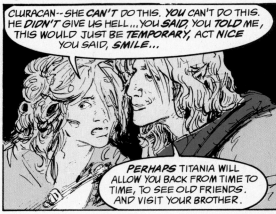

CLURACAN-- SHE *CAN'T* DO THIS. *YOU* CAN'T DO THIS. HE *DIDN'T* GIVE US HELL... YOU *SAID*, YOU *TOLD ME*, THIS WOULD JUST BE *TEMPORARY*, ACT *NICE* YOU SAID, *SMILE*...

PERHAPS TITANIA WILL ALLOW YOU BACK FROM TIME TO TIME, TO SEE OLD FRIENDS. AND VISIT YOUR BROTHER.

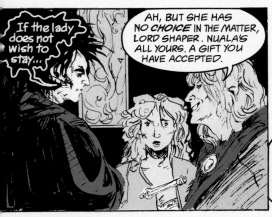

If the lady does not wish to stay...

AH, BUT SHE HAS NO *CHOICE* IN THE MATTER, LORD SHAPER. NUALA'S ALL YOURS. A GIFT YOU HAVE ACCEPTED.

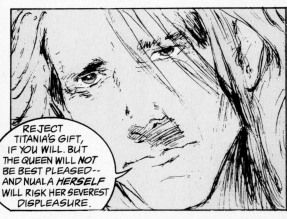

REJECT TITANIA'S GIFT, IF YOU WILL. BUT THE QUEEN WILL *NOT* BE BEST PLEASED-- AND NUALA *HERSELF* WILL RISK HER SEVEREST DISPLEASURE.

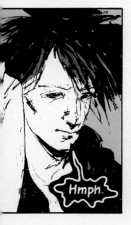

Hmph.

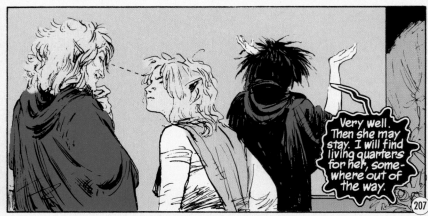

Very well. Then she may stay. I will find living quarters for her, somewhere out of the way.

207

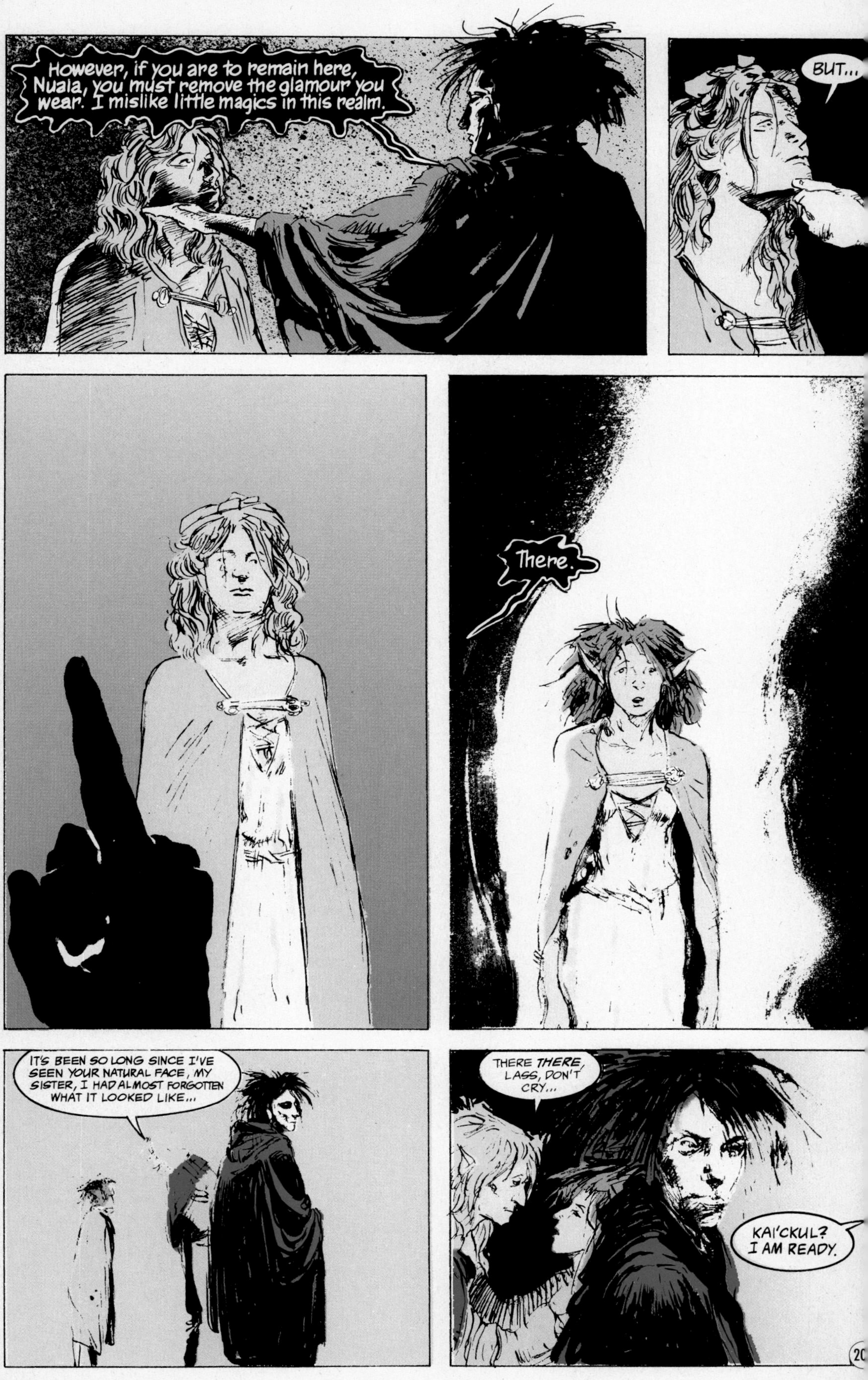
However, if you are to remain here, Nuala, you must remove the glamour you wear. I mislike little magics in this realm.
BUT...
There.
IT'S BEEN SO LONG SINCE I'VE SEEN YOUR NATURAL FACE, MY SISTER, I HAD ALMOST FORGOTTEN WHAT IT LOOKED LIKE...
THERE *THERE*, LASS, DON'T CRY...
KAI'CKUL? I AM READY.

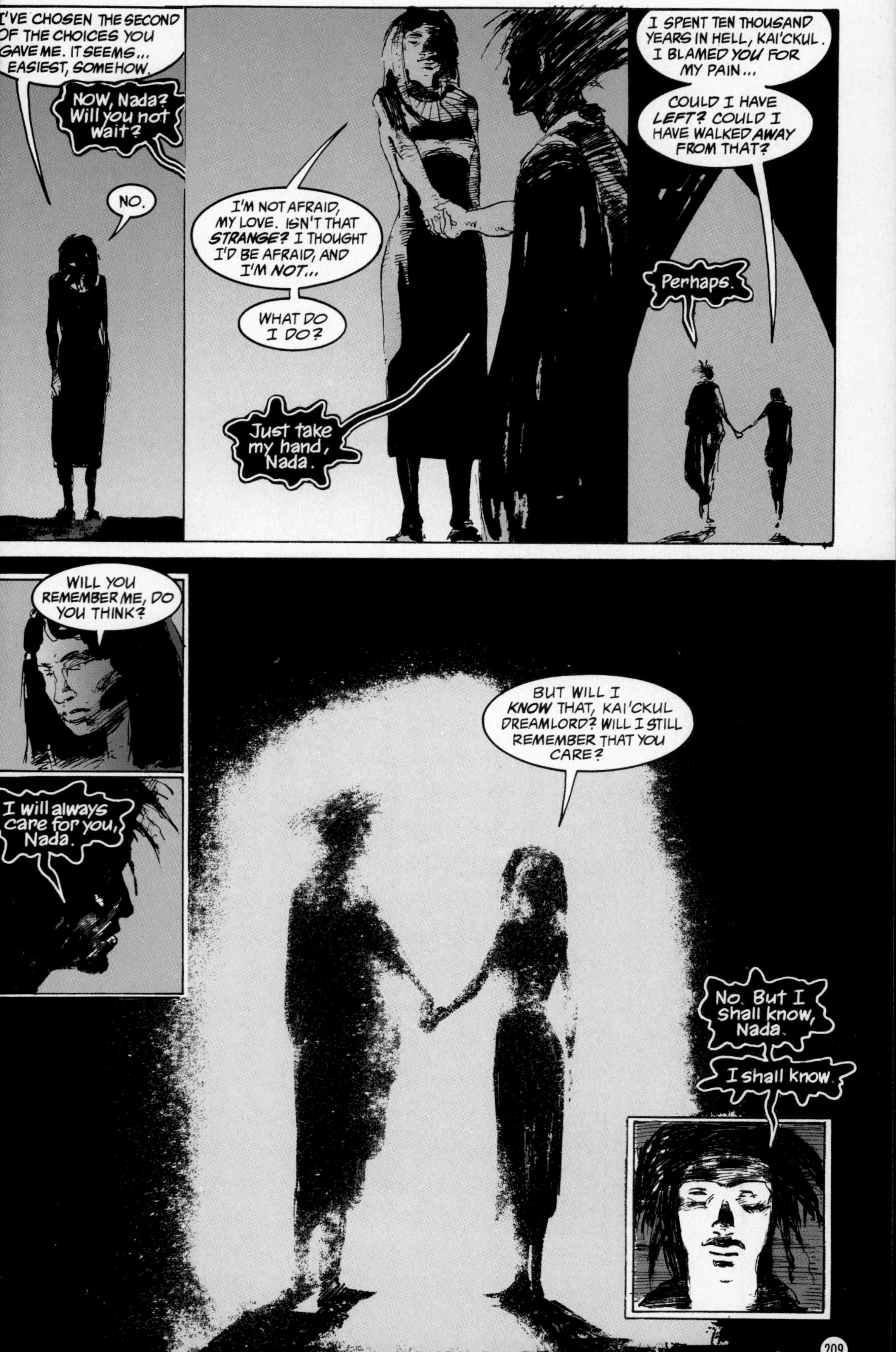
I'VE CHOSEN THE SECOND OF THE CHOICES YOU GAVE ME. IT SEEMS... EASIEST, SOMEHOW.
NOW, Nada? Will you not wait?
NO.
I'M NOT AFRAID, MY LOVE. ISN'T THAT STRANGE? I THOUGHT I'D BE AFRAID, AND I'M NOT...
WHAT DO I DO?
Just take my hand, Nada.
I SPENT TEN THOUSAND YEARS IN HELL, KAI'CKUL. I BLAMED YOU FOR MY PAIN...
COULD I HAVE LEFT? COULD I HAVE WALKED AWAY FROM THAT?
Perhaps.
WILL YOU REMEMBER ME, DO YOU THINK?
I will always care for you, Nada.
BUT WILL I KNOW THAT, KAI'CKUL DREAMLORD? WILL I STILL REMEMBER THAT YOU CARE?
No. But I shall know, Nada.
I shall know.

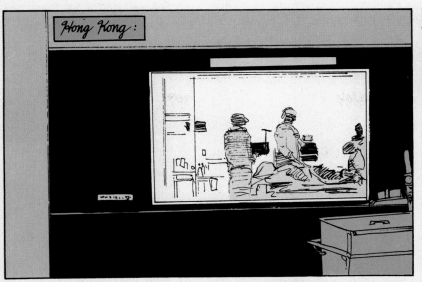

Hong Kong :

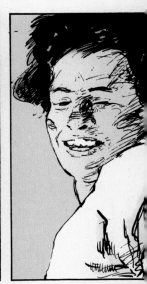

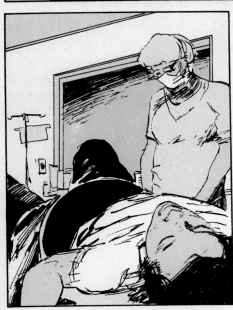

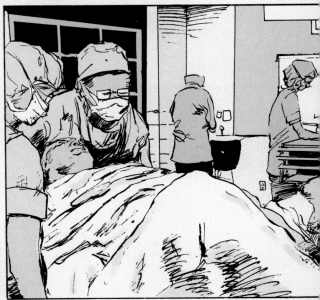

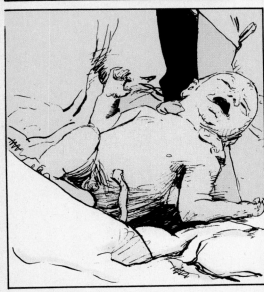

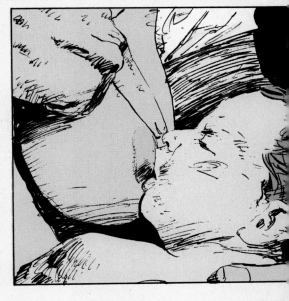

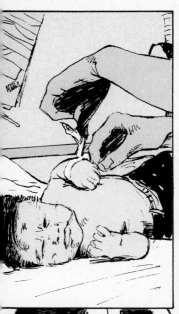

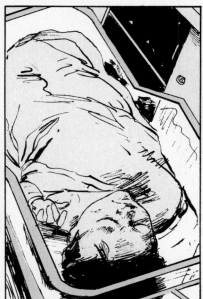

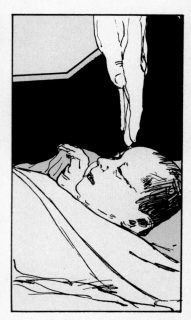

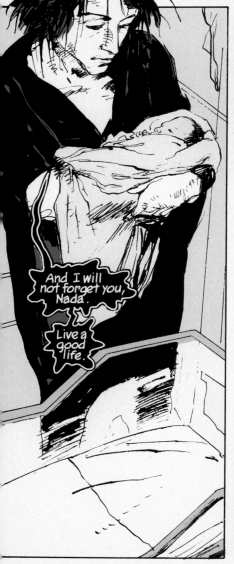

And I will not forget you, Nada.

Live a good life.

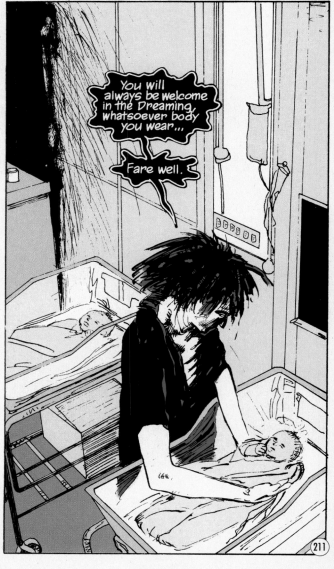

You will always be welcome in the Dreaming, whatsoever body you wear...

Fare well.

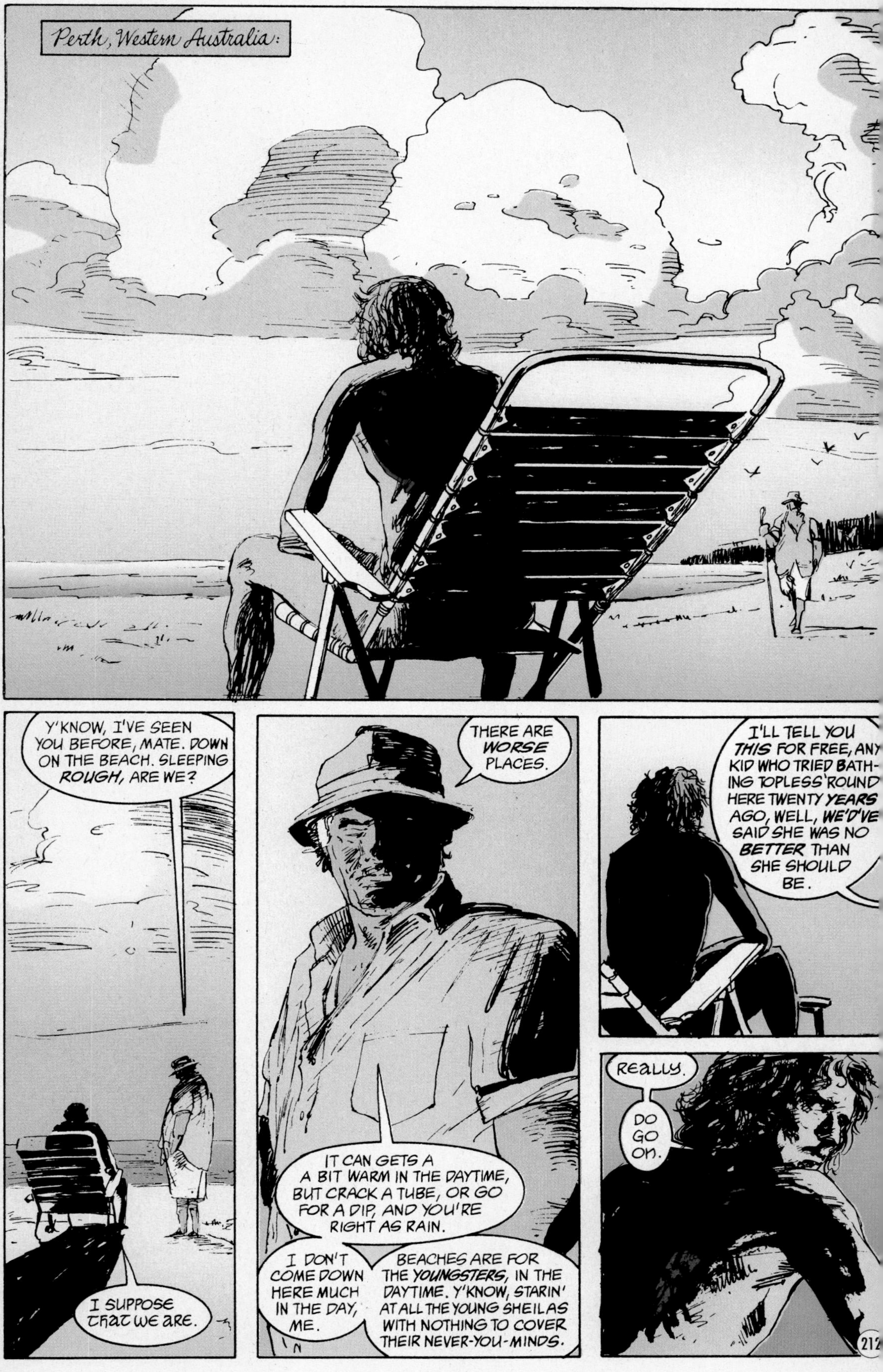
Perth, Western Australia:
Y'KNOW, I'VE SEEN YOU BEFORE, MATE. DOWN ON THE BEACH. SLEEPING ROUGH, ARE WE?
I SUPPOSE THAT WE ARE.
THERE ARE WORSE PLACES.
IT CAN GETS A A BIT WARM IN THE DAYTIME, BUT CRACK A TUBE, OR GO FOR A DIP, AND YOU'RE RIGHT AS RAIN.
I DON'T COME DOWN HERE MUCH IN THE DAY, ME.
BEACHES ARE FOR THE YOUNGSTERS, IN THE DAYTIME. Y'KNOW, STARIN' AT ALL THE YOUNG SHEILAS WITH NOTHING TO COVER THEIR NEVER-YOU-MINDS.
I'LL TELL YOU THIS FOR FREE, ANY KID WHO TRIED BATHING TOPLESS 'ROUND HERE TWENTY YEARS AGO, WELL, WE'D'VE SAID SHE WAS NO BETTER THAN SHE SHOULD BE.
REALLY.
DO GO ON.

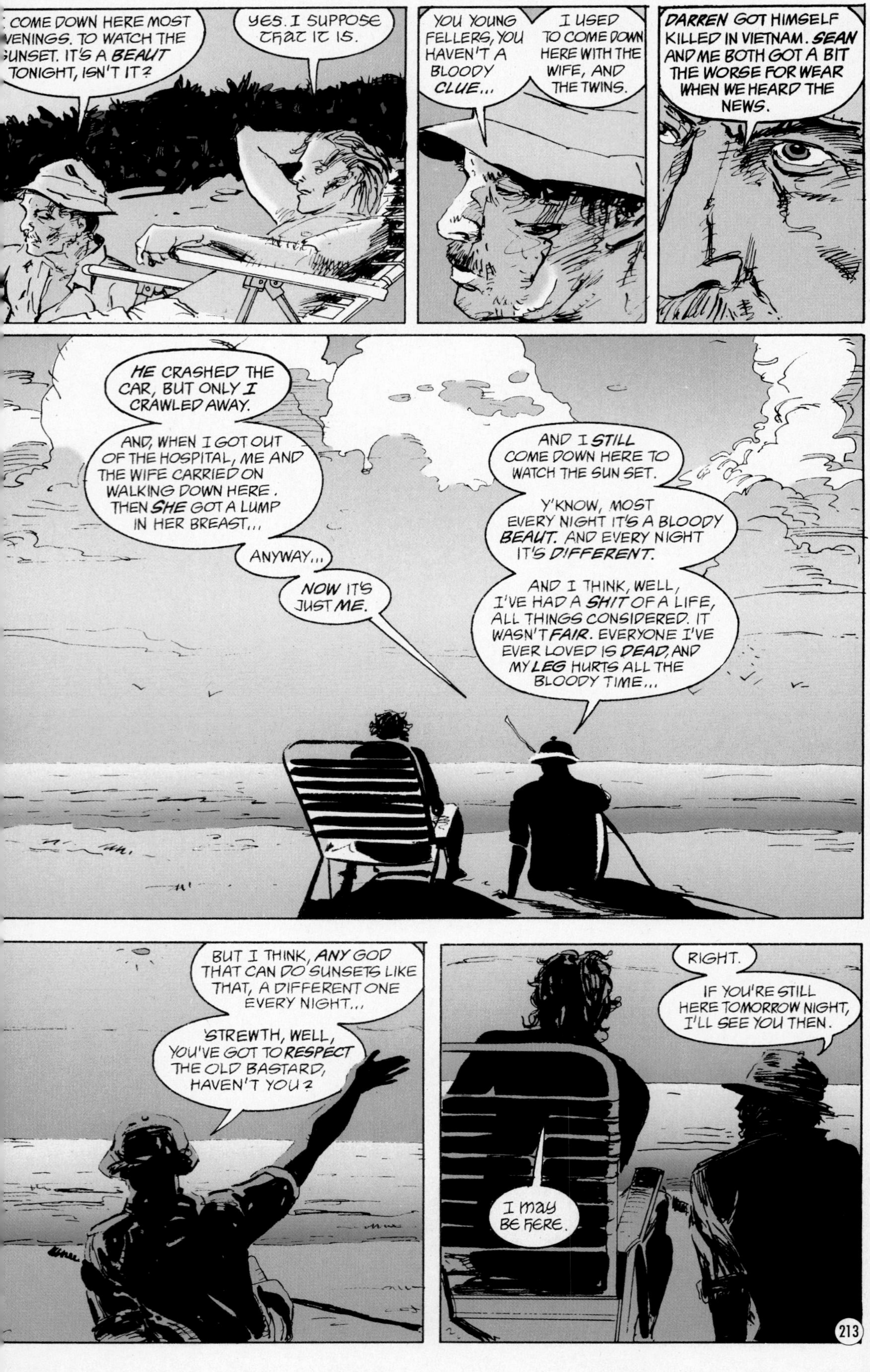
I COME DOWN HERE MOST EVENINGS. TO WATCH THE SUNSET. IT'S A BEAUT TONIGHT, ISN'T IT?
YES. I SUPPOSE THAT IT IS.
YOU YOUNG FELLERS, YOU HAVEN'T A BLOODY CLUE...
I USED TO COME DOWN HERE WITH THE WIFE, AND THE TWINS.
DARREN GOT HIMSELF KILLED IN VIETNAM. SEAN AND ME BOTH GOT A BIT THE WORSE FOR WEAR WHEN WE HEARD THE NEWS.
HE CRASHED THE CAR, BUT ONLY I CRAWLED AWAY.
AND, WHEN I GOT OUT OF THE HOSPITAL, ME AND THE WIFE CARRIED ON WALKING DOWN HERE. THEN SHE GOT A LUMP IN HER BREAST...
ANYWAY...
NOW IT'S JUST ME.
AND I STILL COME DOWN HERE TO WATCH THE SUN SET.
Y'KNOW, MOST EVERY NIGHT IT'S A BLOODY BEAUT. AND EVERY NIGHT IT'S DIFFERENT.
AND I THINK, WELL, I'VE HAD A SHIT OF A LIFE, ALL THINGS CONSIDERED. IT WASN'T FAIR. EVERYONE I'VE EVER LOVED IS DEAD, AND MY LEG HURTS ALL THE BLOODY TIME...
BUT I THINK, ANY GOD THAT CAN DO SUNSETS LIKE THAT, A DIFFERENT ONE EVERY NIGHT...
'STREWTH, WELL, YOU'VE GOT TO RESPECT THE OLD BASTARD, HAVEN'T YOU?
RIGHT.
IF YOU'RE STILL HERE TOMORROW NIGHT, I'LL SEE YOU THEN.
I may be here.

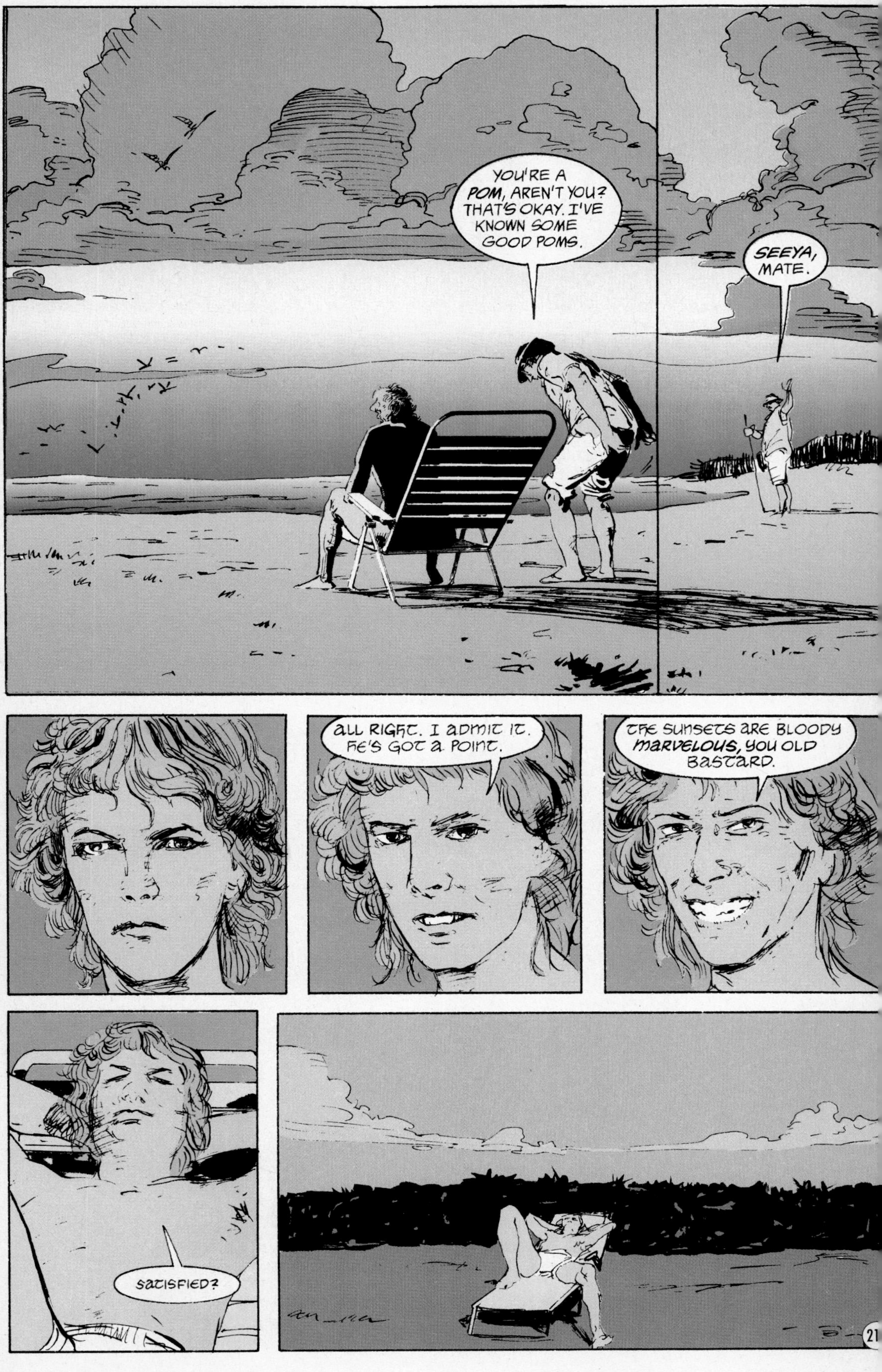
YOU'RE A POM, AREN'T YOU? THAT'S OKAY. I'VE KNOWN SOME GOOD POMS.
SEEYA, MATE.
ALL RIGHT. I ADMIT IT. HE'S GOT A POINT.
THE SUNSETS ARE BLOODY MARVELOUS, YOU OLD BASTARD.
SATISFIED?

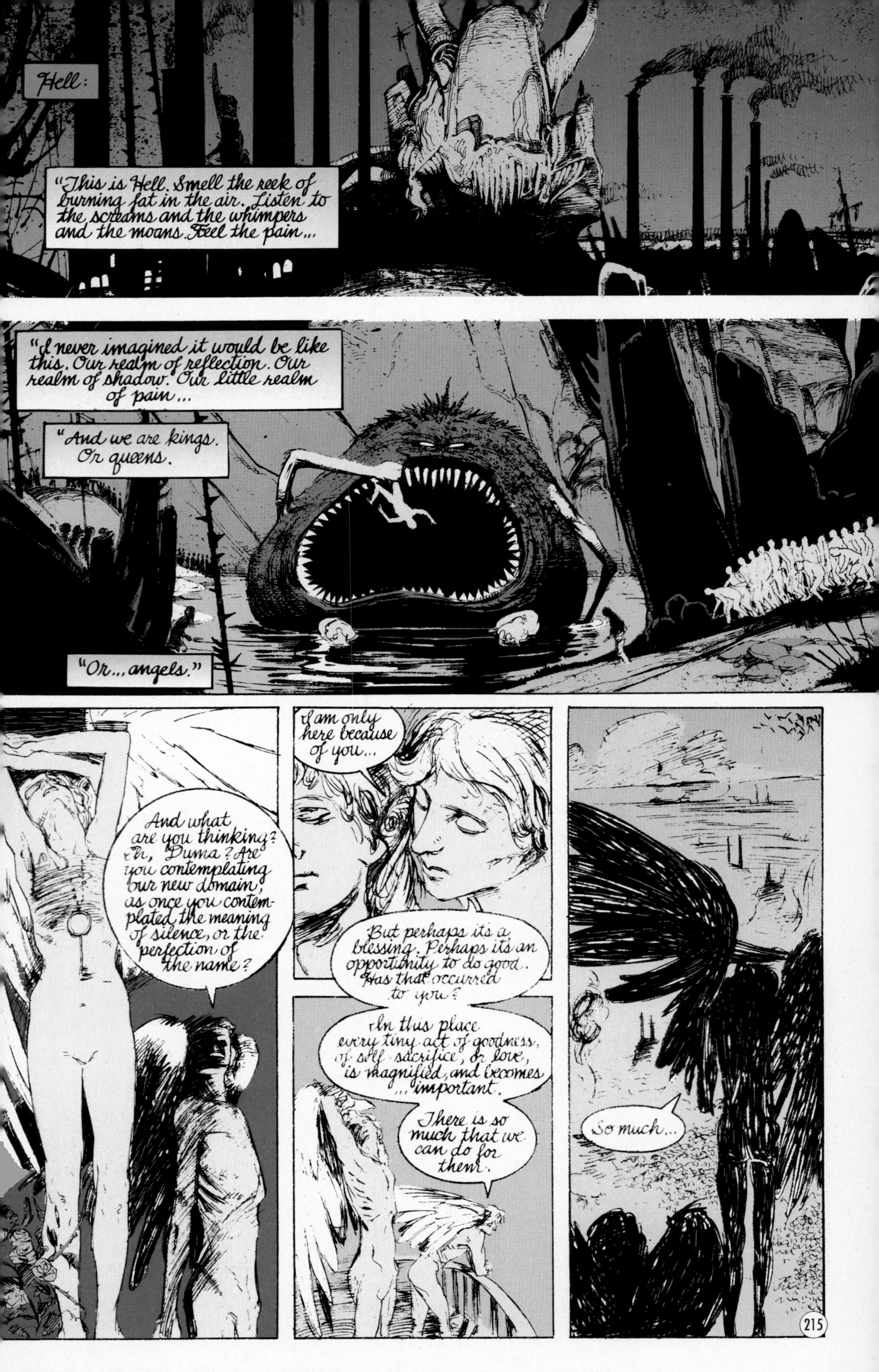
Hell:
"This is Hell. Smell the reek of burning fat in the air. Listen to the screams and the whimpers and the moans. Feel the pain...
"I never imagined it would be like this. Our realm of reflection. Our realm of shadow. Our little realm of pain...
"And we are kings. Or queens.
"Or... angels."
And what are you thinking? Eh, Duma? Are you contemplating our new domain, as once you contemplated the meaning of silence, or the perfection of the name?
I am only here because of you...
But perhaps its a blessing. Perhaps its an opportunity to do good. Has that occurred to you?
In this place every tiny act of goodness, of self sacrifice, or love, is magnified, and becomes ...important.
There is so much that we can do for them.
So much...

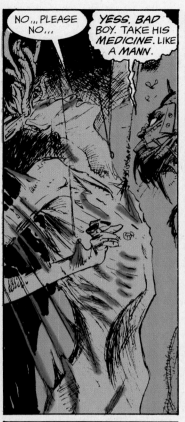

NO...PLEASE NO...

YESS. BAD BOY. TAKE HIS MEDICINE. LIKE A MANN.

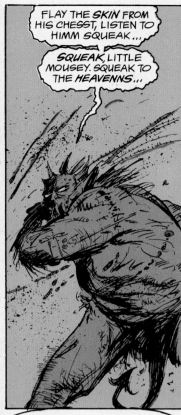

FLAY THE *SKIN* FROM HIS *CHESST*, LISTEN TO HIMM SQUEAK...

SQUEAK, LITTLE MOUSEY. SQUEAK TO THE *HEAVENNS*...

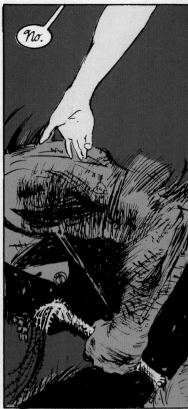

No.

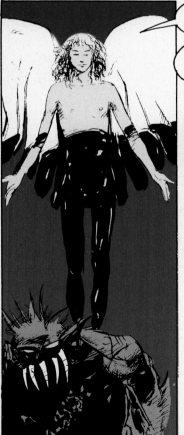

That was the old Hell. That was a place of mindless torture and purposeless pain.

There will be no more wanton violence; no further suffering, inflicted without reason or explanation.

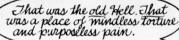

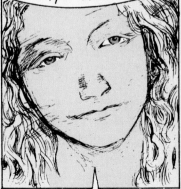

We *will* hurt you. And we are *not* sorry.

But we do *not* do it to punish you. We do it to *redeem* you.

Because afterward, you'll be a better person...

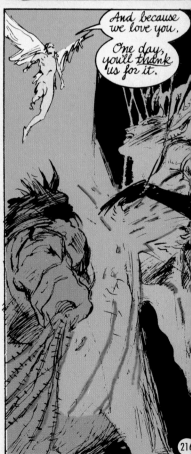

And because we love you. One day, you'll thank us for it.

21

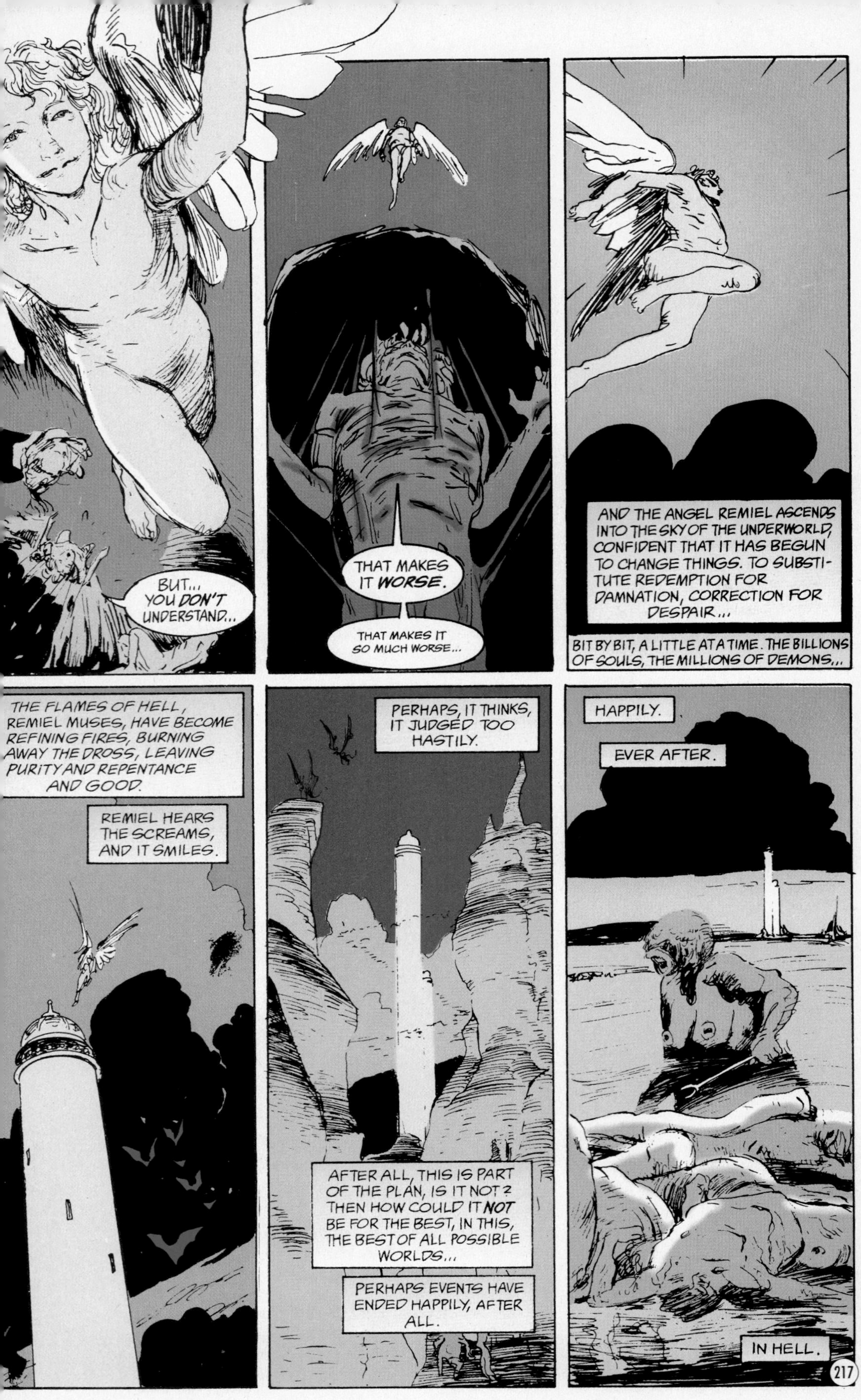

BUT... YOU DON'T UNDERSTAND...
THAT MAKES IT WORSE.
THAT MAKES IT SO MUCH WORSE...
AND THE ANGEL REMIEL ASCENDS INTO THE SKY OF THE UNDERWORLD, CONFIDENT THAT IT HAS BEGUN TO CHANGE THINGS. TO SUBSTITUTE REDEMPTION FOR DAMNATION, CORRECTION FOR DESPAIR...
BIT BY BIT, A LITTLE AT A TIME. THE BILLIONS OF SOULS, THE MILLIONS OF DEMONS...
THE FLAMES OF HELL, REMIEL MUSES, HAVE BECOME REFINING FIRES, BURNING AWAY THE DROSS, LEAVING PURITY AND REPENTANCE AND GOOD.
REMIEL HEARS THE SCREAMS, AND IT SMILES.
PERHAPS, IT THINKS, IT JUDGED TOO HASTILY.
AFTER ALL, THIS IS PART OF THE PLAN, IS IT NOT? THEN HOW COULD IT NOT BE FOR THE BEST, IN THIS, THE BEST OF ALL POSSIBLE WORLDS...
PERHAPS EVENTS HAVE ENDED HAPPILY, AFTER ALL.
HAPPILY.
EVER AFTER.
IN HELL.

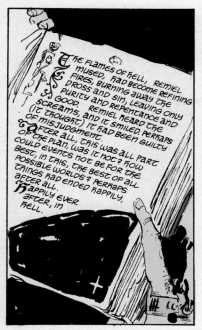

HE FLAMES OF HELL, REMIEL MUSED, HAD BECOME REFINING FIRES, BURNING AWAY THE DROSS AND SIN, LEAVING ONLY PURITY AND REPENTANCE AND GOOD. REMIEL HEARD THE SCREAMS, AND IT SMILED, PERHAPS (IT THOUGHT) IT HAD BEEN GUILTY OF MISJUDGMENT.

AFTER ALL, THIS WAS ALL PART OF THE PLAN, WAS IT NOT? HOW COULD EVENTS NOT BE FOR THE BEST, IN THIS, THE BEST OF ALL POSSIBLE WORLDS? PERHAPS THINGS HAD ENDED HAPPILY, AFTER ALL.

HAPPILY EVER AFTER, IN HELL.

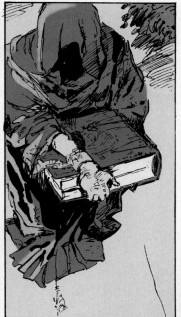

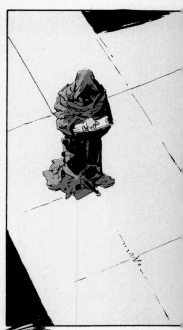

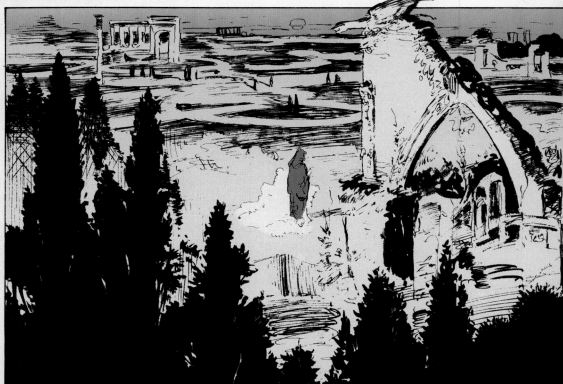

October knew, of course, that the action of turning a page, of ending a chapter or of shutting a book, did not end a tale.

Having admitted that, he would also avow that happy endings were never difficult to find: "It is simply a matter," he explained to April, "of finding a sunny place in a garden, where the light is golden and the grass is soft; somewhere to rest, to stop reading, and to be content."

--from The Man Who Was October by G. K. Chesterton /Library of Dreams

b i o g r a p h i e s

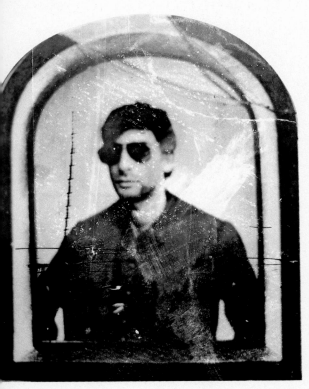

NEIL GAIMAN
writer

To set certain popular misconceptions to rest once and for all:

1) He was not found wandering the sewers of London as a child during the winter of 1864, unable to say anything more than "Powerful big rats, gentlemen."

2) He was never exhibited in public houses to the curious; only briefly in July, 1865, to selected gentlemen of standing from the scientific and literary community.

3) He did not have a vestigial tail.

4) He did indeed have what most people would commonly understand as "eyes."

5) He was not actually the pilot of the Zeppelin, although he did disappear for good following the explosion.

6) There is quite obviously no "underground kingdom beneath London inhabited by huge, intelligent rodents." And even if there were, any suggestion of Neil's involvement in the mazy territorial negotiations between Londons Above and Below can be considered a joke, and in poor taste at that.

7) He was afraid of neither mirrors nor street conjurers.

8) There were no tooth-marks on the bones.

KELLEY JONES
penciller
episodes 1,2,3,5,6

When he was born, in 1802, Kelley Jones had ry appearance of being in his mid-nineties. He onished physicians by growing younger with h year that passed. This photograph, taken in seventieth year, appears to be that of a man is twenties. He died as an infant in 1888, killed a nursery fire. A recording of his voice reciting ats's '*To Autumn*' was discovered on the tele-ne answering machine of a taxi company in ronto in 1979, but was erased by a temporary retary who failed to understand its worth.

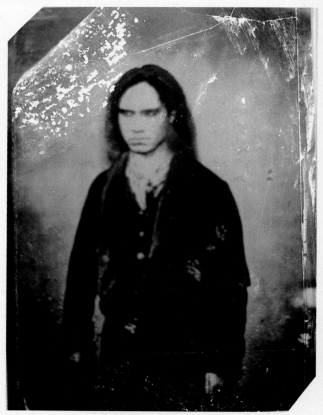

by NEIL GAIMAN

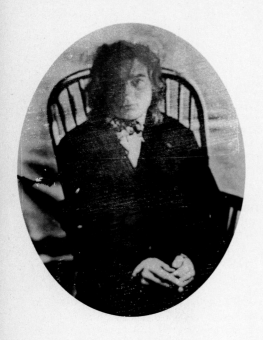

MIKE DRINGENBERG
penciller
episodes 0,∞

"... all of the people were coming and I said to them and I said, there's no hope for me here, none of them have faces, always walking, and I never saw any of them before, and they keep touching m in the night, always in the night, sometimes when the rain comes, and no-one sees them but me, grey eyes maybe screaming, and I sa to them, and I said to them ..."

P. CRAIG RUSSELL
inker
episode 3

The details of his black life and dubious death are written in certain books, and the foolish and the curious may seek them out. Nothing could induce us to elaborate here: by comparison Gilles de Rais was an angel in human form, and de Sade a weak and simpering child. The world is well rid of him—if rid of him it truly is.

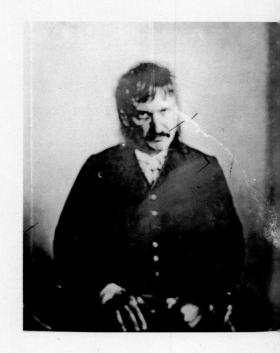

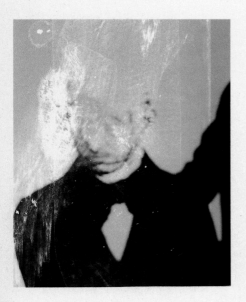

MATT WAGNER
penciller
episode 4

Matt Wagner was the only man to be elected posthumously to t United States Senate. He served three terms before being narrowly defeated by a living candidate in 1874, whereupon he retired from public life. Until recently his jawbone was on display in the Smithsonian Institution.

GEORGE PRATT
inker
episodes 5,∞

ocumented cases of spontaneous human combustion are
; however, in all the annals of this phenomenon, only
rge Pratt was able to combust on cue. As a thaumaturgic
sic Hall 'turn,' Mister Pratt would ignite on stage, in front
paying audience, whereupon Millicent Wirth, his lover
assistant, would extinguish the blaze with a patent liquid
ratt's own invention. This photograph was taken of
mbustible George' the afternoon before his final perfor-
ace, in Boston, in 1901. 'Miss Millie's' subsequent trial
acquittal was a *cause célèbre* for many weeks. Fifty years
she filled a bathtub with gasoline and climbed into it,
ed, holding a lighted taper.

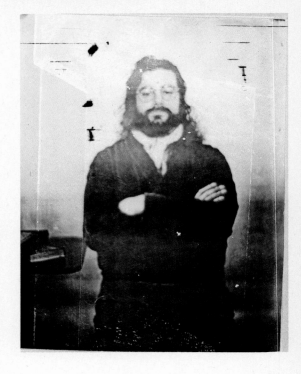

MALCOLM JONES III
inker
episodes 0,1,2

This photograph of one of Malcolm Jones's three homunculi was
originally published in the *Journal of the American Society for Psychical
Knowledge*. Measuring no more than six inches in height, these tiny
creatures were, it is said, capable of human speech, and were wholly
subordinate to Jones's will. None of them survived Jones by more than
a week, disintegrating to dried blood, rose petals and ashes.

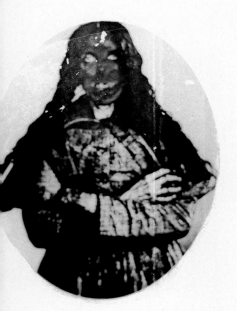

DICK GIORDANO
inker
episode 6

npresario, shipping magnate, oil baron, surgeon, and
anthropist. One Thursday morning in November, 1893,
rdano took his usual table at the Savoy Hotel and requested
waiter bring him 'a newspaper, a bootjack, the Bible, a pint of
gar, a paper of pins, and some barley sugar.' Upon the wait-
refusal to comply with this extraordinary request, Giordano's
dissolved into silent tears. "Aye, me, sir," he said, "you have
lemned an honest man to his doom." Thereupon he hailed a
and was heard to tell the driver to take him to his office, a
ney of no more than fifteen minutes. He was, of course, never
again, although his tiepin was cut from the stomach of a
ty-five pound sturgeon caught in the Black Sea on the first
of World War One.

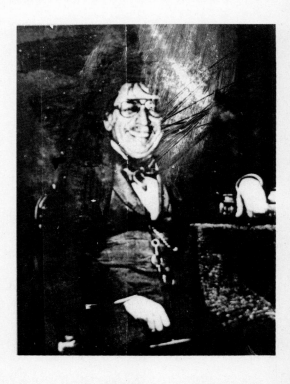

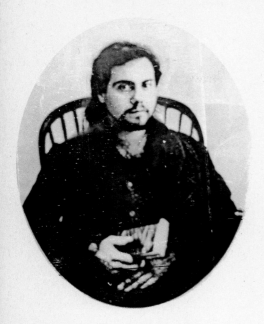

DANIEL VOZZO
colourist
episodes 2,3,4,5,6,∞

Professor Vozzo's handbook, *Ten Thousand Important Quest[ions] Resolved for the Modern Gentleman*, issued in monthly parts fro[m] October 1889 on, contained essays on such vital subjects as: *"Is dancing, as usually conducted, compatible with a high standard of morality?" "Was the purchase of Alaska by this government wise?" "Does the study of physical sciences militate against religious belief?" "Has our government a right to disfranchise the polygamists of Uta[h]"*

Not satisfied with resolving these questions, and many other[s] of equal import, by 1894 he began to address such issues as: *"Is there a purpose to existence?"* and *"What is the composition of the Philosopher's Stone?"*

At this time Vozzo began to complain of being followed by women with the faces of animals. All copies of the latter installm[ent] of his handbook were bought up by an anonymous cartel, and destroyed, and shortly thereafter Vozzo was removed to a priva[te] asylum. He is still there, and he has not aged, although on the ad[vice] of a long-dead physician his tongue was surgically removed, and [is] permitted no writing materials.

STEVE OLIFF
colourist
episodes 0,1

Best known for his revolutionary embalming techniques. Upon his death in 1897 his collection of perfectly preserved schoolchildren was donated to the Royal College of Surgeons. It may be inspected by prior appointment, although several of the older boys were damaged by falling masonry during the Blitz, and have been removed from the permanent exhibition.

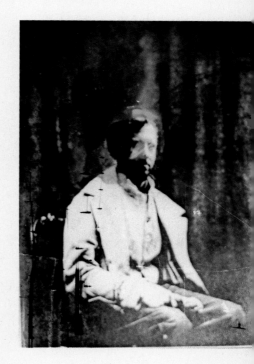

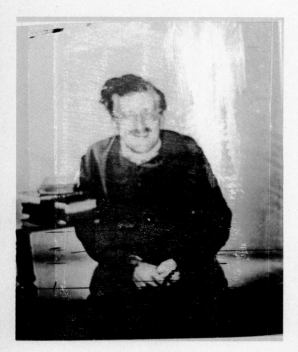

TODD KLEIN
letterer

Was never convicted of any capital crime, for reasons that remain shrouded in mystery.

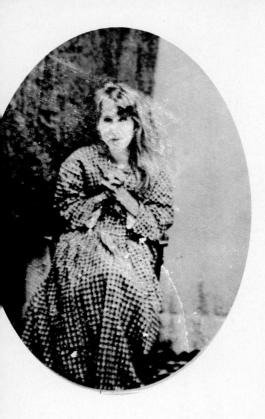

KAREN BERGER
editor

They say she done them all of them in. They say she done it with an axe.

ALISA KWITNEY
assistant editor

According to an old New York folk-tale, Alisa Kwitney appears in a bathroom mirror to people in the final stages of *delirium tremens*, and pleads with them to mend their ways. In another version of the same story she can be induced (by threatening to break the mirror) to reveal winning lottery ticket numbers.

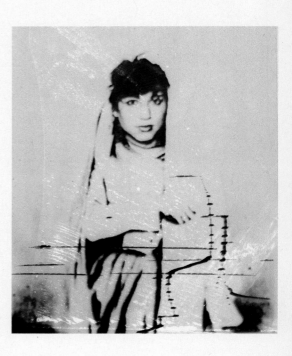

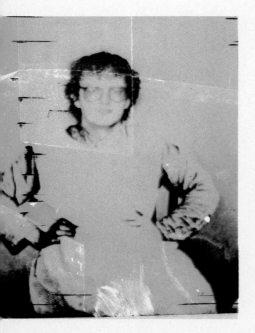

TOM PEYER
assistant editor

Notorious for his cross-dressing during a period when society frowned on such hobbies, Peyer (the illegitimate son of Francis Egerton, the Eighth Earl of Bridgewater and self-styled Prince of the Holy Roman Empire), was arrested at the outbreak of the Crimean War for singing an obscene ballad in a public place while dressed as a washerwoman. The ballad, in the *Parlarie* Argot, went as follows:

> *Nanti dinarly; the omee of the khazi*
> *Says due bionc peroney, manjaree on the cross.*
> *We'll all have to scarper the latty in the morning*
> *Before the bona omee of the khazi shakes his doss.*

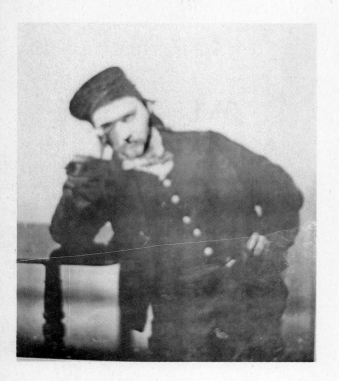

DAVE McKEAN
covers and design

This photograph, found in the Hanussen collection, appears at a hasty first glance to be a portrait of a bearded man in a hat, his coat glittering with five brass buttons. A second, and more careful look reveals that this is simply an illusion: we are looking from above at a snowy landscape: the 'coat' is a river, the 'buttons' stepping stones, the 'face' an island, and a fallen tree, the 'hat' a small body of water in the distance. Photographic illusions of this kind were popular with our forefathers; to our more sophisticated eyes, however, the deception is transparent, and once we see it for what it is, we are unable to see the face that once we thought we saw. The seagull in the foreground is extremely blurred, due to the lengthy exposures Victorian photography demanded.

HARLAN ELLISON
introduction

Harlan Ellison is the author of fifty-eight books and is listed in the *Swedish National Encyclopedia*.

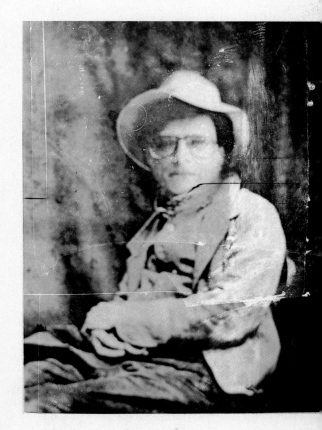